EVERYMAN'S LIBRARY

EVERYMAN,
I WILL GO WITH THEE,
AND BE THY GUIDE,
IN THY MOST NEED
TO GO BY THY SIDE

HONORÉ de BALZAC

Cousin Bette

Translated from the French by James Waring
with an Introduction by Michael Tilby

EVERYMAN'S LIBRARY

15

This book is one of 250 volumes in Everyman's Library
which have been distributed to 4500 state schools
throughout the United Kingdom.
The project has been supported by a grant of £4 million
from the Millennium Commission.

First included in Everyman's Library, 1991
Introduction, Bibliography and Chronology © David Campbell
Publishers Ltd., 1991
Typography by Peter B. Willberg

ISBN 1-85715-015-5

A CIP catalogue record for this book is available from the
British Library

Published by Everyman Publishers plc,
Gloucester Mansions, 140A Shaftesbury Avenue,
London WC2H 8HD

Distributed by Random House (UK) Ltd.,
20 Vauxhall Bridge Road, London SW1V 2SA

COUSIN BETTE

INTRODUCTION

Towards the end of his life, Arnold Bennett, whose admiration for Balzac as a novelist had previously been unqualified, confessed that he was no longer able to regard either *Eugénie Grandet* or *Old Goriot* as masterpieces. Yet he predicted that *Cousin Bette* would 'victoriously survive'. On this occasion, as on so many others, Bennett displayed an unerring sense of what the average reader might most be expected to admire. *Cousin Bette* continues to exert a widespread appeal and is rightly seen as one of Balzac's most powerful representations of the moral and social universe of which he himself was part. At the time of its composition in 1846, his life had scarcely longer to run than Bennett's would have at the moment of his remark. Yet he was only forty-seven. *Cousin Bette* is indisputably the work of a novelist at the height of his powers. The road to maturity as a creative artist had nonetheless been long. It was only after much initial uncertainty, and after stumbling at a relatively late stage upon the idea of linking his novels (both those already written and those still to be conceived) in the manner of a vast anatomy of contemporary French society, that Balzac had begun to appreciate fully the unique role his novels could play in laying bare the infrastructures of that world. In such central works as *Old Goriot* (1835) and *Lost Illusions* (1837–43), he had embarked on what was essentially a process of discovery, using the device of an ambitious young hero fresh from the provinces as a sounding-board to reveal the increasingly complex and gruesome realities of Parisian society in this post-Napoleonic age. The discoveries made, the Balzac of the 1840s was left with convictions. In 1842, the appearance of his lengthy 'Foreword' to *The Human Comedy* had established, not just his attempt to root his practice in analogies with certain scientific models, but also the reactionary hue of his moral and political standpoints. The answer to the moral disintegration now afflicting society, he maintained, was to be found in the twin pillars of legitimate monarchy (in contrast to what he saw as the failed monarchy of the 'Citizen

King' Louis-Philippe) and the Catholic Church, while many current ills were, in his view, to be attributed to the disastrous undermining of the family, a theme which was to dominate *Cousin Bette* some four years later.

Balzac's practice in *Cousin Bette* is instantly reminiscent of the numerous novels and stories that had so far made up *The Human Comedy*, but his art was provided with a new impetus by his desire on this occasion to court a more popular audience. The fictions of Eugène Sue had revealed the opportunities that now existed for reaching a wide reading public as a result of the demand for serialized fiction provided by the new phenomenon of the mass-circulation newspaper. *Cousin Bette* duly appeared in forty-one instalments in the *Le Constitutionnel* between 8 October and 3 December 1846. Not only was Balzac seeking to emulate the commercial success of the author of *The Mysteries of Paris*, he was motivated by what he saw as the need to correct the socialist tendencies manifest in Sue's fiction. He was not unaware that it was one of his own works of fiction, *The Old Maid* (1836), that had in fact been the first contemporary novel to be offered to the public in serial form. What Sue had appreciated, however, was that the serialized novel was a genre in itself. The newspaper medium did not merely entail the division of a novel into equal segments but required of the novelist that he actually compose his fiction in terms of the need for each segment to centre on a dramatic situation, the outcome of which was delayed until the following instalment. Accordingly, of all the works in *The Human Comedy*, *Cousin Bette* is the novel with the most obviously dynamic and intricate plot. Moreover, it is endowed with an extraordinary momentum that is responsible for the fact that the characters are in the end destroyed by the very forces that they have themselves unleashed.

In contrast to many of Balzac's other novels, which open with lengthy background descriptions, *Cousin Bette* is designed to involve the reader from the outset in the dramatic existence of its characters. The serial instalment had no place for the extensive preamble that seeks to provide the reader with an exhaustive account of all the information required for an understanding of subsequent events in their historical, geographical, social and psychological contexts. Instead, such information, which was too important to Balzac's purpose to be abandoned altogether, had to be interspersed with the dramatic dialogue in discreet segments motivated by the reader's instinctive desire to know more, rather than by the novelist's conviction of the need to deliver a lecture. Much of *Cousin Bette* proceeds by means of conversations, and Balzac reveals a newly acquired talent for assigning to the characters themselves the task of furnishing the reader with at least some of the details that had hitherto been considered by him the province of his own narrative voice. The result is a remarkably streamlined composition that reflects the novelist's awareness of the need not to distract the reader from essentials.

This does not mean that Balzac was obliged to sacrifice complexity to this new requirement for instant drama. His justly celebrated device of characters who reappear from novel to novel, sometimes to the fore, sometimes as background figures, and sometimes merely as names that are mentioned by other characters, had been in operation for more than ten years. Thus, he had at his disposal in *Cousin Bette* a fictional Paris already populated by a range of figures whose lives had been partly or wholly narrated by him in earlier stories. The cast of the novel indeed contains numerous individuals already known to his regular readers. However, the central characters are for the most part new creations, though the military exploits of Marshal Hulot would have been familiar to readers of *The Chouans*, Balzac's novel of counter-revolution in Brittany at the turn of the century. Knowledge of the other stories in *The Human Comedy* is certainly not needed for an understanding of the characters and events in *Cousin Bette*. The mere existence of identifiable characters beyond the explicit action of the novel allows the situations and exploits of the central characters to acquire considerable resonance. It is not necessary to be familiar with the rise to power of Rastignac or with the commercial standing of Crevel's former boss, César Birotteau, to experience the effect of Balzac's being able to allude to them with such familiarity, though of course our enjoyment may be heightened by an ability to share in this familiarity. (The one case perhaps where both understanding and appreciation are curtailed if a name means nothing to us is that of Madame Nourrisson's nephew, who is none other than the former convict turned Chief of Police, Vautrin, the most powerful and most ambiguous personage in the entire *Human Comedy* and a constant reminder of the way the world that Balzac is depicting has blurred the distinction between good and evil.) What is important is that Balzac communicates to us the sense that he regards his reappearing characters as figures who are well known. Thus characters who fulfil minor roles can, if they are recurring characters, avoid appearing purely functional or the performers of a cameo part. When a banker is needed to lend money to Hector Hulot or a doctor to attend the dying Valérie Marneffe, Balzac has at his immediate disposal a Baron Nucingen or a Dr Bianchon, just as Rastignac owes his brief mention solely to the need to provide Wenceslas with a prominent and influential customer.

It is, then, Balzac's particular achievement to have broken with the assumption that the interest of a literary character is necessarily exhausted by the story that makes him or her a central figure in a given novel. By the same token, he was led to devise compositions that were not dominated by a single character. *Cousin Bette* is an excellent example. The title suggests that what we are about to read is the story of Lisbeth Fischer. And so it is. *Cousin Bette* illustrates the behaviour of one type of 'poor relation', behaviour that contrasts totally with that of the poor relation in its companion volume *Cousin Pons* (which, though begun shortly before *Cousin Bette*, was not completed until the following year). But, as the subtitle of the novel suggests, it is also the story of the 'Prodigal Father' (Hector Hulot). The proliferation of characters and the complex intertwining of their ambitions in fact serve to shift the emphasis away from an attempt to understand or judge the motives of a particular character to a concern with the ways in which their collective behaviour provides a microcosm of Parisian society under the July Monarchy.

Within *The Human Comedy*, *Cousin Bette* is assigned, uncontroversially, to the category of 'scenes of Parisian life'. On numerous occasions in the novel we are given a sense of the uniqueness of the contemporary Parisian setting. Baron Hulot is described as 'a mere cypher in that immense stir of men and interests and things which makes Paris at once a paradise and a hell'. (Balzac's choice of *The Human Comedy* as his overall title was intended as a conscious echo of Dante's *Divine Comedy*.) For Crevel, whose rise to position and fame gives him good reason to know, 'Paris is a town whither every man of energy ... comes to meet his kind; talent swarms here without hearth or home, and energy equal to anything, even to making a fortune.' In the case of several of the characters it is conveyed to us that they are to be understood first and foremost in terms of their being Parisians. The conception of the capital as a bustling chaos of contradictions indicates the extent to which Balzac's concern is with the contemporary, while the changes of address that accompany the rise and fall of the protagonists' fortunes contribute to the sensation of Paris as the location of perpetual movement.

The transformation of the city following the July Revolution of 1830 continued to be effected by the 'new money' amassed by the commercial bourgeoisie. The Balzacian narrator deplores the consequent lack of taste of the *nouveaux riches*: 'we should have in Paris ten Venices if our retired merchants had had the instinct for fine things characteristic of the Italians'. Yet it is recognized that, for all the violent contrasts which make the capital so disturbing a place, the Parisians – and by dint of long years of residence in the capital Balzac himself may be regarded as an honorary Parisian – 'love their Paris in their heart'. What remains striking is the way Balzac sees Paris as a totality. No character exists in isolation from the rest. It is specifically the Hulot family that is seen as caught in the web spun by Bette, but the spider's web could also serve as an image of Parisian society as a whole. The individual self is seen as a social being who cannot accomplish any significant act outside the social (and economic) organism of which he is condemned to be part and who has little, if any, immunity against the effects of the values and behaviour of that world.

This shift away from the individual to the collective is potentially paradoxical in view of the fact that the hallmark of the age in Balzac's eyes is its rampant individualism. Balzac's characters may represent certain types such as the *roué* or the

parvenu, but they are always individualized. What character-
izes this society as observed by Balzac is precisely a newly
found concern with the unique and individual. Once Wenceslas Steinbock's talent has received society's cachet, the rich
amateurs des arts seek only to possess a sculpture of which there
are no copies and the mould of which has been destroyed. In
every respect Balzac's art is based on a recognition of the
individual. His characters possess unique physical (and physi-
ognomic) characteristics, the rooms they inhabit are seen as a
reflection of individual taste (and more besides). Their deportment has an individuality that may, as in the case of Crevel's
studied pose in the manner of Napoleon (immortalized in the
portrait by the subject of one of Balzac's slightly earlier stories,
Pierre Grassou), invite recourse to the art of the caricaturist.
Although their ways of expressing themselves may betray
certain Balzacian family likenesses, Balzac is the first of the
great French novelists to see characterization in terms of an
individual's highly distinctive way of speaking. What a
character is saying is not always as important a consideration
as the way in which his actual mode of speech conveys aspects
of his personality. That Balzac is concerned, even obsessed,
with categorization is not in doubt, but rather than betraying
a tendency to think solely in general terms, this demands to be
seen as a defensive response to the almost alarming proliferation of individual cases. He is aware of the way underlying
similarities may be explained by such shared notions as
fashion. (During the short period he spent as a journalist in the
months prior to and following the July Revolution, one of his
chief outlets was a new periodical entitled *La Mode*.) But such
categories serve only to sharpen the ways in which personality
and taste remain individual.

It was the rapid changes in fashion in the decades following
the Revolution of 1789 that so fascinated Balzac. Fashion for
him possessed a resolutely historical and political dimension.
The changes were undeniably connected to the frequent
changes of political régime; they shared the same labels. It is a
measure of Adeline Hulot's political naïveté in the widest sense
of the term that she is unable to see how dated her First
Empire interior furnishings appear to the eyes of her more

worldly visitors. Her illusions are dependent on a denial of historical change, on the pretence that things are as they always have been. The majority of the characters we meet are living exemplars, on the other hand, of the way the age is characterized by the manifold possibilities for change. The individual is not seen as limited by origins or class. A residual snobbery may lead to the occasional snub, but an individual's station in the Paris of the July Monarchy is largely determined by his own efforts. If the individual is endowed with the necessary will-power and talent, the indications are that he can occupy virtually any position that he desires, provided that his will-power and talent take into account the central role of money in the realization of an individual's desires. The Paris of the 1830s and 1840s was, according to Balzac's version of contemporary history, a constant encouragement to ambition, and, more specifically, to selfish greed.

For Balzac, egoism was the dominant characteristic of the modern world. In *Cousin Bette* we witness the havoc wreaked by individual desires that are allowed to go unchecked. Bette and Hulot may embody diametrically opposed responses to desire – that of the hoarder and that of the spendthrift – but both are equally self-centred. It is evident that Hulot's lack of self-restraint has a disastrous effect on the family's fortunes in every sense. His own survival is thoroughly ambiguous. On his return to the family, the prodigal father whose charm has ensured him the indulgence of others on so many occasions is descibed as 'a most agreeable old man, a ruin but full of wit, having retained no more of his vice than made it an added social grace'. But the context is one in which Adeline and her children see only what they wish to see; the narrator is led to point out that they conveniently forget that Hulot has been responsible for the death of two uncles. Their unwillingness to face facts is borne out by his courting of the kitchen maid and his marriage to her only days after Adeline's death. On the one hand, his indefatigable desire confers on him a stature that is denied to lesser mortals. On the other, the depths to which he now stoops reveal that he is little more than a grotesque automaton. Valérie had earlier told him that she cannot pronounce his Christian name without thinking of the *Iliad*.

But our final image of the Hector of Balzac's epic is of a thoroughly mock-heroic figure.

Bette's sexual repression is seen as having no less destructive a force than Hulot's erotic monomania. It inevitably leads to its own perverse forms of excess For much of the novel, aided and abetted by Valérie Marneffe (the 'axe'), Bette (the 'hand that wields the axe') remains in control of the fate of all those around her, including herself. But in the end the forces so skilfully set in motion by her, and which depend for their effect not so much on their intrinsic power as on her being able to rely on the moral putridness of individuals bent on satisfying their desires, and on the secure knowledge that those less tainted are condemned to impotence (at least until they accept the help of the diabolical Madame Nourrisson), escape her control. As the narrator points out, her downfall was the ironic consequence of having been too successful in her desire for vengeance. Her aim was not to destroy, but to enjoy the suffering she has caused. The terminal disaster may be one of the more improbable events in this novel, all of which bear at least a superficial resemblance to popular melodrama, yet the underlying sense of the way in which society is destroyed from within by individuals exploiting the possibilities for the realization of their selfish desires takes us well and truly out of the realm of the purely fictional.

If the world Balzac depicts is revealed as a world out of control, it is viewed throughout as a society which is essentially false and unnatural. At the basic level of plot, the emphasis in *Cousin Bette* is on deception. The success of Bette's plotting is dependent on her convincing the world that she is everybody's friend. In perfecting this strategy she comes close to being a 'double agent', as she feeds genuine information to the family in order to confirm in their eyes Valérie's status as the 'enemy'. She is at home in vastly different spheres; other characters instinctively confide in her. She sits as one of the family at table and finds herself invited to Crevel's house. At the same time, she affects an easy relationship with the servants. Forced to earn her living, she has been both in charge of other workers and a simple employee herself. Yet she does not truly belong to any one of these roles, being perpetually either inferior or superior to those with whom she finds herself. It is significant that her apartment in the rue du Doyenné is insufficient of a natural setting for it to reveal much about her personality. When she moves to the rue Vaneau, it is to all intents and purposes to become part of Valérie's household. Moreover she has been settled there by Hulot in the hope that she will be his eyes and ears. In short, she belongs everywhere and nowhere. Yet it is her very independence and ambiguous status that constitute the basis of her power.

Valérie Marneffe is no less skilled in the art of deception. Above all, she possesses the actress's skill in creating an illusion of reality in the mind of her audience. (In view of the undeniable appeal she exerts in the exercise of her creative talents, it is easy to understand why the great positivist critic and thinker Hippolyte Taine should have alleged 'Balzac is in love with his Valérie.') Not only does she manage to persuade each of her lovers that he is the father of her child, in a masterly performance she serves Crevel his come-uppance when he is led to mistake her fake piety for a real instance of penitence. Crevel, for all his own eloquence, is doubtless a gullible spectator, but such is the widespread perversion of values that there is in the novel as a whole a more general inability to distinguish between the genuine and the feigned. At one point even Bette has to ask Valérie whether she is telling the truth or play-acting. Not that the theme is confined to the depiction of Valérie. When Adeline visits Josépha, the latter has to emphasize that her reaction to Adeline's plight is not an example of her prowess as an actress but a genuine homage paid to her visitor by a fellow woman.

The world of *Cousin Bette* is an illicit world characterized by furtive activity. The majority of the characters possess a secret. (The very word itself recurs on numerous occcasions.) Balzac's careful attention to Parisian topography (the path of degradation trodden by Hulot is underscored by his various changes of address – he ends up in a street that is within walking distance of the Père Lachaise cemetery, where Balzac himself was to be buried only a few years later) may give a superficial impression of the vastness of the expanding modern capital, but Paris in the novel is experienced first and foremost as a city of interiors in which the characters indulge their passions, or engage in destructive plotting, behind closed doors. Even the rare scenes that take place in the open retain the pervasive air of furtiveness. The carefully chosen detour made by Bette (which the narrator calls 'this illogical route ... traced by the logic of passion, always the foe of legs') when she walks to Crevel's house in the rue des Saussayes is designed to allow her to spy on Wenceslas undetected. The effect throughout is stifling, and not, as might have been expected from the recognition of the size of the capital, one of expansiveness. No location is able to escape infection by this feverish activity. Adeline's initial above in the rue de l'Université is in essence the location of 'non-desire', a world from which all erotic energy has been drained; unconsciously, Adeline has allowed it to become a shrine to a memory of an earlier period of happiness. Yet is is not allowed to become a refuge from the world. Not only does it harbour, in the person of Bette, the instrument of its own destruction, it is invaded by Crevel who both introduces illicit desire and opens the occupant's eyes to unwelcome truths.

The key to the love-nest acquired by Crevel in the rue du Dauphin for his assignations with Valérie is given appropriate prominence in this world of furtive activity. Bette gives it to Hulot and tells him to have several copies made. It opens the door but it also locks it again behind the couple. As such, it is a pointer to the way the plot is concerned precisely with the unmasking of secrets. It is Bette herself who ill-advisedly reveals to Hortense the existence of her protégé Wenceslas, but in most cases the secret is revealed by others in the know or it is directly uncovered by an unexpected arrival or intrusion, as when the police gain admission to Crevel's love-nest and surprise Hulot with Valérie (a doubtless intentional echo of a fate that had befallen an individual with a not dissimilar name: Victor Hugo). The characters at least begin by assuming that the secret lives are just that. Their delusions are encouraged by the reluctance of characters such as Adeline to face up to the discoveries they make about the illicit activities of others. Concern for the family honour is responsible for Johann Fischer sacrificing his own well-being to an attempt to ensure that the illicit remains hidden from public view. Much of the reader's pleasure stems from the way the truth is gradually revealed to us and from our realization that we possess an overall picture that is more complete than the view aailable to the individual characters themselves, with the possible exception of the master spy and ambiguous defender of law and order, Vautrin, who may be said to stand outside the fiction in every sense.

The world of *Cousin Bette* is conveyed to us in terms of a constant opposition between appearances and reality. The justification for the extravagances of the novel resides in the way in which the reader is thereby educated by Balzac in the interpretation of signs. Explicit admiration is expressed for those characters who possess an infallible sense of the meaning of the sights with which they are presented. The 'sharp eyes' of the Parisian concierges allow them to know unerringly when not to impede the progress of a caller. The police officer whose capacity for dissection earns him a comparison with a surgeon is by training a physiognomist. Thus on Marneffe's face he reads 'mean speculation ... stamped in every line'. As for the perspicacious Valérie, her insights into human character and behaviour are seen as characteristic of 'the Parisian half-breed, who spends her days stretched on a sofe, turning the lantern of her detective spirit on the obscurest depths of souls, sentiments, and intrigues'.

The false world that Balzac holds up for the reader's edification is one that is seen to threaten its own destruction by its commitment to rampant inflation in monetary terms. *Cousin Bette* can be seen as an awesome illustration of the effects of the infamous exhortation to the unenfranchized by Louis-Philippe's Minister of Finance, Guizot: 'Make yourselves rich.' (The rest of Guizot's phrase – 'through work and your savings' – proved altogether less memorable.) The rise of Célestin Crevel shows him to have been a model pupil. It is *en connaissance de cause* that he tells Adeline that their reigning monarch was not Louis-Philippe but 'the holy, venerated, substantial, delightful, obliging, beautiful, noble, ever-youthful, and all-powerful five franc piece'. Power in the world of *Cousin Bette* is incontrovertibly associated with money. It is money that brings about Hulot's downfall, allows Bette to keep Wenceslas in subservience, and causes Adeline ultimately to offer herself to Crevel. Balzac's financial realism is legendary and there is no doubting the effectiveness of his relating the plot to the realities of contemporary financial and legal practice. But it is not simply a question of charting the materialist values of the rising bourgeoisie. Alongside Crevel, who translates into his private life the economic equivalent of the *juste-milieu* political philosophy of the July Monarchy and thereby remains in possession of an adequate portion of his wealth, we witness the devastating effects on the Hulot household of a system that, through the re-negotiability of mortgages, insurance policies and, above all, IOUs, allows Hulot to spend vast sums of money he does not possess. He is thus able to create for himself a life that has no more solidity than a dream. Caught up, as he is, in this spiral of deception, his final recourse to culpable fraud is all but inevitable. The fact remains that Balzac's dismay is directed more at the false precepts on which the relationships in the new bourgeois world were based, than at a literal case of transgressing the law. The plethora of epithets accumulated by Crevel to depict the prestige of the five-franc piece is an indirect indication of the inflationary principles that Balzac saw afflicting contemporary French society. Alongside the various instances of gambling in the novel and the speculative investments in which Crevel excels, there would appear to be a nostalgic preference, on Balzac's part, for the solidity of the gold coins in Cousin Bette's purse.

The flimsy irreality that is mistaken for a solid world by characters who are nothing other than the embodiment of desire is consistently seen by Balzac as a façade reminiscent of theatrical decor. Although he succeeded in completing a small number of plays, he remained throughout his career a frustrated man of the theatre. *Cousin Bette*, the product of the author's conscious desire to woo a popular audience, is arguably the most theatrical of all his novels. The settings of the encounters not infrequently recall the stage. As Crevel makes a dramatic entrance in the very first scene, Hortense and Bette exit into the garden. When, some one hundred and fifty pages into the novel, we are told, to our surprise, that what has gone before is only to be regarded as the introduction to the story, a parallel is drawn with the prologue of a classical tragedy. The climactic scenes between Crevel and Adeline, and between Crevel and the consummate actress Valérie, are self-consciously theatrical in the manner of contemporary melodrama. Crevel's love-nest is duly constructed so that it has two entrances, one at the front through the shop of a furniture-dealer and the second 'through a door in the wall of the passage, so ingeniously hidden as to be almost invisible'. The police officer appropriately tells Hulot: 'The farce is played out.' In other words, Balzac draws indiscriminately on fundamentally distinct forms of drama in order to evoke a hybrid genre appropriate to the contradictory nature of the world he has set out to portray and to the ambivalent effect it has upon the observer.

A similar mixing of theatrical genres may be seen in the profusion of references made by the characters, and above all by the Balzacian narrator himself, to well-known plays and theatrical characters. Allusions to the works of Molière, Corneille, Racine and Shakespeare, which variously take the form of quotations, misquotations and parodies, are especially prominent. The references in fact add little by way of explanation or enlightenment. As much as any features that they might be deemed to have in common, it is the inappropriateness of such comparisons – the puniness of the modern characters alongside the grandeur of their classical counterparts – that strikes the reader. As such, the device deserves to be seen as part of the prominent comic texture of Balzac's writing. The particular prominence of the allusions to Shakespeare's characters (Richard III, Lady Macbeth, Othello, Iago – who is so unfamiliar a name to one of the ladies of easy virtue (Carabine) that she thinks the speaker has pronounced the word *magot*, which is not only the French for a 'Barbary ape' but also means, familiarly, a 'nest-egg', a constant preoccupation of her kind and a word that had indeed already been pronounced in the novel by Lisbeth), as with the mixing of examples from both French tragedy and comedy, reinforces the extent to which Balzac saw the necessity for a hybrid idiom. Shakespeare, for long neglected by the French, had taken on a new significance in France in the early nineteenth century, precisely as a result of his being felt to foreshadow the tensions at the heart of Romantic aesthetics. Victor Hugo in the 'Preface' to his play *Cromwell* (1827) had pointed out that the world was not uniformly beautiful when viewed from a human perspective, that ugliness existed alongside the beautiful. In a formulation that was destined to enjoy a wide currency, he added that the grotesque was the obverse of the sublime. 'Sublime and grotesque' – these two epithets could indeed be said to account for much of the nature of Balzac's highly theatrical writing.

Lest we be tempted to criticize the author of *Cousin Bette* for falling into melodrama, it is necessary to stress that in this novel he in fact makes conscious and ironic play with melodramatic stereotypes. Neither the melodrama as such or the exaggerated idiom that represents the norm is designed to be taken literally by the reader. Balzac's symbolic representation of the contemporary moral universe requires a mode of excess. Through recourse to a melodrama that ridicules itself ('Water! my head is burning, I am going mad!' cries Bette after seeing the lithograph that reveals that Wenceslas' 'Samson' group is the property of Mademoiselle Hulot d'Ervy), Balzac distances us from the purely fictional and directs us to the metaphorical significance of the theatrical in his novel. It is said of Valérie that she knowingly acts out a part as if she were in a melodrama. In this world of false appearances her audience is all too likely to confuse the theatrical for the real. The novel invites a constant reflection on the relationship between the theatrical and the behaviour discernible in contemporary society. When Josépha hides Adeline behind a curtain prior to the entrance of the shameless mother of Olympe Bijou, she tells her: 'Hide there, and you will hear everything. It is a scene that is played quite as often in real life as on the stage.' As for Adeline herself, it is through the extended theatrical metaphor that her naïveté is most tellingly conveyed. After her desperate but abortive attempt to prostitute herself to Crevel she wryly observes, 'I played my part very badly, did I not?' Thus, theatricality is as central to the indictment of the society of the July Monarchy as it is to Balzac's desire to entertain. In part it was simply a question of taking over an idiom that was already in use. Louis-Philippe himself, having decided to retain Charles X's conquest of Algiers, had duly declared: 'It is our opera box, but a terribly expensive one.'

The theatre further possessed associations with immorality that Balzac was happy to exploit. The dividing line between actresses or opera singers, such as Josépha, and courtesans was thin indeed. Prostitution is one of the most prominent of all the extended metaphors in *The Human Comedy* as well as providing many literal examples of its profession. In *Cousin Bette* Balzac takes full advantage of the way the concept of prostitution unites sex, money and the theatre. The French text makes us sharply aware of the closeness of luxury (*luxe*) and lust (*luxure*). The destructive potential of the new and specifically Parisian forms of prostitution may be seen in the name Balzac gives to the courtesan kept by Crevel: Héloïse *Brisetout* or 'Breaks up Everything'.

Throughout the novel characters are seen to destroy, either consciously or unwittingly, the sacrosanct nature of the family. This is most obviously true in the case of Bette's attempt to avenge her status as the 'poor relation' and in the activities that earn Hulot the label of 'prodigal father', but in addition to this betrayal from within, the family is sullied by the misappropriation of its labels to designate relationships out-side the family. Thus, Bette is said to become Valérie's 'aunt'. Others such as Crevel, who admittedly has one foot in the family through the marriage of his daughter to Victorin Hulot, refer to her familiarly as 'Cousin Bette', thereby degrading the special bond of kinship. The evil Madame Nourrisson (whose name is presumably meant to allude ironically to the sustenance provided by *une nourrice* or wet-nurse) passes off her accomplice as her niece. Since she herself is literally Vautrin's aunt, we end up being offered a doubly perverted image of a family united in evil. Crevel pledges himself not to harm the interests of his only daughter (named Célestine in his own image) through unduly profligate expen-diture on Valérie or by re-marrying, but this leads to a grotesque, not to say faintly incestuous, identification of the

two women in his own mind, while his unquestioning accep-
tance of Valérie's claim that he is the father of her newly
conceived child threatens to have the very consequence that
he had sought to avoid: 'I am a father! It seems to me that I
love my poor Célestine the less.' Valérie's grotesque and far-
fetched achievement of convincing all four lovers in her life
that the child in her womb is theirs serves to highlight Balzac's
suggestion of the disruptive force of illegitimacy. In her own
case, Balzac suggests that her behaviour has much to do with
the false position in which she had found herself as the
illegitimate daughter of one of Napoleon's most famous
lieutenants, even though the latter had during his lifetime
been generous in his provision and patronage.

Balzac's quarrel is specifically with the France of the July
Monarchy. It is unlikely to be coincidental that his novel
featuring a libertine of advanced years appeared at a time
when Louis-Philippe had reached his mid-seventies, especially
if a rapprochement is made between the names Adeline and
Adélaïde, the Citizen King's sister and confidante (even if the
reminiscence of Hugo being found *in flagrante delicto* suggests
the name of Adèle Hugo in addition). But if the revolutions of
1848 and the deposal of Louis-Philippe were a mere two years
away, Balzac was no revolutionary. It is with two earlier
periods of French history – the *ancien régime* and the age of
Napoleon – that present-day France is consistently contrasted.
If Crevel likes to think of himself and of Hulot rather grandly
as two men of the eighteenth century, we cannot but mock his
pretension. The mockery is given an extra dimension when
later it is said that Crevel now regards the eighteenth century
as being rather too small for him: it is with the image of no less
a figure than Louis XIV that he now finds himself at home.
The intrigue of Laclos' epistolary novel *Dangerous Liaisons* is a
further explicit point of comparison, but just how unflattering
the comparison is for the 1840s is conveyed by the description
of Valérie Marneffe as 'a middle-class Madame de Merteuil'.

Crevel's affectation of a Napoleonic pose makes him alone
the butt of our ridicule at such moments. The Napoleonic era
itself is not implicated and indeed functions as an age of
principles against which the present must be judged. At one

moment in *Cousin Bette* the narrator steps back from his narrative and gives the reader a potted history of France since the Revolution. His view is expressed in a forthright and unambiguous fashion. Under the Restoration, the aristocracy is seen as having been ever mindful of its fate during the Revolution. As a result it has become 'thrifty, prudent, and stay-at-home, in short bourgeoise and penurious'. Eighteen-thirty is seen as crowning the work of 1793:

> In France, henceforth, there will be great names, but no great houses, unless there should be political changes which we can hardly foresee. Everything takes the stamp of individuality. The wisest invest in annuities.

The narrator concludes with the statement: 'The Family has been destroyed.' Adeline indeed dates her husband's infidelities from the dissolution of the Empire. Hector Hulot, as the trusted protégé of the late Emperor, betrays not just his family, but the memory of Napoleon himself. His contemporaries, starting with his brother, Marshal Hulot, and including his wife's uncle, the unfortunate Johann Fischer, are shown as continuing to revere the Emperor's memory. Marshal Hulot is a by-word for fidelity, it being claimed that Napoleon had said of him: 'That brave old Hulot is the most obstinate republican, but he will never be false to me.' Similarly, we learn that Valérie's father, General Montcornet, allegedly one of Napoleon's most trusted lieutenants and now dead, retains the respect of the whole community. Even Monsieur Rivet, who is the epitome of the tradesman and delivers an encomium for the sound commercial principles advocated by Louis-Philippe's régime, recalls the General with enthusiasm: 'Ah!,' he tells Bette, 'the house has supplied many a uniform to General Montcornet; he soon blackened them with the smoke of cannon. A brave man he was! and he paid on the nail.' The implication to be gleaned from the various posthumous tributes to General Montcornet is that men of that ilk are no longer to be found in the France of Louis-Philippe. The project for a commemorative statue leads Hortense to imagine it portraying Montcornet as the 'embodied ideal of bravery, the type of the cavalry officer, of courage *à la Murat*'. It is no coincidence that it is this monument that Wenceslas will universally be regarded as having botched.

The fault of those loyal to Napoleon's memory, if fault it be, is that they are unable to come to terms with what Balzac regards as their country's moral decline. Marshal Hulot is suitably afflicted with deafness, though his retirement affords no protection from the insidious effects of contemporary behaviour. Adeline, who humbly describes herself as Josephine to her Napoleon, endeavours to retain her belief that they are still living in an age of probity. She cannot therefore bring herself to criticize her husband. To that extent she may be held responsible in part for their decline. We see similar indulgence shown by the Prince de Wissembourg, who out of respect for his past Napoleonic association with Hector Hulot, agrees to Marneffe's quite unjustifiable promotion, the Director of Personnel having earlier absented himself on leave so that Hulot might be given a free path. This is the public equivalent of Adeline's indulgence towards her husband's infidelity to her.

An important reinterpretation of *Cousin Bette* has made much of the moral ambiguity of the novel, emphasizing Balzac's provocative overturning of the simplistic notions of good and evil that inform the stereotypes that he borrows as his starting-point from popular melodrama. In a powerful argument, Christopher Prendergast[1] invites us to reflect on the fact that the upright Victorin ends up conniving with the evil Madame Nourrisson. He likewise develops the observation present in the text that Adeline's moral rectitude plays its part in the sequence of events that threaten to destroy the family. Yet this is an argument that must be handled with care. Balzac is undoubtedly offering us a more complex and ambiguous vision than that which had been the stock-in-trade on the 'boulevard du Crime' (as the boulevard du Temple, site of many of the popular theatres in Paris, was popularly dubbed). His very subject matter obliges him to engage with the grotesque logic by which Beauty attracts Ugliness and Good attracts Evil. (This is just one of the fundamental elements in his vision that he shares with his contemporary Baudelaire, the first edition of whose collected poems, *Les*

Fleurs du mal, would appear a mere ten years later.) He is supremely aware of the ironies by which evil can come of apparent good; for all General Montcornet's heroic status in the novel, it is made clear that the life of luxury that he provided for Valérie's mother is at least indirectly responsible for the future behaviour of their illegitimate daughter. It is quite comprehensible that Balzac's depiction of Adeline as 'sublime' should raise questions instead of being accepted by us as an unproblematical label. Yet this does not mean that the way she is presented authorizes us to see the fiction as encouraging some kind of moral balance sheet. Balzac's concern is not with the distribution of blame but rather with illustrating the consequences produced by a number of explosive starting-points. It is for this reason also that to try and mitigate Bette's crime on the grounds that she has been mistreated by her family may also be regarded as inappropriate. Balzac's interest in the individual stops short of such judgements. His concern is with the way in which his fiction illustrates what he regards to be the motive forces that together give contemporary society its distinct moral and political colour. Thus in the case of Adeline, it is otiose to suggest that had she been in a position to take lessons from a Josépha, she might have been able to offer her husband greater fulfilment within the marital home. The salient point to note about the requirement to be not just a wife and a mistress but all women in one is that this is recognized to be an all but impossible ideal. To achieve it, Balzac makes perfectly clear, would be nothing less than a stroke of genius.

The whole thrust of Balzac's fictional presentation of contemporary society is deeply pessimistic. The very nature of the plot points us towards the inability of the individual to arrest the momentum generated by the conflicting self-interest of the individuals and groups which together reveal the fragmented nature of the modern bourgeois world. The *Human Comedy*'s most famous doctor, Hector Bianchon (whose attendance the dying Balzac is alleged to have requested), provides a diagnosis that leaves little room for any hope of far-reaching reform. Speaking to Adeline, who is now engaged in charitable works, he observes:

'We medical men have the pleasure now and again of a successful cure, as you have that of saving a family from the horrors of hunger, depravity, or misery, and of restoring it to social respectability. But what comfort can the magistrate find, the police agent, or the attorney, who spend their lives in investigating the basest schemes of self-interest...?'

When asked as to the cause of the 'deep-seated evil' that permeates society, Bianchon is confident in his answer:

'The decay of religion ... and the preeminence of finance, which is simply solidified selfishness. Money used not to be everything; there were some kinds of superiority that ranked above it – nobility, genius, service done to the State. But nowadays the law takes wealth as the universal standard, and regards it as the measure of public capacity.'

Balzac's novels usually take the form of an education and in the case of *Cousin Bette*, it is arguably Adeline who, by virtue of her extreme lack of familiarity with the world, receives the fullest education in the novel, starting with the very first scene, during which, for all her protestations to the contrary, Crevel succeeds in revealing truths about her husband's behaviour that were not in fact known to her. Balzac had long had the reputation of being 'le romancier de la femme'. His postbag confirmed that his readership was largely female and it would seem that he instinctively paid attention to the female perspective. The key scene in this respect is clearly the visit Adeline makes to Josépha. Despite the apparent emphasis in the novel on male desire, the women who are the objects of the male protagonists' sexual ambitions are rarely seen through lustful eyes. Thus our intimate acquaintance with Josépha in the privacy of her apartment is gained through the eyes of the female figure who bears least resemblance to her. The angel or madonna figure is fascinated by her antithesis. The notion of a performance for a female audience is specifically introduced when Josépha instructs her maid to 'do my hair in a way to astonish a woman'. She duly succeeds in her aim. But if it is customary to think of this as a scene in which Adeline's eyes are opened, the surprise is mutual. Faced with the unaffected behaviour of her visitor – she had originally equated Adeline with a mere role, that of Virtue to her Vice – Josépha responds by setting aside the role that she has so successfully played in society and speaks to Adeline 'woman to woman'. One might add that the descriptions of interiors are essentially in the form of attention to furnishings, while much attention is paid to the clothes of their female inhabitants. If the touchstone is provided by fashion, the descriptions are designed less to reveal the female as an object of desire and more as a revelation to other women of the resourceful use of artifice that is responsible for a successful ensnarement of the gullible male. The theme appears in a nicely ironic version when we are shown Valérie's creative talents at work in the remarkable transformation of the hitherto dowdy Bette. At such moments we are almost literally back-stage.

Although Valérie's relations with men are first and foremost sexual, we rarely see her exclusively in erotic terms. When she is first glimpsed by Hulot in the street, it is certainly her shapely posterior that mesmerizes him. But the satisfaction she procures Hulot and Crevel turns essentially on their ability to think of her as a possession. Hulot, who has been overwhelmed, as his wife will be in due course, by the luxury of Josépha's abode, delights in contemplating the rue Vaneau apartment, less as a location for the satisfaction of desire and more for its tangible signs of the luxury that he has purchased for his latest mistress. It is her clothes and furnishings rather than her body which are lovingly described. An apparent contrast is offered by a brief description of her in the presence of Crevel: 'Valérie took off her combing-wrapper; she was in her shift, and she wriggled into the dressing-gown like a snake.' Yet, ironically, Crevel's preoccupation with the need to find two hundred thousand francs thwarts any erotic response on his part (just as potentially the most explicit sexual scene of all, when Hulot is in bed with Valérie in the rue du Dauphin, ends up with the male lover covered in ridicule). Thus the scene fails to function as the presentation of Valérie as the object of male desire. Instead, it is characterized by the close complicity between Valérie and her pock-marked maid, Reine, a complicity that is sealed by the exchange of a meaningful smile, one that has the additional effect of signifying the exclusion of the third party present. In the case of

Valérie's dalliance with Wenceslas, the focus is on the strate-
gies she adopts in her pursuit of him, as, for example, in the
description of her manner of offering him a cup of tea in
public. If there is a highly charged description of the 'ex-
sculptor' lacing her stays in front of the blazing log fire, it is
more a statement of her post-coital fulfilment than a
communication of any effect she has on her lover:

> This is a moment when a woman who is neither too fat nor too
> thin, but, like Valérie, elegant and slender, displays divine beauty.
> The rosy skin, moistly soft, invites the sleepiest eye. The lines of her
> figure, so little hidden, are so charmingly outlined by the white pleats
> of the shift and the support of the stays, that she is irresistible – like
> everything that must be parted from.
> With a happy face smiling at the glass, a foot impatiently marking
> time, a hand put up to restore order among the tumbled curls, and
> eyes expressive of gratitude; with the glow of satisfaction which, like a
> sunset, warms the least details of the countenance – everything makes
> such a moment a mine of memories.

The single perspective of Valérie contemplating herself in the
mirror excludes the external gaze of the male. When after this
moment of self-absorption we are made aware again of
Wenceslas, it is as a figure made fun of by her for his lack of
expertise in lacing her stays. If the description explicitly shows
us a female viewed by a woman who happens in this instance
to be the same person, it would seem that it is also, more
generally, a mirror that offers the female reader an image,
albeit idealized, of her own distinctive female sexuality, thereby forming part of the wider concern in this novel with the
processes by which the female sex as a whole is led to become
more fully self-aware.

The moment at which Valérie is experienced most
obviously as an object of male desire appropriately coincides
with the renewed presence in Paris of her highly theatrical
Brazilian lover, Baron Henri Montès de Montéjanos:

> That evening, by one of those strokes of luck which come to pretty
> women, Valérie was charmingly dressed. Her white bosom gleamed
> under a lace tucker of rusty white, which showed off the satin texture

of her beautiful shoulders – for Parisian women, Heaven knows how, have some way of preserving their fine flesh and remaining slender. She wore a black velvet gown that looked as if it might at any moment slip off her shoulders, and her hair was dressed with lace and drooping flowers. Her arms, not fat but dimpled, were graced by deep ruffles to her sleeves. She was like a luscious fruit coquettishly served in a handsome dish, and making the knife-blade long to be cutting it.

Dressed to kill, indeed. But, even here, the description is impersonal rather than offered as an indication of the desire aroused in a particular male onlooker.

In contrast, the description of the sixteen-year-old Olympe Bijou is introduced specifically in terms of the impact she makes on Hulot, the protector she has been assigned by the sympathetic Josépha. Nevertheless the description is unmistakably that of the narrator, for the impulse to see her as the embodiment of the contradictory constituents of Parisian moral life, the comparison that is made with a painting and more especially with the eyes of a Raphael virgin, together with the ability to put a price per metre on the cloth from which her best frock was made, owe nothing to Hulot who, we are asked to accept, can merely feast his eyes. It may well be a scene to cause this aged *roué* to rub his hands, but the truly distinctive response is that of Josépha. For the well-meaning procuress sees in Olympe not only the features that will make Hulot an eager customer, but a mirror offering her a memory of her own earlier life.

Male desire in *Cousin Bette* thus provides rather less of Balzac's subject matter than one might have assumed. In the case of Hulot and Crevel it is identified with features that make them humorous or even ridiculous figures. That Balzac's concern is more with his female characters (and his female readers) would seem an uncontroversial conclusion to draw from the examples so far discussed. It remains a concern that exhibits a number of further dimensions.

The references in the novel to the superiority of women over men are numerous. It may be a question of certain types of women as opposed to certain types of men, the unscrupulous courtesans, for instance, who know how to 'tyrannize old men'. It is specifically in the lower social strata, we are told, that women are not only superior to their menfolk but invariably wield the power. On the other hand, a tribute to Valérie's talents becomes a pretext for a generalization about the superiority of all Parisian women: Crevel initiated her into the ways of the money markets but 'like every Parisian woman, she had soon outstripped her master'. It is Josépha who sees society as being directed from behind the scenes by women: 'Governments are guided by the men, whom we privately guide.' Such a claim could certainly be made with regard to the plot of *Cousin Bette*.

Male/female stereotypes are consistently overturned in the novel. The reference to Laclos' *Dangerous Liaisons*, like so many of the literary allusions, possesses its fair share of irony. It is true that Laclos' Madame de Mertueil, in Robert Niklaus' words, 'surpasses Valmont in wickedness and *libertinage*',[2] but Valmont nonetheless remains an impressive villain. The libertines in *Cousin Bette* are, on the other hand, characterized more by their weakness than by their strength. Generally speaking, the principal male characters are seen to be pusillanimous alongside the scheming females. The impossible relationship that Bette comes close to achieving with Wenceslas casts him in the female role. His beauty, his passivity are part of a more widespread femininity, whereas it is Bette's masculine qualities which are stressed. It was, we are told, 'as though Nature had blundered in the distribution of sex'. The ambiguity of this 'strange alliance' is fully brought out by Balzac when he has Bette oscillate between possible female roles with regard to Wenceslas. She thinks of herself as friend, as mother and as lover, though in her advanced state of virginity, imagining herself in this latter role causes her to think of herself as deranged, which is the starting-point for a convincing representation in detail of the contradictions contained within her state of desire. If this grotesque but hesitant relationship is replaced for Wenceslas by one more reminiscent of the traditional idyll, it is nonetheless Hortense who sets out to steal him from her cousin. His creativity is ultimately at threat from the world of easy sensual gratification offered by such women as Valérie. Hence the irony of Valérie's exhortation to him to complete the story of Samson by creating a bronze of Delilah cutting the 'Jewish Hercules's' hair.

Bette is above all a realist who is able to see that her relationship with Wenceslas could never be a source of lasting fulfilment. Balzac's determination to treat the reader to the most complicated of plots leads to a split in her attentions. For reasons that have almost nothing to do with affection, her marriage ambitions are centred on the affable person of the Marshal, while her previously repressed emotions find an outlet in her relationship with Valérie. The satisfaction she derives from this friendship is in no small measure due to the lack of a male presence, as Balzac, sharing the fascination of the Romantic age with the figure of the lesbian, makes no effort to hide:

> As may be seen, these women were but one ... She really adored Valérie; she had taken her to be her child, her friend, her love; she found her docile as Creoles are, yielding from voluptuous indolence; she chattered with her morning after morning with more pleasure than with Wenceslas; they could laugh together over the mischief they plotted, and over the folly of men, and count up the swelling interest on their respective savings.
>
> Indeed, in this new enterprise and new affection, Lisbeth had found food for her activity that was far more satisfying than her insane passion for Wenceslas. The joys of gratified hatred are the fiercest and strongest the heart can know. Love is the gold, hatred the iron of the mine of feeling that lies buried in us. And then Valérie was, to Lisbeth, Beauty in all its glory – the beauty she worshipped, as we worship what we have not, beauty far more plastic to her than that of Wenceslas, who had always been cold to her and distant.

Paradoxically, it is precisely in this response by Bette to her new friend, with its more than passing resemblance to some of the highly charged poems of Baudelaire, that the reader is given the strongest sense of the erotic charms that we can only assume Valérie possesses for her male entourage.

It is the apparent imprecision concerning the nature of the relationship between Bette and Valérie ('her friend, her child, her love') that draws our attention to its true nature, which must remain heavily suggested rather than stated directly. Indeed, the Balzacian narrator would seem already to have pre-empted discussion by discarding the very hypothesis that his description goes on to suggest. For the passage from which we have quoted is preceded by the seemingly categorical statement:

> Lisbeth and Valérie offered the touching spectacle of one of those friendships between women, so cordial and so improbable, that men always too keen-tongued in Paris, forthwith slander them. The contrast between Lisbeth's dry masculine nature and Valérie's creole prettiness encouraged calumny. And Madame Marneffe had unconsciously given weight to the scandal by the care she took of her friend, with matrimonial views, which were, as will be seen, to complete Lisbeth's revenge.

Yet the very fact of raising the question is enough to lodge the idea in the reader's mind and encourage him to consider the evidence. We may stop short of affixing labels and assigning characters and their responses to particular categories, but it is beyond doubt that Balzac displays in *Cousin Bette* an acute awareness of the ambiguities of sexual attraction and their effect on other realms of behaviour, especially when the desire remains to a significant degree repressed.

The unlikeliness of the combination of Bette and Valérie, the perverse affection deriving from the destructive ambitions that constitute the very origins of their alliance, the illustration they provide of the grotesque logic by which the beautiful and the ugly exercise a mutual attraction, together make the relationship a perfect reflection of Balzac's image of Paris as a city of contrasts. A sense of the hybrid permeates the very form of *Cousin Bette* down to the novelist's highly unconventional use of language. The nature of Balzac's project in *The Human Comedy* might suggest the need for an essentially unproblematical use of language, a more or less literal recording of events in a style that reflects the concern with verifiable fact and accurate categories of explanation. Yet Balzac's pretensions to an analytical language that would allow him to be considered a social scientist on the model of the natural scientists he sought to emulate (principally Geoffroy de Saint-Hilaire) were – fortunately – incompatible with his impulse to write imaginative fiction generated by the workings of his creative imagination.

As only the reader of the original French can fully appreciate, *Cousin Bette* reveals an author who delights in the rich and colourful variety of language. But direct contact with the original French is not necessary to realize that language itself forms part of Balzac's actual subject matter. As such, it is the replacement of the sense of a universal French language by a proliferation of different styles of linguistic usage that engages the novelist's attention. He refers precisely to 'the various styles of conversation invented since 1830'. Like so much else in this novel, language is seen by him partly in terms of contemporary fashion. The age of individualism is seen as bringing with it an appreciation of such linguistic phenomena as professional slang (e.g. the 'stage argot' explicitly mentioned), which maintains the exclusivity of a particular group. It also appears responsible for a linguistic inventiveness that betrays itself through the delight in puns and word play that unites several of the principal characters. (Faced with the list of things that Hulot is without (*sans*), Josépha not only asks him whether he is 'sans culotte', she plays on the homophony of 'bien des sans' ('a lot of *sans*') and 'bien décent' ('fully decent').) For his narration, Balzac displays a similar delight in language for its own sake. Instead of adopting a consistent idiom connoting a precise degree of seriousness, he combines in playful fashion elements of the high and the low, the learned and the popular, the ancient (he takes obvious relish in a phrase quoted from Rabelais) and the ephemeral. It is precisely the self-conscious superficiality of this narrative language that serves as an indication that the significance of the fiction is not to be encountered at the level of explicit enunciation.

The Balzac novel is *sui generis*. The scope of the author's undertaking defied expression in terms of existing literary models. It was necessary for his novels to accommodate the lecture and the anecdote as well as those elements demanded by the basic fiction itself. The multi-faceted nature of his subject matter and his determination to allow its ironies and paradoxes a free play within his composition called for a combination of seemingly incompatible modes of writing. What he saw before him was a perverse and unnatural world that required him to respond with both pathos and farce, a sense of the sublime and of the ridiculous. At various moments, a particular tone might be felt to dominate, but the lesson afforded by *The Human Comedy* is that the world frequently requires such contradictory responses to co-exist. Faced with a totality that could not be described simply, Balzac's strategy is to direct the reader's attention away from the literal events and statements towards a reading in terms of the network of significant contrasts and the interplay of the positive and negative implications of features that are seen constantly to interrelate. To this end, he sought in *Cousin Bette* not to minimize the fictional, but on the contrary to give it an exaggerated prominence; the language that he adopts for the recounting of the basic fiction has the appearance of a quasi-parodic borrowing of a stereotypical idiom. For the nature of the perverse and contradictory society he felt himself to inhabit could best be suggested by the way it was at odds with existing fictional categories, all of which may fairly be regarded as idealist by implication. Whether it be the moral schematism of melodrama (a genre already in decline by the 1840s) or the naïve wish-fulfilment of the fairy story, which in *Cousin Bette*, as in so many other novels by Balzac, provides an explicit model for comparison, Balzac's consistent practice is to show how at every level the complexity of contemporary French society is imbued with an ambiguity that offers a telling contrast with the suppositions on which fictional stereotypes were based. Thus if we are to understand the significance of a novel such as *Cousin Bette*, we must be prepared not merely to listen to what we are told, but to recognize the contrasts the fiction presents with our expectations and to engage with the implications of such contrasts through a process of constant comparison and differentiation.

Michael Tilby

NOTES

———

1. See Christopher Prendergast, *Balzac: Fiction and Melo-drama*, Edward Arnold, 1978, Chapter V.

2. Robert Niklaus, *A Literary History of France. The Eighteenth Century 1715–1789*, Ernest Benn, 1970, p. 364.

SELECT BIBLIOGRAPHY

———

Cousin Bette is one half of a diptych that Balzac entitled *The Poor Relations*, the other half of which is formed by *Cousin Pons*. Though rarely considered to be in the first rank of Balzac's achievements, *Cousin Pons* will be of special interest to the reader who is familiar with *Cousin Bette*.

The 'Avant-Propos' (or 'Foreword') to *La Comédie humaine* sets out the principles that Balzac considered to underlie his vast project and will be found in the first volume of all editions of *The Human Comedy*.

The French text of a good number of Balzac's novels exists in various modern paperback editions (e.g. Garnier-Flammarion, Folio, Le Livre de poche). The authoritative scholarly edition of *La Comédie humaine* is that in twelve volumes published by Gallimard in their *Bibliothèque de la Pléiade* series (Paris, 1976–80). *La Cousine Bette* will be found in Volume VII, with an introduction and highly informative notes by Anne-Marie Meininger. Volume I is prefaced by an excellent introductory essay by Pierre-Georges Castex entitled 'L'Univers de la *Comédie humaine*'.

The story of Balzac's often idiosyncratic life is told very readably by ANDRÉ MAUROIS in *Prometheus: The Life of Balzac*, The Bodley Head, 1965. V. S. PRITCHETT, *Balzac*, Chatto & Windus, 1973, is a handsome volume, lavishly illustrated. GRAHAM ROBB, *Balzac*, Picador, 1994, makes use of the latest scholarship and is compelling reading.

The most convenient study in which to find descriptions of the individual works in the *Human Comedy* is H. J. HUNT, *Balzac's 'Comédie humaine'*, Athlone Press, 1959.

An accessible introduction to Balzac's ideas and preoccupations is given by F. W. J. HEMMINGS, *An Interpretation of 'La Comédie humaine'*, Random House, New York, 1971.

A very useful work of reference that allows the reader to identify the various texts in which a character's story is traced is ANTHONY R. PUGH, *Balzac's Recurring Characters*, Duckworth, 1975.

The most complete scholarly consideration of the genesis of *La Cousine Bette* is that by ANDRÉ LORANT, *'Les Parents pauvres' de Honoré de Balzac. Etude historique et critique*, 2 vols., Droz, Geneva, 1967.

DAVID BELLOS, *Balzac: 'La Cousine Bette'*, Grant & Cutler: *Critical Guides to French Texts*, 1980, is aimed at the reader who is coming to the novel for the first time.

A more demanding, and highly compelling, reinterpretation of the novel is given by CHRISTOPHER PRENDERGAST in Chapter V of *Balzac: Fiction and melodrama*, Edward Arnold, 1978. Also of considerable interest from this perspective is PETER BROOKS, *The Melodramatic Imagination*, Yale University Press, New Haven, Conn., 1976.

The serious student of the novel will also need to engage with the important interpretative essay by FREDRIC JAMESON, '*La Cousine Bette* and allegorical realism' in *Publications of the Modern Language Association of America [PMLA]*, January 1971, pp. 241–54.

A range of critical essays (in French) devoted to *La Cousine Bette* and *Le Cousin Pons* will be found in FRANÇOISE VAN ROSSUM-GUYON and MICHIEL VAN BREDERODE, eds., *Balzac et 'Les Parents pauvres'*, SEDES, Paris, 1981, which also contains a comprehensive list of the scholarly and critical articles written on the two novels prior to 1980.

General critical discussions of Balzac include:

JAMES, HENRY, 'Honoré de Balzac' in James, *Literary Criticism: French Writers. Other European Writers. The Prefaces to the New York Edition*, Cambridge University Press, *The Library of America*, 1984, pp. 31–151.

PROUST, MARCEL, *By Way of Sainte-Beuve*, translated by Sylvia Townsend Warner, Chatto & Windus, 1958.

BARDÈCHE, MAURICE, *Une Lecture de Balzac*, Les Sept Couleurs, Paris, 1964.

KANES, MARTIN, *Balzac's Comedy of Words*, Princeton University Press, Princeton, NJ, 1975.

BERSANI, LEO, *Balzac to Beckett*, Oxford University Press, 1970.

BARTHES, ROLAND, *S/Z*, translated by Richard Miller, Cape, 1975 – a justly celebrated structuralist analysis of Balzac's previously little-read story, *Sarrasine*.

Three important works of Marxist criticism:

LUKÁCS, GEORG, *Studies in European Realism*, Merlin Press, 1972.

BARBÉRIS, PIERRE, *Balzac: Une Mythologie réaliste*, Larousse, Paris, 1971.

— *Le Monde de Balzac*, Arthaud, Paris, 1973.

Balzac, ed. MICHAEL TILBY, Longman, 1995, is an anthology of essays and extracts devoted to Balzac by a wide range of nineteenth- and twentieth-century critics and scholars.

The periodical *L'Année balzacienne* (a single volume annually: Presses universitaires de France, Paris) is always a treasure-house of information about Balzac and his work and provides a forum for new and often stimulating critical readings.

C H R O N O L O G Y

———

DATE	AUTHOR'S LIFE	LITERARY CONTEXT
1799	Born in Tours, 20 May.	Death of Beaumarchais.
1800		Madame de Staël: *De la littérature.*
1801		
1802		Births of A. Dumas *père* and Victor Hugo.
		Chateaubriand: *Le Génie du christianisme.*
1803		Death of Laclos.
		Birth of Mérimée.
1804		Birth of George Sand and Sainte-Beuve.
1805		Chateaubriand: *René.*
1807	Enters the Collège des Oratoriens in Vendôme, where he remains a boarder for six years.	
1808		Birth of G. de Nerval.
1810		Birth of Musset.
		Madame de Staël: *De l'Allemagne.*
1811		Birth of Gautier.
1814	Joins his family in Paris.	Death of the Marquis de Sade.
1815		
1816	Registers with the Faculty of Law in Paris and takes post as a clerk in a solicitor's office.	Constant: *Adolphe.*
1817		Death of Madame de Staël.
1818	Goes to work for another solicitor.	
1819	Bachelor of Law. Forsakes a legal career for his literary ambitions. *Cromwell*, a tragedy, severely criticized by a family friend and left unpublished in his lifetime.	Chénier: *Oeuvres complètes.*
1820	Begins two ambitious literary works of a philosophical nature (*Falthurne* and *Sténie*) which remain unfinished.	Lamartine: *Méditations poétiques.*

Coup d'état of the 18 Brumaire.

The Concordat.

Napoleon is crowned Emperor.

First abdication of Napoleon; first Restoration of the monarchy (Louis XVIII).
The Hundred Days. The Battle of Waterloo. The Congress of Vienna. The second Restoration (Louis XVIII – 1815–24).

DATE	AUTHOR'S LIFE	LITERARY CONTEXT
1821		Birth of Baudelaire and Flaubert.
1822	Publishes (in collaboration) two pot-boilers, *L'Héritière de Birague* and *Jean-Louis*, and (single-handed) *Clothilde de Lusignan* under the anagrammatic pseudonym Lord R'Hoone. Two further novels (*Le Centenaire* and *Le Vicaire des Ardennes*) under the pseudonym Horace de Saint-Aubin.	Victor Hugo: *Odes et Poésies diverses*. Stendhal: *De l'amour*.
1823	Horace de Saint-Aubin: *La Dernière Fée*.	Birth of Renan. Stendhal: *Racine et Shakespeare*.
1824	Horace de Saint-Aubin: *Annette et le criminel*.	
1825	Horace de Saint-Aubin: *Wann-Chlore* (the last of his youthful pot-boilers).	
1826	Establishes himself as a printer in Paris.	Vigny: *Cinq-Mars*.
1827		Victor Hugo: *Préface de Cromwell*.
1828	Abandons his new career amid heavy debts and returns to writing.	Birth of Taine and Verne.
1829	Honoré Balzac: *Le Dernier Chouan ou la Bretagne en 1800* (later *Les Chouans*), the first of his novels to be incorporated in *La Comédie humaine*. 'A Young Bachelor': *Physiologie du mariage*.	Mérimée: *Mateo Falcone*. Victor Hugo: *Les Orientales*, and *Le Dernier Jour d'un condamné*. Musset: *Contes d'Espagne et d'Italie*.
1830	Prolific activity as a journalist and begins to sign his work Honoré de Balzac. Eight short stories, six of which are 'scenes of private life' and two, 'philosophical tales'.	Death of Constant. Victor Hugo: *Hernani*. Stendhal: *Le Rouge et le Noir*.
1831	*Le Peau de chagrin*. Further short stories.	Victor Hugo: *Notre-Dame de Paris* and *Les Feuilles d'automne*.
1832	*Le Colonel Chabert*, *La Femme de trente ans*, *Le Curé de Tours*, and the largely autobiographical *Louis Lambert*. Other short stories, including the first of his *Contes drolatiques* in the manner of Rabelais.	George Sand: *Indiana*.

CHRONOLOGY

Villèle forms a government.

Charles X (1824–30).

Fall of Villèle.

Polignac becomes chief minister; takes repressive measures.

The capture of Algiers. The July Revolution. Accession of Louis-Philippe (1830–48).

DATE	AUTHOR'S LIFE	LITERARY CONTEXT
1833	The beginning of a long correspondence with a married Polishwoman living in the Ukraine, Madame Hanska ('L'Etrangère'). *Le Médecin de campagne, L'Illustre Gaudissart, Eugénie Grandet.*	
1834	*La Recherche de l'absolu. Histoire des Treize.*	Musset: *Lorenzaccio.* Sainte-Beuve: *Volupté.*
1835	His collected *Scènes de la vie privée* and *Etudes philosophiques*, with important prefaces written to the author's order by Félix Davin. *Le Père Goriot, Melmoth réconcilié, Séraphita.*	Vigny: *Servitude et grandeur militaires* and *Chatterton.* Gautier: *Mademoiselle de Maupin.*
1836	Travels to Turin. *Le Lys dans la vallée, Facino Cane.*	Musset: *Confession d'un enfant du siècle.*
1837	New visit to Italy. *La Vieille Fille, Illusions perdues* (first part), *César Birotteau.*	Mérimée: *La Vénus d'Ille.*
1838	Again travels to Italy (including Sardinia). *Les Employés, La Maison Nucingen, La Torpille* (part of *Splendeurs et misères des courtisanes*).	
1839	President of the Société des Gens de Lettres. Two plays, including *Vautrin.* Candidate for the French Academy, but steps down in favour of Victor Hugo, who is not elected. *Le Cabinet des antiques, Gobseck, Une Fille d'Eve, Massimila Doni, Béatrix* (first part), *Les Secrets de la princesse de Cadignan, Illusions perdues* (second part).	Stendhal: *La Chartreuse de Parme.*
1840	First performance of *Vautrin* (banned by the authorities two days later). Founds the short-lived *Revue parisienne* and writes for it an important essay on Stendhal's *La Chartreuse de Parme.* Moves to 47 rue Raynouard (now the home of a Balzac museum). *Pierrette, Pierre Grassou, Z. Marcas, Un Prince de la Bohême.*	Birth of Zola. Mérimée: *Colomba.*
1841	*Le Curé de village.* Contract for *La Comédie humaine.*	

CHRONOLOGY

HISTORICAL EVENTS

Fieschi's assassination attempt on Louis-Philippe.

Uprising attempt of Louis-Napoleon Bonaparte in Strasbourg.

Revolt in Algiers begins. Louis Blanc: *L'Organisation du travail.*
Louis-Napoleon Bonaparte: *Les Idées napoléoniennes.*

Louis-Napoleon Bonaparte makes second failed coup.
Government of Thiers (March). Mehemet Ali crisis (October).
Government of Guizot (to 1848). Proudhon: *Qu'est-ce que la propriété?*

DATE	AUTHOR'S LIFE	LITERARY CONTEXT
1842	First performance of *Les Ressources de Quinola. L'Avant-Propos de la Comédie humaine*, *Mémoires de deux jeunes mariées*, *Albert Savarus, La Fausse Maîtresse*, *Autre étude de femme, Ursule Mirouët*, *Un Début dans la vie, La Rabouilleuse.*	Death of Stendhal. Birth of Mallarmé. Sue: *Les Mystères de Paris* (to 1843). George Sand: *Consuelo.*
1843	Visits St Petersburg to stay with Madame Hanska (widowed in 1841). Returns via Germany. First performance of *Paméla Giraud; Une Ténébreuse Affaire, La Muse du département, Honorine*, *Illusions perdues* (final part).	Victor Hugo: *Les Burgraves.*
1844	*Modeste Mignon, Les Paysans* (first part), *Béatrix* (second part).	Birth of A. France and Verlaine. A. Dumas *père: Les Trois Mousquétaires.*
1845	Travels with Madame Hanska. Candidate for the French Academy (unsuccessful). *Un Homme d'affaires, Les Comédiens sans le savoir.*	A. Dumas *père: Le Comte de Monte-Cristo.* Mérimée: *Carmen.*
1846	Madame Hanska's child still-born. *Petites misères de la vie conjugale, L'Envers de l'histoire contemporaine* (first episode), *La Cousine Bette.*	George Sand: *La Mare au diable.*
1847	Madame Hanska in Paris for three months. Balzac visits her in the Ukraine in the autumn. *Le Cousin Pons, La Dernière Incarnation de Vautrin* (final part of *Splendeurs et misères des courtisanes*).	Lamartine: *Histoire des Girondins.* Michelet: *Histoire de la Révolution.*
1848	Witnesses the February Revolution in Paris. First performance of *La Marâtre*. Goes to the Ukraine in September, where he remains until spring of 1850. *L'Envers de l'histoire contemporaine* (second episode).	Death of Chateaubriand. Birth of Huysmans. George Sand: *François le Champi* and *La Petite Fadette.*
1849	Fails twice more to secure election to the French Academy. Suffers several heart-attacks.	Sainte-Beuve: *Causeries du lundi.*
1850	In March marries Madame Hanska. They return to Paris in May. Balzac dies in August.	Birth of Maupassant.

CHRONOLOGY

HISTORICAL EVENTS

Guizot's railway law. Railway mania in France (to 1846).

France and Morocco at war.

Anglo-French expedition against Madagascar.

Economic crisis in France. Teste trial discredits government. Algerian revolt suppressed.

February Revolution. The fall of Louis-Philippe. June Days: workers' uprising in Paris suppressed. Second Republic (1848–51). Year of Revolutions in Europe.

Election of Legislative Assembly. French restore Pius IX; fall of Roman republic.

THE POOR RELATIONS

PART I
COUSIN BETTE

The Prodigal Father

It is neither to the Roman Prince, nor to the representative of the illustrious house of Cajetani, which has given more than one Pope to the Christian Church, that I dedicate this short portion of a long history; it is to the learned commentator of Dante.

It was you who led me to understand the marvellous framework of ideas on which the great Italian poet built his poem, the only work which the moderns can place by that of Homer. Till I heard you, the Divine Comedy *was to me a vast enigma to which none had found the clue — the commentators least of all. Thus, to understand Dante is to be as great as he; but every form of greatness is familiar to you.*

A French savant would make a reputation, earn a professor's chair and a dozen decorations, by publishing in a dogmatic volume the improvised lecture by which you lent enchantment to one of those evenings which are rest after seeing Rome. You do not know, perhaps, that most of our professors live on Germany, on England, on the East, or on the North, as an insect lives on a tree; and, like the insect, become an integral part of it, borrowing their merit from that of what they feed on. Now, Italy hitherto has not yet been worked out in public lectures. No one will ever give me credit for my literary honesty. Merely by plundering you I might have been as learned as three Schlegels in one, whereas I mean to remain a humble Doctor of the Faculty of Social Medicine, a veterinary surgeon for incurable maladies. Were it only to lay a token of gratitude at the feet of my cicerone, I would fain add your illustrious name to those of Porcia, of San-Severino, of Pareto, of di Negro, and of Belgiojoso, who will represent in this 'Human Comedy' the close and constant alliance between Italy and France, to which

Bandello did honour in the same way in the sixteenth century – Bandello, the bishop and author of some strange tales indeed, who left us the splendid collection of romances whence Shakespeare derived many of his plots and even complete characters, word for word.

The two sketches I dedicate to you are the two eternal aspects of one and the same fact. Homo duplex, *said the great Buffon: why not add* Res duplex? *Everything has two sides, even virtue. Hence Molière always shows us both sides of every human problem; and Diderot, imitating him, once wrote, 'This is not a mere tale' – in what is perhaps Diderot's masterpiece, where he shows us the beautiful picture of Mademoiselle de Lachaux sacrificed by Gardanne, side by side with that of a perfect lover dying for his mistress.*

In the same way, these two romances form a pair, like twins of opposite sexes. This is a literary vagary to which a writer may for once give way, especially as part of a work in which I am endeavouring to depict every form that can serve as a garb to mind.

Most human quarrels arise from the fact that both wise men and dunces exist who are so constituted as to be incapable of seeing more than one side of any fact or idea, while each asserts that the side he sees is the only true and right one. Thus it is written in the Holy Book, 'God will deliver the world over to divisions.' I must confess that this passage of Scripture alone should persuade the Papal See to give you the control of the two Chambers to carry out this text which found its commentary in 1814, in the decree of Louis XVIII.

May your wit and the poetry that is in you extend a protecting hand over these two histories of The Poor Relations

Of your affectionate humble servant,

De Balzac.

PARIS, *August – September* 1846.

COUSIN BETTE

ONE DAY, about the middle of July 1838, one of the carriages, then lately introduced to Paris cabstands, and known as *Milords*, was driving down the Rue de l'Université, conveying a stout man of middle height in the uniform of a captain of the National Guard.

Among the Paris crowd, who are supposed to be so clever, there are some men who fancy themselves infinitely more attractive in uniform than in their ordinary clothes, and who attribute to women so depraved a taste that they believe they will be favourably impressed by the aspect of a busby and of military accoutrements.

The countenance of this Captain of the Second Company beamed with a self-satisfaction that added splendour to his ruddy and somewhat chubby face. The halo of glory that a fortune made in business gives to a retired tradesman sat on his brow, and stamped him as one of the elect of Paris – at least a retired deputy-mayor of his quarter of the town. And you may be sure that the ribbon of the Legion of Honour was not missing from his breast, gallantly padded *à la Prussienne*. Proudly seated in one corner of the *milord*, this splendid person let his gaze wander over the passers-by, who, in Paris, often thus meet an ingratiating smile meant for sweet eyes that are absent.

The vehicle stopped in the part of the street between the Rue de Bellechasse and the Rue de Bourgogne, at the door of a large, newly-built house, standing on part of the courtyard of an ancient mansion that had a garden. The old house remained in its original state, beyond the courtyard curtailed by half its extent.

Only from the way in which the officer accepted the assistance of the coachman to help him out, it was plain that he was past fifty. There are certain movements so undisguisedly heavy that they are as tell-tale as a register of birth. The captain put on his lemon-coloured right-hand glove, and, without any question to the gatekeeper, went up the outer steps to the ground floor of the new house with a look that proclaimed, 'She is mine!'

The *concierges* of Paris have sharp eyes; they do not stop visitors who wear an order, have a blue uniform, and walk ponderously; in short, they know a rich man when they see him.

This ground floor was entirely occupied by Monsieur le Baron Hulot d'Ervy, Commissary General under the Republic, retired army contractor, and at the present time at the head of one of the most important departments of the War Office, Councillor of State, officer of the Legion of Honour, and so forth.

This Baron Hulot had taken the name of d'Ervy – the place of his birth – to distinguish him from his brother, the famous General Hulot, Colonel of the Grenadiers of the Imperial Guard, created by the Emperor Comte de Forzheim after the campaign of 1809. The Count, the elder brother, being responsible for his junior, had, with paternal care, placed him in the commissariat, where, thanks to the services of the two brothers, the Baron deserved and won Napoleon's good graces. After 1807, Baron Hulot was Commissary General for the army in Spain.

Having rung the bell, the citizen-captain made strenuous efforts to pull his coat into place, for it had rucked up as much at the back as in front, pushed out of shape by the working of a piriform stomach. Being admitted as soon as the servant in livery saw him, the important and imposing personage followed the man, who opened the door of the drawing-room, announcing –

'Monsieur Crevel.'

On hearing the name, singularly appropriate to the figure of the man who bore it, a tall, fair woman, evidently young-looking for her age, rose as if she had received an electric shock.

'Hortense, my darling, go into the garden with your Cousin Bette,' she said hastily to her daughter, who was working at some embroidery at her mother's side.

After curtseying prettily to the captain, Mademoiselle Hortense went out by a glass door, taking with her a withered-looking spinster, who looked older than the Baroness, though she was five years younger.

'They are settling your marriage,' said Cousin Bette in the girl's ear, without seeming at all offended at the way in which the Baroness had dismissed them, counting her almost as zero.

The cousin's dress might, at need, have explained this free-and-easy demeanour. The old maid wore a merino gown of a dark plum colour, of which the cut and trimming dated from the year of the Restoration; a little worked collar, worth perhaps three francs; and a common straw hat with blue satin ribbons edged with straw plait, such as the old-clothes buyers wear at market. On looking down at her kid shoes, made, it was evident, by the veriest cobbler, a stranger would have hesitated to recognise Cousin Bette as a member of the family, for she looked exactly like a journeywoman sempstress. But she did not leave the room without bestowing a little friendly nod on Monsieur Crevel, to which that gentleman responded by a look of mutual understanding.

'You are coming to us to-morrow I hope, Mademoiselle Fischer?' said he.

'You have no company?' asked Cousin Bette.

'My children and yourself, no one else,' replied the visitor.

'Very well,' replied she; 'depend on me.'

'And here am I, Madame, at your orders,' said the citizen-captain, bowing again to Madame Hulot.

He gave such a look at Madame Hulot as Tartuffe casts at Elmire – when a provincial actor plays the part and thinks it necessary to emphasise its meaning – at Poitiers, or at Coutances.

'If you will come into this room with me, we shall be more conveniently placed for talking business than we are in this room,' said Madame Hulot, going to an adjoining room, which, as the apartment was arranged, served as a card-room.

It was divided by a slight partition from a boudoir looking out on the garden, and Madame Hulot left her visitor to himself for a minute, for she thought it wise to shut the window and the door of the boudoir, so that no one should get in and listen. She even took the precaution of shutting the glass door of the drawing-room, smiling on her daughter and her cousin, whom she saw seated in an old summer-house at the end of the garden. As she came back she left the card-room door open, so as to hear if any one should open that of the drawing-room to come in.

As she came and went, the Baroness, seen by nobody, allowed her face to betray all her thoughts, and any one who could have seen her would have been shocked to see her agitation. But when she finally came back from the glass door of the drawing-room, as she entered the card-room, her face was hidden behind the impenetrable reserve which every woman, even the most candid, seems to have at her command.

During all these preparations – odd, to say the least – the National Guardsman studied the furniture of the room in which he found himself. As he noted the silk curtains, once red, now faded to dull purple by the sunshine, and frayed in the pleats by long wear; the carpet, from which the hues had faded; the discoloured gilding of the furniture; and the silk seats, discoloured in patches, and wearing into strips – expressions of scorn, satisfaction, and hope dawned in succession without disguise on his stupid tradesman's face. He looked at himself in the glass over an old clock of the Empire, and was contemplating the general effect, when the rustle of her silk skirt announced the Baroness. He at once struck an attitude.

After dropping on to a sofa, which had been a very handsome one in the year 1809, the Baroness, pointing to an armchair with the arms ending in bronze sphinxes' heads, while the paint was peeling from the wood, which showed through in many places, signed to Crevel to be seated.

'All the precautions you are taking, Madame, would seem full of promise to a—'

'To a lover,' said she, interrupting him.

'The word is too feeble,' said he, placing his right hand on his heart, and rolling his eyes in a way which almost always makes a woman laugh when she, in cold blood, sees such a look. 'A lover! A lover? Say a man bewitched—'

'Listen, Monsieur Crevel,' said the Baroness, too anxious to be able to laugh, 'you are fifty – ten years younger than Monsieur Hulot, I know; but at my age a woman's follies ought to be justified by beauty, youth, fame, superior merit – some one of the splendid qualities which can dazzle us to the point of making us forget all else – even at our age. Though you may have fifty thousand francs a year, your age counter-balances your fortune; thus you have nothing whatever of what a woman looks for—'

'But love!' said the officer, rising and coming forward. 'Such love as—'

'No, Monsieur, such obstinacy!' said the Baroness, inter-rupting him to put an end to his absurdity.

'Yes, obstinacy,' said he, 'and love; but something stronger still – a claim—'

'A claim!' cried Madame Hulot, rising sublime with scorn, defiance, and indignation. 'But,' she went on, 'this will bring us to no issues; I did not ask you to come here to discuss the matter which led to your banishment in spite of the connec-tion between our families—'

'I had fancied so.'

'What! still?' cried she. 'Do you not see, Monsieur, by the entire ease and freedom with which I can speak of lovers and love, of everything least creditable to a woman, that I am perfectly secure in my own virtue? I fear nothing – not even to shut myself in alone with you. Is that the conduct of a weak woman? You know full well why I begged you to come.'

'No, Madame,' replied Crevel, with an assumption of great coldness. He pursed up his lips, and again struck an attitude.

'Well, I will be brief, to shorten our common discomfort,' said the Baroness, looking at Crevel.

Crevel made an ironical bow, in which a man who knew the race would have recognised the graces of a bagman.

'Our son married your daughter—'

'And if it were to do again—' said Crevel.

'It would not be done at all, I suspect,' said the Baroness hastily. 'However, you have nothing to complain of. My son is not only one of the leading pleaders of Paris, but for the last year he has sat as Deputy, and his maiden speech was brilliant enough to lead us to suppose that ere long he will be in office. Victorin has twice been called upon to report on important measures; and he might even now, if he chose, be made Attorney-General in the Court of Appeal. So, if you mean to say that your son-in-law has no fortune—'

'Worse than that, Madame, a son-in-law whom I am obliged to maintain,' replied Crevel. 'Of the five hundred thousand francs that formed my daughter's marriage portion, two hundred thousand have vanished – God knows how! – in paying the young gentleman's debts, in furnishing his house splendaciously – a house costing five hundred thousand francs, and bringing in scarcely fifteen thousand, since he occupies the larger part of it, while he owes two hundred and sixty thousand francs of the purchase-money. The rent he gets barely pays the interest on the debt. I have had to give my daughter twenty thousand francs this year to help her to make both ends meet. And then my son-in-law, who was making thirty thousand francs a year at the Assizes, I am told, is going to throw that up for the Chamber—'

'This again, Monsieur Crevel, is beside the mark; we are wandering from the point. Still, to dispose of it finally, it may be said that if my son gets into office, if he has you made an officer of the Legion of Honour and councillor of the municipality of Paris, you, as a retired perfumer, will not have much to complain of—'

'Ah! there we are again, Madame! Yes, I am a tradesman, a shopkeeper, a retail dealer in almond-paste, eau-de-Portugal, and hair-oil, and was only too much honoured when my only daughter was married to the son of Monsieur le Baron Hulot d'Ervy – my daughter will be a Baroness! This is Regency, Louis xv., Œil-de-bœuf – quite tip-top! – very good. I love

Célestine as a man loves his only child – so well indeed, that, to preserve her from having either brother or sister, I resigned myself to all the privations of a widower – in Paris, and in the prime of life, Madame. But you must understand that, in spite of this extravagant affection for my daughter, I do not intend to reduce my fortune for the sake of your son, whose expenses are not wholly accounted for – in my eyes, as an old man of business.'

'Monsieur, you may at this day see in the Ministry of Commerce Monsieur Popinot, formerly a druggist in the Rue des Lombards—'

'And a friend of mine, Madame,' said the ex-perfumer. 'For I, Célestin Crevel, foreman once to old César Birotteau, bought up the said César Birotteau's stock; and he was Popinot's father-in-law. Why, that very Popinot was no more than a shopman in the establishment, and he is the first to remind me of it; for he is not proud, to do him justice, to men in a good position with an income of sixty thousand francs in the funds.'

'Well, then, Monsieur, the notions you term "Regency" are quite out of date at a time when a man is taken at his personal worth; and that is what you did when you married your daughter to my son.'

'But you do not know how the marriage was brought about!' cried Crevel. 'Oh, that cursed bachelor life! But for my misconduct, my Célestine might at this day be Vicomtesse Popinot!'

'Once more have done with recriminations over accomplished facts,' said the Baroness anxiously. 'Let us rather discuss the complaints I found on your strange behaviour. My daughter Hortense had a chance of marrying; the match depended entirely on you; I believed you felt some sentiments of generosity; I thought you would do justice to a woman who has never had a thought in her heart for any man but her husband, that you would have understood how necessary it is for her not to receive a man who may compromise her, and that for the honour of the family with which you are allied you would have been eager to promote Hortense's settlement with

Monsieur le Conseiller Lebas. – And it is you, Monsieur, you who have hindered the marriage.'

'Madame,' said the ex-perfumer, 'I acted the part of an honest man. I was asked whether the two hundred thousand francs to be settled on Mademoiselle Hortense would be forthcoming. I replied exactly in these words: "I would not answer for it. My son-in-law, to whom the Hulots had promised the same sum, was in debt; and I believe that if Monsieur Hulot d'Ervy were to die to-morrow, his widow would have nothing to live on." – There, fair lady.'

'And would you have said as much, Monsieur,' asked Madame Hulot, looking Crevel steadily in the face, 'if I had been false to my duty?'

'I should not be in a position to say it, dearest Adeline,' cried this singular adorer, interrupting the Baroness, 'for you would have found the amount in my pocket-book.'

And adding action to word, the fat guardsman knelt down on one knee and kissed Madame Hulot's hand, seeing that his speech had filled her with speechless horror, which he took for hesitancy.

'What, buy my daughter's fortune at the cost of—? Rise, Monsieur – or I ring the bell.'

Crevel rose with great difficulty. This fact made him so furious that he again struck his favourite attitude. Most men have some habitual position by which they fancy that they show to the best advantage the good points bestowed on them by nature. This attitude in Crevel consisted in crossing his arms like Napoleon, his head showing three-quarters face, and his eyes fixed on the horizon, as the painter has shown the Emperor in his portrait.

'To be faithful,' he began with well-acted indignation, 'so faithful to a liber—'

'To a husband who is worthy of such fidelity,' Madame Hulot put in, to hinder Crevel from saying a word she did not choose to hear.

'Come, Madame; you wrote to bid me here, you ask the reasons for my conduct, you drive me to extremities with your imperial airs, your scorn, and your contempt! Any one might think I was a negro. But I repeat it, and you may believe me, I have a right to – to make love to you, for— But, no; I love you well enough to hold my tongue.'

'You may speak, Monsieur. In a few days I shall be eight-and-forty; I am no prude; I can hear whatever you can say.'

'Then will you give me your word of honour as an honest woman – for you are, alas for me! an honest woman – never to mention my name or to say that it was I who betrayed the secret?'

'If that is the condition on which you speak, I will swear never to tell any one from whom I heard the horrors you propose to tell me, not even my husband.'

'I should think not indeed, for only you and he are concerned.'

Madame Hulot turned pale.

'Oh, if you still really love Hulot, it will distress you. Shall I say no more?'

'Speak, Monsieur; for by your account you wish to justify in my eyes the extraordinary declarations you have chosen to make me, and your persistency in tormenting a woman of my age, whose only wish is to see her daughter married, and then – to die in peace—'

'You see; you are unhappy.'

'I, Monsieur?'

'Yes, beautiful, noble creature!' cried Crevel. 'You have indeed been too wretched!'

'Monsieur, be silent and go – or speak to me as you ought.'

'Do you know, Madame, how Master Hulot and I first made acquaintance? – At our mistresses', Madame.'

'Oh, Monsieur!'

'Yes, Madame, at our mistresses',' Crevel repeated in a melodramatic tone, and leaving his position to wave his right hand.

'Well, and what then?' said the Baroness coolly, to Crevel's great amazement.

Such mean seducers cannot understand a great soul.

'I, a widower five years since,' Crevel began, in the tone of a man who has a story to tell, 'and not wishing to marry again for the sake of the daughter I adore, not choosing either to cultivate any such connection in my own establishment, though I had at the time a very pretty lady-accountant, I set up, "on her own account," as they say, a little sempstress of fifteen – really a miracle of beauty, with whom I fell desperately in love. And in fact, Madame, I asked an aunt of my own, my mother's sister, whom I sent for from the country, to live with the sweet creature and keep an eye on her, that she might behave as well as might be in this rather – what shall I say? – shady? – no, delicate position.

'The child, whose talent for music was striking, had masters, she was educated – I had to give her something to do. Besides, I wished to be at once her father, her benefactor, and – well, out with it – her lover; to kill two birds with one stone, a good action and a sweet heart. For five years I was very happy. The girl had one of those voices that make the fortune of a theatre; I can only describe her by saying that she is a Duprez in petticoats. It cost me two thousand francs a year only to cultivate her talent as a singer. She made me music-mad; I took a box at the opera for her and for my daughter, and went there alternate evenings with Célestine or Josépha.

'What, the famous singer?'

'Yes, Madame,' said Crevel with pride, 'the famous Josépha owes everything to me. – At last, in 1834, when the child was twenty, believing that I had attached her to me for ever, and being very weak where she was concerned, I thought I would give her a little amusement, and I introduced her to a pretty little actress, Jenny Cadine, whose life had been somewhat like her own. This actress also owed everything to a protector who had brought her up in leading-strings. That protector was Baron Hulot.'

'I know that,' said the Baroness, in a calm voice without the least agitation.

'Bless me!' cried Crevel, more and more astounded. 'Well! But do you know that your monster of a husband took Jenny Cadine in hand at the age of thirteen?'

'What then?' said the Baroness.

'As Jenny Cadine and Josépha were both aged twenty when they first met,' the ex-tradesman went on, 'the Baron had been playing the part of Louis xv. to Mademoiselle de Romans ever since 1826, and you were twelve years younger then—'

'I had my reasons, Monsieur, for leaving Monsieur Hulot his liberty.'

'That falsehood, Madame, will surely be enough to wipe out every sin you have ever committed, and to open to you the gates of Paradise,' replied Crevel, with a knowing air that brought the colour to the Baroness's cheeks. 'Sublime and adored woman, tell that to those who will believe it, but not to old Crevel, who has, I may tell you, feasted too often as one of four with your rascally husband not to know what your high merits are! Many a time has he blamed himself when half tipsy as he has expatiated on your perfections. Oh, I know you well! – A libertine might hesitate between you and a girl of twenty. I do not hesitate—'

'Monsieur!'

'Well, I say no more. But you must know, saintly and noble woman, that a husband when he is screwed, will tell his mistress many things about his wife which make the slut split with laughter.'

Tears of shame hanging to Madame Hulot's long lashes checked the National Guardsman. He stopped short, and forgot his attitude.

'To proceed,' said he. 'We became intimate, the Baron and I, through the two hussies. The Baron, like all bad lots, is very pleasant, a thoroughly jolly good fellow. Yes, he took my fancy, the old rascal. He could be so funny! – Well, enough of those reminiscences. We got to be like brothers. The scoundrel – quite Regency in his notions – tried indeed to deprave me altogether, preached Saint-Simonism as to women, and all sorts of lordly ideas; but, you see, I was fond enough of my girl to have married her, only I was afraid of having children.

'Then between two old daddies, such friends as – as we were, what more natural than that we should think of our children marrying each other? – Three months after his son had married my Célestine, Hulot – I don't know how I can utter the wretch's name! he has cheated us both, Madame – well, the villain did me out of my little Josépha. The scoundrel knew that he was supplanted in the heart of Jenny Cadine by a young lawyer and by an artist – only two of them! – for the girl had more and more of a howling success, and he stole my sweet little girl, a perfect darling – but you must have seen her at the opera; he got her an engagement there. Your husband is not so well behaved as I am. I am ruled as straight as a sheet of music-paper. He had dropped a good deal of money on Jenny Cadine, who must have cost him near on thirty thousand francs a year. Well, I can only tell you that he is ruining himself outright for Josépha.

'Josépha, Madame, is a Jewess. Her name is Mirah, the anagram of Hiram, an Israelite mark that stamps her, for she was a foundling picked up in Germany, and the inquiries I have made prove that she is the illegitimate child of a rich Jew banker. The life of the theatre, and, above all, the teaching of Jenny Cadine, Madame Schontz, Malaga, and Carabine, as to the way to treat an old man, have developed, in the child whom I had kept in a respectable and not too expensive way of life, all the native Hebrew instinct for gold and jewels – for the golden calf.

'So this famous singer, hungering for plunder, now wants to be rich – very rich. She tried her 'prentice hand on Baron Hulot, and soon plucked him bare – plucked him, ay, and singed him to the skin. The miserable man, after trying to vie with one of the Kellers and with the Marquis d'Esgrignon, both perfectly mad about Josépha, to say nothing of unknown worshippers, is about to see her carried off by that very rich Duke, who is such a patron of the arts. Oh, what is his name? – a dwarf. – Ah, the Duc d'Hérouville. This fine gentleman insists on having Josépha for his very own, and all that set are talking about it; the Baron knows nothing of it as yet; for it is the same in the thirteenth arrondissement as in every other: the lover, like the husband, is last to get the news.

'Now, do you understand my claim? Your husband, dear lady, has robbed me of my joy in life, the only happiness I have known since I became a widower. Yes, if I had not been so unlucky as to come across that old rip, Josépha would still be mine; for I, you know, should never have placed her on the stage. She would have lived obscure, well conducted, and mine. Oh! if you could but have seen her eight years ago, slight and wiry, with the golden skin of an Andalusian, as they say, black hair as shiny as satin, an eye that flashed lightning under long brown lashes, the style of a duchess in every movement, the modesty of a dependent, decent grace, and the pretty ways of a wild fawn. And by that Hulot's doing all this charm and purity has been degraded to a man-trap, a money-box for five-franc pieces! The girl is the Queen of Trollops; and nowadays she humbugs every one – she who knew nothing, not even that word.'

At this stage the retired perfumer wiped his eyes, which were full of tears. The sincerity of his grief touched Madame Hulot, and roused her from the meditation into which she had sunk.

'Tell me, Madame, is a man of fifty-two likely to find such another jewel? At my age love costs thirty thousand francs a year. It is through your husband's experience that I know the price, and I love Célestine too truly to be her ruin. When I saw you, at the first evening party you gave in our honour, I wondered how that scoundrel Hulot could keep a Jenny Cadine – you had the manner of an Empress. You do not look thirty,' he went on. 'To me, Madame, you look young, and you are beautiful. On my word of honour, that evening I was struck to the heart. I said to myself, "If I had not Josépha, since old Hulot neglects his wife, she would fit me like a glove." Forgive me – it is a reminiscence of my old business. The perfumer will crop up now and then, and that is what keeps me from standing to be elected deputy.

'And then, when I was so abominably deceived by the Baron, for really between old rips like us our friend's mistress should be sacred, I swore I would have his wife. It is but justice. The Baron could say nothing; we are certain of impunity. You showed me the door like a mangy dog at the first words I uttered as to the state of my feelings; you only made my passion – my obstinacy, if you will – twice as strong, and you shall be mine.'

'Indeed; how?'

'I do not know; but it will come to pass. You see, Madame, an idiot of a perfumer – retired from business – who has but one idea in his head, is a stronger man than a clever fellow who has a thousand. I am smitten with you, and you are the means of my revenge; it is like being in love twice over. I am speaking to you quite frankly, as a man who knows what he means. I speak coldly to you, just as you do to me, when you say, "I never will be yours." In fact, as they say, I play the game with the cards on the table. Yes, you shall be mine, sooner or later; if you were fifty, you should still be my mistress. And it will be; for I expect anything from your husband!'

Madame Hulot looked at this vulgar intriguer with such a fixed stare of terror, that he thought she had gone mad, and he stopped.

'You insisted on it, you heaped me with scorn, you defied me – and I have spoken,' said he, feeling that he must justify the ferocity of his last words.

'Oh, my daughter, my daughter,' moaned the Baroness in a voice like a dying woman's.

'Oh! I have forgotten all else,' Crevel went on. 'The day when I was robbed of Josépha I was like a tigress robbed of her cubs; in short, as you see me now. – Your daughter? Yes, I regard her as the means of winning you. Yes, I put a spoke in her marriage – and you will not get her married without my help! Handsome as Mademoiselle Hortense is, she needs a fortune—'

'Alas! yes,' said the Baroness, wiping her eyes.

'Well, just ask your husband for ten thousand francs,' said Crevel, striking his attitude once more. He waited a minute, like an actor who has made a point.

'If he had the money, he would give it to the woman who will take Josépha's place,' he went on, emphasising his tones. 'Does a man ever pull up on the road he has taken? In the first place, he is too sweet on women. There is a happy medium in all things, as our King has told us. And then his vanity is implicated! He is a handsome man! – He would bring you all to ruin for his pleasure; in fact, you are already on the high road to the workhouse. Why, look, never since I first set foot in your house have you been able to do up your drawing-room furniture. "Hard up" is the word shouted by every slit in the stuff. Where will you find a son-in-law who would not turn his back in horror of the ill-concealed evidence of the most cruel misery there is – that of people in decent society? I have kept shop, and I know. There is no eye so quick as that of the Paris tradesman to detect real wealth from its sham. – You have no money,' he said, in a lower voice. 'It is written everywhere, even on your man-servant's coat.

'Would you like me to disclose any more hideous mysteries that are kept from you?'

'Monsieur,' cried Madame Hulot, whose handkerchief was wet through with her tears, 'enough, enough!'

'My son-in-law, I tell you, gives his father money, and this is what I particularly wanted to come to when I began by speaking of your son's expenses. But I keep an eye on my daughter's interests, be easy.'

'Oh, if I could but see my daughter married, and die!' cried the poor woman, quite losing her head.

'Well, then, this is the way,' said the ex-perfumer.

Madame Hulot looked at Crevel with a hopeful expression, which so completely changed her countenance, that this alone ought to have touched the man's feelings and have led him to abandon his monstrous schemes.

'You will still be handsome ten years hence,' Crevel went on, with his arms folded; 'be kind to me, and Mademoiselle

Hulot will marry. Hulot has given me the right, as I have explained to you, to put the matter crudely, and he will not be angry. In three years I have saved the interest on my capital, for my dissipations have been restricted. I have three hundred thousand francs in the bank over and above my invested fortune – they are yours—'

'Go,' said Madame Hulot. 'Go, Monsieur, and never let me see you again. But for the necessity in which you placed me to learn the secret of your cowardly conduct with regard to the match I had planned for Hortense – yes, cowardly!' she repeated, in answer to a gesture from Crevel. 'How can you load a poor girl, a pretty innocent creature, with such a weight of enmity? But for the necessity that goaded me as a mother, you would never have spoken to me again, never again have come within my doors. Thirty-two years of an honourable and loyal life shall not be swept away by a blow from Monsieur Crevel—'

'The retired perfumer, successor to César Birotteau at the *Queen of the Roses*, Rue Saint-Honoré,' added Crevel, in mocking tones. 'Deputy-mayor, captain in the National Guard, Chevalier of the Legion of Honour – exactly what my predecessor was!'

'Monsieur,' said the Baroness, 'if, after twenty years of constancy, Monsieur Hulot is tired of his wife, that is nobody's concern but mine. As you see, he has kept his infidelity a mystery, for I did not know that he had succeeded you in the affections of Mademoiselle Josépha—'

'Oh! it has cost him a pretty penny, Madame. His singing-bird has cost him more than a hundred thousand francs in these two years. Ah, ha! you have not seen the end of it!'

'Have done with all this, Monsieur Crevel. I will not, for your sake, forgo the happiness a mother knows who can embrace her children without a single pang of remorse in her heart, who sees herself respected and loved by her family; and I will give up my soul to God unspotted—'

'Amen!' exclaimed Crevel, with the diabolical rage that embitters the face of these pretenders when they fail for the second time in such an attempt. 'You do not yet know the latter end of poverty – shame, disgrace. – I have tried to warn you; I could have saved you, you and your daughter. Well, you must study the modern parable of the *Prodigal Father* from A to Z. Your tears and your pride move me deeply,' said Crevel, seating himself, 'for it is frightful to see the woman one loves weeping. All I can promise you, dear Adeline, is to do nothing against your interests or your husband's. Only never send to me for information. That is all.'

'What is to be done?' cried Madame Hulot.

Up till now the Baroness had bravely faced the three-fold torment which this explanation inflicted on her; for she was wounded as a woman, as a mother, and as a wife. In fact, so long as her son's father-in-law was insolent and offensive, she had found strength in her resistance to the aggressive tradesman; but the sort of good-nature he showed, in spite of his exasperation as a mortified adorer and as a humiliated National Guardsman, broke down her nerve, strung to the point of snapping. She wrung her hands, melted into tears, and was in a state of such helpless dejection, that she allowed Crevel to kneel at her feet, kissing her hands.

'Good God! what will become of us!' she went on, wiping away her tears. 'Can a mother sit still and see her child pine away before her eyes? What is to be the fate of that splendid creature, as strong in her pure life under her mother's care as she is by every gift of nature? There are days when she wanders round the garden, out of spirits without knowing why; I find her with tears in her eyes—'

'She is one-and-twenty,' said Crevel.

'Must I place her in a convent?' asked the Baroness. 'But in such cases religion is impotent to subdue nature, and the most piously trained girls lose their head! – Get up, pray, Monsieur; do you not understand that everything is final between us? that I look upon you with horror? that you have crushed a mother's last hopes—'

'But if I were to restore them,' asked he.

Madame Hulot looked at Crevel with a frenzied expression that really touched him. But he drove pity back to the depths of his heart; she had said, 'I look upon you with horror.'

Virtue is always a little too rigid; it overlooks the shades and instincts by help of which we are able to tack when in a false position.

'So handsome a girl as Mademoiselle Hortense does not find a husband nowadays if she is penniless,' Crevel remarked, resuming his starchest manner. 'Your daughter is one of those beauties who rather alarm intending husbands; like a thoroughbred horse, which is too expensive to keep up to find a ready purchaser. If you go out walking with such a woman on your arm, every one will turn to look at you, and follow and covet his neighbour's wife. Such success is a source of much uneasiness to men who do not want to be killing lovers; for, after all, no man kills more than one. In the position in which you find yourself there are just three ways of getting your daughter married: Either by my help – and you will have none of it! That is one. – Or by finding some old man of sixty, very rich, childless, and anxious to have children; that is difficult, still such men are to be met with. Many old men take up with a Josépha, a Jenny Cadine, why should not one be found who is ready to make a fool of himself under legal formalities? If it were not for Célestine and our two grandchildren, I would marry Hortense myself. That is two. – The last way is the easiest—'

Madame Hulot raised her head, and looked uneasily at the ex-perfumer.

'Paris is a town whither every man of energy – and they sprout like saplings on French soil – comes to meet his kind; talent swarms here without hearth or home, and energy equal to anything, even to making a fortune. Well, these youngsters – your humble servant was such an one in his time, and how many he has known! What had du Tillet or Popinot twenty years since? They were both pottering round in Daddy Birotteau's shop, with not a penny of capital but their determination to get on, which, in my opinion, is the best capital a man can have. Money may be eaten through, but you don't eat through your determination. Why, what had I? The will to get on, and plenty of pluck. At this day du Tillet is a match for the greatest folks; little Popinot, the richest druggist of the Rue des Lombards, became a deputy, now he is in office. – Well, one of these free lances, as we say on the stock market, of the pen, or of the brush, is the only man in Paris who would marry a penniless beauty, for they have courage enough for anything. Monsieur Popinot married Mademoiselle Birotteau without asking for a farthing. Those men are madmen, to be sure! They trust in love as they trust in good luck and brains! – Find a man of energy who will fall in love with your daughter, and he will marry without a thought of money. You must confess that by way of an enemy I am not ungenerous, for this advice is against my own interests.'

'Oh, Monsieur Crevel, if you would indeed be my friend and give up your ridiculous notions—'

'Ridiculous? Madame, do not run yourself down. Look at yourself – I love you, and you will come to be mine. The day will come when I shall say to Hulot, "You took Josépha, I have taken your wife!"'

'It is the old law of tit-for-tat! And I will persevere till I have attained my end, unless you should become extremely ugly. – I shall succeed; and I will tell you why,' he went on, resuming his attitude, and looking at Madame Hulot. 'You will not meet with such an old man, or such a young lover,' he said after a pause, 'because you love your daughter too well to hand her over to the manœuvres of an old libertine, and because you – the Baronne Hulot, sister of the old Lieute-nent-General who commanded the veteran Grenadiers of the Old Guard – will not condescend to take a man of spirit wherever you may find him; for he might be a mere craftsman, as many a millionaire of to-day was ten years ago, a working artisan, or the foreman of a factory.

'And then, when you see the girl, urged by her twenty years, capable of dishonouring you all, you will say to yourself, "It will be better that I should fall! If Monsieur Crevel will but keep my secret, I will earn my daughter's portion – two hundred thousand francs for ten years' attachment to that old glove-seller – old Crevel!" – I disgust you no doubt, and what I am saying is horribly immoral, you think? But if you happened to have been bitten by an overwhelming passion, you would find a thousand arguments in favour of yielding – as women do when they are in love. – Yes, and Hortense's interests will suggest to your feelings such terms of surrendering your conscience—'

'Hortense has still an uncle.'

'What! Old Fischer? He is winding up his concerns, and that again is the Baron's fault; his rake is dragged over every till within his reach.'

'Comte Hulot—'

'Oh, Madame, your husband has already made thin air of the old General's savings. He spent them in furnishing his singer's rooms. – Now, come; am I to go without a hope?'

'Good-bye, Monsieur. A man easily gets over a passion for a woman of my age, and you will fall back on Christian principles. God takes care of the wretched—'

The Baroness rose to oblige the captain to retreat, and drove him back into the drawing-room.

'Ought the beautiful Madame Hulot to be living amid such squalor?' said he, and he pointed to an old lamp, a chandelier bereft of its gilding, the threadbare carpet, the very rags of wealth which made the large room, with its red, white, and gold, look like a corpse of Imperial festivities.

'Monsieur, virtue shines on it all. I have no wish to owe a handsome abode to having made of the beauty you are pleased to ascribe to me *a man-trap* and *a money-box for five-franc pieces*!'

The captain bit his lip as he recognised the words he had used to vilify Josépha's avarice.

'And for whom are you so magnanimous?' said he. By this time the Baroness had got her rejected admirer as far as the door. – 'For a libertine!' said he, with a lofty grimace of virtue and superior wealth.

'If you are right, my constancy has some merit, Monsieur. That is all.'

After bowing to the officer as a woman bows to dismiss an importunate visitor, she turned away too quickly to see him once more fold his arms. She unlocked the doors she had closed, and did not see the threatening gesture which was Crevel's parting greeting. She walked with a proud, defiant step, like a martyr to the Coliseum, but her strength was exhausted; she sank on the sofa in her blue room, as if she were ready to faint, and sat there with her eyes fixed on the tumbledown summer-house, where her daughter was gossiping with Cousin Bette.

From the first days of her married life to the present time the Baroness had loved her husband, as Joséphine in the end had loved Napoleon, with an admiring, maternal, and cowardly devotion. Though ignorant of the details given her by Crevel, she knew that for twenty years past Baron Hulot had been anything rather than a faithful husband; but she had sealed her eyes with lead, she had wept in silence, and no word of reproach had ever escaped her. In return for this angelic sweetness, she had won her husband's veneration and something approaching to worship from all who were about her.

A wife's affection for her husband and the respect she pays him are infectious in a family. Hortense believed her father to be a perfect model of conjugal affection; as to their son, brought up to admire the Baron, whom everybody regarded as one of the giants who so effectually backed Napoleon, he knew that he owed his advancement to his father's name, position, and credit; and besides, the impressions of childhood exert an enduring influence. He still was afraid of his father; and if he had suspected the misdeeds revealed by Crevel, as he was too much overawed by him to find fault, he would have found excuses in the view every man takes of such matters.

It now will be necessary to give the reasons for the extraordinary self-devotion of a good and beautiful woman; and this, in a few words, is her past history.

Three brothers, simple labouring men, named Fischer, and living in a village situated on the furthest frontier of Lorraine, were compelled by the Republican conscription to set out with the so-called army of the Rhine.

In 1799 the second brother, André, a widower, and Madame Hulot's father, left his daughter to the care of his elder brother, Pierre Fischer, disabled from service by a wound received in 1797, and made a small private venture in the military transport service, an opening he owed to the favour of Hulot d'Ervy, who was high in the commissariat. By a very obvious chance Hulot, coming to Strasbourg, saw the Fischer family. Adeline's father and his younger brother were at that time contractors for forage in the province of Alsace.

Adeline, then sixteen years of age, might be compared with the famous Madame du Barry, like her, a daughter of Lorraine. She was one of those perfect and striking beauties – a woman like Madame Tallien, finished with peculiar care by Nature, who bestows on them all her choicest gifts – distinction, dignity, grace, refinement, elegance, flesh of a superior texture, and a complexion mingled in the unknown laboratory where good luck presides. These beautiful creatures all have something in common: Bianca Capella, whose portrait is one of Bronzino's masterpieces; Jean Goujon's Venus, painted from the famous Diane de Poitiers; Signora Olympia, whose picture adorns the Doria gallery; Ninon, Madame du Barry, Madame Tallien, Mademoiselle Georges, Madame Récamier, – all these women who preserved their beauty in spite of years, of passion, and of their life of excess and pleasure, have in figure, frame, and in the character of their beauty certain striking resemblances, enough to make one believe that there is in the ocean of generations an Aphrodisian current whence every such Venus is born, all daughters of the same salt wave.

Adeline Fischer, one of the loveliest of this race of goddesses, had the splendid type, the flowing lines, the exquisite texture of a woman born a queen. The fair hair that our mother Eve received from the hand of God, the form of an

Empress, an air of grandeur, and an august line of profile, with her rural modesty, made every man pause in delight as she passed, like amateurs in front of a Raphael; in short, having once seen her, the Commissariat officer made Mademoiselle Adeline Fischer his wife as quickly as the law would permit, to the great astonishment of the Fischers, who had all been brought up in the fear of their betters.

The eldest, a soldier of 1792, severely wounded in the attack on the lines at Wissembourg, adored the Emperor Napoleon and everything that had to do with the *Grande Armée*. André and Johann spoke with respect of Commissary Hulot, the Emperor's protégé, to whom indeed they owed their prosperity; for Hulot d'Ervy, finding them intelligent and honest, had taken them from the army provision waggons to place them in charge of a government contract needing despatch. The brothers Fischer had done further service during the campaign of 1804. At the peace Hulot had secured for them the contract for forage from Alsace, not knowing that he would presently be sent to Strasbourg to prepare for the campaign of 1806.

This marriage was like an Assumption to the young peasant girl. The beautiful Adeline was translated at once from the mire of her village to the paradise of the Imperial Court; for the contractor, one of the most conscientious and hardworking of the Commissariat staff, was made a Baron, obtained a place near the Emperor, and was attached to the Imperial Guard. The handsome rustic bravely set to work to educate herself for love of her husband, for she was simply crazy about him; and, indeed, the Commissariat officer was as a man a perfect match for Adeline as a woman. He was one of the picked corps of fine men. Tall, well-built, fair, with beautiful blue eyes full of irresistible fire and life, his elegant appearance made him remarkable by the side of d'Orsay, Forbin, Ouvrard; in short, in the battalion of fine men that surrounded the Emperor. A conquering 'buck,' and holding the ideas of the Directoire with regard to women, his career of gallantry was interrupted for some long time by his conjugal affection.

To Adeline the Baron was from the first a sort of god who could do no wrong. To him she owed everything: fortune – she had a carriage, a fine house, every luxury of the day; happiness – he was devoted to her in the face of the world; a title, for she was a Baroness; fame, for she was spoken of as the beautiful Madame Hulot – and in Paris! Finally, she had the honour of refusing the Emperor's advances, for Napoleon made her a present of a diamond necklace, and always remembered her, asking now and again, 'And is the beautiful Madame Hulot still a model of virtue?' in the tone of a man who might have taken his revenge on one who should have triumphed where he had failed.

So it needs no great intuition to discern what were the motives in a simple, guileless, and noble soul for the fanaticism of Madame Hulot's love. Having fully persuaded herself that her husband could do her no wrong, she made herself in the depths of her heart the humble, abject, and blindfold slave of the man who had made her. It must be noted, too, that she was gifted with great good sense – the good sense of the people, which made her education sound. In society she spoke little, and never spoke evil of any one; she did not try to shine; she thought out many things, listened well, and formed herself on the model of the best-conducted women of good birth.

In 1815 Hulot followed the lead of the Prince de Wissembourg, his intimate friend, and became one of the officers who organised the improvised troops whose rout brought the Napoleonic cycle to a close at Waterloo. In 1816 the Baron was one of the men best hated by the Feltre administration, and was not reinstated in the Commissariat till 1823, when he was needed for the Spanish war. In 1830 he took office as the fourth wheel of the coach, at the time of the levies, a sort of conscription made by Louis Philippe on the old Napoleonic soldiery. From the time when the younger branch ascended the throne, having taken an active part in bringing that about, he was regarded as an indispensable authority at the War Office. He had already won his Marshal's bâton, and the

King could do no more for him unless by making him minister or a peer of France.

From 1818 till 1823, having no official occupation, Baron Hulot had gone on active service to womankind. Madame Hulot dated her Hector's first infidelities from the grand *finale* of the Empire. Thus, for twelve years the Baroness had filled the part in her household of *prima donna assoluta*, without a rival. She still could boast of the old-fashioned, inveterate affection which husbands feel for wives who are resigned to be gentle and virtuous helpmates; she knew that if she had a rival, that rival would not subsist for two hours under a word of reproof from herself; but she shut her eyes, she stopped her ears, she would know nothing of her husband's proceedings outside his home. In short, she treated her Hector as a mother treats a spoilt child.

Three years before the conversation reported above, Hortense, at the Théâtre des Variétés, had recognised her father in a lower tier stage-box with Jenny Cadine, and had exclaimed –

'There is papa!'

'You are mistaken, my darling; he is at the Marshal's,' the Baroness replied.

She too had seen Jenny Cadine; but instead of feeling a pang when she saw how pretty she was, she said to herself, 'That rascal Hector must think himself very lucky.'

She suffered nevertheless; she gave herself up in secret to rages of torment; but as soon as she saw Hector, she always remembered her twelve years of perfect happiness, and could not find it in her to utter a word of complaint. She would have been glad if the Baron would have taken her into his confidence; but she never dared to let him see that she knew of his kicking over the traces, out of respect for her husband. Such an excess of delicacy is never met with but in those grand creatures, daughters of the soil, whose instinct it is to take blows without ever returning them; the blood of the early martyrs still lives in their veins. Well-born women, their husbands' equals, feel the impulse to annoy them, to mark the points of their tolerance, like points at billiards, by some

stinging word, partly in a spirit of diabolical malice, and to
secure the upper hand or the right of turning the tables.

The Baroness had an ardent admirer in her brother-in-law,
Lieutenant-General Hulot, the venerable Colonel of the
Grenadiers of the Imperial Infantry Guard, who was to have
a Marshal's bâton in his old age. This veteran, after having
served from 1830 to 1834 as Commandant of the military
division, including the departments of Brittany, the scene of
his exploits in 1799 and 1800, had come to settle in Paris near
his brother, for whom he had a fatherly affection.

This old soldier's heart was in sympathy with his sister-in-
law; he admired her as the noblest and saintliest of her sex.
He had never married, because he hoped to find a second
Adeline, though he had vainly sought for her through twenty
campaigns in as many lands. To maintain her place in the
esteem of this blameless and spotless old republican – of
whom Napoleon had said, 'That brave old Hulot is the
most obstinate republican, but he will never be false to me'
– Adeline would have endured griefs even greater than those
that had just come upon her. But the old soldier, seventy-two
years of age, battered by thirty campaigns, and wounded for
the twenty-seventh time at Waterloo, was Adeline's admirer,
and not a 'protector.' The poor old Count, among other
infirmities, could only hear through a speaking trumpet.

So long as Baron Hulot d'Ervy was a fine man, his flirta-
tions did not damage his fortune; but when a man is fifty, the
Graces claim payment. At that age love becomes vice; insens-
ate vanities come into play. Thus, at about that time, Adeline
saw that her husband was incredibly particular about his dress;
he dyed his hair and whiskers, and wore a belt and stays. He
was determined to remain handsome at any cost. This care of
his person, a weakness he had once mercilessly mocked at, was
carried out in the minutest details.

At last Adeline perceived that the Pactolus poured out
before the Baron's mistresses had its source in her pocket.
In eight years he had dissipated a considerable amount of
money; and so effectually, that, on his son's marriage two

years previously, the Baron had been compelled to explain to his wife that his pay constituted their whole income.

'What shall we come to?' asked Adeline.

'Be quite easy,' said the official, 'I will leave the whole of my salary in your hands, and I will make a fortune for Hortense, and some savings for the future, in business.'

The wife's deep belief in her husband's power and superior talents, in his capabilities and character, had, in fact, for the moment allayed her anxiety.

What the Baroness's reflections and tears were after Crevel's departure may now be clearly imagined. The poor woman had for two years past known that she was at the bottom of a pit, but she had fancied herself alone in it. How her son's marriage had been finally arranged she had not known; she had known nothing of Hector's connection with the grasping Jewess; and, above all, she hoped that no one in the world knew anything of her troubles. Now, if Crevel went about so ready to talk of the Baron's excesses, Hector's reputation would suffer. She could see, under the angry ex-perfumer's coarse harangue, the odious gossip behind the scenes which had led to her son's marriage. Two reprobate hussies had been the priestesses of this union planned at some orgy amid the degrading familiarities of two tipsy old sinners.

'And has he forgotten Hortense!' she wondered. 'But he sees her every day; will he try to find her a husband among his good-for-nothing sluts?'

At this moment it was the mother that spoke rather than the wife, for she saw Hortense laughing with her Cousin Bette – the reckless laughter of heedless youth; and she knew that such hysterical laughter was quite as distressing a symptom as the tearful reverie of solitary walks in the garden.

Hortense was like her mother, with golden hair that waved naturally, and was amazingly long and thick. Her skin had the lustre of mother-of-pearl. She was visibly the offspring of a true marriage, of a pure and noble love in its prime. There was a passionate vitality in her countenance, a brilliancy of feature, a full fount of youth, a fresh vigour and abundance of health, which radiated from her with electric flashes. Hortense invited the eye.

When her eye, of a deep ultramarine blue, liquid with the moisture of innocent youth, rested on a passer-by, he was involuntarily thrilled. Nor did a single freckle mar her skin, such as those with which many a white and golden maid pays toll for her milky whiteness. Tall, round without being fat, with a slender dignity as noble as her mother's, she really deserved the name of goddess, of which old authors were so lavish. In fact, those who saw Hortense in the street could hardly restrain the exclamation, 'What a beautiful girl!'

She was so genuinely innocent, that she could say to her mother –

'What do they mean, mamma, by calling me a beautiful girl when I am with you? Are not you much handsomer than I am?'

And, in point of fact, at seven-and-forty the Baroness might have been preferred to her daughter by amateurs of sunset beauty; for she had not yet lost any of her charms, by one of those phenomena which are especially rare in Paris, where Ninon was regarded as scandalous, simply because she thus seemed to enjoy such an unfair advantage over the plainer women of the seventeenth century.

Thinking of her daughter brought her back to the father; she saw him sinking by degrees, day after day, down to the social mire, and even dismissed some day from his appointment. The idea of her idol's fall, with a vague vision of the disasters prophesied by Crevel, was such a terror to the poor woman, that she became rapt in the contemplation like an ecstatic.

Cousin Bette, from time to time, as she chatted with Hortense, looked round to see when they might return to the drawing-room; but her young cousin was pelting her with questions, and at the moment when the Baroness opened the glass door she did not happen to be looking.

Lisbeth Fischer, though the daughter of the eldest of the three brothers, was five years younger than Madame Hulot; she was far from being as handsome as her cousin, and had been desperately jealous of Adeline. Jealousy was the fundamental passion of this character, marked by eccentricities – a word invented by the English to describe the craziness not of the asylum, but of respectable households. A native of the Vosges, a peasant in the fullest sense of the word, lean, brown, with shining black hair and thick eyebrows joining in a tuft, with long, strong arms, thick feet, and some moles on her narrow simian face – such is a brief description of the elderly virgin.

The family, living all under one roof, had sacrificed the common-looking girl to the beauty, the bitter fruit to the splendid flower. Lisbeth worked in the fields, while her cousin was indulged; and one day, when they were alone together, she had tried to destroy Adeline's nose, a truly Greek nose, which the old mothers admired. Though she was beaten for this misdeed, she persisted nevertheless in tearing the favourite's gowns and crumpling her collars.

At the time of Adeline's wonderful marriage, Lisbeth had bowed to fate, as Napoleon's brothers and sisters bowed before the splendour of the throne and the force of authority.

Adeline, who was extremely sweet and kind, remembered Lisbeth when she found herself in Paris, and invited her there in 1809, intending to rescue her from poverty by finding her a husband. But seeing that it was impossible to marry the girl out of hand, with her black eyes and sooty brows, unable too to read or write, the Baron began by apprenticing her to a business; he placed her as a learner with the embroiderers to the Imperial Court, the well-known Pons Brothers.

Lisbeth, called Bette for short, having learned to embroider in gold and silver, and possessing all the energy of a mountain race, had determination enough to learn to read, write, and keep accounts; for her cousin the Baron had pointed out the necessity for these accomplishments if she hoped to set up in business as an embroiderer.

She was bent on making a fortune; in two years she was another creature. In 1811 the peasant woman had become a very presentable, skilled, and intelligent forewoman.

Her department, that of gold and silver lace-work, as it is called, included epaulettes, sword-knots, aiguillettes; in short, the immense mass of glittering ornaments that sparkled on the rich uniforms of the French army and civil officials. The Emperor, a true Italian in his love of dress, had overlaid the coats of all his servants with silver and gold, and the Empire included a hundred and thirty-three Departments. These ornaments, usually supplied to tailors who were solvent and wealthy paymasters, were a very secure branch of trade.

Just when Cousin Bette, the best hand in the house of Pons Brothers, where she was forewoman of the embroidery department, might have set up in business on her own account, the Empire collapsed. The olive-branch of peace held out by the Bourbons did not reassure Lisbeth; she feared a diminution of this branch of trade, since henceforth there were to be but the eighty-six Departments to plunder, instead of a hundred and thirty-three, to say nothing of the immense reduction of the army. Utterly scared by the ups and downs of industry, she refused the Baron's offers of help, and he thought she must be mad. She confirmed this opinion by quarrelling with Monsieur Rivet, who bought the business of Pons Brothers, and with whom the Baron wished to place her in partnership; she would be no more than a workwoman. Thus the Fischer family had relapsed into the precarious mediocrity from which Baron Hulot had raised it.

The three brothers Fischer, who had been ruined by the abdication at Fontainebleau, in despair joined the irregular troops in 1815. The eldest, Lisbeth's father, was killed. Adeline's father, sentenced to death by court-martial, fled to Germany, and died at Trèves in 1820. Johann, the youngest, came to Paris, a petitioner to the queen of the family, who was said to dine off gold and silver plate, and never to be seen at a party but with diamonds in her hair as big as hazel-nuts, given to her by the Emperor.

Johann Fischer, then aged forty-three, obtained from Baron Hulot a capital of ten thousand francs with which to start a small business as forage-dealer at Versailles, under the patron-age of the War Office, through the influence of the friends, still in office, of the late Commissary-General.

These family catastrophes, Baron Hulot's dismissal, and the knowledge that he was a mere cypher in that immense stir of men and interests and things which makes Paris at once a paradise and a hell, quite quelled Lisbeth Fischer. She gave up all idea of rivalry and comparison with her cousin after feeling her great superiority; but envy still lurked in her heart, like a plague-germ that may hatch and devastate a city if the fatal bale of wool is opened in which it is concealed.

Now and again, indeed, she said to herself –

'Adeline and I are the same flesh and blood, our fathers were brothers – and she is in a mansion, while I am in a garret.'

But every New Year Lisbeth had presents from the Baron and Baroness; the Baron, who was always good to her, paid for her firewood in the winter; old General Hulot had her to dinner once a week; and there was always a cover laid for her at her cousin's table. They laughed at her no doubt, but they never were ashamed to own her. In short, they had made her independent in Paris, where she lived as she pleased.

The old maid had, in fact, a terror of any kind of tie. Her cousin had offered her a room in her own house – Lisbeth suspected the halter of domestic servitude; several times the Baron had found a solution of the difficult problem of her marriage; but though tempted in the first instance, she would presently decline, fearing lest she should be scorned for her want of education, her general ignorance, and her poverty; finally, when the Baroness suggested that she should live with their uncle Johann, and keep house for him, instead of the upper servant, who must cost him dear, Lisbeth replied that that was the very last way she should think of marrying.

Lisbeth Fischer had the sort of strangeness in her ideas which is often noticeable in characters that have developed late, in savages, who think much and speak little. Her peasant's wit had acquired a good deal of Parisian asperity from hearing the talk of workshops and mixing with workmen and work-women. She, whose character had a marked resemblance to that of the Corsicans, worked upon without fruition by the instincts of a strong nature, would have liked to be the protectress of a weak man; but, as a result of living in the capital, the capital had altered her superficially. Parisian polish became rust on this coarsely tempered soul. Gifted with a cunning which had become unfathomable, as it always does in those whose celibacy is genuine, with the originality and sharpness with which she clothed her ideas, in any other position she would have been formidable. Full of spite, she was capable of bringing discord into the most united family.

In early days, when she indulged in certain secret hopes which she confided to none, she took to wearing stays, and dressing in the fashion, and so shone in splendour for a short time, that the Baron thought her marriageable. Lisbeth at that stage was the piquante brunette of old-fashioned novels. Her piercing glance, her olive skin, her reed-like figure, might invite a half-pay major; but she was satisfied, she would say laughing, with her own admiration.

And, indeed, she found her life pleasant enough when she had freed it from practical anxieties, for she dined out every evening after working hard from sunrise. Thus she had only her rent and her midday meal to provide for; she had most of her clothes given her, and a variety of very acceptable stores, such as coffee, sugar, wine, and so forth.

In 1837, after living for twenty-seven years, half maintained by the Hulots and her Uncle Fischer, Cousin Bette, resigned to being nobody, allowed herself to be treated so. She herself refused to appear at any grand dinners, preferring the family party, where she held her own and was spared all slights to her pride.

Wherever she went – at General Hulot's, at Crevel's, at the house of the young Hulots, or at Rivet's (Pons' successor, with whom she made up her quarrel, and who made much of her), and at the Baroness's table – she was treated as one of the family; in fact, she managed to make friends of the servants by making them an occasional small present, and always gossiping with them for a few minutes before going into the drawing-room. This familiarity, by which she uncompromisingly put herself on their level, conciliated their servile good-nature, which is indispensable to a parasite. 'She is a good, steady woman,' was everybody's verdict.

Her willingness to oblige, which knew no bounds when it was not demanded of her, was indeed, like her assumed bluntness, a necessity of her position. She had at length understood what her life must be, seeing that she was at everybody's mercy; and needing to please everybody, she would laugh with young people, who liked her for a sort of wheedling flattery which always wins them; guessing and taking part with their fancies, she would make herself their spokeswoman, and they thought her a delightful *confidante*, since she had no right to find fault with them.

Her absolute secrecy also won her the confidence of their seniors; for, like Ninon, she had certain manly qualities. As a rule, our confidence is given to those below rather than above us. We employ our inferiors rather than our betters in secret transactions, and they thus become the recipients of our inmost thoughts, and look on at our meditations; Richelieu thought he had achieved success when he was admitted to the Council. This penniless woman was supposed to be so dependent on every one about her, that she seemed doomed to perfect silence. She herself called herself the Family Confessional.

The Baroness only, remembering her ill-usage in childhood by the cousin who, though younger, was stronger than herself, never wholly trusted her. Besides, out of sheer modesty, she would never have told her domestic sorrows to any one but God.

It may here be well to add that the Baron's house preserved all its magnificence in the eyes of Lisbeth Fischer, who was not struck, as the parvenu perfumer had been, with the penury stamped on the shabby chairs, the dirty hangings, and the ripped silk. The furniture we live with is in some sort like our own person; seeing ourselves every day, we end, like the Baron, by thinking ourselves but little altered, and still youthful, when others see that our head is covered with chinchilla, our forehead scarred with circumflex accents, our stomach assuming the rotundity of a pumpkin. So these rooms, always blazing in Bette's eyes with the Bengal fire of Imperial victory, were to her perennially splendid.

As time went on, Lisbeth had contracted some rather strange old-maidish habits. For instance, instead of following the fashions, she expected the fashion to accept her ways and yield to her always out-of-date notions. When the Baroness gave her a pretty new bonnet, or a gown in the fashion of the day, Betty remade it completely at home, and spoilt it by producing a dress of the style of the Empire or of her old Lorraine costume. A thirty-franc bonnet came out a rag, and the gown a disgrace. On this point, Lisbeth was as obstinate as a mule; she would please no one but herself, and believed herself charming; whereas this assimilative process – harmonious, no doubt, in so far as that it stamped her for an old maid from head to foot – made her so ridiculous, that, with the best will in the world, no one could admit her on any smart occasion.

This refractory, capricious, and independent spirit, and the inexplicable wild shyness of the woman for whom the Baron had four times found a match – an employé in his office, a retired major, an army contractor, and a half-pay captain – while she had refused an army lacemaker, who had since made his fortune, had won her the name of the Nanny Goat, which the Baron gave her in jest. But this nickname only met the peculiarities that lay on the surface, the eccentricities which each of us displays to his neighbours in social life. This woman, who, if closely studied, would have shown the most savage traits of the peasant class, was still the girl who had clawed her cousin's nose, and who, if she had not been trained to reason, would perhaps have killed her in a fit of jealousy.

It was only her knowledge of the laws and of the world that enabled her to control the swift instinct with which country folks, like wild men, reduce impulse to action. In this alone, perhaps, lies the difference between natural and civilised man. The savage has only impulse; the civilised man has impulses and ideas. And in the savage the brain retains, as we may say, but few impressions, it is wholly at the mercy of the feeling that rushes in upon it; while in the civilised man, ideas sink into the heart and change it; he has a thousand interests and many feelings, where the savage has but one at a time. This is the cause of the transient ascendency of a child over its parents, which ceases as soon as it is satisfied; in the man who is still one with nature, this cause is constant. Cousin Bette, a savage of Lorraine, somewhat treacherous too, was of this class of natures, which are commoner among the lower orders than is supposed, accounting for the conduct of the populace during revolutions.

At the time when this *Drama* opens, if Cousin Bette would have allowed herself to be dressed like other people; if, like the women of Paris, she had been accustomed to wear each fashion in its turn, she would have been presentable and acceptable, but she preserved the stiffness of a stick. Now a woman devoid of all the graces, in Paris simply does not exist. The fine but hard eyes, the severe features, the Calabrian fixity of complexion which made Lisbeth like a figure by Giotto, and of which a true Parisian would have taken advantage, above all, her strange way of dressing, gave her such an extraordinary appearance that she sometimes looked like one of those monkeys in petticoats taken about by little Savoyards. As she was well known in the houses connected by family ties which she frequented, and restricted her social efforts to that little circle, as she liked her own home, her singularities no longer astonished anybody; and out of doors they were lost in the immense stir of Paris street-life, where only pretty women are ever looked at.

Hortense's laughter was at this moment caused by a victory won over her Cousin Lisbeth's perversity; she had just wrung from her an avowal she had been hoping for these three years

past. However secretive an old maid may be, there is one
sentiment which will always avail to make her break her fast
from words, and that is her vanity. For the last three years,
Hortense, having become very inquisitive on such matters, had
pestered her cousin with questions, which, however, bore the
stamp of perfect innocence. She wanted to know why her
cousin had never married. Hortense, who knew of the five
offers that she had refused, had constructed her little romance;
she supposed that Lisbeth had had a passionate attachment,
and a war of banter was the result. Hortense would talk of
'We young girls!' when speaking of herself and her cousin.

Cousin Bette had on several occasions answered in the same
tone – 'And who says I have not a lover?' So Cousin Bette's
lover, real or fictitious, became a subject of mild jesting. At last,
after two years of this petty warfare, the last time Lisbeth had
come to the house Hortense's first question had been –

'And how is your lover?'

'Pretty well, thank you,' was the answer. 'He is rather ailing,
poor young man.'

'He has delicate health?' asked the Baroness, laughing.

'I should think so! He is fair. A sooty thing like me can love
none but a fair man with a colour like the moon.'

'But who is he? What does he do?' asked Hortense. 'Is he a
prince?'

'A prince of artisans, as I am queen of the bobbin. Is a
poor woman like me likely to find a lover in a man with a fine
house and money in the funds, or in a duke of the realm, or
some Prince Charming out of a fairy tale?'

'Oh, I should so much like to see him!' cried Hortense,
smiling.

'To see what a man can be like who can love the Nanny
Goat?' retorted Lisbeth.

'He must be some monster of an old clerk, with a goat's
beard!' Hortense said to her mother.

'Well, then, you are quite mistaken, Mademoiselle.'

'Then you mean that you really have a lover?' Hortense
exclaimed in triumph.

'As sure as you have not!' retorted Lisbeth, nettled.

'But if you have a lover, why don't you marry him, Lisbeth?' said the Baroness, shaking her head at her daughter. 'We have been hearing rumours about him these three years. You have had time to study him; and if he has been faithful so long, you should not persist in a delay which must be hard upon him. After all, it is a matter of conscience; and if he is young, it is time to take a brevet of dignity.'

Cousin Bette had fixed her gaze on Adeline, and seeing that she was jesting, she replied –

'It would be marrying hunger and thirst; he is a workman, I am a workwoman. If we had children, they would be workmen. – No, no; we love each other spiritually; it is less expensive.'

'Why do you keep him in hiding?' Hortense asked.

'He wears a round jacket,' replied the old maid, laughing.

'You truly love him?' the Baroness inquired.

'I believe you! I love him for his own sake, the dear cherub. For four years his home has been in my heart.'

'Well, then, if you love him for himself,' said the Baroness gravely, 'and if he really exists, you are treating him criminally. You do not know how to love truly.'

'We all know that from our birth,' said Lisbeth.

'No, there are women who love and yet are selfish, and that is your case.'

Cousin Bette's head fell, and her glance would have made any one shiver who had seen it; but her eyes were on her reel of thread.

'If you would introduce your so-called lover to us, Hector might find him employment, or put him in a position to make money.'

'That is out of the question,' said Cousin Bette.

'And why?'

'He is a sort of Pole – a refugee—'

'A conspirator?' cried Hortense. 'What luck for you! – Has he had any adventures?'

'He has fought for Poland. He was a professor in the school where the students began the rebellion; and as he had been placed there by the Grand Duke Constantine, he has no hope of mercy—'

'A professor of what?'

'Of fine arts.'

'And he came to Paris when the rebellion was quelled?'

'In 1833. He came through Germany on foot.'

'Poor young man! And how old is he?'

'He was just four-and-twenty when the insurrection broke out – he is twenty-nine now.'

'Fifteen years your junior,' said the Baroness.

'And what does he live on?' asked Hortense.

'His talent.'

'Oh, he gives lessons?'

'No,' said Cousin Bette; 'he gets them, and hard ones too!'

'And his Christian name – is it a pretty name?'

'Wenceslas.'

'What a wonderful imagination you old maids have!' exclaimed the Baroness. 'To hear you talk, Lisbeth, one might really believe you.'

'You see, mamma, he is a Pole, and so accustomed to the knout that Lisbeth reminds him of the joys of his native land.'

They all three laughed, and Hortense sang *Wenceslas! idole de mon âme!* instead of *O Mathilde.*

Then for a few minutes there was a truce.

'These children,' said Cousin Bette, looking at Hortense as she went up to her, 'fancy that no one but themselves can have lovers.'

'Listen,' Hortense replied, finding herself alone with her cousin, 'if you prove to me that Wenceslas is not a pure invention, I will give you my yellow cashmere shawl.'

'He is a Count.'

'Every Pole is a Count!'

'But he is not a Pole; he comes from Liva – Litha—'

'Lithuania?'

'No.'

'Livonia?'

'Yes, that's it!'

'But what is his name?'

'I wonder if you are capable of keeping a secret.'

'Cousin Bette, I will be as mute!—'

'As a fish?'

'As a fish.'

'By your life eternal?'

'By my life eternal!'

'No, by your happiness in this world?'

'Yes.'

'Well, then, his name is Wenceslas Steinbock.'

'One of Charles XII.'s Generals was named Steinbock.'

'He was his grand-uncle. His own father settled in Livonia after the death of the King of Sweden; but he lost all his fortune during the campaign of 1812, and died, leaving the poor boy at the age of eight without a penny. The Grand Duke Constantine, for the honour of the name of Steinbock, took him under his protection and sent him to school.'

'I will not break my word,' Hortense replied; 'prove his existence, and you shall have the yellow shawl. The colour is most becoming to dark skins.'

'And you will keep my secret?'

'And tell you mine.'

'Well, then, the next time I come you shall have the proof.'

'But the proof will be the lover,' said Hortense.

Cousin Bette, who, since her first arrival in Paris, had been bitten by a mania for shawls, was bewitched by the idea of owning the yellow cashmere given to his wife by the Baron in 1808, and handed down from mother to daughter after the manner of some families in 1830. The shawl had been a good deal worn ten years ago; but the costly object, now always kept in its sandalwood box, seemed to the old maid ever new, like the drawing-room furniture. So she brought in her handbag a present for the Baroness's birthday, by which she proposed to prove the existence of her romantic lover.

This present was a silver seal formed of three little figures back to back, wreathed with foliage, and supporting the Globe. They represented Faith, Hope, and Charity; their feet rested on monsters rending each other, among them the symbolical serpent. In 1846, now that such immense strides have been made in the art of which Benvenuto Cellini was the master, by Mademoiselle de Fauveau, Wagner, Jeanest, Froment-Meurice, and wood-carvers like Liénard, this little masterpiece would amaze nobody; but at that time a girl who understood the silversmiths' art stood astonished as she held the seal which Lisbeth put into her hands, saying –

'There! what do you think of that?'

In design, attitude, and drapery the figures were of the school of Raphael; but the execution was in the style of the Florentine metal-workers – the school created by Donatello, Brunelleschi, Ghiberti, Benvenuto Cellini, John of Bologna, and others. The French masters of the Renaissance had never invented more strangely twining monsters than these that symbolised the evil passions. The palms, ferns, reeds, and foliage that wreathed the Virtues showed a style, a taste, a handling that might have driven a practised craftsman to despair; a scroll floated above the three figures; and on its surface, between the heads, were a W, a chamois, and the word *fecit*.

'Who carved this?' asked Hortense.

'Well, just my lover,' replied Lisbeth. 'There are ten months' work in it; I could earn more at making sword-knots. – He told me that Steinbock means a rock goat, a chamois, in German. And he intends to mark all his work in that way. – Ah, ha! I shall have the shawl.'

'What for?'

'Do you suppose I could buy such a thing, or order it? Impossible! Well, then, it must have been given to me. And who would make me such a present? A lover!'

Hortense, with an artfulness that would have frightened Lisbeth Fischer if she had detected it, took care not to express all her admiration, though she was full of the delight which every soul that is open to a sense of beauty must feel on seeing a faultless piece of work – perfect and unexpected.

'On my word,' said she, 'it is very pretty.'

'Yes, it is pretty,' said her cousin; 'but I like an orange-coloured shawl better. – Well, child, my lover spends his time in doing such work as that. Since he came to Paris he has turned out three or four little trifles in that style, and that is the fruit of four years' study and toil. He has served as apprentice to founders, metal-casters, and goldsmiths. – There, he has paid away thousands and hundreds of francs. And my gentleman tells me that in a few months now he will be famous and rich—'

'Then you often see him?'

'Bless me, do you think it is all a fable? I told you truth in jest.'

'And he is in love with you?' asked Hortense eagerly.

'He adores me,' replied Lisbeth very seriously. 'You see, child, he had never seen any women but the washed-out, pale things they all are in the north, and a slender, brown, youthful thing like me warmed his heart. – But, mum; you promised, you know!'

'And he will fare like the five others,' said the girl ironically, as she looked at the seal.

'Six others, Miss. I left one in Lorraine, who, to this day, would fetch the moon down for me.'

'This one does better than that,' said Hortense; 'he has brought down the sun.'

'Where can that be turned into money?' asked her cousin. 'It takes wide lands to benefit by the sunshine.'

These witticisms, fired in quick retort, and leading to the sort of giddy play that may be imagined, had given cause for the laughter which had added to the Baroness's troubles by making her compare her daughter's future lot with the present, when she was free to indulge the light-heartedness of youth.

'But to give you a gem which cost him six months of work, he must be under some great obligations to you?' said Hortense, in whom the silver seal had suggested very serious reflections.

'Oh, you want to know too much at once!' said her cousin. 'But, listen, I will let you into a little plot.'

'Is your lover in it too?'

'Oh, ho! you want so much to see him! But, as you may suppose, an old maid like Cousin Bette, who had managed to keep a lover for five years, keeps him well hidden. – Now, just let me alone. You see, I have neither cat nor canary, neither a dog nor a parrot, and the old Nanny Goat wanted something to pet and tease—so I treated myself to a Polish Count.'

'Has he a moustache?'

'As long as that,' said Lisbeth, holding up her shuttle filled with gold thread. She always took her lace-work with her, and worked till dinner was served.

'If you ask too many questions, you will be told nothing,' she went on. 'You are but two-and-twenty, and you chatter more than I do though I am forty-two – not to say forty-three.'

'I am listening; I am a wooden image,' said Hortense.

'My lover has finished a bronze group ten inches high,' Lisbeth went on. 'It represents Samson slaying a lion, and he has kept it buried till it is so rusty that you might believe it to be as old as Samson himself. This fine piece is shown at the shop of one of the old curiosity sellers on the Place du Carrousel, near my lodgings. Now, your father knows Monsieur Popinot, the Minister of Commerce and Agriculture, and the Comte de Rastignac, and if he would only mention the group to them as a fine antique he had seen by chance! It seems that such things take the fancy of your grand folks, who don't care so much about gold lace, and that my man's fortune would be made if one of them would buy or even look at the wretched piece of metal. The poor fellow is sure that it might be mistaken for old work, and that the rubbish is worth a great deal of money. And then, if one of the ministers should purchase the group, he would go to pay his respects, and prove that he was the maker, and be almost carried in triumph! Oh! he believes he has reached the pinnacle; poor young man, and he is as proud as two newly-made Counts.'

'Michael Angelo over again; but, for a lover, he has kept his head on his shoulders!' said Hortense. 'And how much does he want for it?'

'Fifteen hundred francs. The dealer will not let it go for less, since he must take his commission.'

'Papa is in the King's household just now,' said Hortense. 'He sees those two ministers every day at the Chamber, and he will do the thing – I undertake that. You will be a rich woman, Madame la Comtesse de Steinbock.'

'No, the boy is too lazy; for whole weeks he sits twiddling with bits of red wax, and nothing comes of it. Why, he spends all his days at the Louvre and the Library, looking at prints and sketching things. He is an idler!'

The cousins chatted and giggled; Hortense laughing a forced laugh, for she was invaded by a kind of love which every girl has gone through – the love of the unknown, love in its vaguest form, when every thought is accreted round some form which is suggested by a chance word, as the efflorescence of hoar-frost gathers about a straw that the wind has blown against the window-sill.

For the past ten months she had made a reality of her cousin's imaginary romance, believing, like her mother, that Lisbeth would never marry; and now, within a week, this visionary being had become Count Wenceslas Steinbock, the dream had a certificate of birth, the wraith had solidified into a young man of thirty. The seal she held in her hand – a sort of Annunciation in which genius shone like an immanent light – had the powers of a talisman. Hortense felt such a surge of happiness, that she almost doubted whether the tale were true; there was a ferment in her blood, and she laughed wildly to deceive her cousin.

'But I think the drawing-room door is open,' said Lisbeth; 'let us go and see if Monsieur Crevel is gone.'

'Mamma has been very much out of spirits these two days. I suppose the marriage under discussion has come to nothing!'

'Oh, it may come on again. He is – I may tell you so much – a Councillor of the Supreme Court. How would you like to be Madame la Présidente? If Monsieur Crevel has a finger in it, he will tell me about it if I ask him. I shall know by to-morrow if there is any hope.'

'Leave the seal with me,' said Hortense; 'I will not show it
– mamma's birthday is not for a month yet; I will give it you
that morning.'

'No, no. Give it back to me; it must have a case.'

'But I will let papa see it, that he may know what he is
talking about to the ministers, for men in authority must be
careful what they say,' urged the girl.

'Well, do not show it to your mother – that is all I ask; for
if she believed I had a lover, she would make game of me.'

'I promise.'

The cousins reached the drawing-room just as the Baroness
turned faint. Her daughter's cry of alarm recalled her to
herself. Lisbeth went off to fetch some salts. When she came
back, she found the mother and daughter in each other's arms,
the Baroness soothing her daughter's fears, and saying –

'It was nothing; a little nervous attack. – There is your
father,' she added, recognising the Baron's way of ringing
the bell. 'Say not a word to him.'

Adeline rose and went to meet her husband, intending to
take him into the garden and talk to him till dinner should be
served of the difficulties about the proposed match, getting
him to come to some decision as to the future, and trying to
hint at some warning advice.

Baron Hector Hulot came in, in a dress at once lawyer-like
and Napoleonic, for Imperial men – men who had been
attached to the Emperor – were easily distinguishable by
their military deportment, their blue coats with gilt buttons,
buttoned to the chin, their black silk stock, and an authoritative demeanour acquired from a habit of command in circumstances requiring despotic rapidity. There was nothing of the
old man in the Baron, it must be admitted; his sight was still so
good, that he could read without spectacles; his handsome
oval face, framed in whiskers that were indeed too black,
showed a brilliant complexion, ruddy with the veins that
characterise a sanguine temperament; and his stomach, kept
in order by a belt, had not exceeded the limits of 'the majestic,' as Brillat-Savarin says. A fine aristocratic air and great

affability served to conceal the libertine with whom Crevel had
had such high times. He was one of those men whose eyes
always light up at the sight of a pretty woman, even of such as
merely pass by, never to be seen again.

'Have you been speaking, my dear?' asked Adeline, seeing
him with an anxious brow.

'No,' replied Hector, 'but I am worn out with hearing
others speak for two hours without coming to a vote. They
carry on a war of words, in which their speeches are like a
cavalry charge which has no effect on the enemy. Talk has
taken the place of action, which goes very much against the
grain with men who are accustomed to marching orders, as I
said to the Marshal when I left him. However, I have enough
of being bored on the ministers' bench; here I may play. –
How' do, la Chèvre! – Good morning, little kid,' and he took
his daughter round the neck, kissed her, and made her sit on
his knee, resting her head on his shoulder, that he might feel
her soft golden hair against his cheek.

'He is tired and worried,' said his wife to herself. 'I shall
only worry him more – I will wait.' – 'Are you going to be at
home this evening?' she asked him.

'No, children. After dinner I must go out. If it had not been
the day when Lisbeth and the children and my brother come
to dinner, you would not have seen me at all.'

The Baroness took up the newspaper, looked down the list
of theatres, and laid it down again when she had seen that
Robert le Diable was to be given at the Opera. Josépha, who had
left the Italian Opera six months since for the French Opera,
was to take the part of Alice.

This little pantomime did not escape the Baron, who looked
hard at his wife. Adeline cast down her eyes and went out into
the garden; her husband followed her.

'Come, what is it, Adeline?' said he, putting his arm round
her waist and pressing her to his side. 'Do not you know that
I love you more than—'

'More than Jenny Cadine or Josépha!' said she, boldly
interrupting him.

'Who put that into your head?' exclaimed the Baron, releasing his wife, and starting back a step or two.

'I got an anonymous letter, which I burnt at once, in which I was told, my dear, that the reason Hortense's marriage was broken off was the poverty of our circumstances. Your wife, my dear Hector, would never have said a word; she knew of your connection with Jenny Cadine, and did she ever complain? – But as the mother of Hortense, I am bound to speak the truth.'

Hulot, after a short silence, which was terrible to his wife, whose heart beat loud enough to be heard, opened his arms, clasped her to his heart, kissed her forehead, and said with the vehemence of enthusiasm –

'Adeline, you are an angel, and I am a wretch—'

'No, no,' cried the Baroness, hastily laying her hand upon his lips to hinder him from speaking evil of himself.

'Yes, for I have not at this moment a sou to give to Hortense, and I am most unhappy. But since you open your heart to me, I may pour into it the trouble that is crushing me. – Your Uncle Fischer is in difficulties, and it is I who dragged him there, for he has accepted bills for me to the amount of twenty-five thousand francs! And all for a woman who deceives me, who laughs at me behind my back, and calls me an old dyed Tom. It is frightful! A vice which costs me more than it would to maintain a family! – And I cannot resist! – I would promise you here and now never to see that abominable Jewess again; but if she wrote me two lines, I should go to her, as we marched into fire under the Emperor.'

'Do not be so distressed,' cried the poor woman in despair, but forgetting her daughter as she saw the tears in her husband's eyes. 'There are my diamonds; whatever happens, save my uncle.'

'Your diamonds are worth scarcely twenty thousand francs nowadays. That would not be enough for old Fischer, so keep them for Hortense; I will see the Marshal to-morrow.'

'My poor dear!' said the Baroness, taking her Hector's hands and kissing them.

This was all the scolding he got. Adeline sacrificed her jewels, the father made them a present to Hortense, she regarded this as a sublime action, and she was helpless.

'He is the master; he could take everything, and he leaves me my diamonds; he is divine!'

This was the current of her thoughts; and indeed the wife had gained more by her sweetness than another perhaps could have achieved by a fit of angry jealousy.

The moralist cannot deny that, as a rule, well-bred though very wicked men are far more attractive and lovable than virtuous men; having crimes to atone for, they crave indulgence by anticipation, by being lenient to the shortcomings of those who judge them, and they are thought most kind. Though there are no doubt some charming people among the virtuous, Virtue considers itself fair enough, unadorned, to be at no pains to please; and then all really virtuous persons, for the hypocrites do not count, have some slight doubts as to their position; they believe that they are cheated in the bargain of life on the whole, and they indulge in acid comments after the fashion of those who think themselves unappreciated.

Hence the Baron, who accused himself of ruining his family, displayed all his charm of wit and his most seductive graces for the benefit of his wife, for his children, and his Cousin Lisbeth.

Then, when his son arrived with Célestine, Crevel's daughter, who was nursing the infant Hulot, he was delightful to his daughter-in-law, loading her with compliments – a treat to which Célestine's vanity was little accustomed, for no moneyed bride more commonplace or more utterly insignificant was ever seen. The grandfather took the baby from her, kissed it, declared it was a beauty and a darling; he spoke to it in baby language, prophesied that it would grow to be taller than himself, insinuated compliments for his son's benefit, and restored the child to the Normandy nurse who had charge of it. Célestine, on her part, gave the Baroness a look, as much as to say, 'What a delightful man!' and she naturally took her father-in-law's part against her father.

After thus playing the charming father-in-law and the indulgent grandpapa, the Baron took his son into the garden, and laid before him a variety of observations full of good sense as to the attitude to be taken up by the Chamber on a certain ticklish question which had that morning come under discussion. The young lawyer was struck with admiration for the depth of his father's insight, touched by his cordiality, and especially by the deferential tone which seemed to place the two men on a footing of equality.

Monsieur Hulot *junior* was in every respect the young Frenchman, as he has been moulded by the Revolution of 1830; his mind infatuated with politics, respectful of his own hopes, and concealing them under an affectation of gravity, very envious of successful men, making sententiousness do the duty of witty rejoinders – the gems of the French language – with a high sense of importance, and mistaking arrogance for dignity.

Such men are walking coffins, each containing a Frenchman of the past; now and again the Frenchman wakes up and kicks against his English-made casing; but ambition stifles him, and he submits to be smothered. The coffin is always covered with black cloth.

'Ah, here is my brother!' said Baron Hulot, going to meet the Count at the drawing-room door.

Having greeted the probable successor of the late Marshal Montcornet, he led him forward by the arm with every show of affection and respect.

The older man, a member of the Chamber of Peers, but excused from attendance on account of his deafness, had a handsome head, chilled by age, but with enough grey hair still to be marked in a circle by the pressure of his hat. He was short, square, and shrunken, but carried his hale old age with a free-and-easy air; and as he was full of excessive activity, which had now no purpose, he divided his time between reading and taking exercise. In a drawing-room he devoted his attention to waiting on the wishes of the ladies.

'You are very merry here,' said he, seeing that the Baron shed a spirit of animation on the little family gathering. 'And yet Hortense is not married,' he added, noticing a trace of melancholy on his sister-in-law's countenance.

'That will come all in good time,' Lisbeth shouted in his ear in a formidable voice.

'So there you are, you wretched seedling that could never blossom,' said he, laughing.

The hero of Forzheim rather liked Cousin Bette, for there were certain points of resemblance between them. A man of the ranks, without any education, his courage had been the sole mainspring of his military promotion, and sound sense had taken the place of brilliancy. Of the highest honour and clean-handed, he was ending a noble life in full contentment in the centre of his family, which claimed all his affections, and without a suspicion of his brother's still undiscovered misconduct. No one enjoyed more than he the pleasing sight of this family party, where there never was the smallest disagreement, for the brothers and sisters were all equally attached, Célestine having been at once accepted as one of the family. But the worthy little Count wondered now and then why Monsieur Crevel never joined the party. 'Papa is in the country,' Célestine shouted, and it was explained to him that the ex-perfumer was away from home.

This perfect union of all her family made Madame Hulot say to herself, 'This, after all, is the best kind of happiness, and who can deprive us of it?'

The General, on seeing his favourite Adeline the object of her husband's attentions, laughed so much about it that the Baron, fearing to seem ridiculous, transferred his gallantries to his daughter-in-law, who at these family dinners was always the object of his flattery and kind care, for he hoped to win Crevel back through her, and make him forgo his resentment.

Any one seeing this domestic scene would have found it hard to believe that the father was at his wits' end, the mother in despair, the son anxious beyond words as to his father's future fate, and the daughter on the point of robbing her cousin of her lover.

At seven o'clock the Baron, seeing his brother, his son, the Baroness, and Hortense all engaged at whist, went off to applaud his mistress at the Opera, taking with him Lisbeth Fischer, who lived in the Rue du Doyenné, and who always made an excuse of the solitude of that deserted quarter to take herself off as soon as dinner was over. Parisians will all admit that the old maid's prudence was but rational.

The existence of the maze of houses under the wing of the old Louvre is one of those protests against obvious good sense which Frenchmen love, that Europe may reassure itself as to the quantum of brains they are known to have, and not be too much alarmed. Perhaps without knowing it, this reveals some profound political idea.

It will surely not be a work of supererogation to describe this part of Paris as it is even now, when we could hardly expect its survival; and our grandsons, who will no doubt see the Louvre finished, may refuse to believe that such a relic of barbarism should have survived for six-and-thirty years in the heart of Paris and in the face of the palace where three dynasties of kings have received, during those thirty-six years, the élite of France and of Europe.

Between the little gate leading to the Bridge of the Carrousel and the Rue du Musée, every one having come to Paris, were it but for a few days, must have seen a dozen of houses with a decayed frontage where the dejected owners have attempted no repairs, the remains of an old block of buildings of which the destruction was begun at the time when Napoleon determined to complete the Louvre. This street, and the blind alley known as the Impasse du Doyenné, are the only passages into this gloomy and forsaken block, inhabited perhaps by ghosts, for there never is anybody to be seen. The pavement is much below the footway of the Rue du Musée, on a level with that of the Rue Froidmanteau. Thus, half sunken by the raising of the soil, these houses are also wrapped in the perpetual shadow cast by the lofty buildings of the Louvre, darkened on that side by the northern blast. Darkness, silence, an icy chill, and the cavernous depth of the soil combine to make these houses a kind of crypt, tombs of the living. As we drive in a hackney cab past this dead-alive spot, and chance to look down the little Rue du Doyenné, a shudder freezes the soul, and we wonder who can live there, and what things may be done there at night, at an hour when the alley is a cut-throat pit, and the vices of Paris run riot there under the cloak of night. This question, frightful in itself, becomes appalling when we note that these dwelling-houses are shut in on the side towards the Rue de Richelieu by marshy ground, by a sea of tumbled paving-stones between them and the Tuileries, by little garden-plots and suspicious-looking hovels on the side of the great galleries, and by a desert of building-stone and old rubbish on the side towards the old Louvre. Henri iii. and his favourites in search of their trunk-hose, and Marguerite's lovers in search of their heads, must dance sarabands by moonlight in this wilderness overlooked by the roof of a chapel still standing there as if to prove that the Catholic religion – so deeply rooted in France – survives all else.

For forty years now has the Louvre been crying out by every gap in these damaged walls, by every yawning window, 'Rid me of these warts upon my face!' This cut-throat lane has no doubt been regarded as useful, and has been thought necessary as symbolising in the heart of Paris the intimate connection between poverty and the splendour that is characteristic of the queen of cities. And indeed these chill ruins, among which the Legitimist newspaper contracted the disease it is dying of – the abominable hovels of the Rue du Musée, and the hoarding appropriated by the shop stalls that flourish there – will perhaps live longer and more prosperously than three successive dynasties.

In 1823 the low rents in these already condemned houses had tempted Lisbeth Fischer to settle there, notwithstanding the necessity imposed upon her by the state of the neighbourhood to get home before nightfall. This necessity, however, was in accordance with the country habits she retained, of rising and going to bed with the sun, an arrangement which saves country folks considerable sums in lights and fuel.

She lived in one of the houses which, since the demolition of the famous Hôtel Cambacérès, command a view of the square.

Just as Baron Hulot set his wife's cousin down at the door of this house, saying, 'Good-night, Cousin,' an elegant-looking woman, young, small, slender, pretty, beautifully dressed, and redolent of some delicate perfume, passed between the wall and the carriage to go in. This lady, without any premeditation, glanced up at the Baron merely to see the lodger's cousin, and the libertine at once felt the swift impression which all Parisians know on meeting a pretty woman, realising, as entomologists have it, their *desiderata;* so he waited to put on one of his gloves with judicious deliberation before getting into the carriage again, to give himself an excuse for allowing his eye to follow the young woman, whose skirts were pleasingly set out by something else than those odious and delusive crinoline bustles.

'That,' said he to himself, 'is a nice little person whose happiness I should like to provide for, as she would certainly secure mine.'

When the unknown fair had gone into the hall at the foot of the stairs going up to the front rooms, she glanced at the gate out of the corner of her eye without precisely looking round, and she could see the Baron riveted to the spot in admiration, consumed by curiosity and desire. This is to every Parisian woman a sort of flower which she smells at with delight, if she meets it on her way. Nay, certain women, though faithful to their duties, pretty, and virtuous, come home much put out if they have failed to cull such a posy in the course of their walk.

The lady ran upstairs, and in a moment a window on the second floor was thrown open, and she appeared at it, but accompanied by a man whose bald head and somewhat scowling looks announced him as her husband.

'If they aren't sharp and ingenious, the cunning jades!' thought the Baron. 'She does that to show me where she lives. But this is getting rather warm, especially for this part of Paris. We must mind what we are at.'

As he got into the *milord*, he looked up, and the lady and the husband hastily vanished, as though the Baron's face had affected them like the mythological head of Medusa.

'It would seem that they know me,' thought the Baron. 'That would account for everything.'

As the carriage went up the Rue du Musée, he leaned forward to see the lady again, and in fact she was again at the window. Ashamed of being caught gazing at the hood under which her admirer was sitting, the unknown started back at once.

'Nanny shall tell me who it is,' said the Baron to himself.

The sight of the Government official had, as will be seen, made a deep impression on this couple.

'Why, it is Baron Hulot, the chief of the department to which my office belongs!' exclaimed the husband as he left the window.

'Well, Marneffe, the old maid on the third floor at the back of the courtyard, who lives with that young man, is his cousin. Is it not odd that we should never have known that till to-day, and now find it out by chance.'

'Mademoiselle Fischer living with a young man?' repeated the husband. 'That is porter's gossip; do not speak so lightly of the cousin of a Councillor of State who can blow hot and cold in the office as he pleases. Now, come to dinner; I have been waiting for you since four o'clock.'

Pretty – very pretty – Madame Marneffe, the natural daughter of Comte Montcornet, one of Napoleon's most famous officers, had, on the strength of a marriage portion of twenty thousand francs, found a husband in an inferior official at the War Office. Through the interest of the famous lieutenant-general – made marshal of France six months before his death – this quill-driver had risen to unhoped-for dignity as head-clerk of his office; but just as he was to be promoted to be deputy-chief, the marshal's death had cut off Marneffe's ambitions and his wife's at the root. The very small salary enjoyed by Sieur Marneffe had compelled the couple to economise in

the matter of rent; for in his hands Mademoiselle Valérie
Fortin's fortune had already melted away – partly in paying
his debts, and partly in the purchase of necessaries for furnishing a house, but chiefly in gratifying the requirements of a
pretty young wife, accustomed in her mother's house to
luxuries she did not choose to dispense with. The situation
of the Rue du Doyenné, within easy distance of the War
Office and the gay part of Paris, smiled on Monsieur and
Madame Marneffe, and for the last four years they had dwelt
under the same roof as Lisbeth Fischer.

Monsieur Jean-Paul-Stanislas Marneffe was one of the class
of employés who escape sheer brutishness by the kind of
power that comes of depravity. The small, lean creature,
with thin hair and a starved beard, an unwholesome pasty
face, worn rather than wrinkled, with red-lidded eyes har-
nessed with spectacles, shuffling in his gait, and yet meaner
in his appearance, realised the type of man that any one would
conceive of as likely to be placed in the dock for an offence
against decency.

The rooms inhabited by this couple had the illusory appearance of sham luxury seen in many Paris homes, and typical of
a certain class of household. In the drawing-room, the furniture covered with shabby cotton velvet, the plaster statuettes
pretending to be Florentine bronze, the clumsy cast chandelier merely lacquered, with cheap glass saucers, the carpet,
whose small cost was accounted for in advancing life by the
quantity of cotton used in the manufacture, now visible to the
naked eye, – everything, down to the curtains, which plainly
showed that worsted damask has not three years of prime,
proclaimed poverty as loudly as a beggar in rags at a church
door.

The dining-room, badly kept by the single servant, had the
sickening aspect of a country inn; everything looked greasy
and unclean.

Monsieur's room, very like a schoolboy's, furnished with
the bed and fittings remaining from his bachelor days, as
shabby and worn as he was, dusted perhaps once a week –

that horrible room where everything was in a litter, with old socks hanging over the horsehair-seated chairs, the pattern outlined in dust, was that of a man to whom home is a matter of indifference, who lives out of doors, gambling in cafés or elsewhere.

Madame's room was an exception to the squalid slovenliness that disgraced the living rooms, where the curtains were yellow with smoke and dust, and where the child, evidently left to himself, littered every spot with his toys. Valérie's room and dressing-room were situated in the part of the house which, on one side of the courtyard, joined the front half, looking out on the street, to the wing forming the inner side of the court backing against the adjoining property. Handsomely hung with chintz, furnished with rosewood, and thickly carpeted, they proclaimed themselves as belonging to a pretty woman – and indeed suggested the kept mistress. A clock in the fashionable style stood on the velvet-covered mantelpiece. There was a nicely fitted cabinet, and the Chinese flower-stands were handsomely filled. The bed, the toilet-table, the wardrobe with its mirror, the little sofa, and all the lady's frippery bore the stamp of fashion or caprice. Though everything was quite third-rate as to elegance or quality, and nothing was absolutely newer than three years old, a dandy would have had no fault to find but that the taste of all this luxury was commonplace. Art, and the distinction that comes of the choice of things that taste assimilates, was entirely wanting. A doctor of social science would have detected a lover in two or three specimens of costly trumpery, which could only have come there through that demi-god – always absent, but always present if the lady is married.

The dinner, four hours behind time, to which the husband, wife, and child sat down, betrayed the financial straits in which the household found itself, for the table is the surest thermometer for gauging the income of a Parisian family. Vegetable soup made with the water haricot beans had been boiled in, a piece of stewed veal and potatoes sodden with water by way of gravy, a dish of haricot beans, and some cheap cherries, served

and eaten in cracked plates and dishes, with the dull-looking
and dull-sounding forks of German silver – was this a banquet
worthy of this pretty young woman? The Baron would
have wept could he have seen it. The dingy decanters could
not disguise the vile hue of wine bought by the pint at the
nearest wineshop. The table-napkins had seen a week's use. In
short, everything betrayed undignified penury, and the equal
indifference of the husband and wife to the decencies of
home. The most superficial observer on seeing them would
have said that these two beings had come to the stage when
the necessity of living had prepared them for any kind of
dishonour that might bring luck to them. Valérie's first
words to her husband will explain the delay that had postponed the dinner by the not disinterested devotion of the
cook.

'Samanon will only take your bills at fifty per cent., and
insists on a lien on your salary as security.'

So poverty, still unconfessed in the house of the superior
official, and hidden under a stipend of twenty-four thousand
francs, irrespective of presents, had reached its lowest stage in
that of the clerk.

'You have caught on with the chief,' said the man, looking
at his wife.

'I rather think so,' replied she, understanding the full meaning of his slang expression.

'What is to become of us?' Marneffe went on. 'The landlord will be down on us to-morrow. And to think of your
father dying without making a will! On my honour, those
men of the Empire all think themselves as immortal as their
Emperor.'

'Poor father!' said she. 'I was his only child, and he was
very fond of me. The Countess probably burned the will. How
could he forget me when he used to give us as much as three
or four thousand-franc notes at once, from time to time?'

'We owe four quarters' rent, fifteen hundred francs. Is the
furniture worth so much? *That is the question*, as Shakespeare
says.'

'Now, good-bye, ducky!' said Valérie, who had only eaten a few mouthfuls of the veal, from which the maid had extracted all the gravy for a brave soldier just home from Algiers. 'Great evils demand heroic remedies.'

'Valérie, where are you off to?' cried Marneffe, standing between his wife and the door.

'I am going to see the landlord,' she replied, arranging her ringlets under her smart bonnet. 'You had better try to make friends with that old maid, if she really is your chief's cousin.'

The ignorance in which the dwellers under one roof can exist as to the social position of their fellow-lodgers is a permanent fact which, as much as any other, shows what the rush of Paris life is. Still, it is easily conceivable that a clerk who goes early every morning to his office, comes home only to dinner, and spends every evening out, and a woman swallowed up in a round of pleasures, should know nothing of an old maid living on the third floor beyond the courtyard of the house they dwell in, especially when she lives as Mademoiselle Fischer did.

Up in the morning before any one else, Lisbeth went out to buy her bread, milk, and live charcoal, never speaking to any one, and she went to bed with the sun; she never had a letter or a visitor, nor chatted with her neighbours. Here was one of those anonymous, entomological existences such as are to be met with in many large tenements where, at the end of four years, you unexpectedly learn that up on the fourth floor there is an old man lodging who knew Voltaire, Pilâtre de Rozier, Beaujon, Marcel, Molé, Sophie Arnould, Franklin, and Robespierre. What Monsieur and Madame Marneffe had just said concerning Lisbeth Fischer they had come to know, in consequence, partly, of the loneliness of the neighbourhood, and of the alliance, to which their necessities had led, between them and the doorkeepers, whose goodwill was too important to them not to have been carefully encouraged.

Now, the old maid's pride, silence, and reserve had engendered in the porter and his wife the exaggerated respect and cold civility which betray the unconfessed annoyance of an inferior. Also, the porter thought himself in all essentials the equal of any lodger whose rent was no more than two hundred and fifty francs. Cousin Bette's confidences to Hortense were true; and it is evident that the porter's wife might be very likely to slander Mademoiselle Fischer in her intimate gossip with the Marneffes, while only intending to tell tales.

When Lisbeth had taken her candle from the hands of worthy Madame Olivier the portress, she looked up to see whether the windows of the garret over her own rooms were lighted up. At that hour, even in July, it was so dark within the courtyard that the old maid could not get to bed without a light.

'Oh, you may be quite easy, Monsieur Steinbock is in his room. He has not been out even,' said Madame Olivier, with meaning.

Lisbeth made no reply. She was still a peasant, in so far that she was indifferent to the gossip of persons unconnected with her. Just as a peasant sees nothing beyond his village, she cared for nobody's opinion outside the little circle in which she lived. So she boldly went up, not to her own room, but to the garret; and this is why. At dessert she had filled her bag with fruit and sweets for her lover, and she went to give them to him, exactly as an old lady brings home a biscuit for her dog.

She found the hero of Hortense's dreams working by the light of a small lamp, of which the light was intensified by the use of a bottle of water as a lens – a pale young man, seated at a workman's bench covered with a modeller's tools, wax, chisels, rough-hewn stone, and bronze castings; he wore a blouse, and had in his hand a little group in red wax, which he gazed at like a poet absorbed in his labours.

'Here, Wenceslas, see what I have brought you,' said she, laying her handkerchief on a corner of the table; then she carefully took the sweetmeats and fruit out of her bag.

'You are very kind, Mademoiselle,' replied the exile in melancholy tones.

'It will do you good, poor boy. You get feverish by working so hard; you were not born to such a rough life.'

Wenceslas Steinbock looked at her with a bewildered air.

'Eat – come, eat,' said she sharply, 'instead of looking at me as you do at one of your images when you are satisfied with it.'

On being thus smacked with words, the young man seemed less puzzled, for this, indeed, was the female Mentor whose tender moods were always a surprise to him, so much more accustomed was he to be scolded.

Though Steinbock was nine-and-twenty, like many fair men, he looked five or six years younger; and seeing his youth, though its freshness had faded under the fatigue and stress of life in exile, by the side of that dry, hard face, it seemed as though Nature had blundered in the distribution of sex. He rose and threw himself into a deep chair of Louis xv. pattern, covered with yellow Utrecht velvet, as if to rest himself. The old maid took a greengage and offered it him.

'Thank you,' said he, taking the plum.

'Are you tired?' said she, giving him another.

'I am not tired with work, but tired of life,' said he.

'What absurd notions you have!' she exclaimed with some annoyance. 'Have you not a good genius to keep an eye on you?' she said, offering him the sweetmeats, and watching him with pleasure as he ate them all. 'You see, I thought of you when dining with my cousin.'

'I know,' said he, with a look at Lisbeth that was at once affectionate and plaintive, 'but for you I should long since have ceased to live. But, my dear lady, artists require relaxation—'

'Ah! there we come to the point!' cried she, interrupting him, her hands on her hips, and her flashing eyes fixed on him. 'You want to go wasting your health in the vile resorts of Paris, like so many artisans, who end by dying in the work-house. No, no. Make a fortune, and then, when you have money in the funds, you may amuse yourself, child; then you will have enough to pay for the doctor and for your pleasure, libertine that you are.'

Wenceslas Steinbock, on receiving this broadside, with an accompaniment of looks that pierced him like a magnetic flame, bent his head. The most malignant slanderer on seeing this scene would at once have understood that the hints thrown out by the Oliviers were false. Everything in this couple, their tone, manner, and way of looking at each other, proved the purity of their private life. The old maid showed the affection of rough but very genuine maternal feeling; the young man submitted, as a respectful son yields to the tyranny of a mother. The strange alliance seemed to be the outcome of a strong will acting constantly on a weak character, on the fluid nature peculiar to the Slavs, which, while it does not hinder them from showing heroic courage in battle, gives them an amazing incoherency of conduct, a moral softness of which physiologists ought to try to detect the causes, since physiologists are to political life what entomologists are to agriculture.

'But if I die before I am rich?' said Wenceslas dolefully.

'Die!' cried she. 'Oh, I will not let you die. I have life enough for both, and I would have my blood injected into your veins if necessary.'

Tears rose to Steinbock's eyes as he heard her vehement and artless speech.

'Do not be unhappy, my little Wenceslas,' said Lisbeth with feeling. 'My cousin Hortense thought your seal quite pretty, I am sure; and I will manage to sell your bronze group, you will see; you will have paid me off, you will be able to do as you please, you will soon be free. Come, smile a little!'

'I can never repay you, Mademoiselle,' said the exile.

'And why not?' asked the peasant woman, taking the Livonian's part against herself.

'Because you not only fed me, lodged me, cared for me in my poverty, but you also gave me strength. You have made me what I am; you have often been stern, you have made me very unhappy—'

'I?' said the old maid. 'Are you going to pour out all your nonsense once more about poetry and the arts, and to crack your fingers and stretch your arms while you spout about the ideal, and beauty, and all your northern madness? – Beauty is not to compare with solid pudding – and that am I! – You have ideas in your brain? What is the use of them? I too have ideas. What is the good of all the fine things you may have in your soul if you can make no use of them? Those who have ideas do not get so far as those who have none, if they don't know which way to go.

'Instead of thinking over your ideas, you must work. – Now, what have you done while I was out?'

'What did your pretty cousin say?'

'Who told you she was pretty?' asked Lisbeth sharply, in a tone hollow with tiger-like jealousy.

'Why, you did.'

'That was only to see your face. Do you want to go trotting after petticoats? You who are so fond of women, well, make them in bronze. Let us see a cast of your desires, for you will have to do without the ladies for some little time yet, and certainly without my cousin, my good fellow. She is not game for your bag; that young lady wants a man with sixty thousand francs a year – and has found him!'

'Why, your bed is not made!' she exclaimed, looking into the adjoining room. 'Poor dear boy, I quite forgot you!'

The sturdy woman pulled off her gloves, her cape and bonnet, and remade the artist's little camp-bed as briskly as any housemaid. This mixture of abruptness, of roughness even, with real kindness, perhaps accounts for the ascendency Lisbeth had acquired over the man whom she regarded as her personal property. Is not our attachment to life based on its alternations of good and evil?

If the Livonian had happened to meet Madame Marneffe instead of Lisbeth Fischer, he would have found a protectress whose complaisance must have led him into some boggy or discreditable path, where he would have been lost. He would certainly never have worked, nor the artist have been hatched out. Thus, while he deplored the old maid's grasping avarice, his reason bid him prefer her iron hand to the life of idleness and peril led by many of his fellow-countrymen.

This was the incident that had given rise to the coalition of female energy and masculine feebleness – a contrast in union said not to be uncommon in Poland.

In 1833 Mademoiselle Fischer, who sometimes worked into the night when business was good, at about one o'clock one morning perceived a strong smell of carbonic acid gas, and heard the groans of a dying man. The fumes and the gasping came from a garret over the two rooms forming her dwelling, and she supposed that a young man who had but lately come to lodge in this attic – which had been vacant for three years – was committing suicide. She ran upstairs, broke in the door by a push with her peasant strength, and found the lodger writhing on a camp-bed in the convulsions of death. She extinguished the brazier; the door was open, the air rushed in, and the exile was saved. Then, when Lisbeth had put him to bed like a patient, and he was asleep, she could detect the motives of his suicide in the destitution of the rooms, where there was nothing whatever but a wretched table, the camp-bed, and two chairs.

On the table lay a document, which she read: –

'I am Count Wenceslas Steinbock, born at Prelia, in Livonia.

'No one is to be accused of my death; my reasons for killing myself are, in the words of Kosciusko, *Finis Poloniæ!*

'The grand-nephew of a valiant General under Charles XII. could not beg. My weakly constitution forbids my taking military service, and I yesterday saw the last of the hundred thalers which I brought with me from Dresden to Paris. I have left twenty-five francs in the drawer of this table to pay the rent I owe to the landlord.

'My parents being dead, my death will affect nobody. I desire that my countrymen will not blame the French Government. I have never registered myself as a refugee, and I have asked for nothing; I have met none of my fellow-exiles; no one in Paris knows of my existence.

'I am dying in Christian beliefs. May God forgive the last of the Steinbocks!

'WENCESLAS.'

Mademoiselle Fischer, deeply touched by the dying man's honesty, opened the drawer and found the five five-franc pieces to pay his rent.

'Poor young man!' cried she. 'And with no one in the world to care about him!'

She went downstairs to fetch her work, and sat stitching in the garret, watching over the Livonian gentleman.

When he awoke his astonishment may be imagined on finding a woman sitting by his bed; it was like the prolongation of a dream. As she sat there, covering aiguillettes with gold thread, the old maid had resolved to take charge of the poor youth whom she had admired as he lay sleeping.

As soon as the young Count was fully awake, Lisbeth talked to give him courage, and questioned him to find out how he might make a living. Wenceslas, after telling his story, added that he owed his position to his acknowledged talent for the fine arts. He had always had a preference for sculpture; the necessary time for study had, however, seemed to him too long for a man without money; and at this moment he was far too weak to do any hard manual labour or undertake an important work in sculpture. All this was Greek to Lisbeth Fischer. She replied to the unhappy man that Paris offered so many openings that any man with will and courage might find a living there. A man of spirit need never perish if he had a certain stock of endurance.

'I am but a poor girl myself, a peasant, and I have managed to make myself independent,' said she in conclusion. 'If you will work in earnest, I have saved a little money, and I will lend you, month by month, enough to live upon; but to live frugally, and not to play ducks and drakes with or squander in the streets. You can dine in Paris for twenty-five sous a day, and I will get you your breakfast with mine every day. I will furnish your rooms and pay for such teaching as you may think necessary. You shall give me formal acknowledgment for the money I may lay out for you, and when you are rich you shall repay me all. But if you do not work, I shall not regard myself as in any way pledged to you, and I shall leave you to your fate.'

'Ah!' cried the poor fellow, still smarting from the bitterness of his first struggle with death, 'exiles from every land may well stretch out their hands to France, as the souls in Purgatory do to Paradise. In what other country is such help to be found, and generous hearts even in such a garret as this? You will be everything to me, my beloved benefactress; I am your slave! Be my sweetheart,' he added, with one of the caressing gestures familiar to the Poles, for which they are unjustly accused of servility.

'Oh, no; I am too jealous, I should make you unhappy; but I will gladly be a sort of comrade,' replied Lisbeth.

'Ah, if only you knew how I longed for some fellow-creature, even a tyrant, who would have something to say to me when I was struggling in the vast solitude of Paris!' exclaimed Wenceslas. 'I regretted Siberia, whither I should be sent by the Emperor if I went home. – Be my Providence! – I will work; I will be a better man than I am, though I am not such a bad fellow!'

'Will you do whatever I bid you?' she asked.

'Yes.'

'Well, then, I will adopt you as my child,' said she lightly. 'Here I am with a son risen from the grave. Come! we will begin at once. I will go out and get what I want; you can dress, and come down to breakfast with me when I knock on the ceiling with the broomstick.'

That day, Mademoiselle Fischer made some inquiries, at the houses to which she carried her work home, as to the business of a sculptor. By dint of many questions she ended by hearing of the studio shop kept by Florent and Chanor, a house that made a special business of casting and finishing decorative bronzes and handsome silver plate. Thither she went with Steinbock, recommending him as an apprentice in sculpture, an idea that was regarded as too eccentric. Their business was to copy the works of the greatest artists, but they did not teach the craft. The old maid's persistent obstinacy so far succeeded that Steinbock was taken on to design ornament. He very soon learned to model ornament, and invented novelties; he had a gift for it.

Five months after he was out of his apprenticeship as a finisher, he made acquaintance with Stidmann, the famous head of Florent's studios. Within twenty months Wenceslas was ahead of his master; but in thirty months the old maid's savings of sixteen years had melted entirely. Two thousand five hundred francs in gold! – a sum with which she had intended to purchase an annuity; and what was there to show for it? A Pole's receipt! And at this moment Lisbeth was working as hard as in her young days to supply the needs of her Livonian.

When she found herself the possessor of a piece of paper instead of her gold louis, she lost her head, and went to consult Monsieur Rivet, who for fifteen years had been his clever head-worker's friend and counsellor. On hearing her story, Monsieur and Madame Rivet scolded Lisbeth, told her she was crazy, abused all refugees whose plots for reconstructing their nation compromised the prosperity of the country and the maintenance of peace; and they urged Lisbeth to find what in trade is called security.

'The only hold you have over this fellow is on his liberty,' observed Monsieur Rivet.

Monsieur Achille Rivet was assessor at the Tribunal of Commerce.

'Imprisonment is no joke for a foreigner,' said he. 'A Frenchman remains five years in prison and comes out, free of his debts to be sure, for he is thenceforth bound only by his conscience, and that never troubles him; but a foreigner never comes out. – Give me your promissory note; my bookkeeper will take it up; he will get it protested; you will both be prosecuted and both be condemned to imprisonment in default of payment; then, when everything is in due form, you must sign a declaration. By doing this your interest will be accumulating, and you will have a pistol always primed to fire at your Pole!'

The old maid allowed these legal steps to be taken, telling her protégé not to be uneasy, as the proceedings were merely to afford a guarantee to a money-lender who agreed to advance them certain sums. This subterfuge was due to the inventive genius of Monsieur Rivet. The guileless artist, blindly trusting to his benefactress, lighted his pipe with the stamped paper, for he smoked, as all men do who have sorrows or energies that need soothing.

One fine day Monsieur Rivet showed Mademoiselle Fischer a schedule, and said to her –

'Here you have Wenceslas Steinbock bound hand and foot, and so effectually, that within twenty-four hours you can have him snug in Clichy for the rest of his days.'

This worthy and honest judge at the Chamber of Commerce experienced that day the satisfaction that must come of having done a malignant good action. Beneficence has so many aspects in Paris that this contradictory expression really represents one of them. The Livonian being fairly entangled in the toils of commercial procedure, the point was to obtain payment; for the illustrious tradesman looked on Wenceslas as a swindler. Feeling, sincerity, poetry, were in his eyes mere folly in business matters.

So Rivet went off to see, in behalf of that poor Mademoiselle Fischer, who, as he said, had been 'done' by the Pole, the rich manufacturers for whom Steinbock had worked. It happened that Stidmann – who, with the help of these distinguished masters of the goldsmiths' art, was raising French work to the perfection it has now reached, allowing it to hold its own against Florence and the Renaissance – Stidmann was in Chanor's private room when the army lace manufacturer called to make inquiries as to 'One Steinbock, a Polish refugee.'

'Whom do you call "One Steinbock"? Do you mean a young Livonian who was a pupil of mine?' cried Stidmann ironically. 'I may tell you, Monsieur, that he is a very great artist. It is said of me that I believe myself to be the Devil. Well, that poor fellow does not know that he is capable of becoming a god.'

'Indeed,' said Rivet, well pleased. And then he added, 'though you take a rather cavalier tone with a man who has the honour to be an Assessor on the Tribunal of Commerce of the Department of the Seine.'

'Your pardon, Consul!' said Stidmann, with a military salute.

'I am delighted,' the Assessor went on, 'to hear what you say. The man may make money then?'

'Certainly,' said Chanor; 'but he must work. He would have a tidy sum by now if he had stayed with us. What is to be done? Artists have a horror of not being free.'

'They have a proper sense of their value and dignity,' replied Stidmann. 'I do not blame Wenceslas for walking alone, trying to make a name, and to become a great man; he had a right to do so! But he was a great loss to me when he left.'

'That, you see,' exclaimed Rivet, 'is what all young students aim at as soon as they are hatched out of the school-egg. Begin by saving money, I say, and seek glory afterwards.'

'It spoils your touch to be picking up coin,' said Stidmann. 'It is Glory's business to bring us wealth.'

'And, after all,' said Chanor to Rivet, 'you cannot tether them.'

'They would eat the halter,' replied Stidmann.

'All these gentlemen have as much caprice as talent,' said Chanor, looking at Stidmann. 'They spend no end of money; they keep their girls, they throw coin out of window, and then they have no time to work. They neglect their orders; we have to employ workmen who are very inferior, but who grow rich; and then they complain of the hard times, while, if they were but steady, they might have piles of gold.'

'You old Lumignon,' said Stidmann, 'you remind me of the publisher before the Revolution who said: "If only I could keep Montesquieu, Voltaire, and Rousseau very poor in my back-shed, and lock up their breeches in a cupboard, what a lot of nice little books they would write to make my fortune." – If works of art could be hammered out like nails, workmen would make them. – Give me a thousand francs, and don't talk nonsense.'

Worthy Monsieur Rivet went home, delighted for poor Mademoiselle Fischer, who dined with him every Monday, and whom he found waiting for him.

'If you can only make him work,' said he, 'you will have more luck than wisdom; you will be repaid, interest, capital, and costs. This Pole has talent, he can make a living; but lock up his trousers and his shoes, do not let him go to the *Chaumière* or the parish of Notre-Dame de Lorette, keep him in leading-strings. If you do not take such precautions, your artist will take to loafing, and if you only knew what these artists mean by loafing! Shocking! Why, I have just heard that they will spend a thousand-franc note in a day!'

This episode had a fatal influence on the home-life of Wenceslas and Lisbeth. The benefactress flavoured the exile's bread with the wormwood of reproof, now that she saw her money in danger, and often believed it to be lost. From a kind mother she became a stepmother; she took the poor boy to task, she nagged him, scolded him for working too slowly, and blamed him for having chosen so difficult a profession. She could not believe that those models in red wax – little figures and sketches for ornamental work – could be of any value. Before long, vexed with herself for her severity, she would try to efface the tears by her care and attention.

Then the poor young man, after groaning to think that he was dependent on this shrew and under the thumb of a peasant of the Vosges, was bewitched by her coaxing ways and by a maternal affection that attached itself solely to the physical and material side of life. He was like a woman who forgives a week of ill-usage for the sake of a kiss and a brief reconciliation.

Thus Mademoiselle Fischer obtained complete power over his mind. The love of dominion that lay as a germ in the old maid's heart developed rapidly. She could now satisfy her pride and her craving for action; had she not a creature belonging to her, to be schooled, scolded, flattered, and made happy, without any fear of a rival? Thus the good and bad sides of her nature alike found play. If she sometimes victimised the poor artist, she had, on the other hand, delicate impulses like the grace of wild flowers; it was a joy to her to provide for all his wants; she would have given her life for him, and Wenceslas knew it. Like every noble soul, the poor fellow forgot the bad points, the defects of the woman who had told him the story of her life as an excuse for her rough ways, and he remembered only the benefits she had done him.

One day, exasperated with Wenceslas for having gone out walking instead of sitting at work, she made a great scene.

'You belong to me,' said she. 'If you were an honest man, you would try to repay me the money you owe as soon as possible.'

The gentleman, in whose veins the blood of the Steinbocks was fired, turned pale.

'Bless me,' she went on, 'we soon shall have nothing to live on but the thirty sous I earn – a poor workwoman!'

The two penniless creatures, worked up by their own war of words, grew vehement; and for the first time the unhappy artist reproached his benefactress for having rescued him from death only to make him lead the life of a galley slave, worse than the bottomless void, where at least, said he, he would have found rest. And he talked of flight.

'Flight!' cried Lisbeth. 'Ah, Monsieur Rivet was right.'

And she clearly explained to the Pole that within twenty-four hours he might be clapped into prison for the rest of his days. It was a crushing blow. Steinbock sank into deep melancholy and total silence.

In the course of the following night, Lisbeth hearing overhead some preparations for suicide, went up to her pensioner's room, and gave him the schedule and a formal release.

'Here, dear child, forgive me,' she said with tears in her eyes. 'Be happy; leave me! I am too cruel to you; only tell me that you will sometimes remember the poor girl who has enabled you to make a living. – What can I say? you are the cause of my ill-humour. I might die; where would you be without me? That is the reason of my being impatient to see you do some saleable work. I do not want my money back for myself, I assure you! I am only frightened at your idleness, which you call meditation; at your ideas, which take up so many hours when you sit gazing at the sky; I want you to get into habits of industry.'

All this was said with an emphasis, a look, and tears that moved the high-minded artist; he clasped his benefactress to his heart and kissed her forehead.

'Keep these pieces,' said he with a sort of cheerfulness. 'Why should you send me to Clichy? Am I not a prisoner here out of gratitude?'

This episode of their secret domestic life had occurred six months previously, and had led to Steinbock's producing three finished works: the seal in Hortense's possession, the group he had placed with the curiosity dealer, and a beautiful clock to which he was putting the last touches, screwing in the last rivets.

This clock represented the twelve Hours, charmingly personified by twelve female figures whirling round in so mad and swift a dance that three little Loves perched on a pile of fruit and flowers could not stop one of them; only the torn skirts of Midnight remained in the hand of the most daring cherub. The group stood on an admirably treated base, ornamented with grotesque beasts. The hours were told by a monstrous mouth that opened to yawn, and each Hour bore some ingeniously appropriate symbol characteristic of the various occupations of the day.

It is now easy to understand the extraordinary attachment of Mademoiselle Fischer for her Livonian; she wanted him to be happy, and she saw him pining, fading away in his attic. The causes of this wretched state of affairs may be easily imagined. The peasant woman watched this son of the North with the affection of a mother, with the jealousy of a wife, and the spirit of a dragon; hence she managed to put every kind of folly or dissipation out of his power by leaving him destitute of money. She longed to keep her victim and companion for herself alone, well conducted perforce, and she had no conception of the cruelty of this senseless wish, since she, for her own part, was accustomed to every privation. She loved Steinbock well enough not to marry him, and too much to give him up to any other woman; she could not resign herself to be no more than a mother to him, though she saw that she was mad to think of playing the other part.

These contradictions, this ferocious jealousy, and the joy of having a man to herself, all agitated her old maid's heart beyond measure. Really in love, as she had been for four years, she cherished the foolish hope of prolonging this impossible and aimless way of life in which her persistence would only be the ruin of the man she thought of as her child. This contest between her instincts and her reason made her unjust and tyrannical. She wreaked on the young man her vengeance for her own lot in being neither young, rich, nor handsome; then, after each fit of rage, recognising herself wrong, she stooped to unlimited humility, infinite tenderness. She never could sacrifice to her idol till she had asserted her power by blows of the axe. In fact, it was the converse of Shakespeare's *Tempest* – Caliban ruling Ariel and Prospero.

As to the poor youth himself, high-minded, meditative, and inclined to be lazy, the desert that his protectress made in his soul might be seen in his eyes, as in those of a caged lion. The penal servitude forced on him by Lisbeth did not fulfil the cravings of his heart. His weariness became a physical malady, and he was dying without daring to ask, or knowing where to procure, the price of some little necessary dissipation. On some days of special energy, when a feeling of utter ill-luck added to his exasperation, he would look at Lisbeth as a thirsty traveller on a sandy shore must look at the bitter sea-water.

These harsh fruits of indigence, and this isolation in the midst of Paris, Lisbeth relished with delight. And besides, she foresaw that the first passion would rob her of her slave. Sometimes she even blamed herself because her own tyranny and reproaches had compelled the poetic youth to become so great an artist of delicate work, and she had thus given him the means of casting her off.

On the day after, these three lives, so differently but so utterly wretched – that of a mother in despair, that of the

Marneffe household, and that of the unhappy exile – were all to be influenced by Hortense's guileless passion, and by the strange outcome of the Baron's luckless passion for Josépha.

Just as Hulot was going into the opera-house, he was stopped by the darkened appearance of the building and of the Rue le Peletier, where there were no gendarmes, no lights, no theatre-servants, no barrier to regulate the crowd. He looked up at the announcement-board, and beheld a strip of white paper, on which was printed the solemn notice —

'CLOSED ON ACCOUNT OF ILLNESS.'

He rushed off to Josépha's lodgings in the Rue Chauchat; for, like all the singers, she lived close at hand.

'Whom do you want, sir?' asked the porter, to the Baron's great astonishment.

'Have you forgotten me?' said Hulot, much puzzled.

'On the contrary, sir, it is because I have the honour to remember you that I ask you, Where are you going?'

A mortal chill fell upon the Baron.

'What has happened?' he asked.

'If you go up to Mademoiselle Mirah's rooms, Monsieur le Baron, you will find Mademoiselle Héloïse Brisetout there – and Monsieur Bixiou, Monsieur Léon de Lora, Monsieur Lousteau, Monsieur de Vernisset, Monsieur Stidmann; and ladies smelling of patchouli – holding a housewarming.'

'Then, where – where is—?'

'Mademoiselle Mirah? – I don't know that I ought to tell you.'

The Baron slipped two five-franc pieces into the porter's hand.

'Well, she is now in the Rue de la Ville l'Évêque, in a fine house, given to her, they say, by the Duc d'Hérouville,' replied the man in a whisper.

Having ascertained the number of the house, Monsieur Hulot called a *milord* and drove to one of those pretty modern houses with double doors, where everything, from the gaslight at the entrance, proclaims luxury.

The Baron, in his blue cloth coat, white neckcloth, nankeen trousers, patent leather boots, and stiffly starched shirt-frill, was supposed to be a guest, though a late arrival, by the janitor of this new Eden. His alacrity of manner and quick step justified the opinion.

The porter rang a bell, and a footman appeared in the hall. This man, as new as the house, admitted the visitor, who said to him in an imperious tone, and with a lordly gesture –

'Take in this card to Mademoiselle Josépha.'

The victim mechanically looked round the room in which he found himself – an anteroom full of choice flowers and of furniture that must have cost twenty thousand francs. The servant, on his return, begged Monsieur to wait in the drawing-room till the company came to their coffee.

Though the Baron had been familiar with Imperial luxury, which was undoubtedly prodigious, while its productions, though not durable in kind, had nevertheless cost enormous sums, he stood dazzled, dumbfounded, in this drawing-room with three windows looking out on a garden like fairyland, one of those gardens that are created in a month with a made soil and transplanted shrubs, while the grass seems as if it must be made to grow by some chemical process. He admired not only the decoration, the gilding, the carving, in the most expensive Pompadour style, as it is called, and the magnificent brocades, all of which any enriched tradesman could have procured for money; but he also noted such treasures as only princes can select and find, can pay for and give away: two pictures by Greuze, two by Watteau, two heads by Vandyck, two landscapes by Ruysdael, and two by le Guaspre, a Rembrandt, a Holbein, a Murillo, and a Titian, two paintings by Teniers, and a pair by Metzu, a Van Huysum, and an Abraham Mignon – in short, two hundred thousand francs' worth of pictures superbly framed. The gilding was worth almost as much as the paintings.

'Ah, ha! Now you understand, my good man?' said Josépha.

She had stolen in on tiptoe through a noiseless door, over Persian carpets, and came upon her adorer, standing lost in amazement – in the stupid amazement when a man's ears tingle so soundly that he hears nothing but that fatal knell.

The words 'my good man,' spoken to an official of such high importance, so perfectly exemplified the audacity with which these creatures pour contempt on the loftiest, that the Baron was nailed to the spot. Josépha, in white and yellow, was so beautifully dressed for the banquet, that amid all this lavish magnificence she still shone like a rarer jewel.

'Isn't this really fine?' said she. 'The Duke has spent all the money on it that he got out of floating a company, of which the shares all sold at a premium. He is no fool, is my little Duke. There is nothing like a man who has been a grandee in his time for turning coals into gold. Just before dinner the notary brought me the title-deeds to sign and the bills receipted! – They are all a first-class set in there – d'Esgrignon, Rastignac, Maxime, Lenoncourt, Verneuil, Laginski, Rochefide, la Palférine, and from among the bankers Nucingen and du Tillet, with Antonia, Malaga, Carabine, and la Schontz; and they all feel for you deeply. – Yes, old boy, and they hope you will join them, but on condition that you forthwith drink up to two bottles full of Hungarian wine, Champagne, or Cape, just to bring you up to their mark. – My dear fellow, we are all so much *on* here, that it was necessary to close the Opera. The manager is as drunk as a cornet-à-pistons; he is hiccuping already.'

'Oh, Josépha!—' cried the Baron.

'Now, can anything be more absurd than explanations?' she broke in with a smile. 'Look here; can you stand six hundred thousand francs which this house and furniture have cost? Can you give me a bond to the tune of thirty thousand francs a year, which is what the Duke has just given me in a packet of common sugared almonds from the grocer's? – a pretty notion that—'

'What an atrocity!' cried Hulot, who in his fury would have given his wife's diamonds to stand in the Duc d'Hérouville's shoes for twenty-four hours.

'Atrocity is my trade,' said she. 'So that is how you take it? Well, why didn't you float a company? Goodness me! my poor dyed Tom, you ought to be grateful to me; I have thrown you over just when you would have spent on me your widow's fortune, your daughter's portion. – What, tears! The Empire is a thing of the past – I hail the coming Empire!'

She struck a tragic attitude, and declaimed –

> 'They call you Hulot! Nay, I know you not—'

And she went into the other room.

Through the door, left ajar, there came, like a lightning-flash, a streak of light with an accompaniment of the crescendo of the orgy and the fragrance of a banquet of the choicest description.

The singer peeped through the partly open door, and seeing Hulot transfixed as if he had been a bronze image, she came one step forward into the room.

'Monsieur,' said she, 'I have handed over the rubbish in the Rue Chauchat to Bixiou's little Héloïse Brisetout. If you wish to claim your cotton nightcap, your boot-jack, your belt, and your wax dye, I have stipulated for their return.'

This insolent banter made the Baron leave the room as precipitately as Lot departed from Gomorrha, but he did not look back like Mrs. Lot.

Hulot went home, striding along in a fury, and talking to himself; he found his family still playing the game of whist at two sous a point, at which he had left them. On seeing her husband return, poor Adeline imagined something dreadful, some dishonour; she gave her cards to Hortense, and led Hector away into the very room where, only five hours since, Crevel had foretold her the utmost disgrace of poverty.

'What is the matter?' she said, terrified.

'Oh, forgive me – but let me tell you all these horrors.' And for ten minutes he poured out his wrath.

'But, my dear,' said the unhappy woman, with heroic courage, 'these creatures do not know what love means – such pure and devoted love as you deserve. How could you, so clearsighted as you are, dream of competing with millions?'

'Dearest Adeline!' cried the Baron, clasping her to his heart.

The Baroness's words had shed balm on the bleeding wounds to his vanity.

'To be sure, take away the Duc d'Hérouville's fortune, and she could not hesitate between us!' said the Baron.

'My dear,' said Adeline with a final effort, 'if you positively must have mistresses, why do you not seek them, like Crevel, among women who are less extravagant, and of a class that can for a time be content with little? We should all gain by that arrangement. – I understand your need – but I do not understand that vanity—'

'Oh, what a kind and perfect wife you are!' cried he. 'I am an old lunatic, I do not deserve to have such a wife!'

'I am simply the Josephine of my Napoleon,' she replied, with a touch of melancholy.

'Josephine was not to compare with you!' said he. 'Come; I will play a game of whist with my brother and the children. I must try my hand at the business of a family man; I must get Hortense a husband, and bury the libertine.'

His frankness so greatly touched poor Adeline, that she said –

'The creature has no taste to prefer any man in the world to my Hector. Oh, I would not give you up for all the gold on earth. How can any woman throw you over who is so happy as to be loved by you?'

The look with which the Baron rewarded his wife's fanaticism confirmed her in her opinion that gentleness and docility were a woman's strongest weapons.

But in this she was mistaken. The noblest sentiments, carried to an excess, can produce mischief as great as do the worst vices. Bonaparte was made Emperor for having fired on the people, at a stone's throw from the spot where Louis XVI. lost his throne and his head because he would not allow a certain Monsieur Sauce to be hurt.

On the following morning, Hortense, who had slept with the seal under her pillow, so as to have it close to her all night, dressed very early, and sent to beg her father to join her in the garden as soon as he should be down.

By about half-past nine, the father, acceding to his daughter's petition, gave her his arm for a walk, and they went along the quays by the Pont Royal to the Place du Carrousel.

'Let us look into the shop windows, papa,' said Hortense, as they went through the little gate to cross the wide square.

'What – here?' said her father, laughing at her.

'We are supposed to have come to see the pictures, and over there' – and she pointed to the stalls in front of the houses at a right angle to the Rue du Doyenné – 'look! there are dealers in curiosities and pictures—'

'Your cousin lives there.'

'I know it; but she must not see us.'

'And what do you want to do?' said the Baron, who, finding himself within thirty yards of Madame Marneffe's windows, suddenly remembered her.

Hortense had dragged her father in front of one of the shops forming the angle of a block of houses built along the front of the Old Louvre, and facing the Hôtel de Nantes. She went into this shop; her father stood outside, absorbed in gazing at the windows of the pretty little lady, who, the evening before, had left her image stamped on the old beau's heart, as if to alleviate the wound he was so soon to receive; and he could not help putting his wife's sage advice into practice.

'I will fall back on a simple little citizen's wife,' said he to himself, recalling Madame Marneffe's adorable graces. 'Such a woman as that will soon make me forget that grasping Josépha.'

Now, this was what was happening at the same moment outside and inside the curiosity shop.

As he fixed his eyes on the windows of his new *belle*, the Baron saw the husband, who, while brushing his coat with his own hands, was apparently on the lookout, expecting to see some one on the square. Fearing lest he should be seen, and subsequently recognised, the amorous Baron turned his back on the Rue du Doyenné, or rather stood at three-quarters face, as it were, so as to be able to glance round from time to time.

This manœuvre brought him face to face with Madame Marneffe, who, coming up from the quay, was doubling the
promontory of houses to go home.

Valérie was evidently startled as she met the Baron's astonished eye, and she responded with a prudish dropping of her
eyelids.

'A pretty woman,' exclaimed he, 'for whom a man would
do many foolish things.'

'Indeed, Monsieur?' said she, turning suddenly, like a
woman who has just come to some vehement decision, 'you
are Monsieur le Baron Hulot, I believe?'

The Baron, more and more bewildered, bowed assent.

'Then, as chance has twice made our eyes meet, and I am
so fortunate as to have interested or puzzled you, I may tell
you that, instead of doing anything foolish, you ought to do
justice. – My husband's fate rests with you.'

'And how may that be?' asked the gallant Baron.

'He is employed in your department in the War Office,
under Monsieur Lebrun, in Monsieur Coquet's room,' said
she, with a smile.

'I am quite disposed, Madame – Madame—?'

'Madame Marneffe.'

'Dear little Madame Marneffe, to do injustice for your sake.
– I have a cousin living in your house; I will go to see her one
day soon – as soon as possible; bring your petition to me in
her rooms.'

'Pardon my boldness, Monsieur le Baron; you must understand that if I dare to address you thus, it is because I have no
friend to protect me—'

'Ah, ha!'

'Monsieur, you misunderstand me,' said she, lowering her
eyelids.

Hulot felt as if the sun had disappeared.

'I am at my wits' end, but I am an honest woman!' she went
on. 'About six months ago my only protector died, Marshal
Montcornet—'

'Ah! You are his daughter?'

'Yes, Monsieur; but he never acknowledged me.'

'That was that he might leave you part of his fortune.'

'He left me nothing; he made no will.'

'Indeed! Poor little woman! The Marshal died suddenly of apoplexy. But, come, Madame, hope for the best. The State must do something for the daughter of one of the Chevalier Bayards of the Empire.'

Madame Marneffe bowed gracefully and went off, as proud of her success as the Baron was of his.

'Where the devil has she been so early?' thought he, watching the flow of her skirts, to which she contrived to impart a somewhat exaggerated grace. 'She looks too tired to have just come from a bath, and her husband is waiting for her. It is strange, and puzzles me altogether.'

Madame Marneffe having vanished within, the Baron wondered what his daughter was doing in the shop. As he went in, still staring at Madame Marneffe's windows, he ran against a young man with a pale brow and sparkling grey eyes, wearing a summer coat of black merino, coarse drill trousers, and tan shoes, with gaiters, rushing away headlong; he saw him run to the house in the Rue du Doyenné, into which he went.

Hortense, on going into the shop, had at once recognised the famous group, conspicuously placed on a table in the middle and in front of the door. Even without the circumstances to which she owed her knowledge of this masterpiece, it would probably have struck her by the peculiar power which we must call the *brio* – the *go* – of great works; and the girl herself might in Italy have been taken as a model for the personification of *Brio*.

Not every work by a man of genius has in the same degree that brilliancy, that glory which is at once patent even to the most ignorant beholder. Thus, certain pictures by Raphael, such as the famous *Transfiguration*, the *Madonna di Foligno*, and the frescoes of the *Stanze* in the Vatican, do not at first captivate our admiration, as do the *Violin-player* in the Sciarra Palace, the portraits of the Doria family, and the

Vision of Ezekiel in the Pitti Gallery, the *Christ bearing His Cross* in the Borghese collection, and the *Marriage of the Virgin* in the Bréra at Milan. The *Saint John the Baptist* of the Tribuna, and *Saint Luke painting the Virgin's portrait* in the Accademia at Rome, have not the charm of the *Portrait of Leo x.* and of the *Virgin* at Dresden.

And yet they are all of equal merit. Nay, more. The *Stanze*, the *Transfiguration*, the panels, and the three easel pictures in the Vatican are in the highest degree perfect and sublime. But they demand a stress of attention, even from the most accomplished beholder, and serious study, to be fully understood; while the *Violin-player*, the *Marriage of the Virgin*, and the *Vision of Ezekiel* go straight to the heart through the portal of sight, and make their home there. It is a pleasure to receive them thus without an effort; if it is not the highest phase of art, it is the happiest. This fact proves that, in the begetting of works of art, there is as much chance in the character of the offspring as there is in a family of children; that some will be happily graced, born beautiful, and costing their mothers little suffering, creatures on whom everything smiles, and with whom everything succeeds; in short, genius, like love, has its fairer blossoms.

This *brio*, an Italian word which the French have begun to use, is characteristic of youthful work. It is the fruit of the impetus and fire of early talent – an impetus which is met with again later in some happy hours; but this particular *brio* no longer comes from the artist's heart; instead of his flinging it into his work as a volcano flings up its fires, it comes to him from outside, inspired by circumstances, by love, or rivalry, often by hatred, and more often still by the imperious need of glory to be lived up to.

This group by Wenceslas was to his later works what the *Marriage of the Virgin* is to the great mass of Raphael's, the first step of a gifted artist taken with the inimitable grace, the eagerness, and delightful overflowingness of a child, whose strength is concealed under the pink-and-white flesh full of dimples which seem to echo to a mother's laughter. Prince

Eugene is said to have paid four hundred thousand francs for this picture, which would be worth a million to any nation that owned no picture by Raphael, but no one would give that sum for the finest of the frescoes, though their value is far greater as works of art.

Hortense restrained her admiration, for she reflected on the amount of her girlish savings; she assumed an air of indifference, and said to the dealer –

'What is the price of that?'

'Fifteen hundred francs,' replied the man, sending a glance of intelligence to a young man seated on a stool in the corner.

The young man himself gazed in a stupefaction at Monsieur Hulot's living masterpiece. Hortense, forewarned, at once identified him as the artist, from the colour that flushed a face pale with endurance; she saw the spark lighted up in his grey eyes by her question; she looked on the thin, drawn features, like those of a monk consumed by asceticism; she loved the red, well-formed mouth, the delicate chin, and the Pole's silky chestnut hair.

'If it were twelve hundred,' said she, 'I would beg you to send it to me.'

'It is antique, Mademoiselle,' the dealer remarked, thinking, like all his fraternity, that, having uttered this *ne plus ultra* of bric-à-brac, there was no more to be said.

'Excuse me, Monsieur,' she replied very quietly, 'it was made this year; I came expressly to beg you, if my price is accepted, to send the artist to see us, as it might be possible to procure him some important commissions.'

'And if he is to have the twelve hundred francs, what am I to get? I am the dealer,' said the man, with candid good-humour.

'To be sure!' replied the girl, with a slight curl of disdain.

'Oh! Mademoiselle, take it; I will make terms with the dealer,' cried the Livonian, beside himself.

Fascinated by Hortense's wonderful beauty and the love of art she displayed, he added –

'I am the sculptor of the group, and for ten days I have come here three times a day to see if anybody would recog-

nise its merit and bargain for it. You are my first admirer –
take it!'

'Come, then, Monsieur, with the dealer, an hour hence. –
Here is my father's card,' replied Hortense.

Then, seeing the shopkeeper go into a back room to wrap
the group in a piece of linen rag, she added in a low voice, to
the great astonishment of the artist, who thought he must be
dreaming –

'For the benefit of your future prospects, Monsieur
Wenceslas, do not mention the name of the purchaser to
Mademoiselle Fischer, for she is our cousin.'

The word cousin dazzled the artist's mind; he had a glimpse
of Paradise whence this daughter of Eve had come to him. He
had dreamed of the beautiful girl of whom Lisbeth had told
him, as Hortense had dreamed of her cousin's lover; and, as
she had entered the shop,

'Ah!' thought he, 'if she could but be like this!'

The look that passed between the lovers may be imagined; it was a flame, for virtuous lovers have no hypocrisies.

'Well, what the deuce are you doing here?' her father asked
her.

'I have been spending twelve hundred francs that I had
saved. Come.' And she took her father's arm.

'Twelve hundred francs?' he repeated.

'To be exact, thirteen hundred; you will lend me the odd
hundred?'

'And on what, in such a place, could you spend so much?'

'Ah! that is the question!' replied the happy girl. 'If I have
got a husband, he is not dear at the money.'

'A husband! In that shop, my child?'

'Listen, dear little father; would you forbid my marrying a
great artist?'

'No, my dear. A great artist in these days is a prince without
a title – he has glory and fortune, the two chief social advantages – next to virtue,' he added, in a smug tone.

'Oh, of course!' said Hortense. 'And what do you think of
sculpture?'

'It is a very poor business,' replied Hulot, shaking his head. 'It needs high patronage as well as great talent, for Government is the only purchaser. It is an art with no demand nowadays, where there are no princely houses, no great fortunes, no entailed mansions, no hereditary estates. Only small pictures and small figures can find a place; the arts are endangered by this need of small things.'

'But if a great artist could find a demand?' said Hortense.

'That indeed would solve the problem.'

'Or had some one to back him?'

'That would be even better.'

'If he were of noble birth?'

'Pooh!'

'A Count.'

'And a sculptor?'

'He has no money.'

'And so he counts on that of Mademoiselle Hortense Hulot?' said the Baron ironically, with an inquisitorial look into his daughter's eyes.

'This great artist, a Count and a sculptor, has just seen your daughter for the first time in his life, and for the space of five minutes, Monsieur le Baron,' Hortense calmly replied. 'Yesterday, you must know, dear little father, while you were at the Chamber, mamma had a fainting fit. This, which she ascribed to a nervous attack, was the result of some worry that had to do with the failure of my marriage, for she told me that to get rid of me—'

'She is too fond of you to have used an expression—'

'So unparliamentary!' Hortense put in with a laugh. 'No, she did not use those words; but I know that a girl old enough to marry and who does not find a husband is a heavy cross for respectable parents to bear. – Well, she thinks that if a man of energy and talent could be found, who would be satisfied with thirty thousand francs for my marriage portion, we might all be happy. In fact, she thought it advisable to prepare me for the modesty of my future lot, and to hinder me from indulging in too fervid dreams. – Which evidently meant an end to the intended marriage, and no settlements for me!'

'Your mother is a very good woman, noble, admirable!' replied the father, deeply humiliated, though not sorry to hear this confession.

'She told me yesterday that she had your permission to sell her diamonds so as to give me something to marry on; but I should like her to keep her jewels, and to find a husband myself. I think I have found the man, the possible husband, answering to mamma's prospectus—'

'There? – in the Place du Carrousel? – and in one morning?'

'Oh, papa, the mischief lies deeper!' said she archly.

'Well, come, my child, tell the whole story to your good old father,' said he persuasively, and concealing his uneasiness.

Under promise of absolute secrecy, Hortense repeated the upshot of her various conversations with her Cousin Bette. Then, when they got home, she showed the much-talked-of seal to her father in evidence of the sagacity of her views. The father, in the depth of his heart, wondered at the skill and acumen of girls who act on instinct, discerning the simplicity of the scheme which her idealised love had suggested in the course of a single night to his guileless daughter.

'You will see the masterpiece I have just bought; it is to be brought home, and that dear Wenceslas is to come with the dealer. – The man who made that group ought to make a fortune; only use your influence to get him an order for a statue, and rooms at the Institut—'

'How you run on!' cried her father. 'Why, if you had your own way, you would be man and wife within the legal period – in eleven days—'

'Must we wait so long?' said she, laughing. 'But I fell in love with him in five minutes, as you fell in love with mamma at first sight. And he loves me as if we had known each other for two years. Yes,' she said in reply to her father's look, 'I read ten volumes of love in his eyes. And will not you and mamma accept him as my husband when you see that he is a man of genius? Sculpture is the greatest of the Arts,' she

cried, clapping her hands and jumping. 'I will tell you everything—'

'What, is there more to come?' asked her father, smiling.

The child's complete and effervescent innocence had
restored her father's peace of mind.

'A confession of the first importance,' said she. 'I loved
him without knowing him; and, for the last hour, since seeing
him, I am crazy about him.'

'A little too crazy!' said the Baron, who was enjoying the
sight of this guileless passion.

'Do not punish me for confiding in you,' replied she. 'It is
so delightful to say to my father's heart, "I love him! I am so
happy in loving him!" – You will see my Wenceslas! His brow
is so sad! The sun of genius shines in his grey eyes – and what
an air he has! What do you think of Livonia? Is it a fine
country? – The idea of Cousin Bette's marrying that young
fellow! She might be his mother. It would be murder! I am
quite jealous of all she has ever done for him. But I don't
think my marriage will please her.'

'See, my darling, we must hide nothing from your mother.'

'I should have to show her the seal, and I promised not to
betray Cousin Lisbeth, who is afraid, she says, of mamma's
laughing at her,' said Hortense.

'You have scruples about the seal, and none about robbing
your cousin of her lover.'

'I promised about the seal – I made no promises about the
sculptor.'

This adventure, patriarchal in its simplicity, came admirably *à
propos* to the unconfessed poverty of the family; the Baron, while
praising his daughter for her candour, explained to her that she
must now leave matters to the discretion of her parents.

'You understand, my child, that it is not your part to
ascertain whether your cousin's lover is a Count, if he has all
his papers properly certified, and if his conduct is a guarantee
for his respectability. – As for your cousin, she refused five
offers when she was twenty years younger; that will prove no
obstacle, I undertake to say.'

'Listen to me, papa; if you really wish to see me married, never say a word to Lisbeth about it till just before the contract is signed. I have been catechising her about this business for the last six months! Well, there is something about her quite inexplicable—'

'What?' said her father, puzzled.

'Well, she looks evil when I say too much, even in joke, about her lover. Make inquiries, but leave me to row my own boat. My confidence ought to reassure you.'

'The Lord said, "Suffer little children to come unto Me." You are one of those who have come back again,' replied the Baron with a touch of irony.

After breakfast the dealer was announced, and the artist with his group. The sudden flush that reddened her daughter's face at once made the Baroness suspicious and then watchful, and the girl's confusion and the light in her eyes soon betrayed the mystery so badly guarded in her simple heart.

Count Steinbock, dressed in black, struck the Baron as a very gentlemanly young man.

'Would you undertake a bronze statue?' he asked, as he held up the group.

After admiring it on trust, he passed it on to his wife, who knew nothing about sculpture.

'It is beautiful, isn't it, mamma?' said Hortense in her mother's ear.

'A statue! Monsieur, it is less difficult to execute a statue than to make a clock like this, which my friend here has been kind enough to bring,' said the artist in reply.

The dealer was placing on the dining-room sideboard the wax model of the twelve Hours that the Loves were trying to delay.

'Leave the clock with me,' said the Baron, astounded at the beauty of the sketch. 'I should like to show it to the Ministers of the Interior and of Commerce.'

'Who is the young man in whom you take so much interest?' the Baroness asked her daughter.

'An artist who could afford to execute this model could get a hundred thousand francs for it,' said the curiosity-dealer, putting on a knowing and mysterious look as he saw that the artist and the girl were interchanging glances. 'He would only need to sell twenty copies at eight thousand francs each – for the materials would cost about a thousand crowns for each example. But if each copy were numbered and the mould destroyed, it would certainly be possible to meet with twenty amateurs only too glad to possess a replica of such a work.'

'A hundred thousand francs!' cried Steinbock, looking from the dealer to Hortense, the Baron, and the Baroness.

'Yes, a hundred thousand francs,' repeated the dealer. 'If I were rich enough, I would buy it of you myself for twenty thousand francs; for by destroying the mould it would become a valuable property. But one of the princes ought to pay thirty or forty thousand francs for such a work to ornament his drawing-room. No man has ever succeeded in making a clock satisfactory alike to the vulgar and to the connoisseur, and this one, sir, solves the difficulty.'

'This is for yourself, Monsieur,' said Hortense, giving six gold pieces to the dealer.

'Never breathe a word of this visit to any one living,' said the artist to his friend, at the door. 'If you should be asked where we sold the group, mention the Duc d'Hérouville, the famous collector in the Rue de Varenne.'

The dealer nodded assent.

'And your name?' said Hulot to the artist when he came back.

'Count Steinbock.'

'Have you the papers that prove your identity?'

'Yes, Monsieur le Baron. They are in Russian and in German, but not legalised.'

'Do you feel equal to undertaking a statue nine feet high?'

'Yes, Monsieur.'

'Well, then, if the persons whom I shall consult are satisfied with your work, I can secure you the commission for the statue of Marshal Montcornet, which is to be erected on his monument at Père-Lachaise. The Minister of War and the old officers of the Imperial Guard have subscribed a sum large enough to enable us to select our artist.'

'Oh! Monsieur, it will make my fortune!' exclaimed Steinbock, overpowered by so much happiness at once.

'Be easy,' replied the Baron graciously. 'If the two ministers to whom I propose to show your group and this sketch in wax are delighted with these two pieces, your prospects of a fortune are good.'

Hortense hugged her father's arm so tightly as to hurt him.

'Bring me your papers, and say nothing of your hopes to anybody, not even to our old Cousin Bette.'

'Lisbeth?' said Madame Hulot, at last understanding the end of all this, though unable to guess the means.

'I could give proof of my skill by making a bust of the Baroness,' added Wenceslas.

The artist, struck by Madame Hulot's beauty, was comparing the mother and daughter.

'Indeed, Monsieur, life may smile upon you,' said the Baron, quite charmed by Count Steinbock's refined and elegant manner. 'You will find out that in Paris no man is clever for nothing, and that persevering toil always finds its reward here.'

Hortense, with a blush, held out to the young man a pretty Algerine purse containing sixty gold pieces. The artist, with something still of a gentleman's pride, responded with a mounting colour easy enough to interpret.

'This, perhaps, is the first money your works have brought you?' said Adeline.

'Yes, Madame – my works of art. It is not the first-fruits of my labour, for I have been a workman.'

'Well, we must hope my daughter's money will bring you good luck,' said she.

'And take it without scruple,' added the Baron, seeing that Wenceslas held the purse in his hand instead of pocketing it. 'The sum will be repaid by some rich man, a prince perhaps, who will offer it with interest to possess so fine a work.'

'Oh, I want it too much myself, papa, to give it up to anybody in the world, even a royal prince!'

'I can make a far prettier thing than that for you, Mademoiselle.'

'But it would not be this one,' replied she; and then, as if ashamed of having said too much, she ran out into the garden.

'Then I shall break the mould and the model as soon as I go home,' said Steinbock.

'Fetch me your papers, and you will hear of me before long, if you are equal to what I expect of you, Monsieur.'

The artist on this could but take leave. After bowing to Madame Hulot and Hortense, who came in from the garden on purpose, he went off to walk in the Tuileries, not bearing – not daring – to return to his attic, where his tyrant would pelt him with questions and wring his secret from him.

Hortense's adorer conceived of groups and statues by the hundred; he felt strong enough to hew the marble himself, like Canova, who was also a feeble man, and nearly died of it. He was transfigured by Hortense, who was to him inspiration made visible.

'Now then,' said the Baroness to her daughter, 'what does all this mean?'

'Well, dear mamma, you have just seen Cousin Lisbeth's lover, who now, I hope, is mine. But shut your eyes, know nothing. Good Heavens! I was to keep it all from you, and I cannot help telling you everything—'

'Good-bye, children!' said the Baron, kissing his wife and daughter; 'I shall perhaps go to call on the Nanny, and from her I shall hear a great deal about our young man.'

'Papa, be cautious!' said Hortense.

'Oh! little girl!' cried the Baroness when Hortense had poured out her poem, of which the morning's adventure was the last canto, 'dear little girl, Artlessness will always be the artfullest puss on earth!'

Genuine passions have an unerring instinct. Set a greedy man before a dish of fruit and he will make no mistake, but take the choicest even without seeing it. In the same way, if you allow a girl who is well brought up to choose a husband for herself, if she is in a position to meet the man of her heart, rarely will she blunder. The act of nature in such cases is known as love at first sight; and in love, first sight is practically second sight.

The Baroness's satisfaction, though disguised under maternal dignity, was as great as her daughter's; for, of the three ways of marrying Hortense of which Crevel had spoken, the best, as she opined, was about to be realised. And she regarded this little drama as an answer by Providence to her fervent prayers.

Mademoiselle Fischer's galley slave, obliged at last to go home, thought he might hide his joy as a lover under his glee as an artist rejoicing over his first success.

'Victory! my group is sold to the Duc d'Hérouville, who is going to give me some commissions,' cried he, throwing the twelve hundred francs in gold on the table before the old maid.

He had, as may be supposed, concealed Hortense's purse; it lay next his heart.

'And a very good thing too,' said Lisbeth. 'I was working myself to death. You see, child, money comes in slowly in the business you have taken up, for this is the first you have earned, and you have been grinding at it for near on five years now. That money barely repays me for what you have cost me since I took your promissory note; that is all I have got by my savings. But be sure of one thing,' she said, after counting the gold, 'this money will all be spent on you. There is enough there to keep us going for a year. In a year you may now be able to pay your debt and have a snug little sum of your own, if you go on in the same way.'

Wenceslas, finding his trick successful, expatiated on the Duc d'Hérouville.

'I will fit you out in a black suit, and get you some new linen,' said Lisbeth, 'for you must appear presentably before your patrons; and then you must have a larger and better apartment than your horrible garret, and furnish it properly. – You look so bright, you are not like the same creature,' she added, gazing at Wenceslas.

'But my work is pronounced a masterpiece.'

'Well, so much the better! Do some more,' said the arid creature, who was nothing but practical, and incapable of understanding the joy of triumph or of beauty in Art. 'Trouble your head no further about what you have sold; make something else to sell. You have spent two hundred francs in money, to say nothing of your time and your labour on that devil of a *Samson*. Your clock will cost you more than two thousand francs to execute. I tell you what, if you will listen to me, you will finish the two little boys crowning the little girl with cornflowers; that would just suit the Parisians. – I will go round to Monsieur Graff the tailor before going to Monsieur Crevel. – Go up now and leave me to dress.'

Next day the Baron, perfectly crazy about Madame Marneffe, went to see Cousin Bette, who was considerably amazed on opening the door to see who her visitor was, for he had never called on her before. She at once said to herself, 'Can it be that Hortense wants my lover?' – for she had heard the evening before, at Monsieur Crevel's, that the marriage with the Councillor of the Supreme Court was broken off.

'What, Cousin! you here? This is the first time you have ever been to see me, and it is certainly not for love of my fine eyes that you have come now.'

'Fine eyes is the truth,' said the Baron; 'you have as fine eyes as I have ever seen—'

'Come, what are you here for? I really am ashamed to receive you in such a kennel.'

The outer room of the two inhabited by Lisbeth served her as sitting-room, dining-room, kitchen, and work-room. The furniture was such as beseemed a well-to-do artisan – walnutwood chairs with straw seats, a small walnut-wood dining table, a work-table, some coloured prints in black wooden frames, short muslin curtains to the windows, the floor well polished and shining with cleanliness, not a speck of dust anywhere, but all cold and dingy, like a picture by Terburg in every particular, even to the grey tone given by a wall paper once blue and now faded to grey. As to the bedroom, no human being had ever penetrated its secrets.

The Baron took it all in at a glance, saw the sign-manual of commonness on every detail, from the cast-iron stove to the household utensils, and his gorge rose at it as he said to himself, 'And *this* is virtue! – What am I here for?' said he aloud. 'You are far too cunning not to guess, and I had better tell you plainly,' cried he, sitting down and looking out across the courtyard through an opening he made in the puckered curtain. 'There is a very pretty woman in the house—'

'Madame Marneffe! Now I understand!' she exclaimed, seeing it all. 'But Josépha?'

'Alas! cousin, Josépha is no more. I was turned out of doors like a discarded footman.'

'And you would like . . . ?' said Lisbeth, looking at the Baron with the dignity of a prude on her guard a quarter of an hour too soon.

'As Madame Marneffe is very much the lady, and the wife of an employé, you can meet her without compromising yourself,' the Baron went on, 'and I should like to see you neighbourly. Oh! you need not be alarmed; she will have the greatest consideration for the cousin of her husband's chief.'

At this moment the rustle of a gown was heard on the stairs and the footstep of a woman wearing the thinnest boots. The sound ceased on the landing. There was a tap at the door, and Madame Marneffe came in.

'Pray excuse me, Mademoiselle, for thus intruding upon you, but I failed to find you yesterday when I came to call; we are near neighbours; and if I had known that you were related to Monsieur le Baron, I should long since have craved your kind interest with him. I saw him come in, so I took the liberty of coming across; for my husband, Monsieur le Baron, spoke to me of a report on the office clerks which is to be laid before the minister to-morrow.'

She seemed quite agitated and nervous – but she had only run upstairs.

'You have no need to play the petitioner, fair lady,' replied the Baron. 'It is I who should ask the favour of seeing you.'

'Very well, if Mademoiselle allows it, pray come!' said Madame Marneffe.

'Yes – go, Cousin, I will join you,' said Lisbeth judiciously.

The Parisienne had so confidently counted on the chief's visit and intelligence, that not only had she dressed herself for so important an interview – she had dressed her room. Early in the day it had been furnished with flowers purchased on credit. Marneffe had helped his wife to polish the furniture, down to the smallest objects, washing, brushing, and dusting everything. Valérie wished to be found in an atmosphere of sweetness, to attract the chief and to please him enough to have a right to be cruel; to tantalise him as a child would, with all the tricks of fashionable tactics. She had gauged Hulot. Give a Paris woman at bay four-and-twenty hours, and she will overthrow a ministry.

The man of the Empire, accustomed to the ways of the Empire, was no doubt quite ignorant of the ways of modern love-making, of the scruples in vogue and the various styles of conversation invented since 1830, which led to the poor weak woman being regarded as the victim of her lover's desires – a Sister of Charity salving a wound, an angel sacrificing herself.

This modern art of love uses a vast amount of evangelical phrases in the service of the Devil. Passion is martyrdom. Both parties aspire to the Ideal, to the Infinite; love is to make them so much better. All these fine words are but a pretext for putting increased ardour into the practical side of it, more frenzy into a fall than of old. This hypocrisy, a characteristic of the times, is a gangrene in gallantry. The lovers are both angels, and they behave, if they can, like two devils.

Love had no time for such subtle analysis between two campaigns, and in 1809 its successes were as rapid as those of the Empire. So, under the Restoration, the handsome Baron, a lady's man once more, had begun by consoling some old friends now fallen from the political firmament, like extinguished stars, and then, as he grew old, was captured by Jenny Cadine and Josépha.

Madame Marneffe had placed her batteries after due study of the Baron's past life, which her husband had narrated in much detail, after picking up some information in the offices. The comedy of modern sentiment might have the charm of novelty to the Baron; Valérie had made up her mind as to her scheme; and we may say the trial of her power that she made this morning answered her highest expectations. Thanks to her manœuvres, sentimental, high-flown, and romantic, Valérie, without committing herself to any promises, obtained for her husband the appointment as deputy head of the office and the Cross of the Legion of Honour.

The campaign was not carried out without little dinners at the *Rocher de Cancale*, parties to the play, and gifts in the form of lace, scarves, gowns, and jewellery. The apartment in the Rue du Doyenné was not satisfactory; the Baron proposed to furnish another magnificently in a charming new house in the Rue Vanneau.

Monsieur Marneffe got a fortnight's leave, to be taken a month hence for urgent private affairs in the country, and a present in money; he promised himself that he would spend both in a little town in Switzerland, studying the fair sex.

While Monsieur Hulot thus devoted himself to the lady he was 'protecting,' he did not forget the young artist. Comte Popinot, Minister of Commerce, was a patron of Art; he paid two thousand francs for a copy of the *Samson* on condition that the mould should be broken, and that there should be no *Samson* but his and Mademoiselle Hulot's. The group was admired by a Prince, to whom the model sketch for the clock was also shown, and who ordered it; but that again was to be unique, and he offered thirty thousand francs for it.

Artists who were consulted, and among them Stidmann, were of opinion that the man who had sketched those two models was capable of achieving a statue. The Marshal Prince de Wissembourg, Minister of War, and President of the Committee for the subscriptions to the monument of Marshal

Montcornet, called a meeting, at which it was decided that the execution of the work should be placed in Steinbock's hands. The Comte de Rastignac, at that time Under-secretary of State, wished to possess a work by the artist, whose glory was waxing amid the acclamations of his rivals. Steinbock sold to him the charming group of two little boys crowning a little girl, and he promised to secure for the sculptor a studio attached to the Government marble-quarries, situated, as all the world knows, at Le Gros-Caillou.

This was success, such success as is won in Paris, that is to say, stupendous success, that crushes those whose shoulders and loins are not strong enough to bear it – as, be it said, not unfrequently is the case. Count Wenceslas Steinbock was written about in all the newspapers and reviews without his having the least suspicion of it, any more than had Mademoiselle Fischer. Every day, as soon as Lisbeth had gone out to dinner, Wenceslas went to the Baroness's and spent an hour or two there, excepting on the evenings when Lisbeth dined with the Hulots.

This state of things lasted for several days.

The Baron, assured of Count Steinbock's titles and position; the Baroness, pleased with his character and habits; Hortense, proud of her permitted love and of her suitor's fame, none of them hesitated to speak of the marriage; in short, the artist was in the seventh heaven, when an indiscretion on Madame Marneffe's part spoilt all.

And this was how.

Lisbeth, whom the Baron wished to see intimate with Madame Marneffe, that she might keep an eye on the couple, had already dined with Valérie; and she, on her part, anxious to have an ear in the Hulot house, made much of the old maid. It occurred to Valérie to invite Mademoiselle Fischer to a house-warming in the new apartments she was about to move into. Lisbeth, glad to have found another house to dine in, and bewitched by Madame Marneffe, had taken a great fancy to Valérie. Of all the persons she had made acquaintance with, no one had taken so much pains to please her. In fact, Madame Marneffe, full of attentions for Mademoiselle Fischer, found herself in the position towards Lisbeth that Lisbeth held towards the Baroness, Monsieur Rivet, Crevel, and the others who invited her to dinner.

The Marneffes had excited Lisbeth's compassion by allowing her to see the extreme poverty of the house, while varnishing it as usual with the fairest colours: their friends were under obligations to them and ungrateful; they had had much illness; Madame Fortin, her mother, had never known of their distress, and had died believing herself wealthy to the end, thanks to their superhuman efforts – and so forth.

'Poor people!' said she to her Cousin Hulot, 'you are right to do what you can for them; they are so brave and so kind! They can hardly live on the thousand crowns he gets as deputy-head of the office, for they have got into debt since Marshal Montcornet's death. It is barbarity on the part of the Government to suppose that a clerk with a wife and family can live in Paris on two thousand four hundred francs a year.'

And so, within a very short time, a young woman who affected regard for her, who told her everything, and consulted her, who flattered her, and seemed ready to yield to her guidance, had become dearer to the eccentric Cousin Lisbeth than all her relations.

The Baron, on his part, admiring in Madame Marneffe such propriety, education, and breeding as neither Jenny Cadine, nor Josépha, nor any friend of theirs had to show, had fallen in love with her in a month, developing a senile passion, a senseless passion, which had an appearance of reason. In fact, he found here neither the banter, nor the orgies, nor the reckless expenditure, nor the depravity, nor the scorn of social decencies, nor the insolent independence which had brought him to grief alike with the actress and the singer. He was spared, too, the rapacity of the courtesan, like unto the thirst of dry sand.

Madame Marneffe, of whom he had made a friend and confidante, made the greatest difficulties over accepting any gift from him.

'Appointments, official presents, anything you can extract from the Government; but do not begin by insulting a woman whom you profess to love,' said Valérie. 'If you do, I shall cease to believe you – and I like to believe you,' she added, with a glance like Saint Theresa leering at heaven.

Every time he made her a present there was a fortress to be stormed, a conscience to be over-persuaded. The hapless Baron laid deep stratagems to offer her some trifle – costly, nevertheless – proud of having at last met with virtue and the realisation of his dreams. In this primitive household, as he assured himself, he was the god as much as in his own. And Monsieur Marneffe seemed at a thousand leagues from suspecting that the Jupiter of his office intended to descend on his wife in a shower of gold; he was his august chief's humblest slave.

Madame Marneffe, twenty-three years of age, a pure and bashful middle-class wife, a blossom hidden in the Rue du Doyenné, could know nothing of the depravity and demoralising harlotry which the Baron could no longer think of without disgust, for he had never known the charm of recalcitrant virtue, and the coy Valérie made him enjoy it to the utmost – all along the line, as the saying goes.

The question having come to this point between Hector and Valérie, it is not astonishing that Valérie should have heard from Hector the secret of the intended marriage between the great sculptor Steinbock and Hortense Hulot. Between a lover on his promotion and a lady who hesitates long before becoming his mistress, there are contests, uttered or unexpressed, in which a word often betrays a thought; as, in fencing, the foils fly as briskly as the swords in duel. Then a prudent man follows the example of Monsieur de Turenne. Thus the Baron had hinted at the greater freedom his daughter's marriage would allow him, in reply to the tender Valérie, who more than once had exclaimed –

'I cannot imagine how a woman can go wrong for a man who is not wholly hers.'

And a thousand times already the Baron had declared that for five-and-twenty years all had been at an end between Madame Hulot and himself.

'And they say she is so handsome!' replied Madame Marneffe. 'I want proof.'

'You shall have it,' said the Baron, made happy by this demand, by which his Valérie committed herself.

Hector had then been compelled to reveal his plans, already being carried into effect in the Rue Vanneau, to prove to Valérie that he intended to devote to her that half of his life which belonged to his lawful wife, supposing that day and night equally divide the existence of civilised humanity. He spoke of decently deserting his wife, leaving her to herself as soon as Hortense should be married. The Baroness would then spend all her time with Hortense or the young Hulot couple; he was sure of her submission.

'And then, my angel, my true life, my real home will be in the Rue Vanneau.'

'Bless me, how you dispose of me!' said Madame Marneffe. 'And my husband—'

'That rag!'

'To be sure, as compared with you so he is!' said she with a laugh.

Madame Marneffe, having heard Steinbock's history, was frantically eager to see the young Count; perhaps she wished to have some trifle of his work while they still lived under the same roof. This curiosity so seriously annoyed the Baron that Valérie swore to him that she would never even look at Wenceslas. But though she obtained, as the reward of her surrender of this wish, a little tea-service of old Sèvres *pâte tendre*, she kept her wish at the bottom of her heart, as if written on tablets.

So one day when she had begged ' *my* Cousin Bette' to come to take coffee with her in her room, she opened on the subject of her lover, to know how she might see him without risk.

'My dear child,' said she, for they called each my dear, 'why have you never introduced your lover to me? Do you know that within a short time he has become famous?'

'He famous?'

'He is the one subject of conversation.'

'Pooh!' cried Lisbeth.

'He is going to execute the statue of my father, and I could be of great use to him and help him to succeed in the work; for Madame Montcornet cannot lend him, as I can, a miniature by Sain, a beautiful thing done in 1809, before the Wagram Campaign, and given to my poor mother – Montcornet when he was young and handsome.'

Sain and Augustin between them held the sceptre of miniature painting under the Empire.

'He is going to make a statue, my dear, did you say?'

'Nine feet high – by the orders of the Minister of War. Why, where have you dropped from that I should tell you the news? Why, the Government is going to give Count Steinbock rooms and a studio at Le Gros-Caillou, the depôt for marble; your Pole will be made the Director, I should not wonder, with two thousand francs a year and a ring on his finger.'

'How do you know all this when I have heard nothing about it?' said Lisbeth at last, shaking off her amazement.

'Now, my dear little Cousin Bette,' said Madame Marneffe, in an insinuating voice, 'are you capable of devoted friendship, put to any test? Shall we henceforth be sisters? Will you swear to me never to have a secret from me any more than I from you – to act as my spy, as I will be yours? – Above all, will you pledge yourself never to betray me either to my husband or to Monsieur Hulot, and never reveal that it was I who told you—?'

Madame Marneffe broke off in this spurring harangue; Lisbeth frightened her. The peasant-woman's face was terrible; her piercing black eyes had the glare of a tiger's; her face was like that we ascribe to a pythoness; she set her teeth to keep them from chattering, and her whole frame quivered convulsively. She had pushed her clenched fingers under her cap to clutch her hair and support her head, which felt too heavy; she was on fire. The smoke of the flame that scorched her seemed to emanate from her wrinkles as from the crevasses rent by a volcanic eruption. It was a startling spectacle.

'Well, why do you stop?' she asked in a hollow voice. 'I will be all to you that I have been to him. – Oh, I would have given him my life-blood!'

'You loved him then?'

'Like a child of my own!'

'Well, then,' said Madame Marneffe, with a breath of relief, 'if you only love him in that way, you will be very happy – for you wish him to be happy?'

Lisbeth replied by a nod as hasty as a mad woman's.

'He is to marry your Cousin Hortense in a month's time.'

'Hortense!' shrieked the old maid, striking her forehead, and starting to her feet.

'Well, but then you were really in love with this young man?' asked Valérie.

'My dear, we are bound for life and death, you and I,' said Mademoiselle Fischer. 'Yes, if you have any love affairs, to me they are sacred. Your vices will be virtues in my eyes. – For I shall need your vices!'

'Then did you live with him?' asked Valérie.

'No; I meant to be a mother to him.'

'I give it up. I cannot understand,' said Valérie. 'In that case you are neither betrayed nor cheated, and you ought to be very happy to see him so well married; he is now fairly afloat. And, at any rate, your day is over. Our artist goes to Madame Hulot's every evening as soon as you go out to dinner.'

'Adeline!' muttered Lisbeth. 'Oh, Adeline, you shall pay for this! I will make you uglier than I am.'

'You are as pale as death!' exclaimed Valérie. 'There is something wrong? – Oh, what a fool I am! The mother and daughter must have suspected that you would raise some obstacles in the way of this affair since they have kept it from you,' said Madame Marneffe. 'But if you did not live with the young man, my dear, all this is a greater puzzle to me than my husband's feelings—'

'Ah, you don't know,' said Lisbeth; 'you have no idea of all their tricks. It is the last blow that kills. And how many such blows have I had to bruise my soul! You don't know that from the time when I could first feel, I have been victimised for Adeline. I was beaten, and she was petted; I was dressed like a scullion, and she had clothes like a lady's; I dug in the garden and cleaned the vegetables, and she – she never stirred a finger for anything but to make up some finery! – She married the Baron, she came to shine at the Emperor's Court, while I stayed in our village till 1809, waiting for four years for a suitable match; they brought me away, to be sure, but only to make me a workwoman, and to offer me clerks or captains like coalheavers for a husband! I have had their leavings for twenty-six years! – And now, like the story in the Old Testament, the poor relation has one ewe-lamb which is all her joy, and the rich man who has flocks covets the ewe-lamb and steals it – without warning, without asking. Adeline has meanly robbed me of my happiness! – Adeline! Adeline! I will see you in the mire, and sunk lower than myself! – And Hortense – I loved her, and she has cheated me. The Baron. – No, it is impossible. Tell me again what is really true of all this.'

'Be calm, my dear child.'

'Valérie, my darling, I will be calm,' said the strange creature, sitting down again. 'One thing only can restore me to reason: give me proofs.'

'Your Cousin Hortense has the *Samson* group – here is a lithograph from it published in a review. She paid for it out of her pocket-money, and it is the Baron who, to benefit his future son-in-law, is pushing him, getting everything for him.'

'Water! – water!' said Lisbeth, after glancing at the print, below which she read, 'A group belonging to Mademoiselle Hulot d'Ervy.' 'Water! my head is burning, I am going mad!'

Madame Marneffe fetched some water. Lisbeth took off her cap, unfastened her black hair, and plunged her head into the basin her new friend held for her. She dipped her forehead into it several times, and checked the incipient inflammation. After this douche she completely recovered her self-command.

'Not a word,' said she to Madame Marneffe as she wiped her face – 'not a word of all this. – You see, I am quite calm; everything is forgotten. I am thinking of something very different.'

'She will be in Charenton to-morrow, that is very certain,' thought Madame Marneffe, looking at the old maid.

'What is to be done?' Lisbeth went on. 'You see, my angel, there is nothing for it but to hold my tongue, bow my head, and drift to the grave, as all water runs to the river. What could I try to do? I should like to grind them all – Adeline, her daughter, and the Baron – all to dust! But what can a poor relation do against a rich family? It would be the story of the earthen pot and the iron pot.'

'Yes, you are right,' said Valérie. 'You can only pull as much hay as you can to your side of the manger. That is all the upshot of life in Paris.'

'Besides,' said Lisbeth, 'I shall soon die, I can tell you, if I lose that boy to whom I fancied I could always be a mother, and with whom I counted on living all my days—'

There were tears in her eyes, and she paused. Such emotion, in this woman made of sulphur and flame, made Valérie shudder.

'Well, at any rate, I have found you,' said Lisbeth, taking Valérie's hand, 'that is some consolation in this dreadful trouble. – We will be true friends; and why should we ever part? I shall never cross your track. No one will ever be in love with me! – Those who would have married me, would only have done it to secure my Cousin Hulot's interest. With energy enough to scale Paradise, to have to devote it to procuring bread and water, a few rags, and a garret! – That is martyrdom, my dear, and I have withered under it.'

She broke off suddenly, and shot a black flash into Madame Marneffe's blue eyes, a glance that pierced the pretty woman's soul, as the point of a dagger might have pierced her heart.

'And what is the use of talking?' she exclaimed in reproof to herself. 'I never said so much before, believe me! The tables will be turned yet!' she added, after a pause. 'As you

so wisely say, let us sharpen our teeth, and pull down all the
hay we can get.'

'You are very wise,' said Madame Marneffe, who had been
frightened by this scene, and had no remembrance of having
uttered this maxim. 'I am sure you are right, my dear child.
Life is not so long after all, and we must make the best of it,
and make use of others to contribute to our enjoyment. Even
I have learned that, young as I am. I was brought up a spoilt
child, my father married ambitiously, and almost forgot me,
after making me his idol and bringing me up like a queen's
daughter! My poor mother, who filled my head with splendid
visions, died of grief at seeing me married to an office clerk
with twelve hundred francs a year, at nine-and-thirty an aged
and hardened libertine, as corrupt as the hulks, looking on me,
as others looked on you, as a means of fortune! – Well, in that
wretched man I have found the best of husbands. He prefers
the squalid sluts he picks up at the street corners, and leaves
me free. Though he keeps all his salary to himself, he never
asks me where I get money to live on—'

And she in her turn stopped short, as a woman does who
feels herself carried away by the torrent of her confessions;
struck, too, by Lisbeth's eager attention, she thought well to
make sure of Lisbeth before revealing her last secrets.

'You see, dear child, how entire is my confidence in you!'
she presently added, to which Lisbeth replied by a most
comforting nod.

An oath may be taken by a look and a nod more solemnly
than in a court of justice.

'I keep up every appearance of respectability,' Valérie went
on, laying her hand on Lisbeth's as if to accept her pledge. 'I
am a married woman, and my own mistress, to such a degree,
that in the morning, when Marneffe sets out for the office, if
he takes it into his head to say good-bye and finds my door
locked, he goes off without a word. He cares less for his
boy than I care for one of the marble children that play at
the feet of one of the river-gods in the Tuileries. If I do not
come home to dinner, he dines quite contentedly with

the maid, for the maid is devoted to Monsieur; and he goes out every evening after dinner, and does not come in till twelve or one o'clock. Unfortunately, for a year past, I have had no ladies' maid, which is as much as to say that I am a widow!

'I have had one passion, once have been happy – a rich Brazilian, who went away a year ago – my only lapse! – He went away to sell his estates, to realise his land, and come back to live in France. What will he find left of his Valérie? A dunghill. Well! it is his fault and not mine; why does he delay coming so long? Perhaps he has been wrecked – like my virtue.'

'Good-bye, my dear,' said Lisbeth abruptly; 'we are friends for ever. I love you, I esteem you, I am wholly yours! My cousin is tormenting me to go and live in the house you are moving to, in the Rue Vanneau; but I would not go, for I saw at once the reasons for this fresh piece of kindness—'

'Yes; you would have kept an eye on me, I know!' said Madame Marneffe.

'That was, no doubt, the motive of his generosity,' replied Lisbeth. 'In Paris, most beneficence is a speculation, as most acts of ingratitude are revenge! To a poor relation you behave as you do to rats to whom you offer a bit of bacon. Now, I will accept the Baron's offer, for this house is grown intolerable to me. You and I have wit enough to hold our tongues about everything that would damage us, and tell all that needs telling. So, no blabbing – and we are friends.'

'Through thick and thin!' cried Madame Marneffe, delighted to have a sheep-dog, a confidante, a sort of respectable aunt. 'Listen to me; the Baron is doing a great deal in the Rue Vanneau—'

'I believe you!' interrupted Lisbeth. 'He has spent thirty thousand francs! Where he got the money, I am sure I don't know, for Josépha the singer bled him dry. – Oh! you are in luck,' she went on. 'The Baron would steal for a woman who held his heart in two little white satin hands like yours!'

'Well, then,' said Madame Marneffe, with the liberality of such creatures, which is mere recklessness, 'look here, my dear child; take away from here everything that may serve your turn in your new quarters – that chest of drawers, that wardrobe and mirror, the carpet, the curtains—'

Lisbeth's eyes dilated with excessive joy; she was incredulous of such a gift.

'You are doing more for me in a breath than my rich relations have done in thirty years!' she exclaimed. 'They have never even asked themselves whether I had any furniture at all. On his first visit, a few weeks ago, the Baron made a rich man's face on seeing how poor I was. – Thank you, my dear; and I will give you your money's worth, you will see how by and by.'

Valérie went out on to the landing with *her* Cousin Bette, and the two women embraced.

'Pouh! How she stinks of hard work!' said the pretty little woman to herself when she was alone. 'I shall not embrace you often, my dear cousin! At the same time, I must look sharp. She must be skilfully managed, for she can be of use, and help me to make my fortune.'

Like the true Creole of Paris, Madame Marneffe abhorred trouble; she had the calm indifference of a cat, which never jumps or runs but when urged by necessity. To her, life must be all pleasure; and the pleasure without difficulties. She loved flowers, provided they were brought to her. She could not imagine going to the play but to a good box, at her own command, and in a carriage to take her there. Valérie inherited these courtesan tastes from her mother, on whom General Montcornet had lavished luxury when he was in Paris, and who for twenty years had seen all the world at her feet; who had been wasteful and prodigal, squandering her all in the luxurious living of which the programme has been lost since the fall of Napoleon.

The grandees of the Empire were a match in their follies for the great nobles of the last century. Under the Restoration the nobility cannot forget that it has been beaten and robbed, and so, with two or three exceptions, it has become thrifty, prudent, and stay-at-home, in short, bourgeoise and penurious. Since then, 1830 has crowned the work of 1793. In France, henceforth, there will be great names, but no great houses, unless there should be political changes which we can hardly foresee. Everything takes the stamp of individuality. The wisest invest in annuities. Family pride is destroyed.

The bitter pressure of poverty which had stung Valérie to the quick on the day when, to use Marneffe's expression, she had 'caught on' with Hulot, had brought the young woman to the conclusion that she would make a fortune by means of her good looks. So, for some days, she had been feeling the need of having a friend about her to take the place of a mother – a devoted friend, to whom such things may be told as must be hidden from a waiting-maid, and who could act, come and go, and think for her, a beast of burden resigned to an unequal share of life. Now, she, quite as keenly as Lisbeth, had understood the Baron's motives for fostering the intimacy between his cousin and herself.

Prompted by the formidable perspicacity of the Parisian half-breed, who spends her days stretched on a sofa, turning the lantern of her detective spirit on the obscurest depths of souls, sentiments, and intrigues, she had decided on making an ally of the spy. This supremely rash step was, perhaps, premeditated; she had discerned the true nature of this ardent creature, burning with wasted passion, and meant to attach her to herself. Thus, their conversation was like the stone a traveller casts into an abyss to demonstrate its depth. And Madame Marneffe had been terrified to find in this old maid a combination of Iago and Richard III., so feeble as she seemed, so humble, and so little to be feared.

For that instant, Lisbeth Fischer had been her real self; that Corsican and savage temperament, bursting the slender bonds that held it under, had sprung up to its terrible height, as the branch of a tree flies up from the hand of a child that has bent it down to gather the green fruit.

To those who study the social world, it must always be a matter of astonishment to see the fulness, the perfection, and the rapidity with which an idea develops in a virgin nature.

Virginity, like every other monstrosity, has its special richness, its absorbing greatness. Life, whose forces are always economised, assumes in the virgin creature an incalculable power of resistance and endurance. The brain is reinforced in the sum-total of its reserved energy. When really chaste natures need to call on the resources of body or soul, and are required to act or to think, they have muscles of steel, or intuitive knowledge in their intelligence – diabolical strength, or the black magic of the Will.

From this point of view the Virgin Mary, even if we regard her only as a symbol, is supremely great above every other type, whether Hindoo, Egyptian, or Greek. Virginity, the mother of great things, *magna parens rerum*, holds in her fair white hands the keys of the upper worlds. In short, that grand and terrible exception deserves all the honours decreed to her by the Catholic Church.

Thus, in one moment, Lisbeth Fischer had become the Mohican whose snares none can escape, whose dissimulation is inscrutable, whose swift decisiveness is the outcome of the incredible perfection of every organ of sense. She was Hatred and Revenge, as implacable as they are in Italy, Spain, and the East. These two feelings, the obverse of friendship and love carried to the utmost, are known only in lands scorched by the sun. But Lisbeth was also a daughter of Lorraine, bent on deceit.

She accepted this detail of her part against her will; she began by making a curious attempt, due to her ignorance. She fancied, as children do, that being imprisoned meant the same thing as solitary confinement. But this is the superlative degree of imprisonment, and that superlative is the privilege of the Criminal Bench.

As soon as she left Madame Marneffe, Lisbeth hurried off to Monsieur Rivet, and found him in his office.

'Well, my dear Monsieur Rivet,' she began, when she had bolted the door of the room. 'You were quite right. Those

Poles! They are low villains – all alike, men who know neither
law nor fidelity.'

'And who want to set Europe on fire,' said the peaceable
Rivet, 'to ruin every trade and every trader for the sake of a
country that is all bog-land, they say, and full of horrible Jews,
to say nothing of the Cossacks and the peasants – a sort of
wild beasts classed by mistake with human beings. Your Poles
do not understand the times we live in; we are no longer
barbarians. War is coming to an end, my dear Mademoiselle;
it went out with the Monarchy. This is the age of triumph for
commerce, and industry, and middle-class prudence, such as
were the making of Holland.

'Yes,' he went on with animation, 'we live in a period when
nations must obtain all they need by the legal extension of
their liberties and by the pacific action of Constitutional
Institutions; that is what the Poles do not see, and I hope—

'You were saying, my dear?—' he added, interrupting
himself when he saw from his workwoman's face that high
politics were beyond her comprehension.

'Here is the schedule,' said Lisbeth. 'If I don't want to lose
my three thousand two hundred and ten francs, I must clap
this rogue into prison.'

'Didn't I tell you so?' cried the oracle of the Saint-Denis
quarter.

The Rivets, successor to Pons Brothers, had kept their shop
still in the Rue des Mauvaises-Paroles, in the ancient Hôtel
Langeais, built by that illustrious family at the time when the
nobility still gathered round the Louvre.

'Yes, and I blessed you on my way here,' replied Lisbeth.

'If he suspects nothing, he can be safe in prison by eight
o'clock in the morning,' said Rivet, consulting the almanac to
ascertain the hour of sunrise; 'but not till the day after to-
morrow, for he cannot be imprisoned till he has had notice
that he is to be arrested by writ, with the option of payment or
imprisonment. And so—'

'What an idiotic law!' exclaimed Lisbeth. 'Of course the
debtor escapes.'

'He has every right to do so,' said the Assessor, smiling. 'So this is the way—'

'As to that,' said Lisbeth, interrupting him, 'I will take the paper and hand it to him, saying that I have been obliged to raise the money, and that the lender insists on this formality. I know my gentleman. He will not even look at the paper; he will light his pipe with it.'

'Not a bad idea, not bad, Mademoiselle Fischer! Well, make your mind easy; the job shall be done. – But stop a minute; to put your man in prison is not the only point to be considered; you only want to indulge in that legal luxury in order to get your money. Who is to pay you?'

'Those who give him money.'

'To be sure; I forgot that the Minister of War had commissioned him to erect a monument to one of our late customers. Ah! the house has supplied many an uniform to General Montcornet; he soon blackened them with the smoke of cannon. A brave man, he was! and he paid on the nail.'

A marshal of France may have saved the Emperor or his country; 'He paid on the nail' will always be the highest praise he can have from a tradesman.

'Very well. And on Saturday, Monsieur Rivet, you shall have the flat tassels. – By the way, I am moving from the Rue du Doyenné; I am going to live in the Rue Vanneau.'

'You are very right. I could not bear to see you in that hole which, in spite of my aversion to the Opposition, I must say is a disgrace; I repeat it, yes! is a disgrace to the Louvre and the Place du Carrousel. I am devoted to Louis-Philippe, he is my idol; he is the august and exact representative of the class on whom he founded his dynasty, and I can never forget what he did for the trimming-makers by restoring the National Guard—'

'When I hear you speak so, Monsieur Rivet, I cannot help wondering why you are not made a deputy.'

'They are afraid of my attachment to the dynasty,' replied Rivet. 'My political enemies are the King's. He has a noble character! They are a fine family; in short,' said he, returning to the charge, 'he is our ideal: morality, economy, everything. But the completion of the Louvre is one of the conditions on which we gave him the crown, and the civil list, which, I admit, had no limits set to it, leaves the heart of Paris in a most melancholy state. – It is because I am so strongly in favour of the middle course that I should like to see the middle of Paris in a better condition. Your part of the town is positively terrifying. You would have been murdered there one fine day. – And so your Monsieur Crevel has been made Major of his division! He will come to us, I hope, for his big epaulette.'

'I am dining with him to-night, and will send him to you.'

Lisbeth believed that she had secured her Livonian to herself by cutting him off from all communication with the outer world. If he could no longer work, the artist would be forgotten as completely as a man buried in a cellar, where she alone would go to see him. Thus she had two happy days, for she hoped to deal a mortal blow at the Baroness and her daughter.

To go to Crevel's house, in the Rue des Saussayes, she crossed the Pont du Carrousel, went along the Quai Voltaire, the Quai d'Orsay, the Rue Bellechasse, Rue de l'Université, the Pont de la Concorde, and the Avenue de Marigny. This illogical route was traced by the logic of passion, always the foe of the legs.

Cousin Bette, as long as she followed the line of the quays, kept watch on the opposite shore of the Seine, walking very slowly. She had guessed rightly. She had left Wenceslas dressing; she at once understood that, as soon as he should be rid of her, the lover would go off to the Baroness's by the shortest road. And, in fact, as she wandered along by the parapet of the Quai Voltaire, in fancy suppressing the river and walking along the opposite bank, she recognised the artist as he came out of the Tuileries to cross the Pont Royal. She there came up with the faithless one, and could follow him unseen, for lovers rarely look behind them. She escorted him as far as Madame Hulot's house, where he went in like an accustomed visitor.

This crowning proof, confirming Madame Marneffe's revelations, put Lisbeth quite beside herself.

She arrived at the newly promoted Major's door in the state of mental irritation which prompts men to commit murder, and found Monsieur Crevel *senior* in his drawing-room awaiting his children, Monsieur and Madame Crevel *junior*.

But Célestin Crevel was so unconscious and so perfect a type of the Parisian parvenu, that we can scarcely venture so unceremoniously into the presence of César Birotteau's successor. Célestin Crevel was a world in himself; and he, even more than Rivet, deserves the honours of the palette by reason of his importance in this domestic drama.

Have you ever observed how in childhood, or at the early stages of social life, we create a model for our own imitation, with our own hands as it were, and often without knowing it? The banker's clerk, for instance, as he enters his master's drawing-room, dreams of possessing such another. If he makes a fortune, it will not be the luxury of the day, twenty years later, that you will find in his house, but the old-fashioned splendour that fascinated him of yore. It is impossible to tell how many absurdities are due to this retrospective jealousy; and in the same way we know nothing of the follies due to the covert rivalry that urges men to copy the type they have set themselves, and exhaust their powers in shining with a reflected light, like the moon.

Crevel was deputy mayor because his predecessor had been; he was Major because he coveted César Birotteau's epaulettes. In the same way, struck by the marvels wrought by Grindot the architect, at the time when Fortune had carried his master to the top of the wheel, Crevel had 'never looked at both sides of a crown-piece,' to use his own language, when he wanted to 'do up' his rooms; he had gone with his purse open and his eyes shut to Grindot, who by this time was quite forgotten. It is impossible to guess how long an extinct reputation may survive, supported by such stale admiration.

So Grindot, for the thousandth time, had displayed his white-and-gold drawing-room panelled with crimson damask. The furniture, of rosewood, clumsily carved, as such work is done for the trade, had in the country been the source of just pride in Paris workmanship on the occasion of an industrial exhibition. The candelabra, the fire-dogs, the fender, the chandelier, the clock, were all in the most unmeaning style of scroll-work; the round table, a fixture in the middle of the room, was a mosaic of fragments of Italian and antique marbles, brought from Rome, where these dissected maps are made of mineralogical specimens – for all the world like tailors' patterns – an object of perennial admiration to Crevel's citizen friends. The portraits of the late lamented Madame Crevel, of Crevel himself, of his daughter and his son-in-law, hung on the walls, two and two; they were the work of Pierre Grassou, the favoured painter of the bourgeoisie, to whom Crevel owed his ridiculous Byronic attitude. The frames, costing a thousand francs each, were quite in harmony with this coffee-house magnificence, which would have made any true artist shrug his shoulders.

Money never yet missed the smallest opportunity of being stupid. We should have in Paris ten Venices if our retired merchants had had the instinct for fine things characteristic of the Italians. Even in our own day a Milanese merchant could leave five hundred thousand francs to the Duomo, to regild the colossal statue of the Virgin that crowns the edifice. Canova, in his will, desired his brother to build a church costing four million francs, and that brother adds something on his own account. Would a citizen of Paris – and they all, like Rivet, love their Paris in their heart – ever dream of building the spires that are lacking to the towers of Notre-Dame? And only think of the sums that revert to the State in property for which no heirs are found.

All the improvements of Paris might have been completed with the money spent on stucco castings, gilt mouldings, and sham sculpture during the last fifteen years by individuals of the Crevel stamp.

Beyond this drawing-room was a splendid boudoir furnished with tables and cabinets in imitation of Boulle.

The bedroom, smart with chintz, also opened out of the
drawing-room. Mahogany in all its glory infested the dining-
room, and Swiss views, gorgeously framed, graced the panels.
Crevel, who hoped to travel in Switzerland, had set his heart
on possessing the scenery in painting till the time should come
when he might see it in reality.

So, as will have been seen, Crevel, the Mayor's deputy, of
the Legion of Honour and of the National Guard, had faithfully reproduced all the magnificence, even as to furniture, of
his luckless predecessor. Under the Restoration, where one
had sunk, this other, quite overlooked, had come to the top –
not by any strange stroke of fortune, but by the force of
circumstance. In revolutions, as in storms at sea, solid treasure
goes to the bottom, and light trifles are floated to the surface.
César Birotteau, a Royalist, in favour and envied, had been
made the mark of bourgeois hostility, while bourgeoisie triumphant found its incarnation in Crevel.

This apartment, at a rent of a thousand crowns, crammed
with all the vulgar magnificence that money can buy, occupied
the first floor of a fine old house between a courtyard and a
garden. Everything was as spick-and-span as the beetles in an
entomological case, for Crevel lived very little at home.

This gorgeous residence was the ambitious citizen's legal
domicile. His establishment consisted of a woman-cook and a
valet; he hired two extra men, and had a dinner sent in by
Chevet, whenever he gave a banquet to his political friends, to
men he wanted to dazzle, or to a family party.

The seat of Crevel's real domesticity, formerly in the Rue
Notre-Dame de Lorette, with Mademoiselle Héloïse Brisetout,
had lately been transferred, as we have seen, to the Rue
Chauchat. Every morning the retired merchant – every ex-
tradesman is a retired merchant – spent two hours in the Rue
des Saussayes to attend to business, and gave the rest of his
time to Mademoiselle Zaïre, which annoyed Zaïre very much.
Orosmanes-Crevel had a fixed bargain with Mademoiselle

Héloïse; she owed him five hundred francs' worth of enjoyment every month, and no 'bills delivered.' He paid separately for his dinner and all extras. This agreement, with certain bonuses, for he made her a good many presents, seemed cheap to the ex-attaché of the great singer; and he would say to widowers who were fond of their daughters, that it paid better to job your horses than to have a stable of your own. At the same time, if the reader remembers the speech made to the Baron by the porter at the Rue Chauchat, Crevel did not escape the coachman and groom.

Crevel, as may be seen, had turned his passionate affection for his daughter to the advantage of his self-indulgence. The immoral aspect of the situation was justified by the highest morality. And then the ex-perfumer derived from this style of living – it was the inevitable, a free-and-easy life, *Régence*, *Pompadour*, *Maréchal de Richelieu*, what not – a certain veneer of superiority. Crevel set up for being a man of broad views, a fine gentleman with an air and grace, a liberal man with nothing narrow in his ideas – and all for the small sum of about twelve to fifteen hundred francs a month. This was the result not of hypocritical policy, but of middle-class vanity, though it came to the same in the end.

On the Bourse Crevel was regarded as a man superior to his time, and especially as a man of pleasure, a *bon vivant*. In this particular Crevel flattered himself that he had overtopped his worthy friend Birotteau by a hundred cubits.

'And is it you?' cried Crevel, flying into a rage as he saw Lisbeth enter the room, 'who have plotted this marriage between Mademoiselle Hulot and your young Count, whom you have been bringing up by hand for her?'

'You don't seem best pleased at it?' said Lisbeth, fixing a piercing eye on Crevel. 'What interest can you have in hindering my cousin's marriage? For it was you, I am told, who hindered her marrying Monsieur Lebas' son.'

'You are a good soul, and to be trusted,' said Crevel. 'Well, then, do you suppose that I will ever forgive Monsieur Hulot for the crime of having robbed me of Josépha – especially when he turned a decent girl, whom I should have married in my old age, into a good-for-nothing slut, a mountebank, an opera singer? – No, no. Never!'

'He is a very good fellow, too, is Monsieur Hulot,' said Cousin Bette.

'Amiable, very amiable – too amiable,' replied Crevel. 'I wish him no harm; but I do wish to have my revenge, and I will have it. It is my one idea.'

'And is that desire the reason why you no longer visit Madame Hulot?'

'Possibly.'

'Ah, ha! then you were courting my fair cousin?' said Lisbeth, with a smile. 'I thought as much.'

'And she treated me like a dog! – worse, like a footman; nay, I might say like a political prisoner. – But I will succeed yet,' said he, striking his brow with his clenched fist.

'Poor man! It would be dreadful to catch his wife deceiving him after being packed off by his mistress.'

'Josépha?' cried Crevel. 'Has Josépha thrown him over, packed him off, turned him out neck and crop? Bravo, Josépha, you have avenged me! I will send you a pair of pearls to hang in your ears, my ex-sweetheart! – I knew nothing of it; for after I had seen you, on the day after that when the fair Adeline had shown me the door, I went to visit the Lebas, at Corbeil, and have but just come back. Héloïse played the very devil to get me into the country, and I have found out the purpose of her game; she wanted me out of the way while she gave a house-warming in the Rue Chauchat, with some artists, and players, and writers. – She took me in! But I can forgive her, for Héloïse amuses me. She is a Déjazet under a bushel. What a character the hussy is! There is the note I found last evening –

'"DEAR OLD CHAP, – I have pitched my tent in the Rue Chauchat. I have taken the precaution of getting a few friends to clean up the paint! All is well. Come when you please, Monsieur; Hagar awaits her Abraham."

'Héloïse will have some news for me, for she has her bohemia at her fingers' end.'

'But Monsieur Hulot took the disaster very calmly,' said Lisbeth.

'Impossible!' cried Crevel, stopping in a parade as regular as the swing of a pendulum.

'Monsieur Hulot is not so young as he was,' Lisbeth remarked significantly.

'I know that,' said Crevel, 'but in one point we are alike: Hulot cannot do without an attachment. He is capable of going back to his wife. It would be a novelty for him, but an end to my vengeance. You smile, Mademoiselle Fischer – ah! perhaps you know something?'

'I am smiling at your notions,' replied Lisbeth. 'Yes, my cousin is still handsome enough to inspire a passion. I should certainly fall in love with her if I were a man.'

'Cut and come again!' exclaimed Crevel. 'You are laughing at me. – The Baron has already found consolation?'

Lisbeth bowed affirmatively.

'He is a lucky man if he can find a second Josépha within twenty-four hours!' said Crevel. 'But I am not altogether surprised, for he told me one evening at supper that when he was a young man he always had three mistresses on hand that he might not be left high and dry – the one he was giving over, the one in possession, and the one he was courting for a future emergency. He had some smart little workwoman in reserve, no doubt – in his fish-pond – his *Parc-aux-cerfs*! He is very Louis xv., is my gentleman. He is in luck to be so handsome! – However, he is ageing; his face shows it. – He has taken up with some little milliner?'

'Dear me, no,' replied Lisbeth.

'Oh!' cried Crevel, 'what would not I do to hinder him from hanging up his hat! I could not win back Josépha; women of that kind never come back to their first love. Besides, it is truly said, such a return is not love. – But, Cousin Bette, I would pay down fifty thousand francs – that is to say, I would spend it – to rob that great good-looking fellow of his mistress, and to show him that a Major with a portly stomach and a brain made to become Mayor of Paris, though he is a grandfather, is not to have his mistress tickled away by a poacher without turning the tables.'

'My position,' said Lisbeth, 'compels me to hear everything and know nothing. You may talk to me without fear; I never repeat a word of what any one may choose to tell me. How can you suppose I should ever break that rule of conduct? No one would ever trust me again.'

'I know,' said Crevel; 'you are the very jewel of old maids. – Still, come, there are exceptions. Look here, the family have never settled an allowance on you?'

'But I have my pride,' said Lisbeth. 'I do not choose to be an expense to anybody.'

'If you will but help me to my revenge,' the tradesman went on, 'I will sink ten thousand francs in an annuity for you. Tell me, my fair cousin, tell me who has stepped into Josépha's shoes, and you will have money to pay your rent, your little breakfast in the morning, the good coffee you love so well – you might allow yourself pure Mocha, heh? And a very good thing is pure Mocha!'

'I do not care so much for the ten thousand francs in an annuity, which would bring me nearly five hundred francs a year, as for absolute secrecy,' said Lisbeth. 'For, you see, my dear Monsieur Crevel, the Baron is very good to me; he is to pay my rent—'

'Oh yes, long may that last! I advise you to trust him,' cried Crevel. 'Where will he find the money?'

'Ah, that I don't know. At the same time, he is spending more than thirty thousand francs on the rooms he is furnishing for this little lady.'

'A lady! What, a woman in society; the rascal, what luck he has! He is the only favourite!'

'A married woman, and quite the lady,' Lisbeth affirmed.

'Really and truly?' cried Crevel, opening wide eyes flashing with envy, quite as much as at the magic words *quite the lady*.

'Yes, really,' said Lisbeth. 'Clever, a musician, three-and-twenty, a pretty, innocent face, a dazzling white skin, teeth like a puppy's, eyes like stars, a beautiful forehead – and tiny feet, I never saw the like, they are not wider than her stay-busk.'

'And ears?' asked Crevel, keenly alive to this catalogue of charms.

'Ears for a model,' she replied.

'And small hands?'

'I tell you, in two words, a gem of a woman – and high-minded, and modest, and refined! A beautiful soul, an angel – and with every distinction, for her father was a Marshal of France—'

'A Marshal of France!' shrieked Crevel, positively bounding with excitement. 'Good Heavens! by the Holy Piper! By all the joys in Paradise! – The rascal! – I beg your pardon, Cousin, I am going crazy! – I think I would give a hundred thousand francs—'

'I dare say you would, and, I tell you, she is a respectable woman – a woman of virtue. The Baron has forked out handsomely.'

'He has not a sou, I tell you.'

'There is a husband he has pushed—'

'Where did he push him?' asked Crevel, with a bitter laugh.

'He is promoted to be second in his office – this husband who will oblige, no doubt; – and his name is down for the Cross of the Legion of Honour.'

'The Government ought to be judicious and respect those who have the Cross by not flinging it broadcast,' said Crevel, with the look of an aggrieved politician. 'But what is there about the man – that old bulldog of a Baron?' he went on. 'It seems to me that I am quite a match for him,' and he struck an attitude as he looked at himself in the glass. 'Héloïse has told me many a time, at moments when a woman speaks the truth, that I was wonderful.'

'Oh,' said Lisbeth, 'women like big men; they are almost always good-natured; and if I had to decide between you and the Baron, I should choose you. Monsieur Hulot is amusing, handsome, and has a figure; but you, you are substantial, and then – you see – you look an even greater scamp than he does.'

'It is incredible how all women, even pious women, take to men who have that about them!' exclaimed Crevel, putting his arm round Lisbeth's waist, he was so jubilant.

'The difficulty does not lie there,' said Bette. 'You must see that a woman who is getting so many advantages will not be unfaithful to her patron for nothing; and it would cost you more than a hundred odd thousand francs, for our little friend can look forward to seeing her husband at the head of his office within two years' time. – It is poverty that is dragging the poor little angel into that pit.'

Crevel was striding up and down the drawing-room in a state of frenzy.

'He must be uncommonly fond of the woman?' he inquired after a pause, while his desires, thus goaded by Lisbeth, rose to a sort of madness.

'You may judge for yourself,' replied Lisbeth. 'I don't believe he has had *that* of her,' said she, snapping her thumbnail against one of her enormous white teeth, 'and he has given her ten thousand francs' worth of presents already.'

'What a good joke it would be!' cried Crevel, 'if I got to the winning post first!'

'Good Heavens! It is too bad of me to be telling you all this tittle-tattle,' said Lisbeth, with an air of compunction.

'No. – I mean to put your relations to the blush. To-morrow I shall invest in your name such a sum in five-per-cents. as will give you six hundred francs a year; but then you must tell me everything – his Dulcinea's name and residence. To you I will make a clean breast of it – I never have had a real lady for a mistress, and it is the height of my ambition. Mahomet's houris are nothing in comparison with what I fancy a woman of fashion must be. In short, it is my dream, my mania, and to such a point, that I declare to you the Baroness Hulot to me will never be fifty,' said he, unconsciously plagiarising one of the greatest wits of the last century. 'I assure you, my good Lisbeth, I am prepared to sacrifice a hundred, two hundred –

Hush! Here are the young people, I see them crossing the courtyard. I shall never have learned anything through you, I give you my word of honour; for I do not want you to lose the Baron's confidence, quite the contrary. He must be amazingly fond of this woman – that old boy.'

'He is crazy about her,' said Lisbeth. 'He could not find forty thousand francs to marry his daughter off, but he has got them somehow for his new passion.'

'And do you think that she loves him?'

'At his age!' said the old maid.

'Oh, what an owl I am!' cried Crevel, 'when I myself allowed Héloïse to keep her artist exactly as Henri IV. allowed Gabrielle her Bellegarde. Alas! old age, old age! – Good morning, Célestine. How do, my jewel? – and the brat? Ah, here he comes; on my honour, he is beginning to be like me! – Good day, Hulot – quite well? We shall soon be having another wedding in the family.'

Célestine and her husband, as a hint to their father, glanced at the old maid, who audaciously asked, in reply to Crevel –

'Indeed – whose?'

Crevel put on an air of reserve which was meant to convey that he would make up for her indiscretions.

'That of Hortense,' he replied; 'but it is not yet quite settled. I have just come from the Lebas, and they were talking of Mademoiselle Popinot as a suitable match for their son, the young councillor, for he would like to get the presidency of a provincial court. – Now, come to dinner.'

By seven o'clock Lisbeth had returned home in an omnibus, for she was eager to see Wenceslas, whose dupe she had been for three weeks, and to whom she was carrying a basket filled with fruit by the hands of Crevel himself, whose attentions were doubled towards *his* Cousin Bette.

She flew up to the attic at a pace that took her breath away, and found the artist finishing the ornamentation of a box to be presented to his adored Hortense. The framework of the lid represented hydrangeas – in French called *Hortensias* –

among which little Loves were playing. The poor lover, to enable him to pay for the materials of the box, of which the panels were of malachite, had designed two candlesticks for Florent and Chanor, and sold them the copyright – two admirable pieces of work.

'You have been working too hard these last few days, my dear fellow,' said Lisbeth, wiping the perspiration from his brow, and giving him a kiss. 'Such laborious diligence is really dangerous in the month of August. Seriously, you may injure your health. Look, here are some peaches and plums from Monsieur Crevel. – Now, do not worry yourself so much; I have borrowed two thousand francs, and, short of some disaster, we can repay them when you sell your clock. At the same time, the lender seems to me suspicious, for he has just sent in this document.'

She laid the writ under the model sketch of the statue of General Montcornet.

'For whom are you making this pretty thing?' said she, taking up the modelled sprays of hydrangea in red wax which Wenceslas had laid down while eating the fruit.

'For a jeweller.'

'For what jeweller?'

'I do not know. Stidmann asked me to make something out of them, as he is very busy.'

'But these,' she said in a deep voice, 'are *Hortensias*. How is it that you have never made anything in wax for me? Is it so difficult to design a pin, a little box – what not, as a keepsake?' and she shot a fearful glance at the artist, whose eyes were happily lowered. 'And yet you say you love me?'

'Can you doubt it, Mademoiselle?'

'That is indeed an ardent *Mademoiselle*! – Why, you have been my only thought since I found you dying – just there. When I saved you, you vowed you were mine. I have never held you to that pledge; but I made a vow to myself! I said to myself, "Since the boy says he is mine, I mean to make him rich and happy!" Well, and I can make your fortune.'

'How?' said the hapless artist, at the height of joy, and too artless to dream of a snare.

'Why, thus,' said she.

Lisbeth could not deprive herself of the savage pleasure of gazing at Wenceslas, who looked up at her with filial affection, the expression really of his love for Hortense, which deluded the old maid. Seeing in a man's eyes, for the first time in her life, the blazing torch of passion, she fancied it was for her that it was lighted.

'Monsieur Crevel will back us to the extent of a hundred thousand francs to start a business, if, as he says, you will marry me. He has queer ideas, has the worthy man. – Well, what do you say to it?' she added.

The artist, as pale as the dead, looked at his benefactress with a lustreless eye, which plainly spoke his thoughts. He stood stupefied and open-mouthed.

'I never before was so distinctly told that I am hideous,' said she, with a bitter laugh.

'Mademoiselle,' said Steinbock, 'my benefactress can never be ugly in my eyes; I have the greatest affection for you. But I am not yet thirty, and—'

'I am forty-three,' said Lisbeth. 'My cousin Adeline is forty-eight, and men are still madly in love with her; but then she is handsome – she is!'

'Fifteen years between us, Mademoiselle! How could we get on together! For both our sakes I think we should be wise to think it over. My gratitude shall be fully equal to your great kindness. – And your money shall be repaid in a few days.'

'My money!' cried she. 'You treat me as if I were nothing but an unfeeling usurer.'

'Forgive me,' said Wenceslas, 'but you remind me of it so often. – Well, it is you who have made me; do not crush me.'

'You mean to be rid of me, I can see,' said she, shaking her head. 'Who has endowed you with this strength of ingratitude – you who are a man made of papier-mâché? Have you ceased to trust me – your good genius? – me, when I have spent so many nights working for you – when I have given you every franc I have saved in my lifetime – when for four years I have shared my bread with you, the bread of a hard-worked woman, and given you all I had, to my very courage.'

'Mademoiselle – no more, no more!' he cried, kneeling before her with uplifted hands. 'Say not another word! In three days I will tell you, you shall know all. – Let me, let me be happy,' and he kissed her hands. 'I love – and I am loved.'

'Well, well, my child, be happy,' she said, lifting him up. And she kissed his forehead and hair with the eagerness that a man condemned to death must feel as he lives through the last morning.

'Ah! you are of all creatures the noblest and best! You are a match for the woman I love,' said the poor artist.

'I love you well enough to tremble for your future fate,' said she gloomily. 'Judas hanged himself – the ungrateful always come to a bad end! You are deserting me, and you will never again do any good work. Consider whether, without being married – for I know I am an old maid, and I do not want to smother the blossom of your youth, your poetry, as you call it, in my arms, that are like vine-stocks – but whether, without being married, we could not get on together? Listen; I have the commercial spirit; I could save you a fortune in the course of ten years' work, for Economy is my name! – while, with a young wife, who would be sheer Expenditure, you would squander everything; you would work only to indulge her. But happiness creates nothing but memories. Even I, when I am thinking of you, sit for hours with my hands in my lap—

'Come, Wenceslas, stay with me. – Look here, I understand all about it: you shall have your mistresses; pretty ones too, like that little Marneffe woman who wants to see you, and who will give you happiness you could never find with me. Then, when I have saved you thirty thousand francs a year in the funds—'

'Mademoiselle, you are an angel, and I shall never forget this hour,' said Wenceslas, wiping away his tears.

'That is how I like to see you, my child,' said she, gazing at him with rapture.

Vanity is so strong a power in us all that Lisbeth believed in her triumph. She had conceded so much when offering him Madame Marneffe. It was the crowning emotion of her life; for the first time she felt the full tide of joy rising in her heart. To go through such an experience again she would have sold her soul to the Devil.

'I am engaged to be married,' Steinbock replied, 'and I love a woman with whom no other can compete or compare. – But you are, and always will be, to me the mother I have lost.'

The words fell like an avalanche of snow on a burning crater. Lisbeth sat down. She gazed with despondent eyes on the youth before her, on his aristocratic beauty – the artist's brow, the splendid hair, everything that appealed to her suppressed feminine instincts, and tiny tears moistened her eyes for an instant and immediately dried up. She looked like one of those meagre statues which the sculptors of the Middle Ages carved on monuments.

'I cannot curse you,' said she, suddenly rising. 'You – you are but a boy. God preserve you!'

She went downstairs and shut herself into her own room.

'She is in love with me, poor creature!' said Wenceslas to himself. 'And how fervently eloquent! She is crazy.'

This last effort on the part of an arid and narrow nature to keep hold on an embodiment of beauty and poetry was, in truth, so violent that it can only be compared to the frenzied vehemence of a shipwrecked creature making a last struggle to reach the shore.

On the next day but one, at half-past four in the morning, when Count Steinbock was sunk in the deepest sleep, he heard a knock at the door of his attic; he rose to open it, and saw two men in shabby clothing, and a third, whose dress proclaimed him a bailiff down on his luck.

'You are Monsieur Wenceslas, Count Steinbock?' said this man.

'Yes, Monsieur.'

'My name is Grasset, sir, successor to Louchard, sheriff's officer—'

'What then?'

'You are under arrest, sir. You must come with us to prison – to Clichy. – Please to get dressed. – We have done the civil, as you see; I have brought no police, and there is a hackney cab below.'

'You are safely nabbed, you see,' said one of the bailiffs; 'and we look to you to be liberal.'

Steinbock dressed and went downstairs, a man holding each arm; when he was in the cab, the driver started without orders, as knowing where he was to go, and within half an hour the unhappy foreigner found himself safely under bolt and bar without even a remonstrance, so utterly amazed was he.

At ten o'clock he was sent for to the prison-office, where he found Lisbeth, who, in tears, gave him some money to feed himself adequately and to pay for a room large enough to work in.

'My dear boy,' said she, 'never say a word of your arrest to anybody, do not write to a living soul; it would ruin you for life; we must hide this blot on your character. I will soon have you out. I will collect the money – be quite easy. Write down what you want for your work. You shall soon be free, or I will die for it.'

'Oh, I shall owe you my life a second time!' cried he, 'for I should lose more than my life if I were thought a bad fellow.'

Lisbeth went off in great glee; she hoped, by keeping her artist under lock and key, to put a stop to his marriage by announcing that he was a married man, pardoned by the efforts of his wife, and gone off to Russia.

To carry out this plan, at about three o'clock she went to the Baroness, though it was not the day when she was due to dine with her; but she wished to enjoy the anguish which Hortense must endure at the hour when Wenceslas was in the habit of making his appearance.

'Have you come to dinner?' asked the Baroness, concealing her disappointment.

'Well, yes.'

'That's well,' replied Hortense. 'I will go and tell them to be punctual, for you do not like to be kept waiting.'

Hortense nodded reassuringly to her mother, for she intended to tell the man-servant to send away Monsieur Steinbock if he should call; the man, however, happened to be out, so Hortense was obliged to give her orders to the maid, and the girl went upstairs to fetch her needle-work and sit in the anteroom.

'And about my lover?' said Cousin Bette to Hortense, when the girl came back. 'You never ask about him now?'

'To be sure, what is he doing?' said Hortense. 'He has become famous. You ought to be very happy,' she added in an undertone to Lisbeth. 'Everybody is talking of Monsieur Wenceslas Steinbock.'

'A great deal too much,' replied she in her clear tones. 'Monsieur is departing. – If it were only a matter of charming him so far as to defy the attractions of Paris, I know my power; but they say that in order to secure the services of such an artist, the Emperor Nicholas has pardoned him—'

'Nonsense!' said the Baroness.

'When did you hear that?' asked Hortense, who felt as if her heart had the cramp.

'Well,' said the villainous Lisbeth, 'a person to whom he is bound by the most sacred ties – his wife – wrote yesterday to tell him so. He wants to be off! Oh, he will be a great fool to give up France to go to Russia!—'

Hortense looked at her mother, but her head sank on one side; the Baroness was only just in time to support her daughter, who dropped fainting, and as white as her lace kerchief.

'Lisbeth! you have killed my child!' cried the Baroness. 'You were born to be our curse!'

'Bless me! what fault of mine is this, Adeline?' replied Lisbeth, as she rose with a menacing aspect, of which the Baroness, in her alarm, took no notice.

'I was wrong,' said Adeline, supporting the girl. 'Ring.'

At this instant the door opened, the women both looked round, and saw Wenceslas Steinbock, who had been admitted by the cook in the maid's absence.

'Hortense!' cried the artist, with one spring to the group of women. And he kissed his betrothed before her mother's eyes, on her forehead, and so reverently, that the Baroness could not be angry. It was a better restorative than any smelling salts. Hortense opened her eyes, saw Wenceslas, and her colour came back. In a few minutes she had quite recovered.

'So this was your secret?' said Lisbeth, smiling at Wenceslas, and affecting to guess the facts from her two cousins' confusion.

'But how did you steal away my lover?' said she, leading Hortense into the garden.

Hortense artlessly told the romance of her love. Her father and mother, she said, being convinced that Lisbeth would never marry, had authorised the Count's visits. Only Hortense, like a full-blown Agnès, attributed to chance her purchase of the group and the introduction of the artist, who, by her account, had insisted on knowing the name of his first purchaser.

Presently Steinbock came out to join the cousins, and thanked the old maid effusively for his prompt release. Lisbeth replied Jesuitically that the creditor having given very vague promises, she had not hoped to be able to get him out before the morrow, and that the person who had lent her the money, ashamed, perhaps, of such mean conduct, had been beforehand with her. The old maid appeared to be perfectly content, and congratulated Wenceslas on his happiness.

'You bad boy!' said she, before Hortense and her mother, 'if you had only told me the evening before last that you loved my cousin Hortense, and that she loved you, you would have spared me many tears. I thought that you were deserting your old friend, your governess; while, on the contrary, you are to become my cousin; henceforth, you will be connected with me, remotely, it is true, but by ties that amply justify the feelings I have for you.' And she kissed Wenceslas on the forehead.

Hortense threw herself into Lisbeth's arms and melted into tears.

'I owe my happiness to you,' said she, 'and I will never forget it.'

'Cousin Bette,' said the Baroness, embracing Lisbeth in her excitement at seeing matters so happily settled, 'the Baron and I owe you a debt of gratitude, and we will pay it. Come and talk things over with me,' she added, leading her away.

So Lisbeth, to all appearance, was playing the part of a good angel to the whole family; she was adored by Crevel and Hulot, by Adeline and Hortense.

'We wish you to give up working,' said the Baroness. 'If you earn forty sous a day, Sundays excepted, that makes six hundred francs a year. Well, then, how much have you saved?'

'Four thousand five hundred francs.'

'Poor Bette!' said her cousin.

She raised her eyes to heaven, so deeply was she moved at the thought of all the labour and privation such a sum must represent accumulated during thirty years.

Lisbeth, misunderstanding the meaning of the exclamation, took it as the ironical pity of the successful woman, and her hatred was strengthened by a large infusion of venom at the very moment when her cousin had cast off her last shred of distrust of the tyrant of her childhood.

'We will add ten thousand five hundred francs to that sum,' said Adeline, 'and put it in trust so that you shall draw the interest for life with reversion to Hortense. Thus, you will have six hundred francs a year.'

Lisbeth feigned the utmost satisfaction. When she went in, her handkerchief to her eyes, wiping away tears of joy, Hortense told her of all the favours that were being showered on Wenceslas, beloved of all the family.

So when the Baron came home, he found his family all present; for the Baroness had formally accepted Wenceslas by the title of Son, and the wedding was fixed, if her husband should approve, for a day a fortnight hence. The moment he came into the drawing-room, Hulot was rushed at by his wife and daughter, who ran to meet him, Adeline to speak to him privately, and Hortense to kiss him.

'You have gone too far in pledging me to this, Madame,' said the Baron sternly. 'You are not married yet,' he added, with a look at Steinbock, who turned pale.

'He has heard of my imprisonment,' said the luckless artist to himself.

'Come, children,' said he, leading his daughter and the young man into the garden; they all sat down on a moss-eaten seat in the summer-house.

'Monsieur le Comte, do you love my daughter as well as I loved her mother?' he asked.

'More, Monsieur,' said the sculptor.

'Her mother was a peasant's daughter, and had not a farthing of her own.'

'Only give me Mademoiselle Hortense just as she is, without a trousseau even—'

'So I should think!' said the Baron, smiling. 'Hortense is the daughter of the Baron Hulot d'Ervy, Councillor of State, high up in the War Office, Grand Commander of the Legion of Honour, and brother to Count Hulot, whose glory is immortal, and who will ere long be Marshal of France! And – she has a marriage portion.'

'It is true,' said the impassioned artist, 'I must seem very ambitious. But if my dear Hortense were a labourer's daughter, I would marry her—'

'That is just what I wanted to know,' replied the Baron. 'Run away, Hortense, and leave me to talk business with Monsieur le Comte. – He really loves you, you see!'

'Oh, papa, I was sure you were only in jest,' said the happy girl.

'My dear Steinbock,' said the Baron, with elaborate grace of diction and the most perfect manners, as soon as he and the artist were alone, 'I promised my son a fortune of two hundred thousand francs, of which the poor boy has never had a sou; and he never will get any of it. My daughter's fortune will also be two hundred thousand francs, for which you will give a receipt—'

'Yes, Monsieur le Baron.'

'You go too fast,' said Hulot. 'Have the goodness to hear me out. I cannot expect from a son-in-law such devotion as I look for from my son. My son knew exactly all I could and would do for his future promotion: he will be a Minister, and will easily make good his two hundred thousand francs. But with you, young man, matters are different. I shall give you a bond for sixty thousand francs in State funds at five per cent. in your wife's name. This income will be diminished by a small charge in the form of an annuity to Lisbeth; but she will not live long; she is consumptive, I know. Tell no one; it is a secret; let the poor soul die in peace. – My daughter will have a trousseau worth twenty thousand francs; her mother will give her six thousand francs' worth of diamonds.'

'Monsieur, you overpower me!' said Steinbock, quite bewildered.

'As to the remaining hundred and twenty thousand francs—'

'Say no more, Monsieur,' said Wenceslas. 'I ask only for my beloved Hortense—'

'Will you listen to me, effervescent youth! – As to the remaining hundred and twenty thousand francs, I have not got them; but you will have them—'

'Monsieur?'

'You will get them from the Government, in payment for commissions which I will secure for you, I pledge you my word of honour. You are to have a studio, you see, at the Government depôt. Exhibit a few fine statues, and I will get you received at the Institute. The highest personages have a regard for my brother and for me, and I hope to succeed in securing for you a commission for sculpture at Versailles up to a quarter of the whole sum. You will have orders from the City of Paris and from the Chamber of Peers; in short, my dear fellow, you will have so many that you will be obliged to get assistants. In that way I shall pay off my debt to you. You must say whether this way of giving a portion will suit you; whether you are equal to it.'

'I am equal to making a fortune for my wife single-handed if all else failed!' cried the artist-nobleman.

'That is what I admire!' cried the Baron. 'High-minded youth that fears nothing. Come,' he added, clasping hands with the young sculptor to conclude the bargain, 'you have my consent. We will sign the contract on Sunday next, and the wedding shall be on the following Saturday, my wife's fête-day.'

'It is all right,' said the Baroness to her daughter, who stood glued to the window. 'Your suitor and your father are embracing each other.'

On going home in the evening, Wenceslas found the solution of the mystery of his release. The porter handed him a thick sealed packet, containing the schedule of his debts, with a signed receipt affixed at the bottom of the writ, and accompanied by this letter: –

'MY DEAR WENCESLAS, – I went to fetch you at ten o'clock this morning to introduce you to a Royal Highness who wishes to see you. There I learned that the duns had had you conveyed to a certain little domain – chief town, *Clichy Castle*.

'So off I went to Léon de Lora, and told him, for a joke, that you could not leave your country quarters for lack of four thousand francs, and that you would spoil your future prospects if you did not make your bow to your royal patron. Happily, Bridau was there – a man of genius, who has known what it is to be poor, and has heard your story. My boy, between them they have found the money, and I went off to pay the Turk who committed treason against genius by putting you in quod. As I had to be at the Tuileries at noon, I could not wait to see you sniffing the outer air. I know you to be a gentleman, and I answered for you to my two friends – but look them up to-morrow.

'Léon and Bridau do not want your cash; they will ask you to do them each a group – and they are right. At least, so thinks the man who wishes he could sign himself your rival, but is only your faithful ally,

'STIDMANN.

'*P.S.* – I told the Prince you were away, and would not return till to-morrow, so he said, "Very good – to-morrow."'

Count Wenceslas went to bed in the sheets of purple, without a rose-leaf to wrinkle them, that Favour can make for us – Favour, the halting divinity who moves more slowly for men of genius than either Justice or Fortune, because Jove has not chosen to bandage her eyes. Hence, lightly deceived by the display of impostors, and attracted by their frippery and trumpets, she spends the time in seeing them and the money in paying them which she ought to devote to seeking out men of merit in the nooks where they hide.

It will now be necessary to explain how Monsieur le Baron Hulot had contrived to count up his expenditure on Hortense's wedding portion, and at the same time to defray the frightful cost of the charming rooms where Madame Marneffe was to make her home. His financial scheme bore that stamp of talent which leads prodigals and men in love into the quagmires where so many disasters await them. Nothing can demonstrate more completely the strange capacity communicated by vice, to which we owe the strokes of skill which ambitious or voluptuous men can occasionally achieve – or, in short, any of the Devil's pupils.

On the day before, old Johann Fischer, unable to pay thirty thousand francs drawn for on him by his nephew, had found himself under the necessity of stopping payment unless the Baron could remit the sum.

This ancient worthy, with the white hairs of seventy years, had such blind confidence in Hulot – who, to the old Bonapartist, was an emanation from the Napoleonic sun – that he was calmly pacing his anteroom with the bank clerk, in the little ground-floor apartment that he rented for eight hundred francs a year as the headquarters of his extensive dealings in corn and forage.

'Marguerite is gone to fetch the money from close by,' said he.

The official, in his grey uniform braided with silver, was so convinced of the old Alsatian's honesty, that he was prepared to leave the thirty thousand francs' worth of bills in his hands; but the old man would not let him go, observing that the clock had not yet struck eight. A cab drew up, the old man rushed into the street, and held out his hand to the Baron with sublime confidence – Hulot handed him out thirty thousand-franc notes.

'Go on three doors further, and I will tell you why,' said Fischer.

'Here, young man,' he said, returning to count out the money to the bank emissary, whom he then saw to the door.

When the clerk was out of sight, Fischer called back the cab containing his august nephew, Napoleon's right hand, and said, as he led him into the house –

'You do not want them to know at the Bank of France that you paid me the thirty thousand francs, after endorsing the bills? – It was bad enough to see them signed by such a man as you!—'

'Come to the bottom of your little garden, Father Fischer,' said the important man. 'You are hearty?' he went on, sitting down under a vine arbour and scanning the old man from head to foot, as a dealer in human flesh scans a substitute for the conscription.

'Ay, hearty enough for a tontine,' said the lean little old man; his sinews were wiry, and his eye bright.

'Does heat disagree with you?'

'Quite the contrary.'

'What do you say to Africa?'

'A very nice country! – The French went there with the little Corporal' (Napoleon).

'To get us all out of the present scrape, you must go to Algiers,' said the Baron.

'And how about my business?'

'An official in the War Office, who has to retire, and has not enough to live on with his pension, will buy your business.'

'And what am I to do in Algiers?'

'Supply the Commissariat with victuals, corn, and forage; I have your commission ready filled in and signed. You can collect supplies in the country at seventy per cent. below the prices at which you can credit us.'

'How shall we get them?'

'Oh, by raids, by taxes in kind, and the Khaliphat. – The country is little known, though we settled there eight years ago; Algeria produces vast quantities of corn and forage. When this produce belongs to Arabs, we take it from them under various pretences; when it belongs to us, the Arabs try to get it back again. There is a great deal of fighting over the corn, and no one ever knows exactly how much each party has stolen from the other. There is not time in the open field to measure the corn as we do in the Paris market, or the hay as it is sold in the Rue d'Enfer. The Arab chiefs, like our Spahis, prefer hard cash, and sell the plunder at a very low price. The Commissariat needs a fixed quantity, and must have it. It winks at exorbitant prices calculated on the difficulty of procuring food, and the dangers to which every form of transport is exposed. That is Algiers from the army contractor's point of view.

'It is a muddle tempered by the ink-bottle, like every incipient government. We shall not see our way through it for another ten years – we who have to do the governing; but private enterprise has sharp eyes. – So I am sending you there to make a fortune; I give you the job, as Napoleon put an impoverished Marshal at the head of a kingdom where smuggling might be secretly encouraged.

'I am ruined, my dear Fischer; I must have a hundred thousand francs within a year.'

'I see no harm in getting it out of the Bedouins,' said the Alsatian calmly. 'It was always done under the Empire—'

'The man who wants to buy your business will be here this morning, and pay you ten thousand francs down,' the Baron went on. 'That will be enough, I suppose, to take you to Africa?'

The old man nodded assent.

'As to capital out there, be quite easy. I will draw the remainder of the money due if I find it necessary.'

'All I have is yours – my very blood,' said old Fischer.

'Oh, do not be uneasy,' said Hulot, fancying that his uncle saw more clearly than was the fact. 'As to our excise dealings, your character will not be impugned. Everything depends on the authority at your back; now I myself appointed the authorities out there; I am sure of them. This, Uncle Fischer, is a dead secret between us. I know you well, and I have spoken out without concealment or circumlocution.'

'It shall be done,' said the old man. 'And it will go on—?'

'For two years. You will have made a hundred thousand francs of your own to live happy on in the Vosges.'

'I will do as you wish; my honour is yours,' said the little old man quietly.

'That is the sort of man I like. – However, you must not go till you have seen your grand-niece happily married. She is to be a Countess.'

But even taxes and raids and the money paid by the War Office clerk for Fischer's business could not forthwith provide sixty thousand francs to give to Hortense, to say nothing of her trousseau, which was to cost about five thousand, and the forty thousand spent – or to be spent – on Madame Marneffe.

Where, then, had the Baron found the thirty thousand francs he had just produced? This was the history.

A few days previously Hulot had insured his life for the sum of a hundred and fifty thousand francs, for three years, in two separate companies. Armed with the policies, of which he paid the premium, he had spoken as follows to the Baron de Nucingen, a peer of the Chamber, in whose carriage he found himself after a sitting, driving home, in fact, to dine with him: –

'Baron, I want seventy thousand francs, and I apply to you. You must find some one to lend his name, to whom I will make over the right to draw my pay for three years; it amounts to twenty-five thousand francs a year – that is, seventy-five thousand francs. – You will say, "But you may die"' – the banker signified his assent. – 'Here, then, is a policy of insurance for a hundred and fifty thousand francs, which I will deposit with you till you have drawn up to eighty thousand francs,' said Hulot, producing the document from his pocket.

'But if you should lose your place?' said the millionaire Baron, laughing.

The other Baron – not a millionaire – looked grave.

'Be quite easy; I only raised the question to show you that I was not devoid of merit in handing you the sum. Are you so very short of cash? for the Bank will take your signature.'

'My daughter is to be married,' said Baron Hulot, 'and I have no fortune – like every one else who remains in office in these thankless times, when five hundred ordinary men seated on benches will never reward the men who devote themselves to the service as handsomely as the Emperor did.'

'Well, well; but you had Josépha on your hands!' replied Nucingen, 'and that accounts for everything. Between ourselves, the Duc d'Hérouville has done you a very good turn by removing that leech from sucking your purse dry. "I have known what it is, and can pity your case,"' he quoted. 'Take a friend's advice: Shut up shop, or you will be done for.'

This dirty business was carried out in the name of one Vauvinet, a small money-lender; one of those jobbers who stand forward to screen great banking houses, like the little fish that is said to attend the shark. This stock-jobber's apprentice was so anxious to gain the patronage of Monsieur le Baron Hulot, that he promised the great man to negotiate bills of exchange for thirty thousand francs at eighty days, and pledged himself to renew them four times, and never pass them out of his hands.

Fischer's successor was to pay forty thousand francs for the house and business, with the promise that he should supply forage to a department close to Paris.

This was the desperate maze of affairs into which a man who had hitherto been absolutely honest was led by his passions – one of the best administrative officials under Napoleon – peculation to pay the money-lenders, and borrowing of the money-lenders to gratify his passions and provide for his daughter. All the efforts of this elaborate prodigality were directed to making a display before Madame Marneffe, and to playing Jupiter to this middle-class Danaë. A man could not expend more activity, intelligence, and presence of mind in the honest acquisition of a fortune than the Baron displayed in shoving his head into a wasp's nest: he did all the business of his department, he hurried on the upholsterers, he talked to the workmen, he kept a sharp lookout on the smallest details of the house in the Rue Vanneau. Wholly devoted to Madame Marneffe, he nevertheless attended the sittings of the Chambers; he was everywhere at once, and neither his family nor anybody else discovered where his thoughts were.

Adeline, quite amazed to hear that her uncle was rescued, and to see a handsome sum figure in the marriage-contract, was not altogether easy, in spite of her joy at seeing her daughter married under such creditable circumstances. But, on the day before the wedding, fixed by the Baron to coincide with Madame Marneffe's removal to her new apartment, Hector allayed his wife's astonishment by this ministerial communication: –

'Now, Adeline, our girl is married; all our anxieties on that subject are at an end. The time is come for us to retire from the world: I shall not remain in office more than three years longer – only the time necessary to secure my pension. Why, henceforth, should we be at any unnecessary expense? Our apartment costs us six thousand francs a year in rent, we have four servants, we eat thirty thousand francs' worth of food in the year. If you want me to pay off my bills – for I have pledged my salary for the sums I needed to give Hortense her little money, and pay off your uncle—'

'You did very right!' said she, interrupting her husband, and kissing his hands.

This explanation relieved Adeline of all her fears.

'I shall have to ask some little sacrifices of you,' he went on, disengaging his hands and kissing his wife's brow. 'I have found in the Rue Plumet a very good flat on the first floor, handsome, splendidly panelled, at only fifteen hundred francs a year, where you would only need one woman to wait on you, and I could be quite content with a boy.'

'Yes, my dear.'

'If we keep house in a quiet way, keeping up a proper appearance of course, we should not spend more than six thousand francs a year, excepting my private account, which I will provide for.'

The generous-hearted woman threw her arms round her husband's neck in her joy.

'How happy I shall be, beginning again to show you how truly I love you!' she exclaimed. 'And what a capital manager you are!'

'We will have the children to dine with us once a week. I, as you know, rarely dine at home. You can very well dine twice a week with Victorin and twice a week with Hortense. And, as I believe, I may succeed in making matters up completely between Crevel and us; we can dine once a week with him. These five dinners and our own at home will fill up the week all but one day, supposing that we may occasionally be invited to dine elsewhere.'

'I shall save a great deal for you,' said Adeline.

'Oh!' he cried, 'you are the pearl of women!'

'My kind, divine Hector, I shall bless you with my latest breath,' said she, 'for you have done well for my dear Hortense.'

This was the beginning of the end of the beautiful Madame Hulot's home; and, it may be added, of her being totally neglected, as Hulot had solemnly promised Madame Marneffe.

Crevel, the important and burly, being invited as a matter of course to the party given for the signing of the marriage-contract, behaved as though the scene with which this drama opened had never taken place, as though he had no grievance against the Baron. Célestin Crevel was quite amiable; he was perhaps rather too much the ex-perfumer, but as a Major he was beginning to acquire majestic dignity. He talked of dancing at the wedding.

'Fair lady,' said he politely to the Baroness, 'people like us know how to forget. Do not banish me from your home; honour me, pray, by gracing my house with your presence now and then to meet your children. Be quite easy; I will never say anything of what lies buried at the bottom of my heart. I behaved, indeed, like an idiot, for I should lose too much by cutting myself off from seeing you.'

'Monsieur, an honest woman has no ears for such speeches as those you refer to. If you keep your word, you need not doubt that it will give me pleasure to see the end of a coolness which must always be painful in a family.'

'Well, you sulky old fellow,' said Hulot, dragging Crevel out into the garden, 'you avoid me everywhere, even in my own house. Are two admirers of the fair sex to quarrel for ever over a petticoat? Come; that is really too plebeian!'

'I, Monsieur, am not such a fine man as you are, and my small attractions hinder me from repairing my losses so easily as you can—'

'Sarcastic!' said the Baron.

'Irony is allowable from the vanquished to the conqueror.'

The conversation, begun in this strain, ended in a complete reconciliation; still Crevel maintained his right to take his revenge.

Madame Marneffe particularly wished to be invited to Mademoiselle Hulot's wedding. To enable him to receive his future mistress in his drawing-room, the great official was obliged to invite all the clerks of his division down to the deputy head-clerks inclusive. Thus a grand ball was a necessity. The Baroness, as a prudent housewife, calculated that an evening party would cost less than a dinner, and allow of a larger number of invitations; so Hortense's wedding was much talked about.

Marshal Prince Wissembourg and the Baron de Nucingen signed in behalf of the bride, the Comtes de Rastignac and Popinot in behalf of Steinbock. Then, as the highest nobility among the Polish emigrants had been civil to Count Steinbock since he had become famous, the artist thought himself bound to invite them. The State Council, and the War Office to which the Baron belonged, and the army, anxious to do honour to the Comte de Forzheim, were all represented by their magnates. There were nearly two hundred indispensable invitations. How natural, then, that little Madame Marneffe was bent on figuring in all her glory amid such an assembly. The Baroness had, a month since, sold her diamonds to set up her daughter's house, while keeping the finest for the trousseau. The sale realised fifteen thousand francs, of which five thousand were sunk in Hortense's clothes. And what was ten thousand francs for the furniture of the young folks' apartment, considering the demands of modern luxury? However, young Monsieur and Madame Hulot, old Crevel, and the Comte de Forzheim made very handsome presents, for the old soldier had set aside a sum for the purchase of plate. Thanks to these contributions, even an exacting Parisian would have been pleased with the rooms the young couple had taken in the Rue Saint-Dominique, near the Invalides. Everything seemed in harmony with their love, pure, honest, and sincere.

At last the great day dawned – for it was to be a great day not only for Wenceslas and Hortense, but for old Hulot too. Madame Marneffe was to give a house-warming in her new apartment the day after becoming Hulot's mistress *en titre*, and after the marriage of the lovers.

Who but has once in his life been a guest at a wedding-ball? Every reader can refer to his reminiscences, and will probably smile as he calls up the images of all that company in their Sunday-best faces as well as their finest frippery.

If any social event can prove the influence of environment, is it not this? In fact, the Sunday-best mood of some reacts so effectually on the rest that the men who are most accustomed to wearing full dress look just like those to whom the party is a high festival, unique in their life. And think too of the serious old men to whom such things are so completely a matter of indifference, that they are wearing their everyday black coats; the long-married men, whose faces betray their sad experience of the life the young pair are but just entering on; and the lighter elements, present as carbonic-acid gas is in champagne; and the envious girls, the women absorbed in wondering if their dress is a success, the poor relations whose parsimonious 'get-up' contrasts with that of the officials in uniform; and the greedy ones, thinking only of the supper; and the gamblers, thinking only of cards.

There are some of every sort, rich and poor, envious and envied, philosophers and dreamers, all grouped like the plants in a flower-bed round the rare, choice blossom, the bride. A wedding-ball is an epitome of the world.

At the liveliest moment of the evening Crevel led the Baron aside, and said in a whisper, with the most natural manner possible –

'By Jove! that's a pretty woman – the little lady in pink who has opened a raking fire on you from her eyes.'

'Which?'

'The wife of that clerk you are promoting, Heaven knows how! – Madame Marneffe.'

'What do you know about it?'

'Listen, Hulot; I will try to forgive you the ill you have done me if only you will introduce me to her – I will take you to Héloïse. Everybody is asking who is that charming creature. Are you sure that it will strike no one how and why her husband's appointment got itself signed? – You happy rascal, she is worth a whole office. – I would serve in her office only too gladly. – Come, Cinna, let us be friends.'

'Better friends than ever,' said the Baron to the perfumer, 'and I promise you I will be a good fellow. Within a month you shall dine with that little angel. – For it is an angel this time, old boy. And I advise you, like me, to have done with the devils.'

Cousin Bette, who had moved to the Rue Vanneau, into a nice little apartment on the third floor, left the ball at ten o'clock, but came back to see with her own eyes the two bonds bearing twelve hundred francs' interest; one of them was the property of the Countess Steinbock, the other was in the name of young Madame Hulot.

It is thus intelligible that Monsieur Crevel should have spoken to Hulot about Madame Marneffe, as knowing what was a secret to the rest of the world; for, as Monsieur Marneffe was away, no one but Lisbeth Fischer, besides the Baron and Valérie, was initiated into the mystery.

The Baron had made a blunder in giving Madame Marneffe a dress far too magnificent for the wife of a subordinate official; other women were jealous alike of her beauty and of her gown. There was much whispering behind fans, for the poverty of the Marneffes was known to every one in the office; the husband had been petitioning for help at the very moment when the Baron had been so smitten with Madame. Also, Hector could not conceal his exultation at seeing Valérie's success; and she, severely proper, very lady-like, and greatly envied, was the object of that strict examination which women so greatly fear when they appear for the first time in a new circle of society.

After seeing his wife into a carriage with his daughter and his son-in-law, Hulot managed to escape unperceived, leaving his son and Célestine to do the honours of the house. He got into Madame Marneffe's carriage to see her home, but he found her silent and pensive, almost melancholy.

'My happiness makes you very sad, Valérie,' said he, putting his arm round her and drawing her to him.

'Can you wonder, my dear,' said she, 'that a hapless woman should be a little depressed at the thought of her first fall from virtue, even when her husband's atrocities have set her free? Do you suppose that I have no soul, no beliefs, no religion? Your glee this evening has been really too barefaced; you have paraded me odiously. Really, a schoolboy would have been less of a coxcomb. And the ladies have dissected me with their side-glances and their satirical remarks. Every woman has some care for her reputation, and you have wrecked mine.

'Oh, I am yours and no mistake! And I have not an excuse left but that of being faithful to you. – Monster that you are!' she added, laughing, and allowing him to kiss her, 'you knew very well what you were doing! Madame Coquet, our chief clerk's wife, came to sit down by me, and admired my lace. "English point!" said she. "Was it very expensive, Madame?" – "I do not know. This lace was my mother's. I am not rich enough to buy the like," said I.'

Madame Marneffe, in short, had so bewitched the old beau, that he really believed she was sinning for the first time for his sake, and that he had inspired such a passion as had led her to this breach of duty. She told him that the wretch Marneffe had neglected her after they had been three days married, and for the most odious reasons. Since then she had lived as innocently as a girl; marriage had seemed to her so horrible. This was the cause of her present melancholy.

'If love should prove to be like marriage—' said she in tears.

These insinuating lies, with which almost every woman in Valérie's predicament is ready, gave the Baron distant visions of the roses of the seventh heaven. And so Valérie coquetted with her lover, while the artist and Hortense were impatiently awaiting the moment when the Baroness should have given the girl her last kiss and blessing.

At seven in the morning the Baron, perfectly happy – for his Valérie was at once the most guileless of girls and the most consummate of demons – went back to release his son and Célestine from their duties. All the dancers, for the most part strangers, had taken possession of the territory, as they do at every wedding-ball, and were keeping up the endless figures of the cotillions, while the gamblers were still crowding round the *bouillotte* tables, and old Crevel had won six thousand francs.

The morning papers, carried round the town, contained this paragraph in the Paris article: –

'The marriage was celebrated this morning, at the Church of Saint-Thomas d'Aquin, between Monsieur le Comte Stein-bock and Mademoiselle Hortense Hulot, daughter of Baron Hulot d'Ervy, Councillor of State, and a Director at the War Office; niece of the famous General Comte de Forzheim. The ceremony attracted a large gathering. There were present some of the most distinguished artists of the day: Léon de Lora, Joseph Bridau, Stidmann, and Bixiou; the magnates of the War Office, of the Council of State, and many members of the two Chambers; also the most distinguished of the Polish exiles living in Paris: Counts Paz, Laginski, and others.

'Monsieur le Comte Wenceslas Steinbock is grand-nephew to the famous general who served under Charles XII., King of Sweden. The young Count, having taken part in the Polish rebellion, found a refuge in France, where his well-earned fame as a sculptor has procured him a patent of naturalisation.'

And so, in spite of the Baron's cruel lack of money, nothing was lacking that public opinion could require, not even the trumpeting of the newspapers over his daughter's marriage, which was solemnised in the same way, in every particular, as his son's had been to Mademoiselle Crevel. This display moderated the reports current as to the Baron's financial position, while the fortune assigned to his daughter explained the need for having borrowed money.

Here ends what is, in a way, the introduction to this story. It is to the drama that follows what the premiss is to a syllogism, what the prologue is to a classical tragedy.

In Paris, when a woman determines to make a business, a trade, of her beauty, it does not follow that she will make a fortune. Lovely creatures may be found there, and full of wit, who are in wretched circumstances, ending in misery a life begun in pleasure. And this is why. It is not enough merely to accept the shameful life of a courtesan with a view to earning its profits, and at the same time to bear the simple garb of a respectable middle-class wife. Vice does not triumph so easily; it resembles genius in so far that they both need a concurrence of favourable conditions to develop the coalition of fortune and gifts. Eliminate the strange prologue of the Revolution, and the Emperor would never have existed; he would have been no more than a second edition of Fabert. Venal beauty, if it finds no amateurs, no celebrity, no cross of dishonour earned by squandering men's fortunes, is Correggio in a hay-loft, is genius starving in a garret. Laïs, in Paris, must first and foremost find a rich man mad enough to pay her price. She must keep up a very elegant style, for this is her shop-sign; she must be sufficiently well bred to flatter the vanity of her lovers; she must have the brilliant wit of a Sophie Arnould, which diverts the apathy of rich men; finally, she must arouse the passions of libertines by appearing to be mistress to one man only who is envied by the rest.

These conditions, which a woman of that class calls being in luck, are difficult to combine in Paris, although it is a city of millionaires, of idlers, of used-up and capricious men.

Providence has, no doubt, vouchsafed protection to clerks and middle-class citizens, for whom obstacles of this kind are at least double in the sphere in which they move. At the same time, there are enough Madame Marneffes in Paris to allow of our taking Valérie to figure as a type in this picture of manners. Some of these women yield to the double pressure of a genuine passion and of hard necessity, like Madame Colleville, who was for long attached to one of the famous orators of the left, Keller the banker. Others are spurred by vanity, like Madame de la Baudraye, who remained almost respectable in spite of her elopement with Lousteau. Some, again, are led astray by the love of fine clothes, and some by the impossibility of keeping a house going on obviously too narrow means. The stinginess of the State – or of Parliament – leads to many disasters and to much corruption.

At the present moment the labouring classes are the fashionable object of compassion; they are being murdered – it is said – by the manufacturing capitalist; but the Government is a hundred times harder than the meanest tradesman, it carries its economy in the article of salaries to absolute folly. If you work harder, the merchant will pay you more in proportion; but what does the State do for its crowd of obscure and devoted toilers?

In a married woman it is an inexcusable crime when she wanders from the path of honour; still, there are degrees even in such a case. Some women, far from being depraved, conceal their fall and remain to all appearance quite respectable, like those two just referred to, while others add to their fault the disgrace of speculation. Thus Madame Marneffe is, as it were, the type of those ambitious married courtesans who from the first accept depravity with all its consequences, and determine to make a fortune while taking their pleasure, perfectly unscrupulous as to the means. But almost always a woman like Madame Marneffe has a husband who is her confederate and accomplice. These Machiavellis in petticoats are the most dangerous of the sisterhood; of every evil class of Parisian woman, they are the worst.

A mere courtesan – a Josépha, a Malaga, a Madame Schontz, a Jenny Cadine – carries in her frank dishonour a warning signal as conspicuous as the red lamp of a house of ill-fame or the flaring lights of a gambling hell. A man knows that they light him to his ruin.

But mealy-mouthed propriety, the semblance of virtue, the hypocritical ways of a married woman who never allows anything to be seen but the vulgar needs of the household, and affects to refuse every kind of extravagance, leads to silent ruin, dumb disaster, which is all the more startling because, though condoned, it remains unaccounted for. It is the ignoble bill of daily expenses and not gay dissipation that devours the largest fortune. The father of a family ruins himself ingloriously, and the great consolation of gratified vanity is wanting in his misery.

This little sermon will go like a javelin to the heart of many a home. Madame Marneffes are to be seen in every sphere of social life, even at Court; for Valérie is a melancholy fact, modelled from the life in the smallest details. And, alas! The portrait will not cure any man of the folly of loving these sweetly-smiling angels, with pensive looks and candid faces, whose heart is a cash-box.

About three years after Hortense's marriage, in 1841, Baron Hulot d'Ervy was supposed to have sown his wild oats, to have 'put up his horses,' to quote the expression used by Louis XV.'s head surgeon, and yet Madame Marneffe was costing him twice as much as Josépha had ever cost him. Still, Valérie, though always nicely dressed, affected the simplicity of a subordinate official's wife; she kept her luxury for her dressing-gowns, her home wear. She thus sacrificed her Parisian vanity to her dear Hector. At the theatre, however, she always appeared in a pretty bonnet and a dress of extreme elegance; and the Baron took her in a carriage to a private box.

Her rooms, the whole of the second floor of a modern house in the Rue Vanneau, between a fore-court and a garden, was redolent of respectability. All its luxury was in good chintz hangings and handsome convenient furniture.

Her bedroom, indeed, was the exception, and rich with such profusion as Jenny Cadine or Madame Schontz might have displayed. There were lace curtains, cashmere hangings, brocade portières, a set of chimney ornaments modelled by Stidmann, a glass cabinet filled with dainty nicknacks. Hulot could not bear to see his Valérie in a bower of inferior magnificence to the dunghill of gold and pearls owned by a Josépha. The drawing-room was furnished with red damask, and the dining-room had carved oak panels. But the Baron, carried away by his wish to have everything in keeping, had, at the end of six months, added solid luxury to mere fashion, and had given her handsome portable property, as, for instance, a service of plate that was to cost more than twenty-four thousand francs.

Madame Marneffe's house had in a couple of years achieved a reputation for being a very pleasant one. Gambling went on there. Valérie herself was soon spoken of as an agreeable and witty woman. To account for her change of style, a rumour was set going of an immense legacy bequeathed to her by her 'natural father,' Marshal Montcornet, and left in trust.

With an eye to the future, Valérie had added religious to social hypocrisy. Punctual at the Sunday services, she enjoyed all the honours due to the pious. She carried the bag for the offertory, she was a member of a charitable association, presented bread for the sacrament, and did some good among the poor, all at Hector's expense. Thus everything about the house was perfectly seemly. And a great many persons maintained that her friendship with the Baron was entirely innocent, supporting the view by the gentleman's mature age, and ascribing to him a Platonic liking for Madame Marneffe's pleasant wit, charming manners, and conversation – such a liking as that of the late lamented Louis XVIII. for a well-turned note.

The Baron always withdrew with the other company at about midnight, and came back a quarter of an hour later.

The secret of this secrecy was as follows. The lodge-keepers of the house were a Monsieur and Madame Olivier, who, under the Baron's patronage, had been promoted from their humble and not very lucrative post in the Rue du Doyenné to the highly-paid and handsome one in the Rue Vanneau. Now, Madame Olivier, formerly a needlewoman in the household of Charles X., who had fallen in the world with the legitimate branch, had three children. The eldest, an under-clerk in a notary's office, was the object of his parents' adoration. This Benjamin, for six years in danger of being drawn for the army, was on the point of being interrupted in his legal career, when Madame Marneffe contrived to have him declared exempt for one of those little malformations which the Examining Board can always discern when requested in a whisper by some power in the ministry. So Olivier, formerly a huntsman to the King, and his wife would have crucified the Lord again for the Baron or for Madame Marneffe.

What could the world have to say? It knew nothing of the former episode of the Brazilian, Monsieur Montès de

Montejanos – it could say nothing. Besides, the world is very indulgent to the mistress of a house where amusement is to be found.

And then to all her charms Valérie added the highly-prized advantage of being an occult power. Claude Vignon, now secretary to Marshal the Prince de Wissembourg, and dreaming of promotion to the Council of State as a Master of Appeals, was constantly seen in her rooms, to which came also some Deputies – good fellows and gamblers. Madame Marneffe had got her circle together with prudent deliberation; only men whose opinions and habits agreed forgathered there, men whose interest it was to hold together and to proclaim the many merits of the lady of the house. Scandal is the true Holy Alliance in Paris. Take that as an axiom. Interests invariably fall asunder in the end; vicious natures can always agree.

Within three months of settling in the Rue Vanneau, Madame Marneffe had entertained Monsieur Crevel, who by that time was Mayor of his *arrondissement* and Officer of the Legion of Honour. Crevel had hesitated; he would have to give up the famous uniform of the National Guard in which he strutted at the Tuileries, believing himself quite as much a soldier as the Emperor himself; but ambition, urged by Madame Marneffe, had proved stronger than vanity. Then Monsieur le Maire had considered his connection with Mademoiselle Héloïse Brisetout as quite incompatible with his political position.

Indeed, long before his accession to the civic chair of the Mayoralty, his gallant intimacies had been wrapped in the deepest mystery. But, as the reader may have guessed, Crevel had soon purchased the right of taking his revenge, as often as circumstances allowed, for having been bereft of Josépha, at the cost of a bond bearing six thousand francs of interest in the name of Valérie Fortin, wife of the Sieur Marneffe, for her sole and separate use. Valérie, inheriting perhaps from her mother the special acumen of the kept woman, read the character of her grotesque adorer at a glance. The phrase 'I never had a lady for a mistress,' spoken by Crevel to Lisbeth, and repeated by Lisbeth to her dear Valérie, had been handsomely discounted in the bargain by which she got her six thousand francs a year in five per cents. And since then she had never allowed her prestige to grow less in the eyes of César Birotteau's erewhile bagman.

Crevel himself had married for money the daughter of a miller of la Brie, an only child indeed, whose inheritance constituted three-quarters of his fortune; for when retail-dealers grow rich, it is generally not so much by trade as through some alliance between the shop and rural thrift. A large proportion of the farmers, corn-factors, dairy-keepers, and market-gardeners in the neighbourhood of Paris, dream of the glories of the desk for their daughters, and look upon a shopkeeper, a jeweller, or a money-changer as a son-in-law after their own heart, in preference to a notary or an attorney, whose superior social position is a ground of suspicion; they are afraid of being scorned in the future by these citizen bigwigs.

Madame Crevel, ugly, vulgar, and silly, had given her husband no pleasures but those of paternity; she had died young. Her libertine husband, fettered at the beginning of his commercial career by the necessity for working, and held in thrall by want of money, had led the life of Tantalus. Thrown in – as he phrased it – with the most elegant women in Paris, he let them out of the shop with servile homage, while admiring their grace, their way of wearing the fashions, and all the nameless charms of what is called breeding. To rise to the level of one of these fairies of the drawing-room was a desire formed in his youth, but buried in the depths of his heart. Thus to win the favours of Madame Marneffe was to him not merely the realisation of his chimera, but, as has been shown, a point of pride, of vanity, of self-satisfaction. His ambition grew with success; his brain was turned with elation; and when the mind is captivated, the heart feels more keenly, every gratification is doubled.

Also, it must be said that Madame Marneffe offered to Crevel a refinement of pleasure of which he had had no idea; neither Josépha nor Héloïse had loved him; and Madame Marneffe thought it necessary to deceive him thoroughly, for this man, she saw, would prove an inexhaustible till. The deceptions of a venal passion are more delightful than the real thing. True love is mixed up with bird-like squabbles, in which the disputants wound each other to the quick; but a quarrel without animus is, on the contrary, a piece of flattery to the dupe's conceit.

The rare interviews granted to Crevel kept his passion at white heat. He was constantly blocked by Valérie's virtuous severity; she acted remorse, and wondered what her father must be thinking of her in the paradise of the brave. Again and again he had to contend with a sort of coldness, which the cunning slut made him believe he had overcome by seeming to surrender to the man's crazy passion; and then, as if ashamed, she entrenched herself once more in her pride of respectability and airs of virtue, just like an Englishwoman, neither more nor less; and she always crushed her Crevel under the weight of her dignity – for Crevel had, in the first instance, swallowed her pretensions to virtue.

In short, Valérie had special veins of affection which made her equally indispensable to Crevel and to the Baron. Before the world she displayed the attractive combination of modest and pensive innocence, of irreproachable propriety, with a bright humour enhanced by the suppleness, the grace and softness of the Creole; but in a *tête-à-tête* she would outdo any courtesan; she was audacious, amusing, and full of original inventiveness. Such a contrast is irresistible to a man of the Crevel type; he is flattered by believing himself sole author of the comedy, thinking it is performed for his benefit alone, and he laughs at the exquisite hypocrisy while admiring the hypocrite.

Valérie had taken entire possession of Baron Hulot; she had persuaded him to grow old by one of those subtle touches of flattery which reveal the diabolical wit of women like her. In all evergreen constitutions a moment arrives when the truth suddenly comes out, as in a besieged town which puts a good face on affairs as long as possible. Valérie, foreseeing the approaching collapse of the old beau of the Empire, determined to forestall it.

'Why give yourself so much bother, my dear old veteran?' said she one day, six months after their doubly adulterous union. 'Do you want to be flirting? To be unfaithful to me? I assure you, I should like you better without your make-up. Oblige me by giving up all your artificial charms. Do you suppose that it is for two sous' worth of polish on your boots that I love you? For your indiarubber belt, your strait-waistcoat, and your false hair? And then, the older you look, the less need I fear seeing my Hulot carried off by a rival.'

And Hulot, trusting to Madame Marneffe's heavenly friendship as much as to her love, intending, too, to end his days with her, had taken this confidential hint, and ceased to dye his whiskers and hair. After this touching declaration from his Valérie, handsome Hector made his appearance one morning perfectly white. Madame Marneffe could assure him that she had a hundred times detected the white line of the growth of the hair.

'And white hair suits your face to perfection,' said she; 'it softens it. You look a thousand times better, quite charming.'

The Baron, once started on this path of reform, gave up his leather waistcoat and stays; he threw off all his bracing. His stomach fell and increased in size. The oak became a tower, and the heaviness of his movements was all the more alarming because the Baron grew immensely older by playing the part of Louis XII. His eyebrows were still black, and left a ghostly reminiscence of Handsome Hulot, as sometimes on the old wall of some feudal building a faint trace of sculpture remains to show what the castle was in the days of its glory. This discordant detail made his eyes, still bright and youthful, all the more remarkable in his tanned face, because it had so long been ruddy with the florid hues of a Rubens; and now a certain discoloration and the deep tension of the wrinkles betrayed the efforts of a passion at odds with natural decay. Hulot was now one of those stalwart ruins in which virile force asserts itself by tufts of hair in the ears and nostrils and on the fingers, as moss grows on the almost eternal monuments of the Roman Empire.

How had Valérie contrived to keep Crevel and Hulot side by side, each tied to an apron-string, when the vindictive Major only longed to triumph openly over Hulot? Without immediately giving an answer to this question, which the course of the story will supply, it may be said that Lisbeth and Valérie had contrived a powerful piece of machinery which tended to this result. Marneffe, as he saw his wife improved in beauty by the setting in which she was enthroned, like the sun at the centre of the sidereal system, appeared, in the eyes of the world, to have fallen in love with her again himself; he was quite crazy about her. Now, though his jealousy made him somewhat of a mar-plot, it gave enhanced value to Valérie's favours. Marneffe meanwhile showed a blind confidence in his chief, which degenerated into ridiculous complaisance. The only person whom he really would not stand was Crevel.

Marneffe, wrecked by the debauchery of great cities, described by Roman authors, though modern decency has no name for it, was as hideous as an anatomical figure in wax. But this disease on feet, clothed in good broadcloth, encased his lath-like legs in elegant trousers. The hollow chest was scented with fine linen, and musk disguised the odours of rotten humanity. This hideous specimen of decaying vice, trotting in red heels – for Valérie dressed the man as beseemed his income, his cross, and his appointment – horrified Crevel, who could not meet the colourless eyes of the Government clerk. Marneffe was an incubus to the Mayor. And the mean rascal, aware of the strange power conferred on him by Lisbeth and his wife, was amused by it; he played on it as on an instrument; and cards being the last resource of a mind as completely played out as the body, he plucked Crevel again and again, the Mayor thinking himself bound to subserviency to the worthy official whom *he was cheating*.

Seeing Crevel a mere child in the hands of that hideous and atrocious mummy, of whose utter vileness the Mayor knew nothing; and seeing him, yet more, an object of deep contempt to Valérie, who made game of Crevel as of some mountebank, the Baron apparently thought him so impossible as a rival that he constantly invited him to dinner.

Valérie, protected by two lovers on guard, and by a jealous husband, attracted every eye, and excited every desire in the circle she shone upon. And thus, while keeping up appearances, she had, in the course of three years, achieved the most difficult conditions of the success a courtesan most cares for and most rarely attains, even with the help of audacity and the glitter of an existence in the light of the sun. Valérie's beauty, formerly buried in the mud of the Rue du Doyenné, now, like a well-cut diamond exquisitely set by Chanor, was worth more than its real value – it could break hearts. Claude Vignon adored Valérie in secret.

This retrospective explanation, quite necessary after the lapse of three years, shows Valérie's balance-sheet. Now for that of her partner, Lisbeth.

Lisbeth Fischer filled the place in the Marneffe household of a relation who combines the functions of a lady companion and a housekeeper; but she suffered from none of the humiliations which, for the most part, weigh upon the women who are so unhappy as to be obliged to fill these ambiguous situations. Lisbeth and Valérie offered the touching spectacle of one of those friendships between women, so cordial and so improbable, that men, always too keen-tongued in Paris, forthwith slander them. The contrast between Lisbeth's dry masculine nature and Valérie's creole prettiness encouraged calumny. And Madame Marneffe had unconsciously given weight to the scandal by the care she took of her friend, with matrimonial views, which were, as will be seen, to complete Lisbeth's revenge.

An immense change had taken place in Cousin Bette; and Valérie, who wanted to smarten her, had turned it to the best account. The strange woman had submitted to stays, and laced tightly; she used bandoline to keep her hair smooth, wore her gowns as the dressmaker sent them home, neat little boots, and grey silk stockings, all of which were included in Valérie's bills, and paid for by the gentleman in possession. Thus furbished up, and wearing the yellow cashmere shawl, Lisbeth would have been unrecognisable by any one who had not seen her for three years.

This other diamond – a black diamond, the rarest of all – cut by a skilled hand, and set as best became her, was appreciated at her full value by certain ambitious clerks. Any one seeing her for the first time might have shuddered involuntarily at the look of poetic wildness which the clever Valérie had succeeded in bringing out by the arts of dress in this Bleeding Nun, framing the ascetic olive face in thick bands of hair as black as the fiery eyes, and making the most of the rigid, slim figure. Lisbeth, like a Virgin by Cranach or Van Eyck, or a Byzantine Madonna stepped out of its frame, had all the stiffness, the precision of those mysterious figures, the more modern cousins of Isis and her sister goddesses sheathed in marble folds by Egyptian sculptors. It was granite, basalt, porphyry, with life and movement.

Saved from want for the rest of her life, Lisbeth was most amiable; wherever she dined she brought merriment. And the Baron paid the rent of her little apartment, furnished, as we know, with the leavings of her friend Valérie's former boudoir and bedroom.

'I began,' she would say, 'as a hungry nanny goat, and I am ending as a *lionne*.'

She still worked for Monsieur Rivet at the more elaborate kinds of gold-trimming, merely, as she said, not to lose her time. At the same time, she was, as we shall see, very full of business; but it is inherent in the nature of country-folks never to give up bread-winning; in this they are like the Jews.

Every morning, very early, Cousin Bette went off to market with the cook. It was part of Lisbeth's scheme that the house-book, which was ruining Baron Hulot, was to enrich her dear Valérie – as it did indeed.

Is there a housewife who, since 1838, has not suffered from the evil effects of Socialist doctrines diffused among the lower classes by incendiary writers? In every household the plague of servants is nowadays the worst of financial afflictions. With very few exceptions, who ought to be rewarded with the Montyon prize, the cook, male or female, is a domestic robber, a thief taking wages, and perfectly barefaced, with the Government for a fence, developing the tendency to dishonesty, which is almost authorised in the cook by the time-honoured jest as to the 'handle of the basket.' The women who formerly picked up their forty sous to buy a lottery ticket now take fifty francs to put into the savings bank. And the smug Puritans who amuse themselves in France with philanthropic experiments fancy that they are making the common people moral!

Between the market and the master's table the servants have their secret toll, and the municipality of Paris is less sharp in collecting the city-dues than the servants are in taking theirs on every single thing. To say nothing of fifty per cent. charged on every form of food, they demand large New Year's premiums from the tradesmen. The best class of dealers tremble before this occult power, and subsidise it without a word — coachmakers, jewellers, tailors, and all. If any attempt is made to interfere with them, the servants reply with impudent retorts, or revenge themselves by the costly blunders of assumed clumsiness; and in these days they inquire into their master's character as, formerly, the master inquired into theirs. This mischief is now really at its height, and the law-courts are beginning to take cognisance of it; but in vain, for it cannot be remedied but by a law which shall compel domestic servants, like labourers, to have a pass-book as a guarantee of conduct. Then the evil will vanish as if by magic. If every servant were obliged to show his pass-book, and if masters were required to state in it the cause of his dismissal, this would certainly prove a powerful check to the evil.

The men who are giving their attention to the politics of the day know not to what lengths the depravity of the lower classes has gone. Statistics are silent as to the startling number of working men of twenty who marry cooks of between forty and fifty enriched by robbery. We shudder to think of the result of such unions from the three points of view of increasing crime, degeneracy of the race, and miserable households.

As to the mere financial mischief that results from domestic peculation, that too is immense from a political point of view. Life being made to cost double, any superfluity becomes impossible in most households. Now superfluity means half the trade of the world, as it is half the elegance of life. Books and flowers are to many persons as necessary as bread.

Lisbeth, well aware of this dreadful scourge of Parisian households, determined to manage Valérie's, promising her every assistance in the terrible scene when the two women had sworn to be like sisters. So she had brought from the depths of the Vosges a humble relation on her mother's side, a very pious and honest soul, who had been cook to the Bishop of Nancy. Fearing, however, her inexperience of Paris ways, and yet more the evil counsel which wrecks such fragile virtue, at first Lisbeth always went to market with Mathurine, and tried to teach her what to buy. To know the real prices of things and command the salesman's respect; to purchase unnecessary delicacies, such as fish, only when they were cheap; to be well informed as to the price current of groceries and provisions, so as to buy when prices are low in anticipation of a rise, – all this housekeeping skill is in Paris essential to domestic economy. As Mathurine got good wages and many presents, she liked the house well enough to be glad to drive good bargains. And by this time Lisbeth had made her quite a match for herself, sufficiently experienced and trustworthy to be sent to market alone, unless Valérie was giving a dinner – which, in fact, was not unfrequently the case. And this was how it came about.

The Baron had at first observed the strictest decorum; but his passion for Madame Marneffe had ere long become so vehement, so greedy, that he would never quit her if he could help it. At first he dined there four times a week; then he thought it delightful to dine with her every day. Six months after his daughter's marriage he was paying her two thousand francs a month for his board. Madame Marneffe invited any one her dear Baron wished to entertain. The dinner was always arranged for six; he could bring in three unexpected guests. Lisbeth's economy enabled her to solve the extraordinary problem of keeping up the table in the best style for a thousand francs a month, giving the other thousand to Madame Marneffe. Valérie's dress being chiefly paid for by Crevel and the Baron, the two women saved another thousand francs a month on this.

And so this pure and innocent being had already accumulated a hundred and fifty thousand francs in savings. She had capitalised her income and monthly bonus, and swelled the amount by enormous interest, due to Crevel's liberality in allowing his 'little Duchess' to invest her money in partnership with him in his financial operations. Crevel had taught Valérie the slang and the procedure of the money market, and, like every Parisian woman, she had soon outstripped her master. Lisbeth, who never spent a sou of her twelve hundred francs, whose rent and dress were given to her, and who never put her hand in her pocket, had likewise a small capital of five or six thousand francs, of which Crevel took fatherly care.

At the same time, two such lovers were a heavy burthen on Valérie. On the day when this drama reopens, Valérie, spurred by one of those incidents which have the effect in life that the ringing of a bell has in inducing a swarm of bees to settle, went up to Lisbeth's rooms to give vent to one of those comforting lamentations – a sort of cigarette blown off from the tongue – by which women alleviate the minor miseries of life.

'Oh, Lisbeth, my love, two hours of Crevel this morning! It is crushing! How I wish I could send you in my place!'

'That, unluckily, is impossible,' said Lisbeth, smiling. 'I shall die a maid.'

'Two old men lovers! Really, I am ashamed sometimes! If my poor mother could see me.'

'You are mistaking me for Crevel!' said Lisbeth.

'Tell me, my little Bette, do you not despise me?'

'Oh! if I had but been pretty, what adventures I would have had!' cried Lisbeth. 'That is your justification.'

'But you would have acted only at the dictates of your heart,' said Madame Marneffe, with a sigh.

'Pooh! Marneffe is a dead man they have forgotten to bury,' replied Lisbeth. 'The Baron is as good as your husband; Crevel is your adorer; it seems to me that you are quite in order – like every other married woman.'

'No, it is not that, dear, adorable thing; that is not where the shoe pinches; you do not choose to understand.'

'Yes I do,' said Lisbeth. 'The unexpressed factor is part of my revenge; what can I do? I am working it out.'

'I love Wenceslas so that I am positively growing thin, and I can never see him,' said Valérie, throwing up her arms. 'Hulot asks him to dinner, and my artist declines. He does not know that I idolise him, the wretch! What is his wife after all? Fine flesh! Yes, she is handsome, but I – I know myself – I am worse!'

'Be quite easy, my child, he will come,' said Lisbeth, in the tone of a nurse to an impatient child. 'He shall.'

'But when?'

'This week perhaps.'

'Give me a kiss.'

As may be seen, these two women were but one. Everything Valérie did, even her most reckless actions, her pleasures, her little sulks, were decided on after serious deliberation between them.

Lisbeth, strangely excited by this harlot existence, advised Valérie on every step, and pursued her course of revenge with pitiless logic. She really adored Valérie; she had taken her to be her child, her friend, her love; she found her docile, as Creoles are, yielding from voluptuous indolence; she chattered with her morning after morning with more pleasure than with Wenceslas; they could laugh together over the mischief they plotted, and over the folly of men, and count up the swelling interest on their respective savings.

Indeed, in this new enterprise and new affection, Lisbeth had found food for her activity that was far more satisfying than her insane passion for Wenceslas. The joys of gratified hatred are the fiercest and strongest the heart can know. Love is the gold, hatred the iron of the mine of feeling that lies buried in us. And then, Valérie was, to Lisbeth, Beauty in all its glory – the beauty she worshipped, as we worship what we have not, beauty far more plastic to her hand than that of Wenceslas, who had always been cold to her and distant.

At the end of nearly three years, Lisbeth was beginning to perceive the progress of the underground mine on which she was expending her life and concentrating her mind. Lisbeth planned, Madame Marneffe acted. Madame Marneffe was the axe, Lisbeth was the hand that wielded it, and that hand was rapidly demolishing the family which was every day more odious to her; for we can hate more and more, just as, when we love, we love better every day.

Love and hatred are feelings that feed on themselves; but of the two, hatred has the longer vitality. Love is restricted within limits of power; it derives its energies from life and from lavishness. Hatred is like death, like avarice; it is, so to speak, an active abstraction, above beings and things.

Lisbeth, embarked on the existence that was natural to her, expended in it all her faculties; governing, like the Jesuits, by occult influences. The regeneration of her person was equally complete; her face was radiant. Lisbeth dreamed of becoming Madame la Maréchale Hulot.

This little scene, in which the two friends had bluntly uttered their ideas without any circumlocution in expressing them, took place immediately on Lisbeth's return from market, whither she had been to procure the materials for an elegant dinner. Marneffe, who hoped to get Coquet's place, was to entertain him and the virtuous Madame Coquet, and Valérie hoped to persuade Hulot, that very evening, to consider the head-clerk's resignation.

Lisbeth dressed to go to the Baroness, with whom she was to dine.

'You will come back in time to make tea for us, my Betty?' said Valérie.

'I hope so.'

'You hope so – why? Have you come to sleeping with Adeline to drink her tears while she is asleep?'

'If only I could!' said Lisbeth, laughing. 'I would not refuse. She is expiating her happiness – and I am glad, for I remember our young days. It is my turn now. She will be in the mire, and I shall be Comtesse de Forzheim!'

Lisbeth set out for the Rue Plumet, where she now went as to the theatre – to indulge her emotions.

The residence Hulot had found for his wife consisted of a large, bare entrance-room, a drawing-room, and a bed and dressing room. The dining-room was next the drawing-room on one side. Two servants' rooms and a kitchen on the third floor completed the accommodation, which was not unworthy of a Councillor of State, high up in the War Office. The house, the courtyard, and the stairs were extremely handsome.

The Baroness, who had to furnish her drawing-room, bed-room, and dining-room with the relics of her splendour, had brought away the best of the remains from the house in the Rue de l'Université. Indeed, the poor woman was attached to these mute witnesses of her happier life; to her they had an almost consoling eloquence. In memory she saw her flowers, as in the carpets she could trace patterns hardly visible now to other eyes.

On going into the spacious anteroom, where twelve chairs, a barometer, a large stove, and long, white cotton curtains, bordered with red, suggested the dreadful waiting-room of a Government office, the visitor felt oppressed, conscious at once of the isolation in which the mistress lived. Grief, like pleasure, infects the atmosphere. A first glance into any home is enough to tell you whether love or despair reigns there.

Adeline would be found sitting in an immense bedroom with beautiful furniture by Jacob Desmalters, of mahogany finished in the Empire style with ormolu, which looks even less inviting than the brass-work of Louis XVI.! It gave one a shiver to see this lonely woman sitting on a Roman chair, a work-table with sphinxes before her, colourless, affecting false

cheerfulness, but preserving her imperial air, as she had preserved the blue velvet gown she always wore in the house. Her
proud spirit sustained her strength and preserved her beauty.

The Baroness, by the end of her first year of banishment to
this apartment, had gauged every depth of misfortune.

'Still, even here my Hector has made my life much handsomer than it should be for a mere peasant,' said she to
herself. 'He chooses that it should be so; his will be done! I
am Baroness Hulot, the sister-in-law of a Marshal of France.
I have done nothing wrong; my two children are settled in
life; I can wait for death, wrapped in the spotless veil of an
immaculate wife and the crape of departed happiness.'

A portrait of Hulot, in the uniform of a Commissary
General of the Imperial Guard, painted in 1810 by Robert
Lefebvre, hung above the work-table, and when visitors were
announced, Adeline threw into a drawer an *Imitation of Jesus
Christ*, her habitual study. This blameless Magdalen thus heard
the Voice of the Spirit in her desert.

'Mariette, my child,' said Lisbeth to the woman who
opened the door, 'how is my dear Adeline to-day?'

'Oh, she looks pretty well, Mademoiselle; but between you
and me, if she goes on in this way, she will kill herself,' said
Mariette in a whisper. 'You really ought to persuade her to live
better. Now, yesterday Madame told me to give her two sous'
worth of milk and a roll for one sou; to get her a herring for
dinner or a bit of cold veal; she had a pound cooked to last her
the week – of course, for the days when she dines at home and
alone. She will not spend more than ten sous a day for her
food. It is unreasonable. If I were to say anything about it to
Monsieur le Maréchal, he might quarrel with Monsieur le
Baron and leave him nothing, whereas you, who are so kind
and clever, can manage things—'

'But why do you not apply to my cousin the Baron?' said
Lisbeth.

'Oh, dear Mademoiselle, he has not been here for three
weeks or more; in fact, not since we last had the pleasure of
seeing you! Besides, Madame has forbidden me, under threat of

dismissal, ever to ask the master for money. But as for grief! –
oh, poor lady, she has been very unhappy. It is the first time
that Monsieur has neglected her for so long. Every time
the bell rang she rushed to the window – but for the last five
days she has sat still in her chair. She reads. Whenever she goes
out to see Madame la Comtesse, she says, "Mariette, if Monsieur comes in," says she, "tell him I am at home, and
send the porter to fetch me; he shall be well paid for his
trouble." '

'Poor soul!' said Lisbeth; 'it goes to my heart. I speak of
her to the Baron every day. What can I do? "Yes," says he,
"Bette, you are right; I am a wretch. My wife is an angel, and I
am a monster! I will go to-morrow—" And he stays with
Madame Marneffe. That woman is ruining him, and he worships her; he lives only in her sight. – I do what I can; if I were
not there, and if I had not Mathurine to depend upon, he
would spend twice as much as he does; and as he has hardly
any money in the world, he would have blown his brains out
by this time. And, I tell you, Mariette, Adeline would die of
her husband's death, I am perfectly certain. At any rate, I pull
to make both ends meet, and prevent my cousin from throwing too much money into the fire.'

'Yes, that is what Madame says, poor soul! She knows how
much she owes you,' replied Mariette. 'She said she had
judged you unjustly for many years—'

'Indeed!' said Lisbeth. 'And did she say anything else?'

'No, Mademoiselle. If you wish to please her, talk to her
about Monsieur le Baron; she envies you your happiness in
seeing him every day.'

'Is she alone?'

'I beg pardon, no; the Marshal is with her. He comes every
day, and she always tells him she saw Monsieur in the morning, but that he comes in very late at night.'

'And is there a good dinner to-day?'

Mariette hesitated; she could not meet Lisbeth's eye. The
drawing-room door opened, and Marshal Hulot rushed out in
such haste that he bowed to Lisbeth without looking at her,

and dropped a paper. Lisbeth picked it up and ran after him downstairs, for it was vain to hail a deaf man; but she managed not to overtake the Marshal, and as she came up again she furtively read the following lines written in pencil: –

'MY DEAR BROTHER, – My husband has given me the money for my quarter's expenses; but my daughter Hortense was in such need of it, that I lent her the whole sum, which was scarcely enough to set her straight. Could you lend me a few hundred francs? For I cannot ask Hector for more; if he were to blame me, I could not bear it.'

'My word!' thought Lisbeth, 'she must be in extremities to bend her pride to such a degree!'

Lisbeth went in. She saw tears in Adeline's eyes, and threw her arm round her neck.

'Adeline, my dearest, I know all,' cried Cousin Bette. 'Here, the Marshal dropped this paper – he was in such a state of mind, and running like a greyhound. – Has that dreadful Hector given you no money since––?'

'He gives it me quite regularly,' replied the Baroness, 'but Hortense needed it, and––'

'And you had not enough to pay for dinner to-night,' said Lisbeth, interrupting her. 'Now I understand why Mariette looked so confused when I said something about the soup. You really are childish, Adeline; come, take my savings.'

'Thank you, my kind cousin,' said Adeline, wiping away a tear. 'This little difficulty is only temporary, and I have provided for the future. My expenses henceforth will be no more than two thousand four hundred francs a year, rent inclusive, and I shall have the money. – Above all, Bette, not a word to Hector. Is he well?'

'As strong as the Pont Neuf, and as gay as a lark; he thinks of nothing but his charmer Valérie.'

Madame Hulot looked out at a tall silver-fir in front of the window, and Lisbeth could not see her cousin's eyes to read their expression.

'Did you mention that it was the day when we all dine together here?'

'Yes. But, dear me! Madame Marneffe is giving a grand dinner; she hopes to get Monsieur Coquet to resign, and that is of the first importance. – Now, Adeline, listen to me. You know that I am fiercely proud as to my independence. Your husband, my dear, will certainly bring you to ruin. I fancied I could be of use to you all by living near this woman, but she is a creature of unfathomable depravity, and she will make your husband promise things which will bring you all to disgrace.' Adeline writhed like a person stabbed to the heart. 'My dear Adeline, I am sure of what I say. I feel it is my duty to enlighten you. – Well, let us think of the future. The Marshal is an old man, but he will last a long time yet – he draws good pay; when he dies his widow would have a pension of six thousand francs. On such an income I would undertake to maintain you all. Use your influence over the good man to get him to marry me. It is not for the sake of being Madame la Maréchale; I value such nonsense at no more than I value Madame Marneffe's conscience; but you will all have bread. I see that Hortense must be wanting it, since you give her yours.'

The Marshal now came in; he had made such haste, that he was mopping his forehead with his bandana.

'I have given Mariette two thousand francs,' he whispered to his sister-in-law.

Adeline coloured to the roots of her hair. Two tears hung on the fringes of the still long lashes, and she silently pressed the old man's hand; his beaming face expressed the glee of a favoured lover.

'I intended to spend the money in a present for you, Adeline,' said he. 'Instead of repaying me, you must choose for yourself the thing you would like best.'

He took Lisbeth's hand, which she held out to him, and so bewildered was he by his satisfaction, that he kissed it.

'That looks promising,' said Adeline to Lisbeth, smiling so far as she was able to smile.

The younger Hulot and his wife now came in.

'Is my brother coming to dinner?' asked the Marshal sharply.

Adeline took up a pencil and wrote these words on a scrap of paper –

'I expect him; he promised this morning that he would be here; but if he should not come, it would be because the Marshal kept him. He is overwhelmed with business.'

And she handed him the paper. She had invented this way of conversing with Marshal Hulot, and kept a little collection of paper scraps and a pencil at hand on the work-table.

'I know,' said the Marshal, 'he is worked very hard over the business in Algiers.'

At this moment, Hortense and Wenceslas arrived, and the Baroness, as she saw all her family about her, gave the Marshal a significant glance understood by none but Lisbeth.

Happiness had greatly improved the artist, who was adored by his wife and flattered by the world. His face had become almost round, and his graceful figure did justice to the advantages which blood gives to men of birth. His early fame, his important position, the delusive eulogies that the world sheds on artists as lightly as we say, 'How d'ye do?' or discuss the weather, gave him that high sense of merit which degenerates into sheer fatuity when talent wanes. The Cross of the Legion of Honour was the crowning stamp of the great man he believed himself to be.

After three years of married life, Hortense was to her husband what a dog is to its master; she watched his every movement with a look that seemed a constant inquiry, her eyes were always on him, like those of a miser on his treasure; her admiring abnegation was quite pathetic. In her might be seen her mother's spirit and teaching. Her beauty, as great as ever, was poetically touched by the gentle shadow of concealed melancholy.

On seeing Hortense come in, it struck Lisbeth that some long suppressed complaint was about to break through the thin veil of reticence. Lisbeth, from the first days of the honeymoon, had been sure that this couple had too small an income for so great a passion.

Hortense, as she embraced her mother, exchanged with her a few whispered phrases, heart to heart, of which the mystery was betrayed to Lisbeth by certain shakes of the head.

'Adeline, like me, must work for her living,' thought Cousin Bette. 'She shall be made to tell me what she will do! Those pretty fingers will know at last, like mine, what it is to work because they must.'

At six o'clock the family party went in to dinner. A place was laid for Hector.

'Leave it so,' said the Baroness to Mariette, 'Monsieur sometimes comes in late.'

'Oh, my father will certainly come,' said Victorin to his mother. 'He promised me he would when we parted at the Chamber.'

Lisbeth, like a spider in the middle of its net, gloated over all these countenances. Having known Victorin and Hortense from their birth, their faces were to her like panes of glass, through which she could read their young souls. Now, from certain stolen looks directed by Victorin on his mother, she saw that some disaster was hanging over Adeline which Victorin hesitated to reveal. The famous young lawyer had some covert anxiety. His deep reverence for his mother was evident in the regret with which he gazed at her.

Hortense was evidently absorbed in her own woes; for a fortnight past, as Lisbeth knew, she had been suffering the first uneasiness which want of money brings to honest souls, and to young wives on whom life has hitherto smiled, and who conceal their alarms. Also Lisbeth had immediately guessed that her mother had given her no money. Adeline's delicacy had brought her so low as to use the fallacious excuses that necessity suggests to borrowers.

Hortense's absence of mind, with her brother's and the Baroness's deep dejection, made the dinner a melancholy meal, especially with the added chill of the Marshal's utter deafness. Three persons gave a little life to the scene: Lisbeth, Célestine, and Wenceslas. Hortense's affection had developed the artist's natural liveliness as a Pole, the somewhat swagger-

ing vivacity and noisy high spirits that characterise these
Frenchmen of the North. His frame of mind and the expression of his face showed plainly that he believed in himself, and
that poor Hortense, faithful to her mother's training, kept all
domestic difficulties to herself.

'You must be content, at any rate,' said Lisbeth to her
young cousin, as they rose from table, 'since your mother
has helped you with her money?'

'Mamma!' replied Hortense in astonishment. 'Oh, poor
mamma! It is for me that she would like to make money.
You do not know, Lisbeth, but I have a horrible suspicion that
she works for it in secret.'

They were crossing the large, dark drawing-room where
there were no candles, all following Mariette, who was carrying
the lamp into Adeline's bedroom. At this instant Victorin just
touched Lisbeth and Hortense on the arm. The two women,
understanding the hint, left Wenceslas, Célestine, the Marshal,
and the Baroness to go on together, and remained standing in
a window-bay.

'What is it, Victorin?' said Lisbeth. 'Some disaster caused
by your father, I dare wager.'

'Yes, alas!' replied Victorin. 'A money-lender named Vauvinet has bills of my father's to the amount of sixty thousand
francs, and wants to prosecute. I tried to speak of the matter
to my father at the Chamber, but he would not understand
me; he almost avoided me. Had we better tell my mother?'

'No, no,' said Lisbeth, 'she has too many troubles; it would
be a deathblow; you must spare her. You have no idea how
low she has fallen. But for your uncle, you would have found
no dinner here this evening.'

'Dear Heaven! Victorin, what wretches we are!' said Hortense to her brother. 'We ought to have guessed what Lisbeth
has told us. My dinner is choking me!'

Hortense could say no more; she covered her mouth with
her handkerchief to smother a sob, and melted into tears.

'I told the fellow Vauvinet to call on me to-morrow,'
replied Victorin, 'but will he be satisfied by my guarantee on

a mortgage? I doubt it. Those men insist on ready money to sweat others on usurious terms.'

'Let us sell out of the funds!' said Lisbeth to Hortense.

'What good would that do?' replied Victorin. 'It would bring fifteen or sixteen thousand francs, and we want sixty thousand.'

'Dear cousin!' cried Hortense, embracing Lisbeth with the enthusiasm of guilelessness.

'No, Lisbeth, keep your little fortune,' said Victorin, pressing the old maid's hand. 'I shall see to-morrow what this man would be up to. With my wife's consent, I can at least hinder or postpone the prosecution – for it would really be frightful to see my father's honour impugned. What would the War Minister say? My father's salary, which he pledged for three years, will not be released before the month of December, so we cannot offer that as a guarantee. This Vauvinet has renewed the bills eleven times; so you may imagine what my father must pay in interest. We must close this pit.'

'If only Madame Marneffe would throw him over!' said Hortense bitterly.

'Heaven forbid!' exclaimed Victorin. 'He would take up some one else; and with her, at any rate, the worst outlay is over.'

What a change in children formerly so respectful, and kept so long by their mother in blind worship of their father! They knew him now for what he was.

'But for me,' said Lisbeth, 'your father's ruin would be more complete than it is.'

'Come in to mamma,' said Hortense; 'she is very sharp, and will suspect something; as our kind Lisbeth says, let us keep everything from her – let us be cheerful.'

'Victorin,' said Lisbeth, 'you have no notion of what your father will be brought to by his passion for women. Try to secure some future resource by getting the Marshal to marry me. Say something about it this evening; I will leave early on purpose.'

Victorin went into the bedroom.

'And you, poor little thing!' said Lisbeth in an undertone to Hortense, 'what can you do?'

'Come to dinner with us to-morrow, and we will talk it over,' answered Hortense. 'I do not know which way to turn; you know how hard life is, and you will advise me.'

While the whole family with one consent tried to persuade the Marshal to marry, and while Lisbeth was making her way home to the Rue Vanneau, one of those incidents occurred which, in such women as Madame Marneffe, are a stimulus to vice by compelling them to exert their energy and every resource of depravity. One fact, at any rate, must however be acknowledged: life in Paris is too full for vicious persons to do wrong instinctively and unprovoked; vice is only a weapon of defence against aggressors – that is all.

Madame Marneffe's drawing-room was full of her faithful admirers, and she had just started the whist-tables, when the footman, a pensioned soldier recruited by the Baron, announced –

'Monsieur le Baron Montès de Montejanos.'

Valérie's heart jumped, but she hurried to the door, exclaiming –

'My cousin!' and as she met the Brazilian, she whispered –

'You are my relation – or all is at an end between us! – And so you were not wrecked, Henri?' she went on audibly, as she led him to the fire. 'I heard you were lost, and have mourned for you these three years.'

'How are you, my good fellow?' said Marneffe, offering his hand to the stranger, whose get-up was indeed that of a Brazilian and a millionaire.

Monsieur le Baron Henri Montès de Montejanos, to whom the climate of the equator had given the colour and stature we expect to see in Othello on the stage, had an alarming look of gloom, but it was a merely pictorial illusion; for, sweet and affectionate by nature, he was predestined to be the victim that a strong man often is to a weak woman. The scorn expressed in his countenance, the muscular strength of his stalwart frame, all his physical powers were shown only to his fellow-men; a form of flattery which women appreciate, nay, which so intoxicates them, that every man with his mistress on his arm assumes a matador swagger that provokes a smile. Very well set up, in a closely fitting blue coat with solid gold buttons, in black trousers, spotless patent evening boots, and gloves of a fashionable hue, the only Brazilian touch in the Baron's costume was a large diamond, worth about a hundred thousand francs, which blazed like a star on a handsome blue silk cravat, tucked into a white waistcoat in such a way as to show corners of a fabulously fine shirt front.

His brow, bossy like that of a satyr, a sign of tenacity in his passions, was crowned by thick jet-black hair like a virgin forest, and under it flashed a pair of hazel eyes, so wild looking as to suggest that before his birth his mother must have been scared by a jaguar.

This fine specimen of the Portuguese race in Brazil took his stand with his back to the fire, in an attitude that showed familiarity with Paris manners; holding his hat in one hand, his elbow resting on the velvet-covered shelf, he bent over Madame Marneffe, talking to her in an undertone, and troubling himself very little about the dreadful people who, in his opinion, were so very much in the way.

This fashion of taking the stage, with the Brazilian's attitude and expression, gave, alike to Crevel and to the Baron, an identical shock of curiosity and anxiety. Both were struck by the same impression and the same surmise. And the manœuvre suggested in each by their very genuine passion was so comical in its simultaneous results, that it made everybody smile who was sharp enough to read its meaning. Crevel, a tradesman and shopkeeper to the backbone, though a mayor of Paris, unluckily, was a little slower to move than his rival partner, and this enabled the Baron to read at a glance Crevel's involuntary self-betrayal. This was a fresh arrow to rankle in the amorous old man's heart, and he resolved to have an explanation from Valérie.

'This evening,' said Crevel to himself too, as he sorted his hand, 'I must know where I stand.'

'You have a heart!' cried Marneffe. 'You have just revoked.'

'I beg your pardon,' said Crevel, trying to withdraw his card. – 'This Baron seems to me very much in the way,' he went on, thinking to himself. 'If Valérie carries on with my Baron, well and good – it is a means to my revenge, and I can get rid of him if I choose; but as for this cousin! – He is one Baron too many; I do not mean to be made a fool of. I will know how they are related.'

That evening, by one of those strokes of luck which come to pretty women, Valérie was charmingly dressed. Her white bosom gleamed under a lace tucker of rusty white, which showed off the satin texture of her beautiful shoulders – for Parisian women, Heaven knows how, have some way of preserving their fine flesh and remaining slender. She wore a black velvet gown that looked as if it might at any moment slip off her shoulders, and her hair was dressed with lace and drooping flowers. Her arms, not fat but dimpled, were graced by deep ruffles to her sleeves. She was like a luscious fruit coquettishly served in a handsome dish, and making the knife-blade long to be cutting it.

'Valérie,' the Brazilian was saying in her ear, 'I have come back faithful to you. My uncle is dead; I am twice as rich as I was when I went away. I mean to live and die in Paris, for you and with you.'

'Lower, Henri, I implore you—'

'Pooh! I mean to speak to you this evening, even if I should have to pitch all these creatures out of window, especially as I have lost two days in looking for you. I shall stay till the last. – I can, I suppose?'

Valérie smiled at her adopted cousin, and said –

'Remember that you are the son of my mother's sister, who married your father during Junot's campaign in Portugal.'

'What, I, Montès de Montejanos, great grandson of a conqueror of Brazil! Tell a lie?'

'Hush, lower, or we shall never meet again.'

'Pray, why?'

'Marneffe, like all dying wretches, who always take up some last whim, has a revived passion for me—'

'That cur?' said the Brazilian, who knew his Marneffe; 'I will settle him!'

'What violence!'

'And where did you get all this splendour?' the Brazilian went on, just struck by the magnificence of the apartment.

She began to laugh.

'Henri! what bad taste!' said she.

She had felt two burning flashes of jealousy which had moved her so far as to make her look at the two souls in purgatory. Crevel, playing against Baron Hulot and Monsieur Coquet, had Marneffe for his partner. The game was even, because Crevel and the Baron were equally absent-minded, and made blunder after blunder. Thus, in one instant, the old men both confessed the passion which Valérie had persuaded them to keep secret for the past three years; but she too had failed to hide the joy in her eyes at seeing the man who had first taught her heart to beat, the object of her first love. The rights of such happy mortals survive as long as the woman lives over whom they have acquired them.

With these three passions at her side – one supported by the insolence of wealth, the second by the claims of possession, and the third by youth, strength, fortune, and priority – Madame Marneffe preserved her coolness and presence of mind, like General Bonaparte when, at the siege of Mantua, he had to fight two armies, and at the same time maintain the blockade.

Jealousy, distorting Hulot's face, made him look as terrible as the late Marshal Montcornet leading a cavalry charge against a Russian square. Being such a handsome man, he had never known any ground for jealousy, any more than Murat knew what it was to be afraid. He had always felt sure that he should triumph. His rebuff by Josépha, the first he had ever met, he ascribed to her love of money; 'he was conquered by millions, and not by a changeling,' he would say when speaking of the Duc d'Hérouville. And now, in one instant, the poison and delirium that the mad passion sheds in a flood had rushed to his heart. He kept turning from the whist-table towards the

fireplace with an action *à la* Mirabeau; and as he laid down his
cards to cast a challenging glance at the Brazilian and Valérie,
the rest of the company felt the sort of alarm mingled with
curiosity that is caused by evident violence ready to break out
at any moment. The sham cousin stared at Hulot as he might
have looked at some big China mandarin.

This state of things could not last; it was bound to end in
some tremendous outbreak. Marneffe was as much afraid of
Hulot as Crevel was of Marneffe, for he was anxious not to die
a mere clerk. Men marked for death believe in life as galley-
slaves believe in liberty; this man was bent on being a first-class
clerk at any cost. Thoroughly frightened by the pantomime of
the Baron and Crevel, he rose, said a few words in his wife's
ear, and then, to the surprise of all, Valérie went into the
adjoining bedroom with the Brazilian and her husband.

'Did Madame Marneffe ever speak to you of this cousin of
hers?' said Crevel to Hulot.

'Never!' replied the Baron, getting up. 'That is enough for
this evening,' said he. 'I have lost two louis – there they are.'

He threw the two gold pieces on to the table, and seated
himself on the sofa with a look which everybody else took as a
hint to go. Monsieur and Madame Coquet, after exchanging
a few words, left the room, and Claude Vignon, in despair,
followed their example. These two departures were a hint to
less intelligent persons, who now found that they were not
wanted. The Baron and Crevel were left together, and spoke
never a word. Hulot at last, ignoring Crevel, went on tiptoe to
listen at the bedroom door; but he bounded back with a
prodigious jump, for Marneffe opened the door and appeared
with a calm face, astonished to find only the two men.

'And the tea?' said he.

'Where is Valérie?' replied the Baron in a rage.

'My wife,' said Marneffe. 'She is gone upstairs to speak to
Mademoiselle your cousin. She will come down directly.'

'And why has she deserted us for that stupid creature?'

'Well,' said Marneffe, 'Mademoiselle Lisbeth came back
from dining with the Baroness with an attack of indigestion,

and Mathurine asked Valérie for some tea for her, so my wife
went up to see what was the matter.'

'And *her* cousin?'

'He is gone.'

'Do you really believe that?' said the Baron.

'I have seen him to his carriage,' replied Marneffe, with a
hideous smirk.

The wheels of a departing carriage were audible in the street.
The Baron, counting Marneffe for nothing, went upstairs to
Lisbeth. An idea flashed through him such as the heart sends
to the brain when it is on fire with jealousy. Marneffe's baseness was so well known to him, that he could imagine the most
degrading connivance between husband and wife.

'What has become of all the ladies and gentlemen?' said
Marneffe, finding himself alone with Crevel.

'When the sun goes to bed, the cocks and hens follow suit,'
said Crevel. 'Madame Marneffe disappeared, and her adorers
departed. Will you play a game of piquet?' added Crevel, who
meant to remain.

He too believed that the Brazilian was in the house.

Monsieur Marneffe agreed. The Mayor was a match for the
Baron. Simply by playing cards with the husband he could stay
on indefinitely; and Marneffe, since the suppression of the
public tables, was quite satisfied with the more limited opportunities of private play.

Baron Hulot went quickly up to Lisbeth's apartment, but the
door was locked, and the usual inquiries through the door took
up time enough to enable the two light-handed and cunning
women to arrange the scene of an attack of indigestion with the
accessories of tea. Lisbeth was in such pain that Valérie was
very much alarmed, and consequently hardly paid any heed to
the Baron's furious entrance. Indisposition is one of the
screens most often placed by women to ward off a quarrel.
Hulot peeped about, here and there, but could see no spot in
Cousin Bette's room where a Brazilian might lie hidden.

'Your indigestion does honour to my wife's dinner, Lisbeth,' said he, scrutinising her, for Lisbeth was perfectly well,

trying to imitate the hiccough of spasmodic indigestion as she drank her tea.

'How lucky it is that dear Bette should be living under my roof!' said Madame Marneffe. 'But for me, the poor thing would have died.'

'You look as if you only half believed it,' added Lisbeth, turning to the Baron, 'and that would be a shame—'

'Why?' asked the Baron. 'Do you know the purpose of my visit?'

And he leered at the door of a dressing-closet from which the key had been withdrawn.

'Are you talking Greek?' said Madame Marneffe, with an appealing look of misprized tenderness and devotedness.

'But it is all through you, my dear cousin; yes, it is your doing that I am in such a state,' said Lisbeth vehemently.

This speech diverted the Baron's attention; he looked at the old maid with the greatest astonishment.

'You know I am devoted to you,' said Lisbeth. 'I am here, that says everything. I am wearing out the last shreds of my strength in watching over your interests, since they are one with our dear Valérie's. Her house costs one-tenth of what any other does that is kept on the same scale. But for me, Cousin, instead of two thousand francs a month, you would be obliged to spend three or four thousand.'

'I know all that,' replied the Baron out of patience; 'you are our protectress in many ways,' he added, turning to Madame Marneffe and putting his arm round her neck. – 'Is not she, my pretty sweet?'

'On my honour,' exclaimed Valérie, 'I believe you are gone mad!'

'Well, you cannot doubt my attachment,' said Lisbeth. 'But I am also very fond of my cousin Adeline, and I found her in tears. She has not seen you for a month. Now that is really too bad; you leave my poor Adeline without a sou. Your daughter Hortense almost died of it when she was told that it is thanks to your brother that we had any dinner at all. There was not even bread in your house this day.

'Adeline is heroically resolved to keep her sufferings to
herself. She said to me, "I will do as you have done!" The
speech went to my heart; and after dinner, as I thought of
what my cousin had been in 1811, and of what she is in 1841 –
thirty years after – I had a violent indigestion. – I fancied I
should get over it; but when I got home, I thought I was
dying—'

'You see, Valérie, to what my adoration of you has brought
me! To crime – domestic crime!'

'Oh! I was wise never to marry!' cried Lisbeth, with savage
joy. 'You are a kind, good man; Adeline is a perfect angel; –
and this is the reward of her blind devotion.'

'An elderly angel!' said Madame Marneffe softly, as she
looked half tenderly, half mockingly, at her Hector, who was
gazing at her as an examining judge gazes at the accused.

'My poor wife!' said Hulot. 'For more than nine months I
have given her no money, though I find it for you, Valérie; but
at what a cost! No one else will ever love you so, and what
torments you inflict on me in return!'

'Torments?' she echoed. 'Then what do you call happiness?'

'I do not yet know on what terms you have been with this
so-called cousin whom you never mentioned to me,' said the
Baron, paying no heed to Valérie's interjection. 'But when he
came in I felt as if a penknife had been stuck into my heart.
Blinded I may be, but I am not blind. I could read his eyes,
and yours. In short, from under that ape's eyelids there flashed
sparks that he flung at you – and your eyes! – Oh! you have
never looked at me so, never! As to this mystery, Valérie, it
shall be cleared up. You are the only woman who ever made
me know the meaning of jealousy, so you need not be surprised by what I say. – But another mystery which has rent its
cloud, and it seems to me infamous—'

'Go on, go on,' said Valérie.

'It is that Crevel, that square lump of flesh and stupidity, is in
love with you, and that you accept his attentions with so good a
grace that the idiot flaunts his passion before everybody.'

'Only three! Can you discover no more?' asked Madame Marneffe.

'There may be more!' retorted the Baron.

'If Monsieur Crevel is in love with me, he is in his rights as a man after all; if I favoured his passion, that would indeed be the act of a coquette, or of a woman who would leave much to be desired on your part. – Well, love me as you find me, or let me alone. If you restore me to freedom, neither you nor Monsieur Crevel will ever enter my doors again. But I will take up with my cousin, just to keep my hand in, in those charming habits you suppose me to indulge. – Good-bye, Monsieur le Baron Hulot.'

She rose, but the Baron took her by the arm and made her sit down again. The old man could not do without Valérie. She had become more imperatively indispensable to him than the necessaries of life; he preferred remaining in uncertainty to having any proof of Valérie's infidelity.

'My dearest Valérie,' said he, 'do you not see how miserable I am? I only ask you to justify yourself. Give me sufficient reasons—'

'Well, go downstairs and wait for me; for I suppose you do not wish to look on at the various ceremonies required by your cousin's state.'

Hulot slowly turned away.

'You old profligate,' cried Lisbeth, 'you have not even asked me how your children are? What are you going to do for Adeline? I, at any rate, will take her my savings to-morrow.'

'You owe your wife white bread to eat at least,' said Madame Marneffe, smiling.

The Baron, without taking offence at Lisbeth's tone, as despotic as Josépha's, got out of the room, only too glad to escape so importunate a question.

The door bolted once more, the Brazilian came out of the dressing-closet, where he had been waiting, and he appeared with his eyes full of tears, in a really pitiable condition. Montès had heard everything.

'Henri, you must have ceased to love me, I know it!' said Madame Marneffe, hiding her face in her handkerchief and bursting into tears.

It was the outcry of real affection. The cry of a woman's despair is so convincing that it wins the forgiveness that lurks at the bottom of every lover's heart – when she is young and pretty, and wears a gown so low that she could slip out at the top and stand in the garb of Eve.

'But why, if you love me, do you not leave everything for my sake?' asked the Brazilian.

This South American born, being logical, as men are who have lived the life of nature, at once resumed the conversation at the point where it had been broken off, putting his arm round Valérie's waist.

'Why?' she repeated, gazing up at Henri, whom she subjugated at once by a look charged with passion, 'why, my dear boy, I am married; we are in Paris, not in the savannah, the pampas, the backwoods of America. – My dear Henri, my first and only love, listen to me. That husband of mine, a second clerk in the War Office, is bent on being a head-clerk and officer of the Legion of Honour; can I help his being ambitious? Now for the very reason that made him leave us our liberty – nearly four years ago, do you remember, you bad boy? – he now abandons me to Monsieur Hulot. I cannot get rid of that dreadful official, who snorts like a grampus, who has fins in his nostrils, who is sixty-three years old, and who has grown ten years older by dint of trying to be young; who is so odious to me that the very day when Marneffe is promoted, and gets his Cross of the Legion of Honour—'

'How much more will your husband get then?'

'A thousand crowns.'

'I will pay him as much in an annuity,' said Baron Montès. 'We will leave Paris and go—'

'Where?' said Valérie, with one of the pretty sneers by which a woman makes fun of a man she is sure of. 'Paris is the only place where we could live happy. I care too much for your love to risk seeing it die out in a *tête-à-tête* in the wilderness.

Listen, Henri, you are the only man I care for in the whole world. Write that down clearly in your tiger's brain.'

For women, when they have made a sheep of a man, always tell him that he is a lion with a will of iron.

'Now, attend to me. Monsieur Marneffe has not five years to live; he is rotten to the marrow of his bones. He spends seven months of the twelve in swallowing drugs and decoctions; he lives wrapped in flannel; in short, as the doctor says, he lives under the scythe, and may be cut off at any moment. An illness that would not harm another man would be fatal to him; his blood is corrupt, his life undermined at the root. For five years I have never allowed him to kiss me – he is poisonous! Some day, and the day is not far off, I shall be a widow. Well, then, I – who have already had an offer from a man with sixty thousand francs a year, I who am as completely mistress of that man as I am of this lump of sugar – I swear to you that if you were as poor as Hulot and as foul as Marneffe, if you beat me even, still you are the only man I will have for a husband, the only man I love, or whose name I will ever bear. And I am ready to give any pledge of my love that you may require.'

'Well, then, to-night—'

'But you, son of the South, my splendid jaguar, come expressly for me from the virgin forest of Brazil,' said she, taking his hand and kissing and fondling it, 'have some consideration for the poor creature you mean to make your wife. – Shall I be your wife, Henri?'

'Yes,' said the Brazilian, overpowered by this unbridled volubility of passion. And he knelt at her feet.

'Well, then, Henri,' said Valérie, taking his two hands and looking straight into his eyes, 'swear to me now, in the presence of Lisbeth, my best and only friend, my sister – that you will make me your wife at the end of my year's widowhood.'

'I swear it.'

'That is not enough. Swear by your mother's ashes and eternal salvation, swear by the Virgin Mary and by all your hopes as a Catholic!'

Valérie knew that the Brazilian would keep that oath even if she should have fallen into the foulest social slough.

The Baron solemnly swore it, his nose almost touching Valérie's white bosom, and his eyes spellbound. He was drunk, drunk as a man is when he sees the woman he loves once more, after a sea voyage of a hundred and twenty days.

'Good. Now be quite easy. And in Madame Marneffe respect the future Baroness de Montejanos. You are not to spend a sou upon me; I forbid it. – Stay here in the outer room; sleep on the sofa. I myself will come and tell you when you may move. – We will breakfast together to-morrow morning, and you can be leaving at about one o'clock as if you had come to call at noon. There is nothing to fear; the gatekeepers love me as much as if they were my father and mother. – Now I must go down and make tea.'

She beckoned Lisbeth, who followed her out on to the landing. There Valérie whispered in the old maid's ear –

'My darkie has come back too soon. I shall die if I cannot avenge you on Hortense!'

'Make your mind easy, my pretty little devil!' said Lisbeth, kissing her forehead. 'Love and Revenge on the same track will never lose the game. Hortense expects me to-morrow; she is in beggary. For a thousand francs you may have a thousand kisses from Wenceslas.'

On leaving Valérie, Hulot had gone down to the porter's lodge and made a sudden invasion there.

'Madame Olivier?'

On hearing the imperious tone of this address, and seeing the action by which the Baron emphasised it, Madame Olivier came out into the courtyard as far as the Baron led her.

'You know that if any one can help your son to a connection by and by, it is I; it is owing to me that he is already third clerk in a notary's office, and is finishing his studies.'

'Yes, Monsieur le Baron; and indeed, sir, you may depend on our gratitude. Not a day passes that I do not pray to God for Monsieur le Baron's happiness.'

'Not so many words, my good woman,' said Hulot, 'but deeds—'

'What can I do, sir?' asked Madame Olivier.

'A man came here to-night in a carriage. Do you know him?'

Madame Olivier had recognised Montès well enough. How could she have forgotten him? In the Rue du Doyenné the Brazilian had always slipped a five-franc piece into her hand as he went out in the morning, rather too early. If the Baron had applied to Monsieur Olivier, he would perhaps have learned all he wanted to know. But Olivier was in bed. In the lower orders the woman is not merely the superior of the man – she almost always has the upper hand. Madame Olivier had long since made up her mind as to which side to take in case of a collision between her two benefactors; she regarded Madame Marneffe as the stronger power.

'Do I know him?' she repeated. 'No, indeed, no. I never saw him before!'

'What! Did Madame Marneffe's cousin never go to see her when she was living in the Rue du Doyenné?'

'Oh! Was it her cousin?' cried Madame Olivier. 'I dare say he did come, but I did not know him again. Next time, sir, I will look at him—'

'He will be coming out,' said Hulot, hastily interrupting Madame Olivier.

'He has left,' said Madame Olivier, understanding the situation. 'The carriage is gone.'

'Did you see him go?'

'As plainly as I see you. He told his servant to drive to the Embassy.'

This audacious statement wrung a sigh of relief from the Baron; he took Madame Olivier's hand and squeezed it.

'Thank you, my good Madame Olivier. But that is not all. – Monsieur Crevel?'

'Monsieur Crevel? What can you mean, sir? I do not understand,' said Madame Olivier.

'Listen to me. He is Madame Marneffe's lover—'

'Impossible, Monsieur le Baron; impossible,' said she, clasping her hands.

'He is Madame Marneffe's lover,' the Baron repeated very positively. 'How do they manage it? I don't know; but I mean to know, and you are to find out. If you can put me on the tracks of this intrigue, your son is a notary.'

'Don't you fret yourself so, Monsieur le Baron,' said Madame Olivier. 'Madame cares for you, and for no one but you; her maid knows that for true, and we say, between her and me, that you are the luckiest man in this world – for you know what Madame is. – Just perfection!

'She gets up at ten every morning; then she breakfasts. Well and good. After that she takes an hour or so to dress; that carries her on till two; then she goes for a walk in the Tuileries in the sight of all men, and she is always in by four to be ready for you. She lives like clockwork. She keeps no secrets from her maid, and Reine keeps nothing from me, you may be sure. Reine can't if she would – along of my son, for she is very sweet upon him. So, you see, if Madame had any intimacy with Monsieur Crevel, we should be bound to know it.'

The Baron went upstairs again with a beaming countenance, convinced that he was the only man in the world to that shameless slut, as treacherous, but as lovely and as engaging, as a siren.

Crevel and Marneffe had begun a second rubber at piquet. Crevel was losing, as a man must who is not giving his thoughts to his game. Marneffe, who knew the cause of the Mayor's absence of mind, took unscrupulous advantage of it; he looked at the cards in reserve, and discarded accordingly; thus, knowing his adversary's hand, he played to beat him. The stake being a franc a point, he had already robbed the Mayor of thirty francs when Hulot came in.

'Hey day!' said he, amazed to find no company. 'Are you alone? Where is everybody gone?'

'Your pleasant temper put them all to flight,' said Crevel.

'No, it was my wife's cousin,' replied Marneffe. 'The ladies and gentlemen supposed that Valérie and Henri might have something to say to each other after three years' separation, and they very discreetly retired. – If I had been in the room, I would have kept them; but then, as it happens, it would have been a mistake, for Lisbeth, who always comes down to make tea at half-past ten, was taken ill, and that upset everything—'

'Then is Lisbeth really unwell?' asked Crevel in a fury.

'So I was told,' replied Marneffe, with the heartless indifference of a man to whom women have ceased to exist.

The Mayor looked at the clock; and, calculating the time, the Baron seemed to have spent forty minutes in Lisbeth's rooms. Hector's jubilant expression seriously incriminated Valérie, Lisbeth, and himself.

'I have just seen her; she is in great pain, poor soul!' said the Baron.

'Then the sufferings of others must afford you much joy, my friend,' retorted Crevel with acrimony, 'for you have come down with a face that is positively beaming. Is Lisbeth likely to die? For your daughter, they say, is her heiress. You are not like the same man. You left this room looking like the Moor of Venice, and you come back with the air of Saint-Preux! – I wish I could see Madame Marneffe's face at this minute—'

'And pray, what do you mean by that?' said Marneffe to Crevel, packing his cards and laying them down in front of him.

A light kindled in the eyes of this man, decrepit at the age of forty-seven; a faint colour flushed his flaccid cold cheeks, his ill-furnished mouth was half open, and on his blackened lips a sort of foam gathered, thick, and as white as chalk. This fury in such a helpless wretch, whose life hung on a thread, and who in a duel would risk nothing while Crevel had everything to lose, frightened the Mayor.

'I said,' repeated Crevel, 'that I should like to see Madame Marneffe's face. And with all the more reason since yours, at this moment, is most unpleasant. On my honour, you are horribly ugly, my dear Marneffe—'

'Do you know that you are very uncivil?'

'A man who has won thirty francs of me in forty-five minutes cannot look handsome in my eyes.'

'Ah, if you had but seen me seventeen years ago!' replied the clerk.

'You were so good-looking?' asked Crevel.

'That was my ruin; now, if I had been like you – I might be a mayor and a peer.'

'Yes,' said Crevel, with a smile, 'you have been too much in the wars; and of the two forms of metal that may be earned by worshipping the god of trade, you have taken the worse – the dross!'[*] And Crevel roared with laughter. Though Marneffe could take offence if his honour were in peril, he always took these rough pleasantries in good part; they were the small coin of conversation between him and Crevel.

'The daughters of Eve cost me dear, no doubt; but, by the powers! "Short and sweet" is my motto.'

'"Long and happy" is more to my mind,' returned Crevel.

Madame Marneffe now came in; she saw that her husband was at cards with Crevel, and only the Baron in the room besides; a mere glance at the municipal dignitary showed her the frame of mind he was in, and her line of conduct was at once decided on.

'Marneffe, my dear boy,' said she, leaning on her husband's shoulder, and passing her pretty fingers through his dingy grey hair, but without succeeding in covering his bald head with it, 'it is very late for you; you ought to be in bed. To-morrow, you know, you must dose yourself by the doctor's orders. Reine will give you your herb tea at seven. If you wish to live, give up your game.'

'We will play it out up to five points,' said Marneffe to Crevel.

'Very good – I have scored two,' replied the Mayor.

'How long will it take you?'

'Ten minutes,' said Marneffe.

'It is eleven o'clock,' replied Valérie. 'Really, Monsieur Crevel, one might fancy you meant to kill my husband. Make haste, at any rate.'

* This dialogue is garnished with puns for which it is difficult to find any English equivalent.

This double-barrelled speech made Crevel and Hulot smile, and even Marneffe himself. Valérie sat down to talk to Hector.

'You must leave, my dearest,' said she in Hulot's ear. 'Walk up and down the Rue Vanneau, and come in again when you see Crevel go out.'

'I would rather leave this room and go into your room through the dressing-room door. You could tell Reine to let me in.'

'Reine is upstairs attending to Lisbeth.'

'Well, suppose then I go up to Lisbeth's rooms?'

Danger hemmed in Valérie on every side; she foresaw a discussion with Crevel, and could not allow Hulot to be in her room, where he could hear all that went on. – And the Brazilian was upstairs with Lisbeth.

'Really, you men, when you have a notion in your head, you would burn a house down to get into it!' exclaimed she. 'Lisbeth is not in a fit state to admit you. – Are you afraid of catching cold in the street? Be off there – or good-night.'

'Good evening, gentlemen,' said the Baron to the other two.

Hulot, when piqued in his old man's vanity, was bent on proving that he could play the young man by waiting for the happy hour in the open air, and he went away.

Marneffe bid his wife good-night, taking her hands with a semblance of devotion. Valérie pressed her husband's hand with a significant glance, conveying –

'Get rid of Crevel.'

'Good-night, Crevel,' said Marneffe. 'I hope you will not stay long with Valérie. Yes! I am jealous – a little late in the day, but it has me hard and fast. I shall come back to see if you are gone.'

'We have a little business to discuss, but I shall not stay long,' said Crevel.

'Speak low. – What is it?' said Valérie, raising her voice, and looking at him with a mingled expression of haughtiness and scorn.

Crevel, as he met this arrogant stare, though he was doing Valérie important services, and had hoped to plume himself on the fact, was at once reduced to submission.

'That Brazilian—' he began, but, overpowered by Valérie's fixed look of contempt, he broke off.

'What of him?' said she.

'That cousin—'

'Is no cousin of mine,' said she. 'He is my cousin to the world and to Monsieur Marneffe. And if he were my lover, it would be no concern of yours. A tradesman who pays a woman to be revenged on another man, is, in my opinion, beneath the man who pays her for love of her. You did not care for me; all you saw in me was Monsieur Hulot's mistress. You bought me as a man buys a pistol to kill his adversary. I wanted bread – I accepted the bargain.'

'But you have not carried it out,' said Crevel, the tradesman once more.

'You want Baron Hulot to be told that you have robbed him of his mistress, to pay him out for having robbed you of Josépha? Nothing can more clearly prove your baseness. You say you love a woman, you treat her like a duchess, and then you want to degrade her? Well, my good fellow, and you are right. This woman is no match for Josépha. That young person has the courage of her disgrace, while I – I am a hypocrite, and deserve to be publicly whipped. – Alas! Josépha is protected by her cleverness and her wealth. I have nothing to shelter me but my reputation; I am still the worthy and blameless wife of a plain citizen; if you create a scandal, what is to become of me? If I were rich, then indeed; but my income is fifteen thousand francs a year at most, I suppose.'

'Much more than that,' said Crevel. 'I have doubled your savings in these last two months by investing in *Orleans*.'

'Well, a position in Paris begins with fifty thousand. And you certainly will not make up to me for the position I should surrender. – What was my aim? I want to see Marneffe a first-class clerk; he will then draw a salary of six thousand francs.

He has been twenty-seven years in his office; within three years I shall have a right to a pension of fifteen hundred francs when he dies. You, to whom I have been entirely kind, to whom I have given your fill of happiness – you cannot wait! – And that is what men call love!' she exclaimed.

'Though I began with an ulterior purpose,' said Crevel, 'I have become your poodle. You trample on my heart, you crush me, you stultify me, and I love you as I never loved in my life. Valérie, I love you as much as I love my Célestine. I am capable of anything for your sake. – Listen, instead of coming twice a week to the Rue du Dauphin, come three times.'

'Is that all! You are quite young again, my dear boy!'

'Only let me pack off Hulot, humiliate him, rid you of him,' said Crevel, not heeding her impertinence! 'Have nothing to say to the Brazilian, be mine alone; you shall not repent of it. To begin with, I will give you eight thousand francs a year, secured by bond, but only as an annuity; I will not give you the capital till the end of five years' constancy—'

'Always a bargain! A tradesman can never learn to give. You want to stop for refreshments on the road of love – in the form of Government bonds! Bah! Shopman, pomatum seller! you put a price on everything! – Hector told me that the Duc d'Hérouville gave Josépha a bond for thirty thousand francs a year in a packet of sugared almonds! And I am worth six of Josépha.

'Oh! to be loved!' she went on, twisting her ringlets round her fingers, and looking at herself in the glass. 'Henri loves me. He would smash you like a fly if I winked at him! Hulot loves me; he leaves his wife in beggary! As for you, go, my good man, be the worthy father of a family. You have three hundred thousand francs over and above your fortune, only to amuse yourself, a hoard, in fact, and you think of nothing but increasing it—'

'For you, Valérie, since I offer you half,' said he, falling on his knees.

'What, still here!' cried Marneffe, hideous in his dressing-gown. 'What are you about?'

'He is begging my pardon, my dear, for an insulting proposal he has dared to make me. Unable to obtain my consent, my gentleman proposed to pay me—'

Crevel only longed to vanish into the cellar, through a trap, as is done on the stage.

'Get up, Crevel,' said Marneffe, laughing, 'you are ridiculous. I can see by Valérie's manner that my honour is in no danger.'

'Go to bed and sleep in peace,' said Madame Marneffe.

'Isn't she clever?' thought Crevel. 'She has saved me. She is adorable!'

As Marneffe disappeared, the Mayor took Valérie's hands and kissed them, leaving on them the traces of tears.

'It shall all stand in your name,' he said.

'That is true love,' she whispered in his ear. 'Well, love for love. Hulot is below, in the street. The poor old thing is waiting to return when I place a candle in one of the windows of my bedroom. I give you leave to tell him that you are the man I love; he will refuse to believe you; take him to the Rue du Dauphin, give him every proof, crush him; I allow it – I order it! I am tired of that old seal; he bores me to death. Keep your man all night in the Rue du Dauphin, grill him over a slow fire, be revenged for the loss of Josépha. Hulot may die of it perhaps, but we shall save his wife and children from utter ruin. Madame Hulot is working for her bread—'

'Oh! poor woman! On my word, it is quite shocking!' exclaimed Crevel, his natural feeling coming to the top.

'If you love me, Célestin,' said she in Crevel's ear, which she touched with her lips, 'keep him there, or I am done for. Marneffe is suspicious; Hector has a key of the outer gate, and will certainly come back.'

Crevel clasped Madame Marneffe to his heart, and went away in the seventh heaven of delight. Valérie fondly escorted him to the landing, and then followed him, like a woman magnetised, down the stairs to the very bottom.

'My Valérie, go back, do not compromise yourself before the porters. – Go back; my life, my treasure, all is yours. – Go in, my duchess!'

'Madame Olivier,' Valérie called gently when the gate was closed.

'Why, Madame! You here?' said the woman in bewilderment.

'Bolt the gates at top and bottom, and let no one in.'

'Very good, Madame.'

Having barred the gate, Madame Olivier told of the bribe that the War Office chief had tried to offer her.

'You behaved like an angel, my dear Olivier; we will talk of that to-morrow.'

Valérie flew like an arrow to the third floor, tapped three times at Lisbeth's door, and then went down to her room, where she gave her instructions to Mademoiselle Reine, for a woman must make the most of the opportunity when a Montès arrives from Brazil.

'By Heaven! only a woman of the world is capable of such love,' said Crevel to himself. 'How she came down those stairs, lighting them up with her eyes, following me! Never did Josépha – Josépha! she is cag-mag!' cried the ex-bagman. 'What have I said? *Cag-mag* – why, I might let the word slip out at the Tuileries! I can never do any good unless Valérie educates me – and I was so bent on being a gentleman. – What a woman she is! She upsets me like a fit of the colic when she looks at me coldly. What grace! What wit! Never did Josépha move me so. And what perfection when you come to know her! – Ha, there is my man!'

He perceived in the gloom of the Rue de Babylone the tall, somewhat stooping figure of Hulot, stealing along close to a hoarding, and he went straight up to him.

'Good morning, Baron, for it is past midnight, my dear fellow. What the devil are you doing here? You are airing yourself under a pleasant drizzle. That is not wholesome at our time of life. Will you let me give you a little piece of advice? Let each of us go home; for, between you and me, you will not see the candle in the window.'

The last words made the Baron suddenly aware that he was sixty-three, and that his cloak was wet.

'Who on earth told you—?' he began.

'Valérie, of course, *our* Valérie, who means henceforth to be *my* Valérie. We are even now, Baron; we will play off the tie when you please. You have nothing to complain of; you know, I always stipulated for the right of taking my revenge; it took you three months to rob me of Josépha; I took Valérie from you in— We will say no more about that. Now I mean to have her all to myself. But we can be very good friends, all the same.'

'Crevel, no jesting,' said Hulot, in a voice choked by rage. 'It is a matter of life and death.'

'Bless me, is that how you take it! – Baron, do you not remember what you said to me the day of Hortense's marriage: "Can two old gaffers like us quarrel over a petticoat? It is too low, too common." We are *Régence*, we agreed, Pompadour, eighteenth century, quite the Maréchal Richelieu, Louis xv., nay, and I may say, *Liaisons dangereuses*!'

Crevel might have gone on with his string of literary allusions; the Baron heard him as a deaf man listens when he is but half deaf. But, seeing in the gaslight the ghastly pallor of his face, the triumphant Mayor stopped short. This was, indeed, a thunderbolt after Madame Olivier's asseverations and Valérie's parting glance.

'Good God! And there are so many other women in Paris!' he said at last.

'That is what I said to you when you took Josépha,' said Crevel.

'Look here, Crevel, it is impossible. Give me some proof. – Have you a key, as I have, to let yourself in?'

And having reached the house, the Baron put the key into the lock; but the gate was immovable; he tried in vain to open it.

'Do not make a noise in the streets at night,' said Crevel coolly. 'I tell you, Baron, I have far better proof than you can show.'

'Proofs! give me proof!' cried the Baron, almost crazy with exasperation.

'Come, and you shall have them,' said Crevel.

And in obedience to Valérie's instructions, he led the Baron away towards the quay, down the Rue Hillerin-Bertin. The unhappy Baron walked on, as a merchant walks on the day before he stops payment; he was lost in conjectures as to the reasons of the depravity buried in the depths of Valérie's heart, and still believed himself the victim of some practical joke. As they crossed the Pont Royal, life seemed to him so blank, so utterly a void, and so out of joint from his financial difficulties, that he was within an ace of yielding to the evil prompting that bid him fling Crevel into the river and throw himself in after.

On reaching the Rue du Dauphin, which had not yet been widened, Crevel stopped before a door in a wall. It opened into a long corridor paved with black-and-white marble, and serving as an entrance-hall, at the end of which there was a flight of stairs and a doorkeeper's lodge, lighted from an inner courtyard, as is often the case in Paris. This courtyard, which was shared with another house, was oddly divided into two unequal portions. Crevel's little house, for he owned it, had additional rooms with a glass skylight, built out on to the adjoining plot, under condition that it should have no story added above the ground floor, so that the structure was entirely hidden by the lodge and the projecting mass of the staircase.

This back building had long served as a store-room, back-shop, and kitchen to one of the shops facing the street. Crevel had cut off these three rooms from the rest of the ground floor, and Grindot had transformed them into an inexpensive private residence. There were two ways in – from the front, through the shop of a furniture-dealer, to whom Crevel let it at a low price, and only from month to month, so as to be able to get rid of him in case of his telling tales, and also through a door in the wall of the passage, so ingeniously hidden as to be almost invisible. The little apartment, comprising a dining-room, drawing-room, and bedroom, all lighted from above, and standing partly on Crevel's ground and partly on his neighbour's, was very difficult to find. With the exception of the second-hand furniture-dealer, the tenants knew nothing of the existence of this little paradise.

The doorkeeper, paid to keep Crevel's secrets, was a capital cook. So Monsieur le Maire could go in and out of his inexpensive retreat at any hour of the night without any fear of being spied upon. By day, a lady, dressed as Paris women dress to go shopping, and having a key, ran no risk in coming to Crevel's lodgings; she would stop to look at the cheapened goods, ask the price, go into the shop, and come out again, without exciting the smallest suspicion if any one should happen to meet her.

As soon as Crevel had lighted the candles in the sitting-room, the Baron was surprised at the elegance and refinement it displayed. The perfumer had given the architect a free hand, and Grindot had done himself credit by fittings in the Pompadour style, which had in fact cost sixty thousand francs.

'What I want,' said Crevel to Grindot, 'is that a duchess, if I brought one there, should be surprised at it.'

He wanted to have a perfect Parisian Eden for his Eve, his 'real lady,' his Valérie, his duchess.

'There are two beds,' said Crevel to Hulot, showing him a sofa that could be made wide enough by pulling out a drawer. 'This is one, the other is in the bedroom. We can both spend the night here.'

'Proof!' was all the Baron could say.

Crevel took a flat candlestick and led Hulot into the adjoining room, where he saw, on a sofa, a superb dressing-gown belonging to Valérie, which he had seen her wear in the Rue Vanneau, to display it before wearing it in Crevel's little apartment. The Mayor pressed the spring of a little writing-table of inlaid work, known as a *bonheur-du-jour*, and took out of it a letter that he handed to the Baron.

'Read that,' said he.

The Councillor read these words written in pencil: –

'I have waited in vain, you old wretch! A woman of my quality does not expect to be kept waiting by a retired perfumer. There was no dinner ordered – no cigarettes. I will make you pay for this!'

'Well, is that her writing?'

'Good God!' gasped Hulot, sitting down in dismay. 'I see all the things she uses – her caps, her slippers. Why, how long since—?'

Crevel nodded that he understood, and took a packet of bills out of the little inlaid cabinet.

'You can see, old man. I paid the decorators in December 1838. In October, two months before, this charming little place was first used.'

Hulot bent his head.

'How the devil do you manage it? I know how she spends every hour of her day.'

'How about her walk in the Tuileries?' said Crevel, rubbing his hands in triumph.

'What then?' said Hulot, mystified.

'Your lady love comes to the Tuileries, she is supposed to be airing herself from one till four. But, hop, skip, and jump, and she is here. You know your Molière? Well, Baron, there is nothing imaginary in your title.'

Hulot, left without a shred of doubt, sat sunk in ominous silence. Catastrophes lead intelligent and strong-minded men to be philosophical. The Baron, morally, was at this moment like a man trying to find his way by night through a forest. This gloomy taciturnity and the change in that dejected countenance made Crevel very uneasy, for he did not wish the death of his colleague.

'As I said, old fellow, we are now even; let us play for the odd. Will you play off the tie by hook and by crook? Come!'

'Why,' said Hulot, talking to himself – 'why is it that out of ten pretty women at least seven are false?'

But the Baron was too much upset to answer his own question. Beauty is the greatest of human gifts for power. Every power that has no counterpoise, no autocratic control, leads to abuses and folly. Despotism is the madness of power; in women the despot is caprice.

'You have nothing to complain of, my good friend; you have a beautiful wife, and she is virtuous.'

'I deserve my fate,' said Hulot. 'I have undervalued my wife and made her miserable, and she is an angel! Oh, my poor Adeline! you are avenged! She suffers in solitude and silence, and she is worthy of my love; I ought – for she is still charming, fair and girlish even— But was there ever a woman known more base, more ignoble, more villainous than this Valérie?'

'She is a good-for-nothing slut,' said Crevel, 'a hussy that deserves whipping on the Place du Châtelet. But, my dear Canillac, though we are such blades, so Maréchal de Richelieu, Louis xv., Pompadour, Madame du Barry, gay dogs, and everything that is most eighteenth century, there is no longer a lieutenant of police.'

'How can we make them love us?' Hulot wondered to himself without heeding Crevel.

'It is sheer folly in us to expect to be loved, my dear fellow,' said Crevel. 'We can only be endured; for Madame Marneffe is a hundred times more profligate than Josépha.'

'And avaricious! She costs me a hundred and ninety-two thousand francs a year!' cried Hulot.

'And how many centimes!' sneered Crevel, with the insolence of a financier who scorns so small a sum.

'You do not love her, that is very evident,' said the Baron dolefully.

'I have had enough of her,' replied Crevel, 'for she has had more than three hundred thousand francs of mine!'

'Where is it? Where does it all go?' said the Baron, clasping his head in his hands.

'If we had come to an agreement, like the simple young men who combine to maintain a twopenny baggage, she would have cost us less.'

'That is an idea!' replied the Baron. 'But she would still be cheating us; for, my burly friend, what do you say to this Brazilian?'

'Ay, old sly fox, you are right, we are swindled like – like shareholders!' said Crevel. 'All such women are an unlimited liability, and we the sleeping partners.'

'Then it was she who told you about the candle in the window?'

'My good man,' replied Crevel, striking an attitude, 'she has fooled us both. Valérie is a— She told me to keep you here. – Now I see it all. She has got her Brazilian! – Oh, I have done with her, for if you hold her hands, she would find a way to cheat you with her feet! There! she is a minx, a jade!'

'She is lower than a prostitute,' said the Baron. 'Josépha and Jenny Cadine were in their rights when they were false to us; they make a trade of their charms.'

'But she, who affects the saint – the prude!' said Crevel. 'I tell you what, Hulot, do you go back to your wife; your money matters are not looking well; I have heard talk of certain notes of hand given to a low usurer whose special line of business is lending to these sluts, a man named Vauvinet. For my part, I am cured of your "real ladies." And, after all, at our time of life what do we want of these swindling hussies, who, to be honest, cannot help playing us false? You have white hair and false teeth; I am of the shape of Silenus. I shall go in for saving. Money never deceives one. Though the Treasury is indeed open to all the world twice a year, it pays you interest, and this woman swallows it. With you, my worthy friend, as Gubetta, as my partner in the concern, I might have resigned myself to a shady bargain – no, a philosophical calm. But with a Brazilian who has possibly smuggled in some doubtful colonial produce—'

'Woman is an inexplicable creature!' said Hulot.

'I can explain her,' said Crevel. 'We are old; the Brazilian is young and handsome.'

'Yes; that, I own, is true,' said Hulot; 'we are older than we were. But, my dear fellow, how is one to do without these pretty creatures – seeing them undress, twist up their hair, smile cunningly through their fingers as they screw up their curl-papers, put on all their airs and graces, tell all their lies, declare that we don't love them when we are worried with business; and they cheer us in spite of everything.'

'Yes, by the Powers. It is the only pleasure in life!' cried Crevel. 'When a saucy little mug smiles at you and says, "My old dear, you don't know how nice you are! I am not like other women, I suppose, who go crazy over mere boys with goats' beards, smelling of smoke, and as coarse as serving-men! For in their youth they are so insolent! – They come in and they bid you good morning, and out they go. – I, whom you think such a flirt, I prefer a man of fifty to these brats. A man who will stick by me, who is devoted, who knows a woman is not to be picked up every day, and appreciates us. – That is what I love you for, you old monster!" – and they fill up these avowals with little pettings and prettinesses and— Faugh! they are as false as the bills on the Hôtel de Ville.'

'A lie is sometimes better than the truth,' said Hulot, remembering sundry bewitching scenes called up by Crevel, who mimicked Valérie. 'They are obliged to act upon their lies, to sew spangles on their stage frocks—'

'And they are ours after all, the lying jades!' said Crevel coarsely.

'Valérie is a witch,' said the Baron. 'She can turn an old man into a young one.'

'Oh yes!' said Crevel, 'she is an eel that wriggles through your hands; but the prettiest eel, as white and sweet as sugar, as amusing as Arnal – and ingenious!'

'Yes, she is full of fun,' said Hulot, who had now quite forgotten his wife.

The colleagues went to bed the best friends in the world, reminding each other of Valérie's perfections, the tones of her voice, her kittenish ways, her movements, her fun, her sallies of wit, and of affection; for she was an artist in love, and had charming impulses, as tenors may sing a scena better one day than another. And they fell asleep, cradled in tempting and diabolical visions lighted by the fires of hell.

At nine o'clock next morning Hulot went off to the War Office, Crevel had business out of town; they left the house together, and Crevel held out his hand to the Baron, saying –

'To show that there is no ill-feeling. For we, neither of us, will have anything more to say to Madame Marneffe?'

'Oh, this is the end of everything,' replied Hulot with a sort of horror.

By half-past ten Crevel was mounting the stairs, four at a time, up to Madame Marneffe's apartment. He found the infamous wretch, the adorable enchantress, in the most becoming morning wrapper, enjoying an elegant little breakfast in the society of the Baron Montès de Montejanos and Lisbeth. Though the sight of the Brazilian gave him a shock, Crevel begged Madame Marneffe to grant him two minutes' speech with her. Valérie led Crevel into the drawing-room.

'Valérie, my angel,' said the amorous Mayor, 'Monsieur Marneffe cannot have long to live. If you will be faithful to me, when he dies we will be married. Think it over. I have rid you of Hulot. – So just consider whether this Brazilian is to compare with a Mayor of Paris, a man who, for your sake, will make his way to the highest dignities, and who can already offer you eighty odd thousand francs a year.'

'I will think it over,' said she. 'You will see me in the Rue du Dauphin at two o'clock, and we can discuss the matter. But be a good boy – and do not forget the bond you promised to transfer to me.'

She returned to the dining-room, followed by Crevel, who flattered himself that he had hit on a plan for keeping Valérie to himself; but there he found Baron Hulot, who, during this short colloquy, had also arrived with the same end in view. He, like Crevel, begged for a brief interview. Madame Marneffe again rose to go to the drawing-room, with a smile at the Brazilian that seemed to say, 'What fools they are! Cannot they see you?'

'Valérie,' said the official, 'my child, that cousin of yours is an American cousin—'

'Oh, that is enough!' she cried, interrupting the Baron. 'Marneffe never has been, and never will be, never can be my husband! The first, the only man I ever loved, has come back quite unexpectedly. It is no fault of mine! But look at Henri and then at yourself. Then ask yourself whether a woman, and a woman in love, can hesitate for a moment. My dear fellow, I am not a kept mistress. From this day forth I refuse to play the part of Susannah between the two Elders. If you really care for me, you and Crevel, you will be our friends; but all else is at an end, for I am six-and-twenty, and henceforth I mean to be a saint, an admirable and worthy wife – as yours is.'

'Is that what you have to say?' answered Hulot. 'Is this the way you receive me when I come like a Pope with my hands full of Indulgences? – Well, your husband will never be a first-class clerk, nor be promoted in the Legion of Honour.'

'That remains to be seen,' said Madame Marneffe, with a meaning look at Hulot.

'Well, well, no temper,' said Hulot in despair. 'I will call this evening, and we will come to an understanding.'

'In Lisbeth's rooms then.'

'Very good – at Lisbeth's,' said the old dotard.

Hulot and Crevel went downstairs together without speaking a word till they were in the street; but outside on the side walk they looked at each other with a dreary laugh.

'We are a couple of old fools,' said Crevel.

'I have got rid of them,' said Madame Marneffe to Lisbeth, as she sat down once more. 'I never loved and I never shall love any man but my Jaguar,' she added, smiling at Henri Montès. 'Lisbeth, my dear, you don't know. Henri has forgiven me the infamy to which I was reduced by poverty.'

'It was my own fault,' said the Brazilian. 'I ought to have sent you a hundred thousand francs.'

'Poor boy!' said Valérie; 'I might have worked for my living, but my fingers were not made for that – ask Lisbeth.'

The Brazilian went away the happiest man in Paris.

At noon Valérie and Lisbeth were chatting in the splendid bedroom where this dangerous woman was giving to her dress those finishing touches which a lady alone can give. The doors were bolted, the curtains drawn over them, and Valérie related in every detail all the events of the evening, the night, the morning.

'What do you think of it all, my darling?' she said to Lisbeth in conclusion. 'Which shall I be when the time comes – Madame Crevel, or Madame Montès?'

'Crevel will not last more than ten years, such a profligate as he is,' replied Lisbeth. 'Montès is young. Crevel will leave you about thirty thousand francs a year. Let Montès wait; he will be happy enough as Benjamin. And so, by the time you are three-and-thirty, if you take care of your looks, you may marry your Brazilian and make a fine show with sixty thousand francs a year of your own – especially under the wing of a Maréchale.'

'Yes, but Montès is a Brazilian; he will never make his mark,' observed Valérie.

'We live in the day of railways,' said Lisbeth, 'when foreigners rise to high positions in France.'

'We shall see,' replied Valérie, 'when Marneffe is dead. He has not much longer to suffer.'

'These attacks that return so often are a sort of physical remorse,' said Lisbeth. 'Well, I am off to see Hortense.'

'Yes – go, my angel!' replied Valérie. 'And bring me my artist. – Three years, and I have not gained an inch of ground! It is a disgrace to both of us! – Wenceslas and Henri – those are my two passions – one for love, the other for fancy.'

'You are lovely this morning,' said Lisbeth, putting her arm round Valérie's waist and kissing her forehead. 'I enjoy all your pleasures, your good fortune, your dresses – I never really lived till the day when we became sisters.'

'Wait a moment, my tiger-cat!' cried Valérie, laughing; 'your shawl is crooked. You cannot put a shawl on yet in spite of my lessons for three years – and you want to be Madame la Maréchale Hulot!'

Shod in prunella boots, over grey silk stockings, in a gown of handsome corded silk, her hair in smooth bands under a very pretty black velvet bonnet, lined with yellow satin, Lisbeth made her way to the Rue Saint-Dominique by the Boulevard des Invalides, wondering whether sheer dejection would at last break down Hortense's brave spirit, and whether Sarmatian instability, taken at a moment when, with such a character, everything is possible, would be too much for Steinbock's constancy.

Hortense and Wenceslas had the ground floor of a house situated at the corner of the Rue Saint-Dominique and the Esplanade des Invalides. These rooms, once in harmony with the honeymoon, now had that half-new, half-faded look that may be called the autumnal aspect of furniture. Newly married folks are as lavish and wasteful, without knowing it or intending it, of everything about them as they are of their affection. Thinking only of themselves, they reck little of the future, which, at a later time, weighs on the mother of a family.

Lisbeth found Hortense just as she had finished dressing a baby Wenceslas, who had been carried into the garden.

'Good morning, Bette,' said Hortense, opening the door herself to her cousin. The cook was gone out, and the house servant, who was also the nurse, was doing some washing.

'Good morning, dear child,' replied Lisbeth, kissing her. 'Is Wenceslas in the studio?' she added in a whisper.

'No; he is in the drawing-room talking to Stidmann and Chanor.'

'Can we be alone?' asked Lisbeth.

'Come into my room.'

In this room, the hangings of pink-flowered chintz with green leaves on a white ground, constantly exposed to the sun, were much faded, as was the carpet. The muslin curtains had not been washed for many a day. The smell of tobacco hung about the room; for Wenceslas, now an artist of repute, and born a fine gentleman, left his cigar-ash on the arms of the chairs and the prettiest pieces of furniture, as a man does to whom love allows everything – a man rich enough to scorn vulgar carefulness.

'Now, then, let us talk over your affairs,' said Lisbeth, seeing her pretty cousin silent in the armchair into which she had dropped. 'But what ails you? You look rather pale, my dear.'

'Two articles have just come out in which my poor Wenceslas is pulled to pieces; I have read them, but I have hidden them from him, for they would completely depress him. The marble statue of Marshal Montcornet is pronounced utterly bad. The bas-reliefs are allowed to pass muster, simply to allow of the most perfidious praise of his talent as a decorative artist, and to give the greater emphasis to the statement that serious art is quite out of his reach! Stidmann, whom I besought to tell me the truth, broke my heart by confessing that his own opinion agreed with that of every other artist, of the critics, and the public. He said to me in the garden before breakfast, "If Wenceslas cannot exhibit a masterpiece next season, he must give up heroic sculpture and be content to execute idyllic subjects, small figures, pieces of jewellery, and high-class goldsmiths' work!" This verdict is dreadful to me, for Wenceslas, I know, will never accept it; he feels he has so many fine ideas.'

'Ideas will not pay the tradesman's bills,' remarked Lisbeth. 'I was always telling him so – nothing but money. Money is only to be had for work done – things that ordinary folks like well enough to buy them. When an artist has to live and keep a family, he had far better have a design for a candlestick on his counter, or for a fender or a table, than for groups or statues. Everybody must have such things, while he may wait months for the admirer of the group – and for his money—'

'You are right, my good Lisbeth. Tell him all that; I have not the courage. – Besides, as he was saying to Stidmann, if he goes back to ornamental work and small sculpture, he must give up all hope of the Institute and grand works of art, and we should not get the three hundred thousand francs' worth of work promised at Versailles and by the City of Paris and the Ministers. That is what we are robbed of by those dreadful articles, written by rivals who want to step into our shoes.'

'And that is not what you dreamed of, poor little puss!' said Lisbeth, kissing Hortense on the brow. 'You expected to find a gentleman, a leader of Art, the chief of all living sculptors. – But that is poetry, you see, a dream requiring fifty thousand francs a year, and you have only two thousand four hundred – so long as I live. After my death three thousand.'

A few tears rose to Hortense's eyes, and Lisbeth drank them with her eyes as a cat laps milk.

This is the history of their honeymoon – the tale will perhaps not be lost on some artists.

Intellectual work, labour in the upper regions of mental effort, is one of the grandest achievements of man. That which deserves real glory in Art – for by Art we must understand every creation of the mind – is courage above all things – a sort of courage of which the vulgar have no conception, and which has never perhaps been described till now.

Driven by the dreadful stress of poverty, goaded by Lisbeth, and kept by her in blinkers, as a horse is, to hinder it from seeing to the right and left of its road, lashed on by that hard woman, the personification of Necessity, a sort of deputy Fate, Wenceslas, a born poet and dreamer, had gone on from conception to execution, and overleaped, without sounding it, the gulf that divides these two hemispheres of Art. To nurse, to dream, to conceive of fine works, is a delightful occupation. It is like smoking a magic cigar or leading the life of a courtesan who follows her own fancy. The work then floats in all the grace of infancy, in the mad joy of conception, with the fragrant beauty of a flower, and the aromatic juices of a fruit enjoyed in anticipation.

The man who can but sketch his purpose beforehand in words is regarded as a wonder, and every artist and writer possesses that faculty. But gestation, fruition, the laborious rearing of the offspring, putting it to bed every night full fed with milk, embracing it anew every morning with the inexhaustible affection of a mother's heart, licking it clean, dressing it a hundred times in the richest garb only to be instantly destroyed; then never to be cast down at the convulsions of this headlong life till the living masterpiece is perfected which in sculpture speaks to every eye, in literature to every intellect, in painting to every memory, in music to every heart! – This is the task of execution. The hand must be ready at every instant to come forward and obey the brain. But the brain has no more a creative power at command than love has a perennial spring.

The habit of creativeness, the indefatigable love of motherhood which makes a mother – that miracle of nature which Raphael so perfectly understood – the maternity of the brain, in short, which is so difficult to develop, is lost with prodigious ease. Inspiration is the opportunity of genius. She does not indeed dance on the razor's edge, she is in the air and flies away with the suspicious swiftness of a crow; she wears no scarf by which the poet can clutch her; her hair is a flame; she vanishes like the lovely rose and white flamingo, the sportsman's despair. And work, again, is a weariful struggle, alike dreaded and delighted in by these lofty and powerful natures who are often broken by it. A great poet of our day has said in speaking of this overwhelming labour, 'I sit down to it in despair, but I leave it with regret.' Be it known to all who are ignorant! If the artist does not throw himself into his work as Curtius sprang into the gulf, as a soldier leads a forlorn hope without a moment's thought, and if when he is in the crater he does not dig on as a miner does when the earth has fallen in on him; if he contemplates the difficulties before him instead of conquering them one by one, like the lovers in fairy tales, who to win their princesses overcome ever new enchantments, the work remains incomplete; it perishes in the studio where creativeness becomes impossible, and the artist looks on at the suicide of his own talent.

Rossini, a brother genius to Raphael, is a striking instance in his poverty-stricken youth, compared with his later years of opulence. This is the reason why the same prize, the same triumph, the same bays are awarded to great poets and to great generals.

Wenceslas, by nature a dreamer, had expended so much energy in production, in study, and in work under Lisbeth's despotic rule, that love and happiness resulted in reaction. His real character reappeared, the weakness, recklessness, and indolence of the Sarmatian returned to nestle in the comfortable corners of his soul, whence the schoolmaster's rod had routed them.

For the first few months the artist adored his wife. Hortense and Wenceslas abandoned themselves to the happy childishness of a legitimate and unbounded passion. Hortense was the first to release her husband from his labours, proud to triumph over her rival, his Art. And, indeed, a woman's caresses scare away the Muse, and break down the sturdy, brutal resolution of the worker.

Six or seven months slipped by, and the artist's fingers had forgotten the use of the modelling tool. When the need for work began to be felt, when the Prince de Wissembourg, president of the committee of subscribers, asked to see the statue, Wenceslas spoke the inevitable byword of the idler, ' I am just going to work on it,' and he lulled his dear Hortense with fallacious promises and the magnificent schemes of the artist as he smokes. Hortense loved her poet more than ever; she dreamed of a sublime statue of Marshal Montcornet. Montcornet would be the embodied ideal of bravery, the type of the cavalry officer, of courage *à la Murat*. Yes, yes; at the mere sight of that statue all the Emperor's victories were to seem a foregone conclusion. And then, such workmanship! The pencil was accommodating and answered to the word.

By way of a statue the result was a delightful little Wenceslas.

When the progress of affairs required that he should go to the studio at Le Gros-Caillou to mould the clay and set up the life-size model, Steinbock found one day that the Prince's clock required his presence in the workshop of Florent and

Chanor, where the figures were being finished; or, again, the light was grey and dull; to-day he had business to do, to-morrow they had a family dinner, to say nothing of indispositions of mind and body, and the days when he stayed at home to toy with his adored wife.

Marshal the Prince de Wissembourg was obliged to be angry to get the clay model finished; he declared that he must put the work into other hands. It was only by dint of endless complaints and much strong language that the committee of subscribers succeeded in seeing the plaster-cast. Day after day Steinbock came home, evidently tired, complaining of this 'hodman's work' and his own physical weakness. During that first year the household felt no pinch; the Countess Steinbock, desperately in love with her husband, cursed the War Minister. She went to see him; she told him that great works of art were not to be manufactured like cannon; and that the State – like Louis XIV., Francis I., and Leo X. – ought to be at the beck and call of genius. Poor Hortense, believing she held a Phidias in her embrace, had the sort of motherly cowardice for her Wenceslas that is in every wife who carries her love to the pitch of idolatry.

'Do not be hurried,' said she to her husband, 'our whole future life is bound up with that statue. Take your time and produce a masterpiece.'

She would go to the studio, and then the enraptured Steinbock wasted five hours out of seven in describing the statue instead of working at it. He thus spent eighteen months in finishing the design, which to him was all-important.

When the plaster was cast and the model complete, poor Hortense, who had looked on at her husband's toil, seeing his health really suffer from the exertions which exhaust a sculptor's frame and arms and hands – Hortense thought the result admirable. Her father, who knew nothing of sculpture, and her mother, no less ignorant, lauded it as a triumph; the War Minister came with them to see it, and, overruled by them, expressed approval of the figure, standing as it did alone, in a favourable light, thrown up against a green baize background.

Alas! at the exhibition of 1841, the disapprobation of the public soon took the form of abuse and mockery in the mouths of those who were indignant with the idol too hastily set up for worship. Stidmann tried to advise his friend, but was accused of jealousy. Every article in a newspaper was to Hortense an outcry of envy. Stidmann, the best of good fellows, got articles written, in which adverse criticism was contravened, and it was pointed out that sculptors altered their works in translating the plaster into marble, and that the marble would be the test.

'In reproducing the plaster sketch in marble,' wrote Claude Vignon, 'a masterpiece may be ruined, or a bad design made beautiful. The plaster is the manuscript, the marble is the book.'

So in two years and a half Wenceslas had produced a statue and a son. The child was a picture of beauty; the statue was execrable.

The clock for the Prince and the price of the statue paid off the young couple's debts. Steinbock had acquired fashionable habits; he went to the play, to the opera; he talked admirably about art; and in the eyes of the world he maintained his reputation as a great artist by his powers of conversation and criticism. There are many clever men in Paris who spend their lives in talking themselves out, and are content with a sort of drawing-room celebrity. Steinbock, emulating these emasculated but charming men, grew every day more averse to hard work. As soon as he began a thing, he was conscious of all its difficulties, and the discouragement that came over him enervated his will. Inspiration, the frenzy of intellectual procreation, flew swiftly away at the sight of this effete lover.

Sculpture – like dramatic art – is at once the most difficult and the easiest of all arts. You have but to copy a model, and the task is done; but to give it a soul, to make it typical by creating a man or a woman – this is the sin of Prometheus. Such triumphs in the annals of sculpture may be counted, as we may count the few poets among men. Michael Angelo, Michel Columb, Jean Goujon, Phidias, Praxiteles, Polycletes,

Puget, Canova, Albert Dürer, are the brothers of Milton, Virgil, Dante, Shakespeare, Tasso, Homer, and Molière. And such an achievement is so stupendous that a single statue is enough to make a man immortal, as Figaro, Lovelace, and Manon Lescaut have immortalised Beaumarchais, Richardson, and the Abbé Prévost.

Superficial thinkers – and there are many in the artist world – have asserted that sculpture lives only by the nude, that it died with the Greeks, and that modern vesture makes it impossible. But, in the first place, the Ancients have left sublime statues entirely clothed – the *Polyhymnia*, the *Julia*, and others, and we have not found one-tenth of all their works; and then, let any lover of art go to Florence and see Michael Angelo's *Penseroso*, or to the Cathedral of Mainz, and behold the *Virgin* by Albert Dürer, who has created a living woman out of ebony, under her threefold drapery, with the most flowing, the softest hair that ever a waiting-maid combed through; let all the ignorant flock thither, and they will acknowledge that genius can give mind to drapery, to armour, to a robe, and fill it with a body, just as a man leaves the stamp of his individuality and habits of life on the clothes he wears.

Sculpture is the perpetual realisation of the fact which once, and never again, was, in painting, called Raphael!

The solution of this hard problem is to be found only in constant persevering toil; for, merely to overcome the material difficulties to such an extent, the hand must be so practised, so dexterous and obedient, that the sculptor may be free to struggle soul to soul with the elusive moral element that he has to transfigure as he embodies it. If Paganini, who uttered his soul through the strings of his violin, spent three days without practising, he lost what he called the *stops* of his instrument, meaning the sympathy between the wooden frame, the strings, the bow, and himself; if he had lost this alliance, he would have been no more than an ordinary player.

Perpetual work is the law of art, as it is the law of life, for art is idealised creation. Hence great artists and perfect poets wait neither for commissions nor for purchasers. They are constantly creating – to-day, to-morrow, always. The result is the habit of work, the unfailing apprehension of the difficulties which keep them in close intercourse with the Muse and her productive forces. Canova lived in his studio, as Voltaire lived in his study; and so must Homer and Phidias have lived.

While Lisbeth kept Wenceslas Steinbock in thraldom in his garret, he was on the thorny road trodden by all these great men, which leads to the Alpine heights of glory. Then happiness, in the person of Hortense, had reduced the poet to idleness – the normal condition of all artists, since to them idleness is fully occupied. Their joy is such as that of the pasha of a seraglio; they revel with ideas, they get drunk at the founts of intellect. Great artists, such as Steinbock, wrapped in reverie, are rightly spoken of as dreamers. They, like opium-eaters, all sink into poverty, whereas if they had been kept up to the mark by the stern demands of life, they might have been great men.

At the same time, these half-artists are delightful; men like them and cram them with praise; they even seem superior to the true artists, who are taxed with conceit, unsociableness, contempt of the laws of society. This is why: Great men are the slaves of their work. Their indifference to outer things, their devotion to their work, make simpletons regard them as egotists, and they are expected to wear the same garb as the dandy who fulfils the trivial evolutions called social duties. These men want the lions of the Atlas to be combed and scented like a lady's poodle.

These artists, who are too rarely matched to meet their fellows, fall into habits of solitary exclusiveness; they are inexplicable to the majority, which, as we know, consists mostly of fools – of the envious, the ignorant, and the superficial.

Now you may imagine what part a wife should play in the life of these glorious and exceptional beings. She ought to be what, for five years, Lisbeth had been, but with the added offering of love, humble and patient love, always ready and always smiling.

Hortense, enlightened by her anxieties as a mother, and driven by dire necessity, had discovered too late the mistakes she had been involuntarily led into by her excessive love. Still, the worthy daughter of her mother, her heart ached at the thought of worrying Wenceslas; she loved her dear poet too much to become his torturer; and she could foresee the hour when beggary awaited her, her child, and her husband.

'Come, come, my child,' said Lisbeth, seeing the tears in her cousin's lovely eyes, 'you must not despair. A glassful of tears will not buy a plate of soup. How much do you want?'

'Well, five or six thousand francs.'

'I have but three thousand at most,' said Lisbeth. 'And what is Wenceslas doing now?'

'He has had an offer to work in partnership with Stidmann at a table service for the Duc d'Hérouville for six thousand francs. Then Monsieur Chanor will advance four thousand to repay Monsieur de Lora and Bridau – a debt of honour.'

'What, you have had the money for the statue and the bas-reliefs for Marshal Montcornet's monument, and you have not paid them yet?'

'For the last three years,' said Hortense, 'we have spent twelve thousand francs a year, and I have but a hundred louis a year of my own. The Marshal's monument, when all the expenses were paid, brought us no more than sixteen thousand francs. Really and truly, if Wenceslas gets no work, I do not know what is to become of us. Oh, if only I could learn to make statues, I would handle the clay!' she cried, holding up her fine arms.

The woman, it was plain, fulfilled the promise of the girl; there was a flash in her eye; impetuous blood, strong with iron, flowed in her veins; she felt that she was wasting her energy in carrying her infant.

'Ah, my poor little thing! a sensible girl should not marry an artist till his fortune is made – not while it is still to make.'

At this moment they heard voices; Stidmann and Wenceslas were seeing Chanor to the door; then Wenceslas and Stidmann came in again.

Stidmann, an artist in vogue in the world of journalists, famous actresses, and courtesans of the better class, was a

young man of fashion whom Valérie much wished to see in
her rooms; indeed, he had already been introduced to her by
Claude Vignon. Stidmann had lately broken off an intimacy
with Madame Schontz, who had married some months since
and gone to live in the country. Valérie and Lisbeth, hearing of
this upheaval from Claude Vignon, thought it well to get
Steinbock's friend to visit in the Rue Vanneau.

Stidmann, out of good feeling, went rarely to the Steinbocks; and as it happened that Lisbeth was not present when
he was introduced by Claude Vignon, she now saw him for the
first time. As she watched this noted artist, she caught certain
glances from his eyes at Hortense, which suggested to her the
possibility of offering him to the Countess Steinbock as a
consolation if Wenceslas should be false to her. In point of
fact, Stidmann was reflecting that if Steinbock were not his
friend, Hortense, the young and superbly beautiful countess,
would be an adorable mistress; it was this very notion, controlled by honour, that kept him away from the house. Lisbeth
was quick to mark the significant awkwardness that troubles a
man in the presence of a woman with whom he will not allow
himself to flirt.

'Very good-looking – that young man,' said she in a whisper to Hortense.

'Oh, do you think so?' she replied. 'I never noticed him.'

'Stidmann, my good fellow,' said Wenceslas, in an undertone to his friend, 'we are on no ceremony, you and I – we
have some business to settle with this old girl.'

Stidmann bowed to the ladies and went away.

'It is settled,' said Wenceslas, when he came in from taking
leave of Stidmann. 'But there are six months' work to be
done, and we must live meanwhile.'

'There are my diamonds,' cried the young Countess, with
the impetuous heroism of a loving woman.

A tear rose in Wenceslas's eye.

'Oh! I am going to work,' said he, sitting down by his wife
and drawing her on to his knee. 'I will do odd jobs – a
wedding chest, bronze groups—'

'But, my children,' said Lisbeth; 'for, as you know, you will be my heirs, and I shall leave you a very comfortable sum, believe me, especially if you help me to marry the Marshal; nay, if we succeed in that quickly, I will take you all to board with me – you and Adeline. We should live very happily together. – But for the moment, listen to the voice of my long experience. Do not fly to the Mont-de-Piété; it is the ruin of the borrower. I have always found that when the interest was due, those who had pledged their things had nothing wherewith to pay up, and then all is lost. I can get you a loan at five per cent. on your note of hand.'

'Oh, we are saved!' said Hortense.

'Well, then, child, Wenceslas had better come with me to see the lender, who will oblige him at my request. It is Madame Marneffe. If you flatter her a little – for she is as vain as a *parvenue* – she will get you out of the scrape in the most obliging way. Come yourself and see her, my dear Hortense.'

Hortense looked at her husband with the expression a man condemned to death must wear on his way to the scaffold.

'Claude Vignon took Stidmann there,' said Wenceslas. 'He says it is a very pleasant house.'

Hortense's head fell. What she felt can only be expressed in one word; it was not pain; it was illness.

'But, my dear Hortense, you must learn something of life!' exclaimed Lisbeth, understanding the eloquence of her cousin's looks. 'Otherwise, like your mother, you will find yourself abandoned in a deserted room, where you will weep like Calypso on the departure of Ulysses, and at an age when there is no hope of Telemachus—' she added, repeating a jest of Madame Marneffe's. 'We have to regard the people in the world as tools which we make use of or let alone, according as they can serve our turn. Make use of Madame Marneffe now, my dears, and let her alone by and by. Are you afraid lest Wenceslas, who worships you, should fall in love with a woman four or five years older than himself, as yellow as a bundle of field peas, and—?'

'I would far rather pawn my diamonds,' said Hortense. 'Oh, never go there, Wenceslas! – It is hell!'

'Hortense is right,' said Steinbock, kissing his wife.

'Thank you, my dearest,' said Hortense, delighted. 'My husband is an angel, you see, Lisbeth. He does not gamble, he goes nowhere without me; if he only could stick to work – oh, I should be too happy. Why take us on show to my father's mistress, a woman who is ruining him and is the cause of troubles that are killing my heroic mother?'

'My child, that is not where the cause of your father's ruin lies. It was his singer who ruined him, and then your marriage!' replied her cousin. 'Bless me! why, Madame Marneffe is of the greatest use to him. – However, I must tell no tales.'

'You have a good word for everybody, dear Bette—'

Hortense was called into the garden by hearing the child cry; Lisbeth was left alone with Wenceslas.

'You have an angel for your wife, Wenceslas!' said she. 'Love her as you ought; never give her cause for grief.'

'Yes, indeed, I love her so well that I do not tell her all,' replied Wenceslas; 'but to you, Lisbeth, I may confess the truth. – If I took my wife's diamonds to the Mont-de-Piété, we should be no further forward.'

'Then borrow of Madame Marneffe,' said Lisbeth. 'Persuade Hortense, Wenceslas, to let you go there, or else, bless me! go there without telling her.'

'That is what I was thinking of,' replied Wenceslas, 'when I refused for fear of grieving Hortense.'

'Listen to me; I care too much for you both not to warn you of your danger. If you go there, hold your heart tight in both hands, for the woman is a witch. All who see her adore her; she is so wicked, so inviting! She fascinates men like a masterpiece. Borrow her money, but do not leave your soul in pledge. I should never be happy again if you were false to Hortense – here she is! not another word! I will settle the matter.'

'Kiss Lisbeth, my darling,' said Wenceslas to his wife. 'She will help us out of our difficulties by lending us her savings.'

And he gave Lisbeth a look which she understood.

'Then, I hope you mean to work, my dear treasure,' said Hortense.

'Yes, indeed,' said the artist. 'I will begin to-morrow.'

'To-morrow is our ruin!' said his wife, with a smile.

'Now, my dear child! say yourself whether some hindrance has not come in the way every day; some obstacle or business?'

'Yes, very true, my love.'

'Here!' cried Steinbock, striking his brow, 'here I have swarms of ideas! I mean to astonish all my enemies. I am going to design a service in the German style of the sixteenth century; the romantic style: foliage twined with insects, sleeping children, newly invented monsters, chimeras – real chimeras, such as we dream of! – I see it all! It will be undercut, light, and yet crowded. Chanor was quite amazed. – And I wanted some encouragement, for the last article on Montcornet's monument had been crushing.'

At a moment in the course of the day when Lisbeth and Wenceslas were left together, the artist agreed to go on the morrow to see Madame Marneffe – he either would win his wife's consent, or he would go without telling her.

Valérie, informed the same evening of this success, insisted that Hulot should go to invite Stidmann, Claude Vignon, and Steinbock to dinner; for she was beginning to tyrannise over him as women of that type tyrannise over old men, who trot round town, and go to make interest with every one who is necessary to the interests or the vanity of their task-mistress.

Next evening Valérie armed herself for conquest by making such a toilet as a French woman can devise when she wishes to make the most of herself. She studied her appearance in this great work as a man going out to fight a duel practises his feints and lunges. Not a speck, not a wrinkle was to be seen. Valérie was at her whitest, her softest, her sweetest. And certain little 'patches' attracted the eye.

It is commonly supposed that the patch of the eighteenth century is out of date or out of fashion; that is a mistake. In these days women, more ingenious perhaps than of yore, invite a glance through the opera-glass by other audacious devices. One is the first to hit on a rosette in her hair with a diamond in the centre, and she attracts every eye for a whole evening; another revives the hair-net, or sticks a dagger through the twist to suggest a garter; this one wears velvet bands round her wrists, that one appears in lace lappets. These valiant efforts, an Austerlitz of vanity or of love, then set the fashion for lower spheres by the time the inventive creatress has originated something new. This evening, which Valérie meant to be a success for her, she had placed three patches. She had washed her hair with some lye, which changed its hue for a few days from gold colour to a duller shade. Madame Steinbock's was almost red, and she would be in every point unlike her. This new effect gave her a piquant and strange appearance, which puzzled her followers so much, that Montès asked her –

'What have you done to yourself this evening?' – Then she put on a rather wide black velvet neck-ribbon, which showed off the whiteness of her skin. One patch took the place of the *assassine* of our grandmothers. And Valérie pinned the sweetest rosebud into her bodice, just in the middle above the stay-busk, and in the daintiest little hollow! It was enough to make every man under thirty drop his eyelids.

'I am as sweet as a sugar-plum,' said she to herself, going through her attitudes before the glass, exactly as a dancer practises her curtseys.

Lisbeth had been to market, and the dinner was to be one of those superfine meals which Mathurine had been wont to cook for her Bishop when he entertained the prelate of the adjoining diocese.

Stidmann, Claude Vignon, and Count Steinbock arrived almost together, just at six. An ordinary, or, if you will, a natural woman would have hastened at the announcement of a name so eagerly longed for; but Valérie, though ready since five o'clock, remained in her room, leaving her three guests together, certain that she was the subject of their conversation or of their secret thoughts. She herself had arranged the drawing-room, laying out the pretty trifles produced in Paris and nowhere else, which reveal the woman and announce her presence: albums bound in enamel or embroidered with beads, saucers full of pretty rings, marvels of Sèvres or Dresden mounted exquisitely by Florent and Chanor, statues, books, all the frivolities which cost insane sums, and which passion orders of the makers in its first delirium – or to patch up its last quarrel.

Besides, Valérie was in the state of intoxication that comes of triumph. She had promised to marry Crevel if Marneffe should die; and the amorous Crevel had transferred to the name of Valérie Fortin bonds bearing ten thousand francs a year, the sum-total of what he had made in railway speculations during the past three years, the returns on the capital of a hundred thousand crowns which he had at first offered to the Baronne Hulot. So Valérie now had an income of thirty-two thousand francs.

Crevel had just committed himself to a promise of far greater magnitude than this gift of his surplus. In the paroxysm of rapture which *his Duchess* had given him from two to four – he gave this fine title to Madame *de* Marneffe to complete the illusion – for Valérie had surpassed herself in the Rue du Dauphin that afternoon, he had thought well to encourage her in her promised fidelity by giving her the prospect of a certain little mansion, built in the Rue Barbette by an imprudent contractor, who now wanted to sell it. Valérie could already see herself in this delightful residence, with a fore-court and a garden, and keeping a carriage!

'What respectable life can ever procure so much in so short a time, or so easily?' said she to Lisbeth as she finished dressing. Lisbeth was to dine with Valérie that evening, to tell Steinbock those things about the lady which nobody can say about herself.

Madame Marneffe, radiant with satisfaction, came into the drawing-room with modest grace, followed by Lisbeth dressed in black and yellow to set her off.

'Good evening, Claude,' said she, giving her hand to the famous old critic.

Claude Vignon, like many another, had become a political personage – a word describing an ambitious man at the first stage of his career. The *political personage* of 1840 represents, in some degree, the *Abbé* of the eighteenth century. No drawing-room circle is complete without one.

'My dear, this is my cousin, Count Steinbock,' said Lisbeth, introducing Wenceslas, whom Valérie seemed to have over-looked.

'Oh yes, I recognised Monsieur le Comte,' replied Valérie, with a gracious bow to the artist. 'I often saw you in the Rue du Doyenné, and I had the pleasure of being present at your wedding. – It would be difficult, my dear,' said she to Lisbeth, 'to forget your adopted son after once seeing him. – It is most kind of you, Monsieur Stidmann,' she went on, 'to have accepted my invitation at such short notice; but necessity knows no law. I knew you to be the friend of both these gentlemen. Nothing is more dreary, more sulky, than a dinner where all the guests are strangers, so it was for their sake that I hailed you in – but you will come another time for mine, I hope? – Say that you will.'

And for a few minutes she moved about the room with Stidmann, wholly occupied with him.

Crevel and Hulot were announced separately, and then a deputy named Beauvisage.

This individual, a provincial Crevel, one of the men created to make up the crowd in the world, voted under the banner of Giraud, a State Councillor, and Victorin Hulot. These two politicians were trying to form a nucleus of progressives in the loose array of the Conservative Party. Giraud himself occasionally spent the evening at Madame Marneffe's, and she flattered herself that she should also capture Victorin Hulot; but the puritanical lawyer had hitherto found excuses for refusing to accompany his father and father-in-law. It seemed to him criminal to be seen in the house of the woman who cost his mother so many tears. Victorin Hulot was to the puritans of political life what a pious woman is among bigots.

Beauvisage, formerly a stocking manufacturer at Arcis, was anxious to *pick up the Paris style*. This man, one of the outer stones of the Chamber, was forming himself under the auspices of this delicious and fascinating Madame Marneffe. Introduced there by Crevel, he had accepted him, at her instigation, as his model and master. He consulted him on every point, took the address of his tailor, imitated him, and tried to strike the same attitudes. In short, Crevel was his Great Man.

Valérie, surrounded by these bigwigs and the three artists, and supported by Lisbeth, struck Wenceslas as a really superior woman, all the more so because Claude Vignon spoke of her like a man in love.

'She is Madame de Maintenon in Ninon's petticoats!' said the veteran critic. 'You may please her in an evening if you have the wit; but as for making her love you – that would be a triumph to crown a man's ambition and fill up his life.'

Valérie, while seeming cold and heedless of her former neighbour, piqued his vanity, quite unconsciously indeed, for she knew nothing of the Polish character. There is in the Slav a childish element, as there is in all these primitively wild nations which have overflowed into civilisation rather than that they have become civilised. The race has spread like an inundation, and has covered a large portion of the globe. It inhabits deserts whose extent is so vast that it expands at its ease; there is no jostling there, as there is in Europe, and civilisation is impossible without the constant friction of minds and interests. The Ukraine, Russia, the plains by the Danube, in short, the Slav nations, are a connecting link between Europe and Asia, between civilisation and barbarism. Thus the Pole, the wealthiest member of the Slav family, has in his character all the childishness and inconsistency of a beardless race. He has courage, spirit, and strength; but, cursed with instability, that courage, strength, and energy have neither method nor guidance; for the Pole displays a variability

COUSIN BETTE   223

resembling that of the winds which blow across that vast plain broken with swamps; and though he has the impetuosity of the snow squalls that wrench and sweep away buildings, like those aerial avalanches he is lost in the first pool and melts into water. Man always assimilates something from the surroundings in which he lives. Perpetually at strife with the Turk, the Pole has imbibed a taste for Oriental splendour; he often sacrifices what is needful for the sake of display. The men dress themselves out like women, yet the climate has given them the tough constitution of Arabs.

The Pole, sublime in suffering, has tired his oppressors' arms by sheer endurance of beating; and, in the nineteenth century, has reproduced the spectacle presented by the early Christians. Infuse only ten per cent. of English cautiousness into the frank and open Polish nature, and the magnanimous white eagle would at this day be supreme wherever the two-headed eagle has sneaked in. A little Machiavelism would have hindered Poland from helping to save Austria, who has taken a share of it; from borrowing from Prussia, the usurer who had undermined it; and from breaking up as soon as a division was first made.

At the christening of Poland, no doubt, the Fairy Carabosse, overlooked by the genii who endowed that attractive people with the most brilliant gifts, came in to say –

'Keep all the gifts that my sisters have bestowed on you; but you shall never know what you wish for!'

If, in its heroic duel with Russia, Poland had won the day, the Poles would now be fighting among themselves, as they formerly fought in their Diets to hinder each other from being chosen King. When that nation, composed entirely of hot-headed dare-devils, has good sense enough to seek a Louis xi. among her own offspring, to accept his despotism and a dynasty, she will be saved.

What Poland has been politically, almost every Pole is in private life, especially under the stress of disaster. Thus Wenceslas Steinbock, after worshipping his wife for three years and knowing that he was a god to her, was so much nettled at

finding himself barely noticed by Madame Marneffe, that he
made it a point of honour to attract her attention. He compared Valérie with his wife and gave her the palm. Hortense
was beautiful flesh, as Valérie had said to Lisbeth; but
Madame Marneffe had spirit in her very shape, and the savour
of vice.

Such devotion as Hortense's is a feeling which a husband
takes as his due; the sense of the immense preciousness of
such perfect love soon wears off, as a debtor, in the course
of time, begins to fancy that the borrowed money is his own.
This noble loyalty becomes the daily bread of the soul, and an
infidelity is as tempting as a dainty. The woman who is
scornful, and yet more the woman who is reputed dangerous,
excites curiosity, as spices add flavour to good food. Indeed,
the disdain so cleverly acted by Valérie was a novelty to
Wenceslas, after three years of too easy enjoyment. Hortense
was a wife; Valérie a mistress.

Many men desire to have two editions of the same work,
though it is in fact a proof of inferiority when a man cannot
make his mistress of his wife. Variety in this particular is a sign
of weakness. Constancy will always be the real genius of love,
the evidence of immense power – the power that makes the
poet! A man ought to find every woman in his wife, as the
squalid poets of the seventeenth century made their Manons
figure as Iris and Chloe.

'Well,' said Lisbeth to the Pole, as she beheld him fascinated, 'what do you think of Valérie?'

'She is too charming,' replied Wenceslas.

'You would not listen to me,' said Betty. 'Oh! my little
Wenceslas, if you and I had never parted, you would have
been that siren's lover; you might have married her when she
was a widow, and you would have had her forty thousand
francs a year—'

'Really?'

'Certainly,' replied Lisbeth. 'Now, take care of yourself; I
warned you of the danger; do not singe your wings in the
candle! – Come, give me your arm, dinner is served.'

No language could be so thoroughly demoralising as this; for if you show a Pole a precipice, he is bound to leap it. As a nation they have the very spirit of cavalry; they fancy they can ride down every obstacle and come out victorious. The spur applied by Lisbeth to Steinbock's vanity was intensified by the appearance of the dining-room, bright with handsome silver plate; the dinner was served with every refinement and extravagance of Parisian luxury.

'I should have done better to take Célimène,' thought he to himself.

All through the dinner Hulot was charming; pleased to see his son-in-law at that table, and yet more happy in the prospect of a reconciliation with Valérie, whose fidelity he proposed to secure by the promise of Coquet's head-clerkship. Stidmann responded to the Baron's amiability by shafts of Parisian banter and an artist's high spirits. Steinbock would not allow himself to be eclipsed by his friend; he too was witty, said amusing things, made his mark, and was pleased with himself; Madame Marneffe smiled at him several times to show that she quite understood him.

The good meal and heady wines completed the work; Wenceslas was deep in what must be called the slough of dissipation. Excited by just a glass too much, he stretched himself on a settee after dinner, sunk in physical and mental ecstasy, which Madame Marneffe wrought to the highest pitch by coming to sit down by him – airy, scented, pretty enough to damn an angel. She bent over Wenceslas and almost touched his ear as she whispered to him –

'We cannot talk over business matters this evening, unless you will remain till the last. Between us – you, Lisbeth, and me – we can settle everything to suit you.'

'Ah, Madame, you are an angel!' replied Wenceslas, also in a murmur. 'I was a pretty fool not to listen to Lisbeth—'

'What did she say?'

'She declared, in the Rue du Doyenné, that you loved me!'

Madame Marneffe looked at him, seemed covered with confusion, and hastily left her seat. A young and pretty woman never rouses the hope of immediate success with impunity. This retreat, the impulse of a virtuous woman who is crushing a passion in the depths of her heart, was a thousand times more effective than the most reckless avowal. Desire was so thoroughly roused in Wenceslas that he doubled his attentions to Valérie. A woman seen by all is a woman wished for. Hence the terrible power of actresses. Madame Marneffe, knowing that she was watched, behaved like an admired actress. She was quite charming, and her success was immense.

'I no longer wonder at my father-in-law's follies,' said Steinbock to Lisbeth.

'If you say such things, Wenceslas, I shall to my dying day repent of having got you the loan of these ten thousand francs. Are you, like all these men,' and she indicated the guests, 'madly in love with that creature? Remember, you would be your father-in-law's rival. And think of the misery you would bring on Hortense.'

'That is true,' said Wenceslas. 'Hortense is an angel; I should be a wretch.'

'And one is enough in the family!' said Lisbeth.

'Artists ought never to marry!' exclaimed Steinbock.

'Ah! that is what I always told you in the Rue du Doyenné. Your groups, your statues, your great works, ought to be your children.'

'What are you talking about?' Valérie asked, joining Lisbeth. – 'Give us tea, Cousin.'

Steinbock, with Polish vainglory, wanted to appear familiar with this drawing-room fairy. After defying Stidmann, Vignon, and Crevel with a look, he took Valérie's hand and forced her to sit down by him on the settee.

'You are rather too lordly, Count Steinbock,' said she, resisting a little. But she laughed as she dropped on to the seat, not without arranging the rosebud pinned into her bodice.

'Alas! if I were really lordly,' said he, 'I should not be here to borrow money.'

'Poor boy! I remember how you worked all night in the Rue du Doyenné. You really were rather a spooney; you married as a starving man snatches a loaf. You knew nothing of Paris, and you see where you are landed. But you turned a deaf ear to Lisbeth's devotion, as you did to the love of a woman who knows her Paris by heart.'

'Say no more!' cried Steinbock; 'I am done for!'

'You shall have your ten thousand francs, my dear Wenceslas; but on one condition,' she went on, playing with his handsome curls.

'What is that?'

'I will take no interest—'

'Madame!'

'Oh! you need not be indignant; you shall make it good by giving me a bronze group. You began the story of Samson; finish it. – Do a Delilah cutting off the Jewish Hercules's hair. And you, who, if you will listen to me, will be a great artist, must enter into the subject. What you have to show is the power of woman. Samson is a secondary consideration. He is the corpse of dead strength. It is Delilah – passion – that ruins everything. How far more beautiful is that *replica* – That is what you call it, I think—' She skilfully interpolated, as Claude Vignon and Stidmann came up to them on hearing her talk of sculpture – 'how far more beautiful than the Greek myth is that *replica* of Hercules at Omphale's feet. – Did Greece copy Judæa, or did Judæa borrow the symbolism from Greece?'

'There, Madame, you raise an important question – that of the date of the various writings in the Bible. The great and immortal Spinoza – most foolishly ranked as an atheist, whereas he gave mathematical proof of the existence of God – asserts that the Book of Genesis and all the political history of the Bible are of the time of Moses, and he demonstrates the interpolated passages by philological evidence. And he was thrice stabbed as he went into the synagogue.'

'I had no idea I was so learned,' said Valérie, annoyed at this interruption to her *tête-à-tête*.

'Women know everything by instinct,' replied Claude Vignon.

'Well, then, you promise me?' she said to Steinbock, taking his hand with the timidity of a girl in love.

'You are indeed a happy man, my dear fellow,' cried Stid-mann, 'if Madame asks a favour of you!'

'What is it?' asked Claude Vignon.

'A small bronze group,' replied Steinbock, 'Delilah cutting off Samson's hair.'

'It is difficult,' remarked Claude Vignon. 'A bed—'

'On the contrary, it is exceedingly easy,' replied Valérie, smiling.

'Ah, ha! teach us sculpture!' said Stidmann.

'You should take Madame for your subject,' replied Vig-non, with a keen glance at Valérie.

'Well,' she went on, 'this is my notion of the composition. Samson on waking finds he has no hair, like many a dandy with a false top-knot. The hero is sitting on the bed, so you need only show the foot of it, covered with hangings and drapery. There he is, like Marius among the ruins of Carthage, his arms folded, his head shaven – Napoleon at Saint-Helena – what you will! Delilah is on her knees, a good deal like Canova's Magdalen. When a hussy has ruined her man, she adores him. As I see it, the Jewess was afraid of Samson in his strength and terrors, but she must have loved him when she saw him a child again. So Delilah is bewailing her sin, she would like to give her lover his hair again. She hardly dares to look at him; but she does look, with a smile, for she reads forgiveness in Samson's weakness. Such a group as this, and one of the ferocious Judith, would epitomise woman. Virtue cuts off your head; vice only cuts off your hair. Take care of your wigs, gentlemen!'

And she left the artists quite overpowered, to sing her praises in concert with the critic.

'It is impossible to be more bewitching!' cried Stidmann.

'Oh! she is the most intelligent and desirable woman I have ever met,' said Claude Vignon. 'Such a combination of beauty and cleverness is so rare.'

'And if you who had the honour of being intimate with Camille Maupin can pronounce such a verdict,' replied Stid-mann, 'what are we to think?'

'If you will make your Delilah a portrait of Valérie, my dear Count,' said Crevel, who had risen for a moment from the card-table, and who had heard what had been said, 'I will give you a thousand crowns for an example – yes, by the Powers! I will shell out to the tune of a thousand crowns!'

'Shell out! What does that mean?' asked Beauvisage of Claude Vignon.

'Madame must do me the honour to sit for it then,' said Steinbock to Crevel. 'Ask her—'

At this moment Valérie herself brought Steinbock a cup of tea. This was more than a compliment, it was a favour. There is a complete language in the manner in which a woman does this little civility; but women are fully aware of the fact, and it is a curious thing to study their movements, their manner, their look, tone, and accent when they perform this apparently simple act of politeness. – From the question, 'Do you take tea?' – 'Will you have some tea?' – 'A cup of tea?' coldly asked, and followed by instructions to the nymph of the urn to bring it, to the eloquent poem of the odalisque coming from the tea-table, cup in hand, towards the pasha of her heart, presenting it submissively, offering it in an insinuating voice, with a look full of intoxicating promises, a physiologist could deduce the whole scale of feminine emotion, from aversion or indifference to Phædra's declaration to Hippolytus. Women can make it, at will, contemptuous to the verge of insult, or humble to the expression of Oriental servility.

And Valérie was more than woman; she was the serpent made woman; she crowned her diabolical work by going up to Steinbock, a cup of tea in her hand.

'I will drink as many cups of tea as you will give me,' said the artist, murmuring in her ear as he rose, and touching her fingers with his, 'to have them given to me thus!'

'What were you saying about sitting?' said she, without betraying that this declaration, so frantically desired, had gone straight to her heart.

'Old Crevel promises me a thousand crowns for a copy of your group.'

'He! a thousand crowns for a bronze group?'

'Yes – if you will sit for Delilah,' said Steinbock.

'He will not be there to see, I hope!' replied she. 'The group would be worth more than all his fortune, for Delilah's costume is rather un-dressy.'

Just as Crevel loved to strike an attitude, every woman has a victorious gesture, a studied movement, which she knows must win admiration. You may see in a drawing-room how one spends all her time looking down at her tucker or pulling up the shoulder-piece of her gown, how another makes play with the brightness of her eyes by glancing up at the cornice. Madame Marneffe's triumph, however, was not face to face like that of other women. She turned sharply round to return to Lisbeth at the tea-table. This ballet-dancer's pirouette, whisking her skirts, by which she had overthrown Hulot, now fascinated Steinbock.

'Your vengeance is secure,' said Valérie to Lisbeth in a whisper. 'Hortense will cry out all her tears, and curse the day when she robbed you of Wenceslas.'

'Till I am Madame la Maréchale I shall not think myself successful,' replied the Cousin; 'but they are all beginning to wish for it. – This morning I went to Victorin's – I forgot to tell you. – The young Hulots have bought up their father's notes of hand given to Vauvinet, and to-morrow they will endorse a bill for seventy-two thousand francs at five per cent., payable in three years, and secured by a mortgage on their house. So the young people are in straits for three years; they can raise no more money on that property. Victorin is dreadfully distressed; he understands his father. And Crevel is capable of refusing to see them; he will be so angry at this piece of self-sacrifice.'

'The Baron cannot have a sou now,' said Valérie, and she smiled at Hulot.

'I don't see where he can get it. But he will draw his salary again in September.'

'And he has his policy of insurance; he has renewed it. Come, it is high time he should get Marneffe promoted. I will drive it home this evening.'

'My dear cousin,' said Lisbeth to Wenceslas, 'go home, I beg. You are quite ridiculous. Your eyes are fixed on Valérie in a way that is enough to compromise her, and her husband is insanely jealous. Do not tread in your father-in-law's footsteps. Go home; I am sure Hortense is sitting up for you.'

'Madame Marneffe told me to stay till the last to settle my little business with you and her,' replied Wenceslas.

'No, no,' said Lisbeth; 'I will bring you the ten thousand francs, for her husband has his eye on you. It would be rash to remain. To-morrow at eleven o'clock bring your note of hand; at that hour that mandarin Marneffe is at his office, Valérie is free. – Have you really asked her to sit for your group? – Come up to my rooms first. – Ah! I was sure of it,' she added, as she caught the look which Steinbock flashed at Valérie, 'I knew you were a profligate in the bud! Well, Valérie is lovely – but try not to bring trouble on Hortense.'

Nothing annoys a married man so much as finding his wife perpetually interposing between himself and his wishes, however transient.

Wenceslas got home at about one in the morning; Hortense had expected him ever since half-past nine. From half-past nine till ten she had listened to the passing carriages, telling herself that never before had her husband come in so late from dining with Florent and Chanor. She sat sewing by the child's cot, for she had begun to save a needlewoman's pay for the day by doing the mending herself. – From ten till half-past, a suspicion crossed her mind; she sat wondering –

'Is he really gone to dinner, as he told me, with Chanor and Florent? He put on his best cravat and his handsomest pin when he dressed. He took as long over his toilet as a woman when she wants to make the best of herself. – I am crazy! He loves me! – And here he is!'

But instead of stopping, the cab she heard went past.

From eleven till midnight Hortense was a victim to terrible alarms; the quarter where they lived was now deserted.

'If he has set out on foot, some accident may have happened,' thought she. 'A man may be killed by tumbling over a kerbstone or failing to see a gap. Artists are so heedless! Or if he should have been stopped by robbers! – It is the first time he has ever left me alone here for six hours and a half! – But why should I worry myself? He cares for no one but me.'

Men ought to be faithful to the wives who love them, were it only on account of the perpetual miracles wrought by true love in the sublime regions of the spiritual world. The woman who loves is, in relation to the man she loves, in the position of a somnambulist to whom the magnetiser should give the painful power, when she ceases to be the mirror of the world, of being conscious as a woman of what she has seen as a somnambulist. Passion raises the nervous tension of a woman to the ecstatic pitch at which presentiment is as acute as the insight of a clairvoyant. A wife knows she is betrayed; she will not let herself say so, she doubts still – she loves so much! She gives the lie to the outcry of her own Pythian power. This paroxysm of love deserves a special form of worship.

In noble souls, admiration of this divine phenomenon will always be a safeguard to protect them from infidelity. How should a man not worship a beautiful and intellectual creature whose soul can soar to such manifestations?

By one in the morning Hortense was in a state of such intense anguish, that she flew to the door as she recognised her husband's ring at the bell, and clasped him in her arms like a mother.

'At last – here you are!' cried she, finding her voice again. 'My dearest, henceforth where you go I go, for I cannot again endure the torture of such waiting. – I pictured you stumbling over a kerbstone, with a fractured skull! Killed by thieves! – No, a second time I know I should go mad. – Have you enjoyed yourself so much? – And without me! – Bad boy!'

'What can I say, my darling? There was Bixiou, who drew fresh caricatures for us; Léon de Lora, as witty as ever; Claude Vignon, to whom I owe the only consolatory article that has come out about the Montcornet statue. There were—'

'Were there no ladies?' Hortense eagerly inquired.

'Worthy Madame Florent—'

'You said the Rocher de Cancale. – Were you at the Florents'?'

'Yes, at their house; I made a mistake.'

'You did not take a coach to come home?'

'No.'

'And you have walked from the Rue des Tournelles?'

'Stidmann and Bixiou came back with me along the boulevards as far as the Madeleine, talking all the way.'

'It is dry then on the boulevards and the Place de la Concorde and the Rue de Bourgogne? You are not muddy at all!' said Hortense, looking at her husband's patent leather boots.

It had been raining, but between the Rue Vanneau and the Rue Saint-Dominique Wenceslas had not got his boots soiled.

'Here – here are five thousand francs Chanor has been so generous as to lend me,' said Wenceslas, to cut short this lawyer-like examination.

He had made a division of the ten thousand-franc notes, half for Hortense and half for himself, for he had five thousand francs' worth of debts of which Hortense knew nothing. He owed money to his foreman and his workmen.

'Now your anxieties are relieved,' said he, kissing his wife. 'I am going to work to-morrow. Yes, I am off to the studio at half-past eight to-morrow morning. So I am going to bed this minute to get up early, by your leave, my pet.'

The suspicion that had dawned in Hortense's mind vanished; she was miles away from the truth. Madame Marneffe! She never thought of her. Her fear for her Wenceslas was that he should fall in with street prostitutes. The names of Bixiou and Léon de Lora, two artists noted for their wild dissipations, had alarmed her.

Next morning she saw Wenceslas go out at nine o'clock, and was quite reassured.

'Now he is at work again,' said she to herself, as she proceeded to dress her boy. 'I see he is quite in the vein! Well, well, if we cannot have the glory of Michael Angelo, we may have that of Benvenuto Cellini!'

Lulled by her own hopes, Hortense believed in a happy future; and she was chattering to her son of twenty months in the language of onomatopœia that amuses babes when, at about eleven o'clock, the cook, who had not seen Wenceslas go out, showed in Stidmann.

'I beg pardon, Madame,' said he. 'Is Wenceslas gone out already?'

'He is at the studio.'

'I came to talk over the work with him.'

'I will send for him,' said Hortense, offering Stidmann a chair.

Thanking Heaven for this piece of luck, Hortense was glad to detain Stidmann to ask some questions about the evening before. Stidmann bowed in acknowledgment of her kindness. The Countess Steinbock rang; the cook appeared, and was desired to go at once and fetch her master from the studio.

'You had an amusing dinner last night?' said Hortense. 'Wenceslas did not come in till past one in the morning.'

'Amusing? not exactly,' replied the artist, who had intended to fascinate Madame Marneffe. 'Society is not very amusing unless one is interested in it. That little Madame Marneffe is clever, but a great flirt.'

'And what did Wenceslas think of her?' asked poor Hortense, trying to keep calm. 'He said nothing about her to me.'

'I will only say one thing,' said Stidmann, 'and that is, that I think her a very dangerous woman.'

Hortense turned as pale as a woman after childbirth.

'So – it was at – at Madame Marneffe's that you dined – and not – not with Chanor?' said she, 'yesterday – and Wenceslas – and he—'

Stidmann, without knowing what mischief he had done, saw that he had blundered.

The Countess did not finish her sentence; she simply fainted away. The artist rang, and the maid came in. When Louise tried to get her mistress into her bedroom, a serious nervous attack came on, with violent hysterics. Stidmann, like any man who by an involuntary indiscretion has overthrown the structure built on a husband's lie to his wife, could not conceive that his words should produce such an effect; he supposed that the Countess was in such delicate health that the slightest contradiction was mischievous.

The cook presently returned to say, unfortunately in loud tones, that her master was not in the studio. In the midst of her anguish, Hortense heard, and the hysterical fit came on again.

'Go and fetch Madame's mother,' said Louise to the cook. 'Quick – run!'

'If I knew where to find Steinbock, I would go and fetch him!' exclaimed Stidmann in despair.

'He is with that woman!' cried the unhappy wife. 'He was not dressed to go to his work!'

Stidmann hurried off to Madame Marneffe's, struck by the truth of this conclusion, due to the second sight of passion.

At that moment Valérie was posed as Delilah. Stidmann, too sharp to ask for Madame Marneffe, walked straight in past the lodge, and ran quickly up to the second floor, arguing thus: 'If I ask for Madame Marneffe, she will be out. If I inquire pointblank for Steinbock, I shall be laughed at to my face. – Take the bull by the horns!'

Reine appeared in answer to his ring.

'Tell Monsieur le Comte Steinbock to come at once, his wife is dying—'

Reine, quite a match for Stidmann, looked at him with blank surprise.

'But, sir – I don't know – did you suppose—'

'I tell you that my friend Monsieur Steinbock is here; his wife is very ill. It is quite serious enough for you to disturb your mistress.' And Stidmann turned on his heel.

'He is there, sure enough!' said he to himself.

And in point of fact, after waiting a few minutes in the Rue Vanneau, he saw Wenceslas come out, and beckoned to him to come quickly. After telling him of the tragedy enacted in the

Rue Saint-Dominique, Stidmann scolded Steinbock for not having warned him to keep the secret of yesterday's dinner.

'I am done for,' said Wenceslas, 'but you are forgiven. I had totally forgotten that you were to call this morning, and I blundered in not telling you that we were to have dined with Florent. – What can I say? That Valérie has turned my head; but, my dear fellow, for her glory is well lost, misfortune well won! She really is! – Good Heavens! – But I am in a dreadful fix. Advise me. What can I say? How can I excuse myself?'

'I! advise you! I don't know,' replied Stidmann. 'But your wife loves you, I imagine? Well, then, she will believe anything. Tell her that you were on your way to me when I was on my way to you; that, at any rate, will set this morning's business right. Good-bye.'

Lisbeth, called down by Reine, ran after Wenceslas and caught him up at the corner of the Rue Hillerin-Bertin; she was afraid of his Polish artlessness. Not wishing to be involved in the matter, she said a few words to Wenceslas, who in his joy hugged her then and there. She had no doubt pushed out a plank to enable the artist to cross this awkward place in his conjugal affairs.

At the sight of her mother, who had flown to her aid, Hortense burst into floods of tears. This happily changed the character of the hysterical attack.

'Treachery, dear mamma!' cried she. 'Wenceslas, after giving me his word of honour that he would not go near Madame Marneffe, dined with her last night, and did not come in till a quarter-past one in the morning. – If you only knew! The day before we had had a discussion, not a quarrel, and I had appealed to him so touchingly. I told him I was jealous, that I should die if he were unfaithful; that I was easily suspicious, but that he ought to have some consideration for my weaknesses, as they came of my love for him; that I had my father's blood in my veins as well as yours; that at the first moment of such a discovery I should be mad, and capable of mad deeds – of avenging myself – of dishonouring us all, him, his child, and myself; that I might even kill him first and myself after – and so on.

'And yet he went there; he is there! – That woman is bent on breaking all our hearts! Only yesterday my brother and Célestin pledged their all to pay off seventy thousand francs on notes of hand signed for that good-for-nothing creature. – Yes, mamma, my father would have been arrested and put into prison. Cannot that dreadful woman be content with having my father, and with all your tears? Why take my Wenceslas? – I will go to see her and stab her!'

Madame Hulot, struck to the heart by the dreadful secrets Hortense was unwittingly letting out, controlled her grief by one of the heroic efforts which a magnanimous mother can make, and drew her daughter's head on to her bosom to cover it with kisses.

'Wait for Wenceslas, my child; all will be explained. The evil cannot be so great as you picture it! – I, too, have been deceived, my dear Hortense; you think me handsome, I have lived blameless; and yet I have been utterly forsaken for three-and-twenty years – for a Jenny Cadine, a Josépha, a Madame Marneffe! – Did you know that?'

'You, mamma, you! You have endured this for twenty—?'

She broke off, staggered by her own thoughts.

'Do as I have done, my child,' said her mother. 'Be gentle and kind, and your conscience will be at peace. On his deathbed a man may say, "My wife has never cost me a pang!" And God, who hears that dying breath, credits it to us. If I had abandoned myself to fury like you, what would have happened? Your father would have been embittered, perhaps he would have left me altogether, and he would not have been withheld by any fear of paining me. Our ruin, utter as it now is, would have been complete ten years sooner, and we should have shown the world the spectacle of a husband and wife living quite apart – a scandal of the most horrible, heartbreaking kind, for it is the destruction of the family. Neither your brother nor you could have married.

'I sacrificed myself, and that so bravely, that, till this last connection of your father's, the world has believed me happy. My serviceable and indeed courageous falsehood has, till now, screened Hector; he is still respected; but this old man's passion is taking him too far, that I see. His own folly, I fear, will break through the veil I have kept between the world and our home. However, I have held that curtain steady for twenty-three years, and have wept behind it – motherless, I, without a friend to trust, with no help but in religion – I have for twenty-three years secured the family honour—'

Hortense listened with a fixed gaze. The calm tones of resignation and of such crowning sorrow soothed the smart of her first wound; the tears rose again and flowed in torrents. In a frenzy of filial affection, overcome by her mother's noble heroism, she fell on her knees before Adeline, took up the hem of her dress and kissed it, as pious Catholics kiss the holy relics of a martyr.

'Nay, get up, Hortense,' said the Baroness. 'Such homage from my daughter wipes out many sad memories. Come to my heart, and weep for no sorrows but your own. It is the despair of my dear little girl, whose joy was my only joy, that broke the solemn seal which nothing ought to have removed from my lips. Indeed, I meant to have taken my woes to the tomb, as a shroud the more. It was to soothe your anguish that I spoke. – God will forgive me!

'Oh! if my life were to be your life, what would I not do? Men, the world, Fate, Nature, God Himself, I believe, make us pay for love with the most cruel grief. I must pay for ten years of happiness with twenty-four years of despair, of ceaseless sorrow, of bitterness—'

'But you had ten years, dear mamma, and I have had but three!' said the self-absorbed girl.

'Nothing is lost yet,' said Adeline. 'Only wait till Wenceslas comes.'

'Mother,' said she, 'he lied, he deceived me. He said, ''I will not go,'' and he went. And that over his child's cradle.'

'For pleasure, my child, men will commit the most cowardly, the most infamous actions – even crimes; it lies in their nature, it would seem. We wives are set apart for sacrifice. I believed my troubles were ended, and they are beginning again, for I never thought to suffer doubly by suffering with my child. Courage – and silence! – My Hortense, swear that you will never discuss your griefs with anybody but me, never let them be suspected by any third person. Oh! be as proud as your mother has been.'

Hortense started; she had heard her husband's step.

'So it would seem,' said Wenceslas, as he came in, 'that Stidmann has been here while I went to see him.'

'Indeed!' said Hortense, with the angry irony of an offended woman who uses words to stab.

'Certainly,' said Wenceslas, affecting surprise. 'We have just met.'

'And yesterday?'

'Well, yesterday I deceived you, my darling love; and your mother shall judge between us.'

This candour unlocked his wife's heart. All really lofty women like the truth better than lies. They cannot bear to see their idol smirched; they want to be proud of the despotism they bow to.

There is a strain of this feeling in the devotion of the Russians to their Czar.

'Now, listen, dear mother,' Wenceslas went on. 'I so truly love my sweet and kind Hortense, that I concealed from her the extent of our poverty. What could I do? She was still nursing the boy, and such troubles would have done her harm; you know what the risk is for a woman. Her beauty, youth, and health are imperilled. Did I do wrong? – She believes that we owe five thousand francs; but I owe five thousand more. The day before yesterday we were in the depths! No one on earth will lend to us artists. Our talents are not less untrustworthy than our whims. I knocked in vain at every door. Lisbeth, indeed, offered us her savings.'

'Poor soul!' said Hortense.

'Poor soul!' said the Baroness.

'But what are Lisbeth's two thousand francs? Everything to her, nothing to us. – Then, as you know, Hortense, she spoke to us of Madame Marneffe, who, as she owes so much to the

Baron, out of a sense of honour, will take no interest. Hortense wanted to send her diamonds to the Mont-de-Piété; they would have brought in a few thousand francs, but we needed ten thousand. Those ten thousand francs were to be had free of interest for a year! – I said to myself, "Hortense will be none the wiser; I will go and get them."

'Then the woman asked me to dinner through my father-in-law, giving me to understand that Lisbeth had spoken of the matter, and I should have the money. Between Hortense's despair on one hand, and the dinner on the other, I could not hesitate. – That is all.

'What! could Hortense, at four-and-twenty, lovely, pure, and virtuous, and all my pride and glory, imagine that, when I have never left her since we married, I could now prefer – what? – a tawny, painted, ruddled creature?' said he, using the vulgar exaggeration of the studio to convince his wife by the vehemence that women like.

'Oh! if only your father had ever spoken so—!' cried the Baroness.

Hortense threw her arms round her husband's neck.

'Yes, that is what I should have done,' said her mother. 'Wenceslas, my dear fellow, your wife was near dying of it,' she went on very seriously. 'You see how well she loves you. And, alas – she is yours!'

She sighed deeply.

'He may make a martyr of her, or a happy woman,' thought she to herself, as every mother thinks when she sees her daughter married. – 'It seems to me,' she said aloud, 'that I am miserable enough to hope to see my children happy.'

'Be quite easy, dear mamma,' said Wenceslas, only too glad to see this critical moment end happily. 'In two months I shall have repaid that dreadful woman. How could I help it,' he went on, repeating this essentially Polish excuse with a Pole's grace; 'there are times when a man would borrow of the Devil. – And, after all, the money belongs to the family. When once she had invited me, should I have got the money at all if I had responded to her civility with a rude refusal?'

'Oh, mamma, what mischief papa is bringing on us!' cried Hortense.

The Baroness laid her finger on her daughter's lips, aggrieved by this complaint, the first blame she had ever uttered of a father so heroically screened by her mother's magnanimous silence.

'Now, good-bye, my children,' said Madame Hulot. 'The storm is over. But do not quarrel any more.'

When Wenceslas and his wife returned to their room after letting out the Baroness, Hortense said to her husband –

'Tell me all about last evening.'

And she watched his face all through the narrative, interrupting him by the questions that crowd on a wife's mind in such circumstances. The story made Hortense reflect; she had a glimpse of the infernal dissipation which an artist must find in such vicious company.

'Be honest, my Wenceslas; Stidmann was there, Claude Vignon, Vernisset. – Who else? In short, it was good fun?'

'I, I was thinking of nothing but our ten thousand francs, and I was saying to myself, "My Hortense will be freed from anxiety."'

This catechism bored the Livonian excessively; he seized a gayer moment to say –

'And you, my dearest, what would you have done if your artist had proved guilty?'

'I,' said she, with an air of prompt decision, 'I should have taken up Stidmann – not that I love him, of course!'

'Hortense!' cried Steinbock, starting to his feet with a sudden and theatrical emphasis. 'You would not have had the chance – I would have killed you!'

Hortense threw herself into his arms, clasping him closely enough to stifle him, and covered him with kisses, saying –

'Ah, you do love me! I fear nothing! – But no more Marneffe. Never go plunging into such horrible bogs.'

'I swear to you, my dear Hortense, that I will go there no more, excepting to redeem my note of hand.'

She pouted at this, but only as a loving woman sulks to get something for it. Wenceslas, tired out with such a morning's work, went off to his studio to make a clay sketch of the *Samson and Delilah*, for which he had the drawings in his pocket.

Hortense, penitent for her little temper, and fancying that her husband was annoyed with her, went to the studio just as the sculptor had finished handling the clay with the impetuosity that spurs an artist when the mood is on him. On seeing his wife, Wenceslas hastily threw the wet wrapper over the group, and putting both arms round her, he said –

'We were not really angry, were we, my pretty puss?'

Hortense had caught sight of the group, had seen the linen thrown over it, and had said nothing; but as she was leaving, she took off the rag, looked at the model, and asked –

'What is that?'

'A group for which I had just had an idea.'

'And why did you hide it?'

'I did not mean you to see it till it was finished.'

'The woman is very pretty,' said Hortense.

And a thousand suspicions cropped up in her mind, as, in India, tall, rank plants spring up in a night-time.

By the end of three weeks, Madame Marneffe was intensely irritated by Hortense. Women of that stamp have a pride of their own; they insist that men shall kiss the devil's hoof; they have no forgiveness for the virtue that does not quail before their dominion, or that even holds its own against them. Now, in all that time Wenceslas had not paid one visit in the Rue Vanneau, not even that which politeness required to a woman who had sat for Delilah.

Whenever Lisbeth had called on the Steinbocks, there had been nobody at home. Monsieur and Madame lived in the studio. Lisbeth, following up the turtledoves to their nest at Le Gros-Caillou, found Wenceslas hard at work, and was informed by the cook that Madame never left Monsieur's side. Wenceslas was a slave to the autocracy of love. So now

Valérie, on her own account, took part with Lisbeth in her hatred of Hortense.

Women cling to a lover that another woman is fighting for, just as much as men do to women round whom many coxcombs are buzzing. Thus any reflections *à propos* to Madame Marneffe are equally applicable to any lady-killing rake; he is, in fact, a sort of male courtesan. Valérie's last fancy was a madness; above all, she was bent on getting her group; she was even thinking of going one morning to the studio to see Wenceslas, when a serious incident arose of the kind which, to a woman of that class, may be called the spoil of war.

This is how Valérie announced this wholly personal event.

She was breakfasting with Lisbeth and her husband.

'I say, Marneffe, what would you say to being a second time a father?'

'You don't mean it – a baby? – Oh, let me kiss you!'

He rose and went round the table; his wife held up her head so that he could just kiss her hair.

'If that is so,' he went on, 'I am head-clerk and officer of the Legion of Honour at once. But you must understand, my dear, Stanislas is not to be the sufferer, poor little man!'

'Poor little man?' Lisbeth put in. 'You have not set your eyes on him these seven months. I am supposed to be his mother at the school; I am the only person in the house who takes any trouble about him.'

'A brat that costs us a hundred crowns a quarter!' said Valérie. 'And he, at any rate, is your own child, Marneffe. You ought to pay for his schooling out of your salary. – The new-comer, far from reminding us of butchers' bills, will rescue us from want.'

'Valérie,' replied Marneffe, assuming an attitude like Crevel, 'I hope that Monsieur le Baron Hulot will take proper charge of his son, and not lay the burden on a poor clerk. I intend to keep him well up to the mark. So take the necessary steps, Madame! Get him to write you letters in which he alludes to his satisfaction, for he is rather backward in coming forward in regard to my appointment.'

And Marneffe went away to the office, where his chief's precious leniency allowed him to come in at about eleven o'clock. And, indeed, he did little enough, for his incapacity was notorious, and he detested work.

No sooner were they alone than Lisbeth and Valérie looked at each other for a moment like Augurs, and both together burst into a loud fit of laughter.

'I say, Valérie – is it the fact?' said Lisbeth, 'or merely a farce?'

'It is a physical fact!' replied Valérie. 'Now, I am sick and tired of Hortense; and it occurred to me in the night that I might fire this infant, like a bomb, into the Steinbock household.'

Valérie went back to her room, followed by Lisbeth, to whom she showed the following letter: –

'WENCESLAS MY DEAR, – I still believe in your love, though it is nearly three weeks since I saw you. Is this scorn? Delilah can scarcely believe that. Does it not rather result from the tyranny of a woman whom, as you told me, you can no longer love? Wenceslas, you are too great an artist to submit to such a dominion. Home is the grave of glory. – Consider now, are you the Wenceslas of the Rue du Doyenné? You missed fire with my father's statue; but in you the lover is greater than the artist, and you have had better luck with his daughter. You are a father, my beloved Wenceslas.

'If you do not come to me in the state I am in, your friends would think very badly of you. But I love you so madly, that I feel I should never have the strength to curse you. May I sign myself as ever,

'YOUR VALÉRIE.'

'What do you say to my scheme for sending this note to the studio at a time when our dear Hortense is there by herself?' asked Valérie. 'Last evening I heard from Stidmann that Wenceslas is to pick him up at eleven this morning to go on business to Chanor's; so that gowk Hortense will be there alone.'

'But after such a trick as that,' replied Lisbeth, 'I cannot continue to be your friend in the eyes of the world; I shall have to break with you, to be supposed never to visit you, or even to speak to you.'

'Evidently,' said Valérie; 'but—'

'Oh! be quite easy,' interrupted Lisbeth; 'we shall often meet when I am Madame la Maréchale. They are all set upon it now. Only the Baron is in ignorance of the plan, but you can talk him over.'

'Well,' said Valérie, 'but it is quite likely that the Baron and I may be on distant terms before long.'

'Madame Olivier is the only person who can make Hortense demand to see the letter,' said Lisbeth. 'And you must send her to the Rue Saint-Dominique before she goes on to the studio.'

'Our beauty will be at home, no doubt,' said Valérie, ringing for Reine to call up Madame Olivier.

Ten minutes after the despatch of this fateful letter, Baron Hulot arrived. Madame Marneffe threw her arms round the old man's neck with kittenish impetuosity.

'Hector, you are a father!' she said in his ear. 'That is what comes of quarrelling and making friends again—'

Perceiving a look of surprise, which the Baron did not at once conceal, Valérie assumed a reserve which brought the old man to despair. She made him wring the proofs from her one by one. When conviction, led on by vanity, had at last entered his mind, she enlarged on Monsieur Marneffe's wrath.

'My dear old veteran,' said she, 'you can hardly avoid getting your responsible editor, our representative partner if you like, appointed head-clerk and officer of the Legion of Honour, for you really have done for the poor man; he adores his Stanislas, the little monstrosity who is so like him, that to me he is insufferable. Unless you prefer to settle twelve hundred francs a year on Stanislas – the capital to be his, and the life-interest payable to me, of course—'

'But if I am to settle securities, I would rather it should be on my own son, and not on the monstrosity,' said the Baron.

This rash speech, in which the words 'my own son' came out as full as a river in flood, was, by the end of an hour, ratified as a formal promise to settle twelve hundred francs a year on the future boy. And this promise became, on Valérie's tongue and in her countenance, what a drum is in the hands of a child; for three weeks she played on it incessantly.

At the moment when Baron Hulot was leaving the Rue Vanneau, as happy as a man who after a year of married life still desires an heir, Madame Olivier had yielded to Hortense, and given up the note she was instructed to give only into the Count's own hands. The young wife paid twenty francs for that letter. The wretch who commits suicide must pay for the opium, the pistol, the charcoal.

Hortense read and re-read the note; she saw nothing but this sheet of white paper streaked with black lines; the universe held for her nothing but that paper; everything was dark around her. The glare of the conflagration that was consuming the edifice of her happiness lighted up the page, for blackest night enfolded her. The shouts of her little Wenceslas at play fell on her ear, as if he had been in the depths of a valley and she on a high mountain. Thus insulted at four-and-twenty, in all the splendour of her beauty, enhanced by pure and devoted love – it was not a stab, it was death. The first shock had been merely on the nerves, the physical frame had struggled in the grip of jealousy; but now certainty had seized her soul, her body was unconscious.

For about ten minutes Hortense sat under the incubus of this oppression. Then a vision of her mother appeared before her, and revulsion ensued; she was calm and cool, and mistress of her reason.

She rang.

'Get Louise to help you, child,' said she to the cook. 'As quickly as you can, pack up everything that belongs to me and everything wanted for the little boy. I give you an hour. When all is ready, fetch a hackney coach from the stand, and call me.

'Make no remarks! I am leaving the house, and shall take Louise with me. You must stay here with Monsieur; take good care of him—'

She went into her room, and wrote the following letter: —

'MONSIEUR LE COMTE, —

'The letter I enclose will sufficiently account for the determination I have come to.

'When you read this, I shall have left your house and have found refuge with my mother, taking our child with me.

'Do not imagine that I shall retrace my steps. Do not imagine that I am acting with the rash haste of youth, without reflection, with the anger of offended affection; you will be greatly mistaken.

'I have been thinking very deeply during the last fortnight of life, of love, of our marriage, of our duties to each other. I have known the perfect devotion of my mother; she has told me all her sorrows! She has been heroical — every day for twenty-three years. But I have not the strength to imitate her, not because I love you less than she loves my father, but for reasons of spirit and nature. Our home would be a hell; I might lose my head so far as to disgrace you — disgrace myself and our child.

'I refuse to be a Madame Marneffe; once launched on such a course, a woman of my temper might not, perhaps, be able to stop. I am, unfortunately for myself, a Hulot, not a Fischer.

'Alone, and absent from the scene of your dissipations, I am sure of myself, especially with my child to occupy me, and by the side of a strong and noble mother, whose life cannot fail to influence the vehement impetuousness of my feelings. There, I can be a good mother, bring our boy up well, and live. Under your roof the wife would oust the mother; and constant contention would sour my temper.

'I can accept a deathblow, but I will not endure for twenty-five years, like my mother. If, at the end of three years of perfect, unwavering love, you can be unfaithful to me with your father-in-law's mistress, what rivals may I expect to have in later years? Indeed, Monsieur, you have begun your career of profligacy much earlier than my father did, the life of dissipation, which is a disgrace to the father of a family, which undermines the respect of his children, and which ends in shame and despair.

'I am not unforgiving. Unrelenting feelings do not beseem erring creatures living under the eye of God. If you win fame and fortune by sustained work, if you have nothing to do with courtesans and ignoble, defiling ways, you will find me still a wife worthy of you.

'I believe you to be too much a gentleman, Monsieur le Comte, to have recourse to the law. You will respect my wishes, and leave me under my mother's roof. Above all, never let me see you there. I have left all the money lent to you by that odious woman. – Farewell.

'HORTENSE HULOT.'

This letter was written in anguish. Hortense abandoned herself to the tears, the outcries of murdered love. She laid down her pen and took it up again, to express as simply as possible all that passion commonly proclaims in this sort of testamentary letter. Her heart went forth in exclamations, wailing and weeping; but reason dictated the words.

Informed by Louise that all was ready, the young wife slowly went round the little garden, through the bedroom and drawing-room, looking at everything for the last time. Then she earnestly enjoined on the cook to take the greatest care for her master's comfort, promising to reward her handsomely if she would be honest. At last she got into the hackney coach to drive to her mother's house, her heart quite broken, crying so much as to distress the maid, and covering little Wenceslas with kisses, which betrayed her still unfailing love for his father.

The Baroness knew already from Lisbeth that the father-in-law was largely to blame for the son-in-law's fault; nor was she surprised to see her daughter, whose conduct she approved, and she consented to give her shelter. Adeline, perceiving that her own gentleness and patience had never checked Hector, for whom her respect was indeed fast diminishing, thought her daughter very right to adopt another course.

In three weeks the poor mother had suffered two wounds of which the pain was greater than any ill-fortune she had hitherto endured. The Baron had placed Victorin and his wife in great difficulties; and then, by Lisbeth's account, he was the cause of his son-in-law's misconduct, and had corrupted Wenceslas. The dignity of the father of the family, so long upheld by her really foolish self-sacrifice, was now overthrown. Though they did not regret the money, the young Hulots were full alike of doubts and uneasiness as regarded the Baron. This sentiment, which was evident enough, distressed the Baroness; she foresaw a break-up of the family tie.

Hortense was accommodated in the dining-room, arranged as a bedroom with the help of the Marshal's money, and the anteroom became the dining-room, as it is in many apartments.

When Wenceslas returned home and had read the two letters, he felt a kind of gladness mingled with regret. Kept so constantly under his wife's eye, so to speak, he had inwardly rebelled against this fresh thraldom, *à la* Lisbeth. Full fed with love for three years past, he too had been reflecting during the last fortnight; and he found a family heavy on his hands. He had just been congratulated by Stidmann on the passion he had inspired in Valérie; for Stidmann, with an under-thought that was not unnatural, saw that he might flatter the husband's vanity in the hope of consoling the victim. And Wenceslas was glad to be able to return to Madame Marneffe.

Still, he remembered the pure and unsullied happiness he had known, the perfections of his wife, her judgment, her innocent and guileless affection, – and he regretted her acutely. He thought of going at once to his mother-in-law's to crave forgiveness; but, in fact, like Hulot and Crevel, he went to Madame Marneffe, to whom he carried his wife's letter to show her what a disaster she had caused, and to discount his misfortune, so to speak, by claiming in return the pleasures his mistress could give him.

He found Crevel with Valérie. The mayor, puffed up with pride, marched up and down the room, agitated by a storm of feelings. He put himself into position as if he were about to speak, but he dared not. His countenance was beaming, and he went now and again to the window, where he drummed on the pane with his fingers. He kept looking at Valérie with a glance of tender pathos. Happily for him, Lisbeth presently came in.

'Cousin Bette,' said he in her ear, 'have you heard the news? I am a father! It seems to me I love my poor Célestine the less. – Oh! what a thing it is to have a child by the woman one idolises! It is the fatherhood of the heart added to that of the flesh! I say – tell Valérie that I will work for that child – it shall be rich. She tells me she has some reason for believing that it will be a boy! If it is a boy, I shall insist on his being called Crevel. I will consult my notary about it.'

'I know how much she loves you,' said Lisbeth. 'But for her sake in the future, and for your own, control yourself. Do not rub your hands every five minutes.'

While Lisbeth was speaking aside on this wise to Crevel, Valérie had asked Wenceslas to give her back her letter, and she was saying things that dispelled all his griefs.

'So now you are free, my dear,' said she. 'Ought any great artist to marry? You live only by fancy and freedom! There, I shall love you so much, beloved poet, that you shall never regret your wife. At the same time, if, like so many people, you want to keep up appearances, I undertake to bring Hortense back to you in a very short time.'

'Oh, if only that were possible!'

'I am certain of it,' said Valérie, nettled. 'Your poor father-in-law is a man who is in every way utterly done for; who wants to appear as though he could be loved, out of conceit, and to make the world believe that he has a mistress; and he is so excessively vain on this point, that I can do what I please with him. The Baroness is still so devoted to her old Hector –

I always feel as if I were talking of the *Iliad* – that these two old folks will contrive to patch up matters between you and Hortense. Only, if you want to avoid storms at home for the future, do not leave me for three weeks without coming to see your mistress – I was dying of it. My dear boy, some consideration is due from a gentleman to a woman he has so deeply compromised, especially when, as in my case, she has to be very careful of her reputation.

'Stay to dinner, my darling – and remember that I must treat you with all the more apparent coldness because you are guilty of this too obvious mishap.'

Baron Montès was presently announced; Valérie rose and hurried forward to meet him; she spoke a few sentences in his ear, enjoining on him the same reserve as she had impressed on Wenceslas; the Brazilian assumed a diplomatic reticence suitable to the great news which filled him with delight, for he, at any rate, was sure of his paternity.

Thanks to these tactics, based on the vanity of man in the lover stage of his existence, Valérie sat down to table with four men, all pleased and eager to please, all charmed, and each believing himself adored; called by Marneffe, who included himself, in speaking to Lisbeth, the five Fathers of the Church.

Baron Hulot alone at first showed an anxious countenance, and this was why. Just as he was leaving the office, the head of the staff of clerks had come to his private room – a General with whom he had served for thirty years – and Hulot had spoken to him as to appointing Marneffe to Coquet's place, Coquet having consented to retire.

'My dear fellow,' said he, 'I would not ask this favour of the Prince without our having agreed on the matter, and knowing that you approved.'

'My good friend,' replied the other, 'you must allow me to observe that, for your own sake, you should not insist on this nomination. I have already told you my opinion. There would be a scandal in the office, where there is a great deal too much talk already about you and Madame Marneffe. This, of course, is between ourselves. I have no wish to touch you on a

sensitive spot, or disoblige you in any way, and I will prove it.
If you are determined to get Monsieur Coquet's place, and he
will really be a loss in the War Office, for he has been here
since 1809, I will go into the country for a fortnight, so as to
leave the field open between you and the Marshal, who loves
you as a son. Then I shall take neither part, and shall have
nothing on my conscience as an administrator.'

'Thank you very much,' said Hulot. 'I will reflect on what
you have said.'

'In allowing myself to say so much, my dear friend, it is
because your personal interest is far more deeply implicated
than any concern or vanity of mine. In the first place, the
matter lies entirely with the Marshal. And then, my good
fellow, we are blamed for so many things, that one more or
less! We are not at the maiden stage in our experience of fault-
finding. Under the Restoration, men were put in simply to give
them places, without any regard for the office. – We are old
friends—'

'Yes,' the Baron put in; 'and it is in order not to impair our
old and valued friendship that I—'

'Well, well,' said the departmental manager, seeing Hulot's
face clouded with embarrassment, 'I will take myself off, old
fellow. – But I warn you! you have enemies – that is to say,
men who covet your splendid appointment, and you have
but one anchor out. Now if, like me, you were a Deputy,
you would have nothing to fear; so mind what you are
about.'

This speech, in the most friendly spirit, made a deep
impression on the Councillor of State.

'But, after all, Roger, what is it that is wrong? Do not make
any mysteries with me.'

The individual addressed as Roger looked at Hulot, took his
hand, and pressed it.

'We are such old friends, that I am bound to give you
warning. If you want to keep your place, you must make a bed
for yourself, and instead of asking the Marshal to give
Coquet's place to Marneffe, in your place I would beg him

to use his influence to reserve a seat for me on the General Council of State; there you may die in peace, and, like the beaver, abandon all else to the pursuers.'

'What, do you think the Marshal would forget—?'

'The Marshal has already taken your part so warmly at a General Meeting of the Ministers, that you will not now be turned out; but it was seriously discussed! So give them no excuse. I can say no more. At this moment you may make your own terms; you may sit on the Council of State and be made a Peer of the Chamber. If you delay too long, if you give any one a hold against you, I can answer for nothing. – Now, am I to go?'

'Wait a little. I will see the Marshal,' replied Hulot, 'and I will send my brother to see which way the wind blows at headquarters.'

The humour in which the Baron came back to Madame Marneffe's may be imagined; he had almost forgotten his fatherhood, for Roger had taken the part of a true and kind friend in explaining the position. At the same time, Valérie's influence was so great that, by the middle of dinner, the Baron was tuned up to the pitch, and was all the more cheerful for having unwonted anxieties to conceal; but the hapless man was not yet aware that in the course of that evening he would find himself in a cleft stick, between his happiness and the danger pointed out by his friend – compelled, in short, to choose between Madame Marneffe and his official position.

At eleven o'clock, when the evening was at its gayest, for the room was full of company, Valérie drew Hector into a corner of her sofa.

'My dear old boy,' said she, 'your daughter is so annoyed at knowing that Wenceslas comes here, that she has left him "planted." Hortense is wrong-headed. Ask Wenceslas to show you the letter the little fool has written to him.

'This division of two lovers, of which I am reputed to be the cause, may do me the greatest harm, for this is how virtuous women undermine each other. It is disgraceful to pose as a victim in order to cast the blame on a woman whose only crime is that she keeps a pleasant house. If you love me, you will clear my character by reconciling the sweet turtle-doves.

'I do not in the least care about your son-in-law's visits; you brought him here – take him away again! If you have any authority in your family, it seems to me that you may very well insist on your wife's patching up this squabble. Tell the worthy old lady from me, that if I am unjustly charged with having caused a young couple to quarrel, with upsetting the unity of a family, and annexing both the father and the son-in-law, I will deserve my reputation by annoying them in my own way! Why, here is Lisbeth talking of throwing me over! She prefers to stick to her family, and I cannot blame her for it. She will throw me over, says she, unless the young people make friends again. A pretty state of things! Our expenses here will be trebled!'

'Oh, as for that!' said the Baron, on hearing of his daughter's strong measures, 'I will have no nonsense of that kind.'

'Very well,' said Valérie. 'And now for the next thing. – What about Coquet's place?'

'That,' said Hector, looking away, 'is more difficult, not to say impossible.'

'Impossible, my dear Hector?' said Madame Marneffe in the Baron's ear. 'But you do not know to what lengths Marneffe will go. I am completely in his power; he is immoral for his own gratification, like most men, but he is excessively vindictive, like all weak and impotent natures. In the position to which you have reduced me, I am in his power. I am bound to be on terms with him for a few days, and he is quite capable of refusing to leave my room any more.'

Hulot started with horror.

'He would leave me alone on condition of being head-clerk. It is abominable – but logical.'

'Valérie, do you love me?'

'In the state in which I am, my dear, the question is the meanest insult.'

'Well, then – if I were to attempt, merely to attempt, to ask the Prince for a place for Marneffe, I should be done for, and Marneffe would be turned out.'

'I thought that you and the Prince were such intimate friends.'

'We are, and he has amply proved it; but, my child, there is authority above the Marshal's – for instance, the whole Council of Ministers. With time and a little tacking, we shall get there. But, to succeed, I must wait till the moment when some service is required of me. Then I can say one good turn deserves another—'

'If I tell Marneffe this tale, my poor Hector, he will play us some mean trick. You must tell him yourself that he has to wait. I will not undertake to do so. Oh! I know what my fate would be. He knows how to punish me! He will henceforth share my room—

'Do not forget to settle the twelve hundred francs a year on the little one!'

Hulot, seeing his pleasures in danger, took Monsieur Marneffe aside, and for the first time derogated from the haughty tone he had always assumed towards him, so greatly was he horrified by the thought of that half-dead creature in his pretty young wife's bedroom.

'Marneffe, my dear fellow,' said he, 'I have been talking of you to-day. But you cannot be promoted to the first-class just yet. We must have time.'

'I will be, Monsieur le Baron,' said Marneffe shortly.

'But, my dear fellow—'

'I *will* be, Monsieur le Baron,' Marneffe coldly repeated, looking alternately at the Baron and at Valérie. 'You have placed my wife in a position that necessitates her making up her differences with me, and I mean to keep her; for, *my dear fellow*, she is a charming creature,' he added, with crushing irony. 'I am master here – more than you are at the War Office.'

The Baron felt one of those pangs of fury which have the effect, in the heart, of a fit of raging toothache, and he could hardly conceal the tears in his eyes.

During this little scene, Valérie had been explaining Marneffe's imaginary determination to Montès, and thus had rid herself of him for a time.

Of her four adherents, Crevel alone was exempted from the rule – Crevel, the master of the little 'bijou' apartment; and he displayed on his countenance an air of really insolent beatitude, notwithstanding the wordless reproofs administered by Valérie in frowns and meaning grimaces. His triumphant paternity beamed in every feature.

When Valérie was whispering a word of correction in his ear, he snatched her hand, and put in –

'To-morrow, my Duchess, you shall have your own little house! The papers are to be signed to-morrow.'

'And the furniture?' said she, with a smile.

'I have a thousand shares in the Versailles *rive gauche* railway. I bought them at twenty-five, and they will go up to three hundred in consequence of the amalgamation of the two lines, which is a secret told to me. You shall have furniture fit for a queen. But then you will be mine alone henceforth?'

'Yes, burly Maire,' said this middle-class Madame de Merteuil. 'But behave yourself; respect the future Madame Crevel.'

'My dear cousin,' Lisbeth was saying to the Baron, 'I shall go to see Adeline early to-morrow; for, as you must see, I cannot, with any decency, remain here. I will go and keep house for your brother the Marshal.'

'I am going home this evening,' said Hulot.

'Very well, you will see me at breakfast to-morrow,' said Lisbeth, smiling.

She understood that her presence would be necessary at the family scene that would take place on the morrow. And the very first thing in the morning she went to see Victorin and to tell him that Hortense and Wenceslas had parted.

When the Baron went home at half-past ten, Mariette and Louise, who had had a hard day, were locking up the apartment. Hulot had not to ring.

Very much put out at this compulsory virtue, the husband went straight to his wife's room, and through the half-open door he saw her kneeling before her Crucifix, absorbed in prayer, in one of those attitudes which make the fortune of the painter or the sculptor who is so happy to invent and then to express them. Adeline, carried away by her enthusiasm, was praying aloud –

'O God, have mercy and enlighten him!'

The Baroness was praying for her Hector.

At this sight, so unlike what he had just left, and on hearing this petition founded on the events of the day, the Baron heaved a sigh of deep emotion. Adeline looked round, her face drowned in tears. She was so convinced that her prayer had been heard, that, with one spring, she threw her arms round Hector with the impetuosity of happy affection. Adeline had given up all a wife's instincts; sorrow had effaced even the memory of them. No feeling survived in her but those of motherhood, of the family honour, and the pure attachment of a Christian wife for a husband who had gone astray – the saintly tenderness which survives all else in a woman's soul.

'Hector!' she said, 'are you come back to us? Has God taken pity on our family?'

'Dear Adeline,' replied the Baron, coming in and seating his wife by his side on a couch, 'you are the saintliest creature I ever knew; I have long known myself to be unworthy of you.'

'You would have very little to do, my dear,' said she, holding Hulot's hand and trembling so violently that it was as though she had a palsy, 'very little to set things in order—'

She dared not proceed; she felt that every word would be a reproof, and she did not wish to mar the happiness with which this meeting was inundating her soul.

'It is Hortense who has brought me here,' said Hulot. 'That child may do us far more harm by her hasty proceeding than my absurd passion for Valérie has ever done. But we will discuss all this to-morrow morning. Hortense is asleep, Mariette tells me; we will not disturb her.'

'Yes,' said Madame Hulot, suddenly plunged into the depths of grief.

She understood that the Baron's return was prompted not so much by the wish to see his family as by some ulterior interest.

'Leave her in peace till to-morrow,' said the mother. 'The poor child is in a deplorable condition; she has been crying all day.'

At nine next morning, the Baron, awaiting his daughter, whom he had sent for, was pacing the large, deserted drawing-room, trying to find arguments by which to conquer the most difficult form of obstinacy there is to deal with – that of a young wife, offended and implacable, as blameless youth ever is, in its ignorance of the disgraceful compromises of the world, of its passions and interests.

'Here I am, papa,' said Hortense in a tremulous voice, and looking pale from her miseries.

Hulot, sitting down, took his daughter round the waist, and drew her down to sit on his knee.

'Well, my child,' said he, kissing her forehead, 'so there are troubles at home, and you have been hasty and headstrong? That is not like a well-bred child. My Hortense ought not to have taken such a decisive step as that of leaving her house and deserting her husband on her own account, and without consulting her parents. If my darling girl had come to see her kind and admirable mother, she would not have given me the cruel pain I feel! – You do not know the world; it is malignantly spiteful. People will perhaps say that your husband sent you back to your parents. Children brought up, as you were, on your mother's lap, remain children longer than others; they know nothing of life. An artless, maidenly passion like yours for Wenceslas, unfortunately, makes no allowances; it acts on every impulse. The little heart is moved, the head follows suit. You would burn down Paris to be revenged, with no thought of the courts of justice!

'When your old father tells you that you have outraged the proprieties, you may take his word for it. – I say nothing of the cruel pain you have given me. It is bitter, I assure you, for you throw all the blame on a woman of whose heart you know nothing, and whose hostility may become disastrous. And you, alas! so full of guileless innocence and purity, can have no suspicions; but you may be vilified and slandered. – Besides, my darling pet, you have taken a foolish jest too seriously. I can assure you, on my honour, that your husband is blameless. Madame Marneffe—'

So far the Baron, artistically diplomatic, had formulated his remonstrances very judiciously. He had, as may be observed, worked up to the mention of this name with superior skill; and yet Hortense, as she heard it, winced as if stung to the quick.

'Listen to me; I have had great experience, and I have seen much,' he went on, stopping his daughter's attempt to speak. 'That lady is very cold to your husband. Yes, you have been made the victim of a practical joke, and I will prove it to you. Yesterday Wenceslas was dining with her—'

'Dining with her!' cried the young wife, starting to her feet, and looking at her father with horror in every feature. 'Yesterday! After having had my letter! Oh, great God! – Why did I not take the veil rather than marry! But now my life is not my own! I have the child!' and she sobbed.

Her weeping went to Madame Hulot's heart. She came out of her room and ran to her daughter, taking her in her arms, and asking her those questions, stupid with grief, which first rose to her lips.

'Now we have tears,' said the Baron to himself, 'and all was going so well! What is to be done with women who cry?'

'My child,' said the Baroness, 'listen to your father! He loves us all – come, come—'

'Come, Hortense, my dear little girl, cry no more, you make yourself too ugly!' said the Baron. 'Now, be a little reasonable. Go sensibly home, and I promise you that Wenceslas shall never set foot in that woman's house. I ask you to make that sacrifice, if it is a sacrifice to forgive the husband you love so small a fault. I ask you – for the sake of my grey hairs, and of the love you owe your mother. You do not want to blight my later years with bitterness and regret?'

Hortense fell at her father's feet like a crazed thing, with the vehemence of despair; her hair, loosely pinned up, fell about her, and she held out her hands with an expression that painted her misery.

'Father,' she said, 'ask my life! Take it if you will, but at least take it pure and spotless, and I will yield it up gladly. Do not ask me to die in dishonour and crime. I am not at all like my husband; I cannot swallow an outrage. If I went back under my husband's roof, I should be capable of smothering him in a fit of jealousy – or of doing worse! Do not exact from me a thing that is beyond my powers. Do not have to mourn for me still living, for the least that can befall me is to go mad. I feel madness close upon me!

'Yesterday, yesterday, he could dine with that woman, after having read my letter? – Are other men made so? My life I give you, but do not let my death be ignominious! – His fault? – a small one! When he has a child by that woman!'

'A child!' cried Hulot, starting back a step or two. 'Come. This is really some fooling.'

At this juncture Victorin and Lisbeth arrived, and stood dumbfounded at the scene. The daughter was prostrate at her father's feet. The Baroness, speechless between her maternal feelings and her conjugal duty, showed a harassed face bathed in tears.

'Lisbeth,' said the Baron, seizing his cousin by the hand and pointing to Hortense, 'you can help me here. My poor child's brain is turned; she believes that her Wenceslas is Madame Marneffe's lover, while all that Valérie wanted was to have a group by him.'

'*Delilah!*' cried the young wife. 'The only thing he had done since our marriage. The man would not work for me or for his son, and he has worked with frenzy for that good-for-nothing creature. – Oh, father, kill me outright, for every word stabs like a knife!'

Lisbeth turned to the Baroness and Victorin, pointing with a pitying shrug to the Baron, who could not see her.

'Listen to me,' said she to him. 'I had no idea – when you asked me to go to lodge over Madame Marneffe and keep house for her – I had no idea of what she was; but many things may be learned in three years. That creature is a prostitute, and one whose depravity can only be compared with that of her infamous and horrible husband. You are the dupe, my lord pot-boiler, of those people; you will be led further by them than you dream of! I speak plainly, for you are at the bottom of a pit.'

The Baroness and her daughter, hearing Lisbeth speak in this style, cast adoring looks at her, such as the devout cast at a Madonna for having saved their life.

'That horrible woman was bent on destroying your son-in-law's home. To what end? – I know not. My brain is not equal to seeing clearly into these dark intrigues – perverse, ignoble, infamous! Your Madame Marneffe does not love your son-in-law, but she will have him at her feet out of revenge. I have just spoken to the wretched woman as she deserves. She is a shameless courtesan; I have told her that I am leaving her house, that I would not have my honour smirched in that muck-heap. – I owe myself to my family before all else.

'I knew that Hortense had left her husband, so here I am. Your Valérie, whom you believe to be a saint, is the cause of this miserable separation; can I remain with such a woman? Our poor little Hortense,' said she, touching the Baron's arm, with peculiar meaning, 'is perhaps the dupe of a wish of such women as these, who, to possess a toy, would sacrifice a family.

'I do not think Wenceslas guilty; but I think him weak, and I cannot promise that he will not yield to her refinements of temptation. – My mind is made up. The woman is fatal to you; she will bring you all to utter ruin. I will not even seem to be concerned in the destruction of my own family, after living there for three years solely to hinder it.

'You are cheated, Baron; say very positively that you will have nothing to say to the promotion of that dreadful Marneffe, and you will see then! There is a fine rod in pickle for you in that case.'

Lisbeth lifted up Hortense and kissed her enthusiastically.

'My dear Hortense, stand firm,' she whispered.

The Baroness embraced Lisbeth with the vehemence of a woman who sees herself avenged. The whole family stood in perfect silence round the father, who had wit enough to know what that silence implied. A storm of fury swept across his brow and face with evident signs; the veins swelled, his eyes were bloodshot, his flesh showed patches of colour. Adeline fell on her knees before him and seized his hands.

'My dear, forgive, my dear!'

'You loathe me!' cried the Baron – the cry of his conscience.

For we all know the secret of our own wrongdoing. We almost always ascribe to our victims the hateful feelings which must fill them with the hope of revenge; and in spite of every effort of hypocrisy, our tongue or our face makes confession under the rack of some unexpected anguish, as the criminal of old confessed under the hands of the torturer.

'Our children,' he went on, to retract the avowal, 'turn at last to be our enemies—'

'Father!' Victorin began.

'You dare to interrupt your father!' said the Baron in a voice of thunder, glaring at his son.

'Father, listen to me,' Victorin went on in a clear, firm voice, the voice of a puritanical deputy. 'I know the respect I owe you too well ever to fail in it, and you will always find me the most respectful and submissive of sons.'

Those who are in the habit of attending the sittings of the Chamber will recognise the tactics of parliamentary warfare in these fine-drawn phrases, used to calm the factions while gaining time.

'We are far from being your enemies,' his son went on. 'I have quarrelled with my father-in-law, Monsieur Crevel, for having rescued your notes of hand for sixty thousand francs from Vauvinet, and that money is, beyond doubt, in Madame Marneffe's pocket. – I am not finding fault with you, father,' said he, in reply to an impatient gesture of the Baron's; 'I simply wish to add my protest to my cousin Lisbeth's, and to point out to you that though my devotion to you as a father is blind and unlimited, my dear father, our pecuniary resources, unfortunately, are very limited.'

'Money!' cried the excitable old man, dropping on to a chair, quite crushed by this argument. 'From my son! – You shall be repaid your money, sir,' said he, rising, and he went to the door.

'Hector!'

At this cry the Baron turned round, suddenly showing his wife a face bathed in tears; she threw her arms round him with the strength of despair.

'Do not leave us thus – do not go away in anger. I have not said a word – not I!'

At this heart-wrung speech the children fell at their father's feet.

'We all love you,' said Hortense.

Lisbeth, as rigid as a statue, watched the group with a superior smile on her lips. Just then Marshal Hulot's voice was heard in the anteroom. The family all felt the importance of secrecy, and the scene suddenly changed. The young people rose, and every one tried to hide all traces of emotion.

A discussion was going on at the door between Mariette and a soldier, who was so persistent that the cook came in.

'Monsieur, a regimental quarter-master, who says he is just come from Algiers, insists on seeing you.'

'Tell him to wait.'

'Monsieur,' said Mariette to her master in an undertone, 'he told me to tell you privately that it has to do with your uncle there.'

The Baron started; he believed that the funds had been sent at last which he had been asking for these two months, to pay up his bills; he left the family-party, and hurried out to the anteroom.

'You are Mounsieur de Paron Hulot?'

'Yes.'

'Your own self?'

'My own self.'

The man, who had been fumbling meanwhile in the lining of his cap, drew out a letter, of which the Baron hastily broke the seal, and read as follows: –

'DEAR NEPHEW, – Far from being able to send you the hundred thousand francs you ask of me, my present position is not tenable unless you can take some decisive steps to save me. We are saddled with a public prosecutor who talks goody, and rhodomontades nonsense about the management. It is impossible to get the black-chokered pump to hold his tongue. If the War Minister allows civilians to feed out of his hand, I am done for. I can trust the bearer; try to get him promoted; he has done us good service. Do not abandon me to the crows!'

This letter was a thunderbolt; the Baron could read in it the intestine warfare between the civil and military authorities, which to this day hampers the Government, and he was required to invent on the spot some palliative for the difficulty that stared him in the face. He desired the soldier to come back next day, dismissing him with splendid promises of promotion, and he returned to the drawing-room. 'Good day and good-bye, brother,' said he to the Marshal. – 'Good-bye, children. – Good-bye, my dear Adeline. – And what are you going to do, Lisbeth?' he asked.

'I? – I am going to keep house for the Marshal, for I must end my days doing what I can for one or another of you.'

'Do not leave Valérie till I have seen you again,' said Hulot in his cousin's ear. – 'Good-bye, Hortense, refractory little puss; try to be reasonable. I have important business to be attended to at once; we will discuss your reconciliation another time. Now, think it over, my child,' said he as he kissed her.

And he went away, so evidently uneasy, that his wife and children felt the gravest apprehensions.

'Lisbeth,' said the Baroness, 'I must find out what is wrong with Hector; I never saw him in such a state. Stay a day or two longer with that woman; he tells her everything, and we can then learn what has so suddenly upset him. Be quite easy; we will arrange your marriage to the Marshal, for it is really necessary.'

'I shall never forget the courage you have shown this morning,' said Hortense, embracing Lisbeth.

'You have avenged our poor mother,' said Victorin.

The Marshal looked on with curiosity at all the display of affection lavished on Lisbeth, who went off to report the scene to Valérie.

This sketch will enable guileless souls to understand what various mischief Madame Marneffes may do in a family, and the means by which they reach poor virtuous wives apparently so far out of their ken. And then, if we only transfer, in fancy, such doings to the upper class of society about a throne, and if we consider what king's mistresses must have cost them, we may estimate the debt owed by a nation to a sovereign who sets the example of a decent and domestic life.

In Paris each ministry is a little town by itself, whence women are banished; but there is just as much detraction and scandal as though the feminine population were admitted there. At the end of three years, Monsieur Marneffe's position was perfectly clear and open to the day, and in every room one and another asked, 'Is Marneffe to be, or not to be, Coquet's successor?' Exactly as the question might have been put to the Chamber, 'Will the estimates pass or not pass?' The smallest initiative on the part of the Board of Management was commented on; everything in Baron Hulot's department was carefully noted. The astute State Councillor had enlisted on his side the victim of Marneffe's promotion, a hard-working clerk, telling him that if he could fill Marneffe's place, he would certainly succeed to it; he had told him that the man was dying. So this clerk was scheming for Marneffe's advancement.

When Hulot went through his anteroom, full of visitors, he saw Marneffe's colourless face in a corner, and sent for him before any one else.

'What do you want of me, my dear fellow?' said the Baron, disguising his anxiety.

'Monsieur le Directeur, I am the laughing-stock of the office, for it has become known that the chief of the clerks has left this morning for a holiday, on the ground of his health. He is to be away a month. Now, we all know what waiting for a month means. You deliver me over to the mockery of my enemies, and it is bad enough to be drummed upon on one side; drumming on both at once, Monsieur, is apt to burst the drum.'

'My dear Marneffe, it takes long patience to gain an end. You cannot be made head-clerk in less than two months, if ever. Just when I must, as far as possible, secure my own position, is not the time to be applying for your promotion, which would raise a scandal.'

'If you are broke, I shall never get it,' said Marneffe coolly. 'And if you get me the place, it will make no difference in the end.'

'Then I am to sacrifice myself for you?' said the Baron.

'If you do not, I shall be much mistaken in you.'

'You are too exclusively Marneffe, Monsieur Marneffe,' said Hulot, rising and showing the clerk the door.

'I have the honour to wish you good morning, Monsieur le Baron,' said Marneffe humbly.

'What an infamous rascal!' thought the Baron. 'This is uncommonly like a summons to pay within twenty-four hours on pain of distraint.'

Two hours later, just when the Baron had been instructing Claude Vignon, whom he was sending to the Ministry of Justice to obtain information as to the judicial authorities under whose jurisdiction Johann Fischer might fall, Reine opened the door of his private room and gave him a note, saying she would wait for the answer.

'Valérie is mad!' said the Baron to himself. 'To send Reine! It is enough to compromise us all, and it certainly compromises that dreadful Marneffe's chances of promotion!'

But he dismissed the minister's private secretary, and read as follows: —

'Oh, my dear friend, what a scene I have had to endure! Though you have made me happy for three years, I have paid dearly for it! He came in from the office in a rage that made me quake. I knew he was ugly; I have seen him a monster! His four real teeth chattered, and he threatened me with his odious presence without respite if I should continue to receive you. My poor, dear old boy, our door is closed against you henceforth. You see my tears; they are dropping on the paper and soaking it; can you read what I write, dear Hector? Oh, to think of never seeing you, of giving you up when I bear in me some of your life, as I flatter myself I have your heart – it is enough to kill me. Think of our little Hector!

'Do not forsake me, but do not disgrace yourself for Marneffe's sake; do not yield to his threats.

'I love you as I have never loved! I remember all the sacrifices you have made for your Valérie; she is not, and never will be, ungrateful; you are, and will ever be, my only husband. Think no more of the twelve hundred francs a year I asked you to settle on the dear little Hector who is to come some months hence; I will not cost you anything more. And besides, my money will always be yours.

'Oh, if you only loved me as I love you, my Hector, you would retire on your pension; we should both take leave of our family, our worries, our surroundings, so full of hatred, and we should go to live with Lisbeth in some pretty country place – in Brittany, or wherever you like. There we should see nobody, and we should be happy away from the world. Your pension and the little property I can call my own would be enough for us. You say you are jealous; well, you would then have your Valérie entirely devoted to her Hector, and you would never have to talk in a loud voice, as you did the other day. I shall have but one child – ours – you may be sure, my dearly loved old veteran.

'You cannot conceive of my fury, for you cannot know how he treated me, and the foul words he vomited on your Valérie. Such words would disgrace my paper; a woman such as I am – Montcornet's daughter – ought never to have heard one of them in her life. I only wish you had been there, that I might have punished him with the sight of the mad passion I felt for you. My father would have killed the wretch; I can only do as women do – love you devotedly! Indeed, my love, in the state of exasperation in which I am, I cannot possibly give up seeing you. I must positively see you, in secret, every day! That is what we are, we women. Your resentment is mine. If you love me, I implore you, do not let him be promoted; leave him to die a second-class clerk!

'At this moment I have lost my head; I still seem to hear him abusing me. Bette, who had meant to leave me, has pity on me, and will stay for a few days.

'My dear kind love, I do not know yet what is to be done. I see nothing for it but flight. I always delight in the country – Brittany, Languedoc, what you will, so long as I am free to love you. Poor dear, how I pity you! Forced now to go back to your old Adeline, to that lachrymal urn – for, as he no doubt told you, the monster means to watch me night and day; he spoke of a detective! Do not come here; he is capable of anything I know, since he could make use of me for the basest purposes of speculation. I only wish I could return you all the things I have received from your generosity.

'Ah! my kind Hector, I may have flirted, and have seemed to you to be fickle, but you did not know your Valérie; she liked to tease you, but she loves you better than any one in the world.

'He cannot prevent your coming to see your cousin; I will arrange with her that we have speech with each other. My dear old boy, write me just a line, pray, to comfort me in the absence of your dear self. (Oh, I would give one of my hands to have you by me on our sofa!) A letter will work like a charm; write me something full of your noble soul; I will return your note to you, for I must be cautious; I should not know where to hide it, he pokes his nose in everywhere. In short, comfort your Valérie, your little wife, the mother of your child. – To think of my having to write to you, when I used to see you every day. As I say to Lisbeth, "I did not

know how happy I was!" A thousand kisses, dear boy. Be true
to your
'VALÉRIE.'

'And tears!' said Hulot to himself as he finished this letter,
'tears which have blotted out her name. – How is she?' said he
to Reine.

'Madame is in bed; she has dreadful spasms,' replied Reine.
'She had a fit of hysterics that twisted her like a withy round a
faggot. It came on after writing. It comes of crying so much.
She heard Monsieur's voice on the stairs.'

The Baron in his distress wrote the following note on office
paper with a printed heading: –

'Be quite easy, my angel, he will die a second-class clerk! –
Your idea is admirable; we will go and live far from Paris,
where we shall be happy with our little Hector; I will retire on
my pension, and I shall be sure to find some good appointment on a railway.

'Ah, my sweet friend, I feel so much the younger for your
letter! I shall begin life again and make a fortune, you will see,
for our dear little one. As I read your letter, a thousand times
more ardent than those of the *Nouvelle Héloïse*, it worked a
miracle! I had not believed it possible that I could love you
more. This evening, at Lisbeth's, you will see

'YOUR HECTOR, FOR LIFE.'

Reine carried off this reply, the first letter the Baron had
written to his 'sweet friend.' Such emotions to some extent
counterbalanced the disasters growling in the distance; but the
Baron, at this moment believing he could certainly avert the
blows aimed at his uncle, Johann Fischer, thought only of
the deficit.

One of the characteristics of the Bonapartist temperament
is a firm belief in the power of the sword, and confidence in
the superiority of the military over civilians. Hulot laughed to
scorn the Public Prosecutor in Algiers, where the War Office

is supreme. Man is always what he has once been. How can the officers of the Imperial Guard forget that time was when the mayors of the largest towns in the Empire and the Emperor's prefects, Emperors themselves on a minute scale, would come out to meet the Imperial Guard, to pay their respects on the borders of the Departments through which it passed, and to do it, in short, the homage due to sovereigns?

At half-past four the Baron went straight to Madame Marneffe's; his heart beat as high as a young man's as he went upstairs, for he was asking himself this question, 'Shall I see her? or shall I not?'

How was he now to remember the scene of the morning when his weeping children had knelt at his feet? Valérie's note, enshrined for ever in a thin pocket-book over his heart, proved to him that she loved him more than the most charming of young men.

Having rung, the unhappy visitor heard within the shuffling slippers and vexatious scraping cough of the detestable master. Marneffe opened the door, but only to put himself into an attitude and point to the stairs, exactly as Hulot had shown him the door of his private room.

'You are too exclusively Hulot, Monsieur Hulot!' said he.

The Baron tried to pass him, Marneffe took a pistol out of his pocket and cocked it.

'Monsieur le Baron,' said he, 'when a man is as vile as I am – for you think me very vile, don't you? – he would be the meanest galley-slave if he did not get the full benefit of his betrayed honour. – You are for war; it will be hot work and no quarter. Come here no more, and do not attempt to get past me. I have given the police notice of my position with regard to you.'

And taking advantage of Hulot's amazement, he pushed him out and shut the door.

'What a low scoundrel!' said Hulot to himself, as he went upstairs to Lisbeth. 'I understand her letter now. Valérie and I will go away from Paris. Valérie is wholly mine for the remainder of my days; she will close my eyes.'

Lisbeth was out. Madame Olivier told the Baron that she was gone to his wife's house, thinking that she would find him there.

'Poor thing! I should never have expected her to be so sharp as she was this morning,' thought Hulot, recalling Lisbeth's behaviour as he made his way from the Rue Vanneau to the Rue Plumet.

As he turned the corner of the Rue Vanneau and the Rue de Babylone, he looked back at the Eden whence Hymen had expelled him with the sword of the law. Valérie, at her window, was watching his departure; as he glanced up, she waved her handkerchief, but the rascally Marneffe hit his wife's cap and dragged her violently away from the window. A tear rose to the great official's eye.

'Oh! to be so well loved! To see a woman so ill used, and to be so nearly seventy years old!' thought he.

Lisbeth had come to give the family the good news. Adeline and Hortense had already heard that the Baron, not choosing to compromise himself in the eyes of the whole office by appointing Marneffe to the first-class, would be turned from the door by the Hulot-hating husband. Adeline, very happy, had ordered a dinner that her Hector was to like better than any of Valérie's; and Lisbeth, in her devotion, was helping Mariette to achieve this difficult result. Cousin Bette was the idol of the hour. Mother and daughter kissed her hands, and had told her with touching delight that the Marshal consented to have her as his housekeeper.

'And from that, my dear, there is but one step to becoming his wife!' said Adeline.

'In fact, he did not say no when Victorin mentioned it,' added the Countess.

The Baron was welcomed home with such charming proofs of affection, so pathetically overflowing with love, that he was fain to conceal his troubles.

Marshal Hulot came to dinner. After dinner, Hector did not go out. Victorin and his wife joined them, and they made up a rubber.

'It is a long time, Hector,' said the Marshal gravely, 'since you gave us the treat of such an evening.'

This speech from the old soldier, who spoiled his brother though he thus implicitly blamed him, made a deep impression. It showed how wide and deep were the wounds in a heart where all the woes he had divined had found an echo. At eight o'clock the Baron insisted on seeing Lisbeth home, promising to return.

'Do you know, Lisbeth, he ill-treats her!' said he in the street. 'Oh, I never loved her so well!'

'I never imagined that Valérie loved you so well,' replied Lisbeth. 'She is frivolous and a coquette, she loves to have attentions paid her, and to have the comedy of love-making performed for her, as she says; but you are her only real attachment.'

'What message did she send me?'

'Why, this,' said Lisbeth. 'She has, as you know, been on intimate terms with Crevel. You must owe her no grudge, for that, in fact, is what has raised her above utter poverty for the rest of her life; but she detests him, and matters are nearly at an end. – Well, she has kept the key of some rooms—'

'Rue du Dauphin!' cried the thrice-blest Baron. 'If it were for that alone, I would overlook Crevel. – I have been there; I know.'

'Here, then, is the key,' said Lisbeth. 'Have another made from it in the course of to-morrow – two if you can.'

'And then,' said Hulot eagerly.

'Well, I will dine at your house again to-morrow; you must give me back Valérie's key, for old Crevel might ask her to return it to him, and you can meet her there the day after; then you can decide what your facts are to be. You will be quite safe, as there are two ways out. If by chance Crevel, who is *Régence* in his habits, as he is fond of saying, should come in by the side street, you would go out through the shop, or *vice versa*.

'You owe all this to me, you old villain; now what will you do for me?'

'Whatever you want.'

'Then you will not oppose my marrying your brother!'

'You! the Maréchale Hulot, the Comtesse de Forzheim?' cried Hector, startled.

'Well, Adeline is a Baroness!' retorted Bette in a vicious and formidable tone. 'Listen to me, you old libertine. You know how matters stand; your family may find itself starving in the gutter—'

'That is what I dread,' said Hulot in dismay.

'And if your brother were to die, who would maintain your wife and daughter? The widow of a Marshal gets at least six thousand francs pension, doesn't she? Well, then, I wish to marry to secure bread for your wife and daughter – old dotard!'

'I had not seen it in that light!' said the Baron. 'I will talk to my brother – for we are sure of you. – Tell my angel that my life is hers.'

And the Baron, having seen Lisbeth go into the house in the Rue du Vanneau, went back to his whist and stayed at home. The Baroness was at the height of happiness, her husband seemed to be returning to domestic habits; for about a fortnight he went to his office at nine every morning, he came in to dinner at six, and spent the evening with his family. He twice took Adeline and Hortense to the play. The mother and daughter paid for three thanksgiving masses, and prayed to God to suffer them to keep the husband and father He had restored to them.

One evening Victorin Hulot, seeing his father retire for the night, said to his mother –

'Well, we are at any rate so far happy that my father has come back to us. My wife and I shall never regret our capital if only this lasts—'

'Your father is nearly seventy,' said the Baroness. 'He still thinks of Madame Marneffe, that I can see; but he will forget her in time. A passion for women is not like gambling, or speculation, or avarice; there is an end to it.'

But Adeline, still beautiful in spite of her fifty years and her sorrows, in this was mistaken. Profligates, men whom

Nature has gifted with the precious power of loving beyond the limits ordinarily set to love, rarely are as old as their age.

During this relapse into virtue Baron Hulot had been three times to the Rue du Dauphin, and had certainly not been the man of seventy. His rekindled passion made him young again, and he would have sacrificed his honour to Valérie, his family, his all, without a regret. But Valérie, now completely altered, never mentioned money, not even the twelve hundred francs a year to be settled on their son; on the contrary, she offered him money, she loved Hulot as a woman of six-and-thirty loves a handsome law-student – a poor, poetical, ardent boy. And the hapless wife fancied she had reconquered her dear Hector!

The fourth meeting between this couple had been agreed upon at the end of the third, exactly as formerly in Italian theatres the play was announced for the next night. The hour fixed was nine in the morning. On the day when the happiness was due for which the amorous old man had resigned himself to domestic rules, at about eight in the morning, Reine came and asked to see the Baron. Hulot, fearing some catastrophe, went out to speak with Reine, who would not come into the anteroom. The faithful waiting-maid gave him the following note: –

'DEAR OLD MAN, – Do not go to the Rue du Dauphin. Our incubus is ill, and I must nurse him; but be there this evening at nine. Crevel is at Corbeil with Monsieur Lebas; so I am sure he will bring no princess to his little palace. I have made arrangements here to be free for the night and get back before Marneffe is awake. Answer me as to all this, for perhaps your long elegy of a wife no longer allows you your liberty as she did. I am told she is still so handsome that you might play me false, you are such a gay dog! Burn this note; I am suspicious of every one.'

Hulot wrote this scrap in reply: –

'My Love, – As I have told you, my wife has not for five-and-twenty years interfered with my pleasures. For you I would give up a hundred Adelines. – I will be in the Crevel sanctum at nine this evening awaiting my divinity. Oh that your clerk might soon die! We should part no more. And this is the dearest wish of

'Your Hector.'

That evening the Baron told his wife that he had business with the Minister at Saint-Cloud, that he would come home at about four or five in the morning; and he went to the Rue du Dauphin. It was towards the end of the month of June.

Few men have in the course of their life known really the dreadful sensation of going to their death; those who have returned from the foot of the scaffold may be easily counted. But some have had a vivid experience of it in dreams; they have gone through it all, to the sensation of the knife at their throat, at the moment when waking and daylight come to release them. – Well, the sensation to which the Councillor of State was a victim at five in the morning in Crevel's handsome and elegant bed, was immeasurably worse than that of feeling himself bound to the fatal block in the presence of ten thousand spectators looking at you with twenty thousand sparks of fire.

Valérie was asleep in a graceful attitude. She was lovely, as a woman is who is lovely enough to look so even in sleep. It is art invading nature; in short, a living picture.

In his horizontal position the Baron's eyes were but three feet above the floor. His gaze, wandering idly, as that of a man who is just awake and collecting his ideas, fell on a door painted with flowers by Jan, an artist disdainful of fame. The Baron did not indeed see twenty thousand flaming eyes, like the man condemned to death; he saw but one, of which the shaft was really more piercing than the thousands on the Public Square.

Now this sensation, far rarer in the midst of enjoyment even than that of a man condemned to death, was one for which many a splenetic Englishman would certainly pay a high price. The Baron lay there, horizontal still, and literally bathed in cold sweat. He tried to doubt the fact; but this murderous eye had a voice. A sound of whispering was heard through the door.

'So long as it is nobody but Crevel playing a trick on me!' said the Baron to himself, only too certain of an intruder in the temple.

The door was opened. The Majesty of the French Law, which in all documents follows next to the King, became visible in the person of a worthy little police-officer supported by a tall Justice of the Peace, both shown in by Monsieur Marneffe. The police functionary, rooted in shoes of which the straps were tied together with flapping bows, ended at top in a yellow skull almost bare of hair, and a face betraying him as a wide awake, cheerful, and cunning dog, from whom Paris life had no secrets. His eyes, though garnished with spectacles, pierced the glasses with a keen mocking glance. The Justice of the Peace, a retired attorney, and an old admirer of the fair sex, envied the delinquent.

'Pray excuse the strong measures required by our office, Monsieur le Baron!' said the constable; 'we are acting for the plaintiff. The Justice of the Peace is here to authorise the visitation of the premises. – I know who you are, and who the lady is who is accused.'

Valérie opened her astonished eyes, gave such a shriek as actresses use to depict madness on the stage, writhed in convulsions on the bed, like a witch of the Middle Ages in her sulphur-coloured frock on a bed of faggots.

'Death, and I am ready! my dear Hector – but a police court? – Oh! never.'

With one bound she passed the three spectators and crouched under the little writing-table, hiding her face in her hands.

'Ruin! Death!' she cried.

'Monsieur,' said Marneffe to Hulot, 'if Madame Marneffe goes mad, you are worse than a profligate; you will be a murderer.'

What can a man do, what can he say, when he is discovered in a bed which is not his, even on the score of hiring, with a woman who is no more his than the bed is? – Well, this: –

'Monsieur the Justice of the Peace, Monsieur the Police Officer,' said the Baron with some dignity, 'be good enough to take proper care of that unhappy woman, whose reason seems to me to be in danger. – You can harangue me afterwards. The doors are locked, no doubt; you need not fear that she will get away, or I either, seeing the costume we wear.'

The two functionaries bowed to the magnate's injunctions.

'You, come here, miserable cur!' said Hulot in a low voice to Marneffe, taking him by the arm and drawing him closer. 'It is not I, but you, who will be the murderer! You want to be head-clerk of your room and officer of the Legion of Honour?'

'That in the first place, Chief!' replied Marneffe, with a bow.

'You shall be all that, only soothe your wife and dismiss these fellows.'

'Nay, nay!' said Marneffe knowingly. 'These gentlemen must draw up their report as eye-witnesses to the fact; without that, the chief evidence in my case, where should I be? The higher official ranks are chokeful of rascalities. You have done me out of my wife, and you have not promoted me, Monsieur le Baron; I give you only two days to get out of the scrape. Here are some letters—'

'Some letters!' interrupted Hulot.

'Yes; letters which prove that you are the father of the child my wife expects to give birth to. – You understand? And you ought to settle on my son a sum equal to what he will lose through this bastard. But I will be reasonable; this does not distress me, I have no mania for paternity myself. A hundred louis a year will satisfy me. By to-morrow I must be Monsieur Coquet's successor and see my name on the list for promotion in the Legion of Honour at the July fêtes, or else – the documentary evidence and my charge against you will be laid before the Bench. I am not so hard to deal with after all, you see.'

'Bless me, and such a pretty woman!' said the Justice of the Peace to the police constable. 'What a loss to the world if she should go mad!'

'She is not mad,' said the constable sententiously. The police is always the incarnation of scepticism. – 'Monsieur le Baron Hulot has been caught by a trick,' he added, loud enough for Valérie to hear him.

Valérie shot a flash from her eye which would have killed him on the spot if looks could effect the vengeance they express. The police-officer smiled; he had laid a snare, and the woman had fallen into it. Marneffe desired his wife to go into the other room and clothe herself decently, for he and the Baron had come to an agreement on all points, and Hulot fetched his dressing-gown and came out again.

'Gentlemen,' said he to the two officials, 'I need not impress on you to be secret.'

The functionaries bowed.

The police-officer rapped twice on the door; his clerk came in, sat down at the '*bonheur-du-jour*,' and wrote what the constable dictated to him in an undertone. Valérie still wept vehemently. When she was dressed, Hulot went into the other room and put on his clothes. Meanwhile the report was written.

Marneffe then wanted to take his wife home; but Hulot, believing that he saw her for the last time, begged the favour of being allowed to speak with her.

'Monsieur, your wife has cost me dear enough for me to be allowed to say good-bye to her – in the presence of you all, of course.'

Valérie went up to Hulot, and he whispered in her ear –

'There is nothing left for us but to fly, but how can we correspond? We have been betrayed—'

'Through Reine,' she answered. 'But, my dear friend, after this scandal we can never meet again. I am disgraced. Besides, you will hear dreadful things about me – you will believe them—'

The Baron made a gesture of denial.

'You will believe them, and I can thank God for that, for then perhaps you will not regret me.'

'He will *not* die a second-class clerk!' said Marneffe to Hulot, as he led his wife away, saying roughly, 'Come, Madame; if I am foolish to you, I do not choose to be a fool to others.'

Valérie left the house, Crevel's Eden, with a last glance at the Baron, so cunning that he thought she adored him. The Justice of the Peace gave Madame Marneffe his arm to the hackney coach with a flourish of gallantry. The Baron, who was required to witness the report, remained quite bewildered, alone with the police-officer. When the Baron had signed, the officer looked at him keenly, over his glasses.

'You are very sweet on the little lady, Monsieur le Baron?'

'To my sorrow, as you see.'

'Suppose that she does not care for you?' the man went on, 'that she is deceiving you?'

'I have long known that, Monsieur – here, in this very spot, Monsieur Crevel and I told each other—'

'Oh! Then you knew that you were in Monsieur le Maire's private snuggery?'

'Perfectly.'

The constable lightly touched his hat with a respectful gesture.

'You are very much in love,' said he. 'I say no more. I respect an inveterate passion, as a doctor respects an inveterate complaint. – I saw Monsieur de Nucingen, the banker, attacked in the same way—'

'He is a friend of mine,' said the Baron. 'Many a time have I supped with his handsome Esther. She was worth the two million francs she cost him.'

'And more,' said the officer. 'That caprice of the old Baron's cost four persons their lives. Oh! such passions as these are like the cholera!'

'What had you to say to me?' asked the Baron, who took this indirect warning very ill.

'Oh! why should I deprive you of your illusions?' replied the officer. 'Men rarely have any left at your age!'

'Rid me of them!' cried the Councillor.

'You will curse the physician later,' replied the officer, smiling.

'I beg of you, Monsieur.'

'Well, then, that woman was in collusion with her husband.'

'Oh!—'

'Yes, sir, and so it is in two cases out of every ten. Oh! we know it well.'

'What proof have you of such a conspiracy?'

'In the first place, the husband!' said the other, with the calm acumen of a surgeon practised in unbinding wounds. 'Mean speculation is stamped in every line of that villainous face. But you, no doubt, set great store by a certain letter written by that woman with regard to the child?'

'So much so, that I always have it about me,' replied Hulot, feeling in his breast-pocket for the little pocket-book which he always kept there.

'Leave your pocket-book where it is,' said the man, as crushing as a thunder-clap. 'Here is the letter. – I now know all I want to know. Madame Marneffe, of course, was aware of what that pocket-book contained?'

'She alone in the world.'

'So I supposed. – Now for the proof you asked for of her collusion with her husband.'

'Let us hear!' said the Baron, still incredulous.

'When we came in here, Monsieur le Baron, that wretched creature Marneffe led the way, and he took up this letter, which his wife, no doubt, had placed on this writing-table,' and he pointed to the *bonheur-du-jour*. 'That evidently was the spot agreed upon by the couple, in case she should succeed in stealing the letter while you were asleep; for this letter, as written to you by the lady, is, combined with those you wrote to her, decisive evidence in a police court.'

He showed Hulot the note that Reine had delivered to him in his private room at the office.

'It is one of the documents in the case,' said the police-agent; 'return it to me, Monsieur.'

'Well, Monsieur,' replied Hulot with bitter expression, 'that woman is profligacy itself in fixed ratios. I am certain at this moment that she has three lovers.'

'That is perfectly evident,' said the officer. 'Oh, they are not all on the streets! When a woman follows that trade in a carriage and a drawing-room, and her own house, it is not a case for francs and centimes, Monsieur le Baron. Mademoiselle Esther, of whom you spoke, and who poisoned herself, made away with millions. – If you will take my advice, you will get out of it, Monsieur. This last little game will have cost you dear. That scoundrel of a husband has the law on his side. And indeed, but for me, that little woman would have caught you again!'

'Thank you, Monsieur,' said the Baron, trying to maintain his dignity.

'Now we will lock up; the farce is played out, and you can send your key to Monsieur the Mayor.'

Hulot went home in a state of dejection bordering on helplessness, and sunk in the gloomiest thoughts. He woke his noble and saintly wife, and poured into her heart the history of the three past years, sobbing like a child deprived of a toy. This confession from an old man young in feeling, this frightful and heartrending narrative, while it filled Adeline with pity, also gave her the greatest joy; she thanked Heaven for this last catastrophe, for in fancy she saw the husband settled at last in the bosom of his family.

'Lisbeth was right,' said Madame Hulot gently and without any useless recrimination, 'she told us how it would be.'

'Yes. If only I had listened to her, instead of flying into a rage, that day when I wanted poor Hortense to go home rather than compromise the reputation of that—Oh! my dear Adeline, we must save Wenceslas. He is up to his chin in that mire!'

'My poor old man, the respectable middle-classes have turned out no better than the actresses,' said Adeline, with a smile.

The Baroness was alarmed at the change in her Hector; when she saw him so unhappy, ailing, crushed under his weight of woes, she was all heart, all pity, all love; she would have shed her blood to make Hulot happy.

'Stay with us, my dear Hector. Tell me what is it that such women do to attract you so powerfully. I too will try. Why have you not taught me to be what you want? Am I deficient in intelligence? Men still think me handsome enough to court my favour.'

Many a married woman, attached to her duty and to her husband, may here pause to ask herself why strong and affectionate men, so tender-hearted to the Madame Marneffes, do not take their wives for the object of their fancies and passions, especially wives like the Baronne Adeline Hulot.

This is, indeed, one of the most recondite mysteries of human nature. Love, which is the debauch of reason, the strong and austere joy of a lofty soul, and pleasure, the vulgar counterfeit sold in the market-place, are two aspects of the same thing. The woman who can satisfy both these devouring appetites is as rare in her sex as a great general, a great writer, a great artist, a great inventor in a nation. A man of superior intellect or an idiot – a Hulot or a Crevel – equally crave for the ideal and for enjoyment; all alike go in search of the mysterious compound, so rare that at last it is usually found to be a work in two volumes. This craving is a depraved impulse due to society.

Marriage, no doubt, must be accepted as a tie; it is life, with its duties and its stern sacrifices on both parts equally. Libertines, who seek for hidden treasure, are as guilty as other evil-doers who are more hardly dealt with than they. These reflections are not a mere veneer of moralising; they show the reason of many unexplained misfortunes. But, indeed, this drama points its own moral – or morals, for they are of many kinds.

The Baron presently went to call on the Marshal Prince de Wissembourg, whose powerful patronage was now his only chance. Having dwelt under his protection for five-and-thirty years, he was a visitor at all hours, and would be admitted to his rooms as soon as he was up.

'Ah! How are you, my dear Hector?' said the great and worthy leader. 'What is the matter? You look anxious. And yet the session is ended. One more over! I speak of that now as I used to speak of a campaign. And indeed I believe the newspapers nowadays speak of the sessions as parliamentary campaigns.'

'We have been in difficulties, I must confess, Marshal; but the times are hard!' said Hulot. 'It cannot be helped; the world was made so. Every phase has its own drawbacks. The worst misfortune in the year 1841 is that neither the King nor the ministers are free to act as Napoleon was.'

The Marshal gave Hulot one of those eagle flashes which in its pride, clearness, and perspicacity showed that, in spite of years, that lofty soul was still upright and vigorous.

'You want me to do something for you?' said he, in a hearty tone.

'I find myself under the necessity of applying to you for the promotion of one of my second clerks to the head of a room – as a personal favour to myself – and his advancement to be officer of the Legion of Honour.'

'What is his name?' said the Marshal, with a look like a lightning flash.

'Marneffe.'

'He has a pretty wife; I saw her on the occasion of your daughter's marriage. – If Roger – but Roger is away! – Hector, my boy, this is concerned with your pleasures. What, you still indulge—? Well, you are a credit to the old Guard. That is what comes of having been in the Commissariat; you have reserves! – But have nothing to do with this little job, my dear boy; it is too strong of the petticoat to be good business.'

'No, Marshal; it is a bad business, for the police courts have a finger in it. Would you like to see me there?'

'The devil!' said the Prince uneasily. 'Go on!'

'Well, I am in the predicament of a trapped fox. You have always been so kind to me, that you will, I am sure, condescend to help me out of the shameful position in which I am placed.'

Hulot related his misadventures, as wittily and as lightly as he could.

'And you, Prince, will you allow my brother to die of grief, a man you love so well; or leave one of your staff in the War Office, a Councillor of State, to live in disgrace. This Marneffe is a wretched creature; he can be shelved in two or three years.'

'How you talk of two or three years, my dear fellow!' said the Marshal.

'But, Prince, the Imperial Guard is immortal.'

'I am the last of the first batch of Marshals,' said the Prince. 'Listen, Hector. You do not know the extent of my attachment to you; you shall see. On the day when I retire from office, we will go together. But you are not a Deputy, my friend. Many men want your place; but for me, you would be out of it by this time. Yes, I have fought many a pitched battle to keep you in it. – Well, I grant you your two requests; it would be too bad to see you riding the bar at your age and in the position you hold. But you stretch your credit a little too far. If this appointment gives rise to discussion, we shall not be held blameless. I can laugh at such things; but you will find it a thorn under your foot. And the next session will see your dismissal. Your place is held out as a bait to five or six influential men, and you have been enabled to keep it solely by the force of my arguments.

'I tell you, on the day when you retire, there will be five malcontents to one happy man; whereas, by keeping you hanging on by a thread for two or three years, we shall secure all six votes. There was a great laugh at the Council meeting; the Veteran of the Old Guard, as they say, was becoming desperately wide awake in parliamentary tactics! I am frank with you. – And you are growing grey; you are a happy man to be able to get into such difficulties as these! How long is it since I – Lieutenant Cottin – had a mistress?'

He rang the bell.

'That police report must be destroyed,' he added.

'Monseigneur, you are as a father to me! I dared not mention my anxiety on that point.'

'I still wish I had Roger here,' cried the Prince, as Mitouflet, his groom of the chambers, came in. 'I was just going to send for him! – You may go, Mitouflet. – Go you, my dear old fellow, go and have the nomination made out; I will sign it. At the same time, that low schemer will not long enjoy the fruit of his crimes. He will be sharply watched, and drummed out of the regiment for the smallest fault. – You are saved this time, my dear Hector; take care for the future. Do not exhaust your friends' patience. You shall have the nomination this morning, and your man shall get his promotion in the Legion of Honour. – How old are you now?'

'Within three months of seventy.'

'What a scapegrace!' said the Prince, laughing. 'It is you who deserve promotion, but, by thunder! we are not under Louis xv.!'

Such is the sense of comradeship that binds the glorious survivors of the Napoleonic phalanx, that they always feel as if they were in camp together, and bound to stand together through thick and thin.

'One more favour such as this,' Hulot reflected as he crossed the courtyard, 'and I am done for!'

The luckless official went to Baron de Nucingen, to whom he now owed a mere trifle, and succeeded in borrowing forty thousand francs, on his salary pledged for two years more; the banker stipulated that in the event of Hulot's retirement on his pension, the whole of it should be devoted to the repayment of the sum borrowed till the capital and interest were all cleared off.

This new bargain, like the first, was made in the name of Vauvinet, to whom the Baron signed notes of hand to the amount of twelve thousand francs.

On the following day, the fateful police report, the husband's charge, the letters – all the papers – were destroyed. The scandalous promotion of Monsieur Marneffe, hardly heeded in the midst of the July fêtes, was not commented on in any newspaper.

Lisbeth, to all appearance at war with Madame Marneffe, had taken up her abode with Marshal Hulot. Ten days after

these events, the banns of marriage were published between
the old maid and the distinguished old officer, to whom, to
win his consent, Adeline had related the financial disaster that
had befallen her Hector, begging him never to mention it to
the Baron, who was, as she said, much saddened, quite
depressed and crushed.

'Alas! he is as old as his years,' she added.

So Lisbeth had triumphed. She was achieving the object
of her ambition, she would see the success of her scheme,
and her hatred gratified. She delighted in the anticipated joy of
reigning supreme over the family who had so long looked
down upon her. Yes, she would patronise her patrons, she
would be the rescuing angel who would dole out a livelihood
to the ruined family; she addressed herself as 'Madame la
Comtesse' and 'Madame la Maréchale,' curtsying in front of
a glass. Adeline and Hortense should end their days in struggling with poverty, while she, a visitor at the Tuileries, would
lord it in the fashionable world.

A terrible disaster overthrew the old maid from the social
heights where she so proudly enthroned herself.

On the very day when the banns were first published, the
Baron received a second message from Africa. Another Alsatian arrived, handed him a letter, after assuring himself that he
spoke to Baron Hulot, and after giving the Baron the address
of his lodgings, bowed himself out, leaving the great man
stricken by the opening lines of this letter: –

'DEAR NEPHEW, – You will receive this letter, by my
calculations, on the 7th of August. Supposing it takes you
three days to send us the help we need, and that it is a fortnight
on the way here, that brings us to the 1st of September.

'If you can act decisively within that time, you will have
saved the honour and the life of yours sincerely, Johann
Fischer.

'This is what I am required to demand by the clerk you
have made my accomplice; for I am amenable, it would seem,

to the law, at the Assizes, or before a council of war. Of course, you understand that Johann Fischer will never be brought to the bar of any tribunal; he will go of his own act to appear at that of God.

'Your clerk seems to me a bad lot, quite capable of getting you into hot water; but he is as clever as any rogue. He says the line for you to take is to call out louder than any one, and to send out an inspector, a special commissioner, to discover who is really guilty, rake up abuses, and make a fuss, in short; but if we stir up the struggle, who will stand between us and the law?

'If your commissioner arrives here by the 1st of September, and you have given him your orders, sending by him two hundred thousand francs to place in our storehouses the supplies we profess to have secured in remote country places, we shall be absolutely solvent and regarded as blameless. You can trust the soldier who is the bearer of this letter with a draft in my name on a house in Algiers. He is a trustworthy fellow, a relation of mine, incapable of trying to find out what he is the bearer of. I have taken measures to guarantee the fellow's safe return. If you can do nothing, I am ready and willing to die for the man to whom we owe our Adeline's happiness!'

The anguish and raptures of passion and the catastrophe which had checked his career of profligacy had prevented Baron Hulot's ever thinking of poor Johann Fischer, though his first letter had given warning of the danger now become so pressing. The Baron went out of the dining-room in such agitation that he literally dropped on to a sofa in the drawing-room. He was stunned, sunk in the dull numbness of a heavy fall. He stared at a flower on the carpet, quite unconscious that he still held in his hand Johann's fatal letter.

Adeline, in her room, heard her husband throw himself on the sofa, like a lifeless mass; the noise was so peculiar that she fancied he had an apoplectic attack. She looked through the door at the mirror, in such dread as stops the breath and hinders motion, and she saw her Hector in the attitude of a man crushed. The Baroness stole in on tiptoe; Hector heard nothing; she went close up to him, saw the letter, took it, read it, trembling in every limb. She went through one of those violent nervous shocks that leave their traces for ever on the sufferer. Within a few days she became subject to a constant trembling, for after the first instant the need for action gave her such strength as can only be drawn from the very well-spring of the vital powers.

'Hector, come into my room,' said she, in a voice that was no more than a breath. 'Do not let your daughter see you in this state! Come, my dear, come!'

'Two hundred thousand francs? Where can I find them? I can get Claude Vignon sent out there as commissioner. He is a clever, intelligent fellow. – That is a matter of a couple of days. – But two hundred thousand francs! My son has not so much; his house is loaded with mortgages for three hundred thousand. My brother has saved thirty thousand francs at most. Nucingen would simply laugh at me! – Vauvinet? – he was not very ready to lend me the ten thousand francs I wanted to make up the sum for that villain Marneffe's boy. No, it is all up with me; I must throw myself at the Prince's feet, confess how matters stand, hear myself told that I am a low scoundrel, and take his broadside so as to go decently to the bottom.'

'But, Hector, this is not merely ruin, it is disgrace,' said Adeline. 'My poor uncle will kill himself. Only kill us – yourself and me; you have a right to do that, but do not be a murderer! Come, take courage; there must be some way out of it.'

'Not one,' said Hulot. 'No one in the Government could find two hundred thousand francs, not if it were to save an Administration! – Oh, Napoleon! where art thou?'

'My uncle! poor man! Hector, he must not be allowed to kill himself in disgrace.'

'There is one more chance,' said he, 'but a very remote one. – Yes, Crevel is at daggers drawn with his daughter. – He has plenty of money, he alone could—'

'Listen, Hector, it will be better for your wife to perish than to leave our uncle to perish – and your brother – the honour of the family!' cried the Baroness, struck by a flash of light. 'Yes, I can save you all. – Good God! what a degrading thought! How could it have occurred to me?'

She clasped her hands, dropped on her knees, and put up a prayer. On rising, she saw such a crazy expression of joy on her husband's face, that the diabolical suggestion returned, and then Adeline sank into a sort of idiotic melancholy.

'Go, my dear, at once to the War Office,' said she, rousing herself from this torpor; 'try to send out a commission; it must be done. Get round the Marshal. And on your return, at five o'clock, you will find – perhaps – yes! you shall find two hundred thousand francs. Your family, your honour as a man, as a State official, a Councillor of State, your honesty – your son – all shall be saved; – but your Adeline will be lost, and you will see her no more. Hector, my dear,' said she, kneeling before him, clasping and kissing his hand, 'give me your blessing! Say fare-well.'

It was so heartrending that Hulot put his arms round his wife, raised her and kissed her, saying –

'I do not understand.'

'If you did,' said she, 'I should die of shame, or I should not have the strength to carry out this last sacrifice.'

'Breakfast is served,' said Mariette.

Hortense came in to wish her parents good morning. They had to go to breakfast and assume a false face.

'Begin without me; I will join you,' said the Baroness.

She sat down to her desk and wrote as follows: –

'MY DEAR MONSIEUR CREVEL, – I have to ask a service of you; I shall expect you this morning, and I count on your gallantry, which is well known to me, to save me from having too long to wait for you. – Your faithful servant,

'ADELINE HULOT.'

'Louise,' said she to her daughter's maid, who waited on her, 'take this note down to the porter and desire him to carry it at once to this address and wait for an answer.'

The Baron, who was reading the news, held out a Republican paper to his wife, pointing to an article, and saying –

'Is there time?'

This was the paragraph, one of the terrible 'notes' with which the papers spice their political bread and butter: –

'A correspondent in Algiers writes that such abuses have been discovered in the commissariat transactions of the province of Oran, that the Law is making inquiries. The peculation is self-evident, and the guilty persons are known. If severe measures are not taken, we shall continue to lose more men through the extortion that limits their rations than by Arab steel or the fierce heat of the climate. We await further information before enlarging on this deplorable business. We need no longer wonder at the terror caused by the establishment of the Press in Africa, as was contemplated by the Charter of 1830.'

'I will dress and go to the Minister,' said the Baron, as they rose from table. 'Time is precious; a man's life hangs on every minute.'

'Oh, mamma, there is no hope for me!' cried Hortense. And, unable to check her tears, she handed to her mother a number of the *Revue des Beaux Arts*.

Madame Hulot's eye fell on a print of the group of 'Delilah' by Count Steinbock, under which were the words, 'The property of Madame Marneffe.'

The very first lines of the article, signed V., showed the talent and friendliness of Claude Vignon.

'Poor child!' said the Baroness.

Alarmed by her mother's tone of indifference, Hortense looked up, saw the expression of a sorrow before which her own paled, and rose to kiss her mother, saying –

'What is the matter, mamma? What is happening? Can we be more wretched than we are already?'

'My child, it seems to me that in what I am going through to-day my past dreadful sorrows are as nothing. When shall I have ceased to suffer?'

'In heaven, mother,' said Hortense solemnly.

'Come, my angel, help me to dress. – No, no; I will not have you help me in this! Send me Louise.'

Adeline, in her room, went to study herself in the glass. She looked at herself closely and sadly, wondering to herself –

'Am I still handsome? Can I still be desirable? Am I not wrinkled?'

She lifted up her fine golden hair, uncovering her temples; they were as fresh as a girl's. She went further; she uncovered her shoulders, and was satisfied; nay, she had a little feeling of pride. The beauty of really handsome shoulders is one of the last charms a woman loses, especially if she has lived chastely.

Adeline chose her dress carefully, but the pious and blameless woman is decent to the end, in spite of her little coquettish graces. Of what use were brand-new grey silk stockings and high-heeled satin shoes when she was absolutely ignorant of the art of displaying a pretty foot at a critical moment, by obtruding it an inch or two beyond a half-lifted skirt, opening horizons to desire. She put on, indeed, her prettiest flowered muslin dress, with a low body and short sleeves; but horrified at so much bareness, she covered her fine arms with clear gauze sleeves and hid her shoulders under an embroidered cape. Her curls, à l'Anglaise, struck her as too fly-away; she subdued their airy lightness by putting on a very pretty cap; but, with or without the cap, would she have known how to twist the golden ringlets so as to show off her taper fingers to admiration?

As to rouge – the consciousness of guilt, the preparations for a deliberate fall, threw this saintly woman into a state of high fever, which, for the time, revived the brilliant colouring of youth. Her eyes were bright, her cheeks glowed. Instead of assuming a seductive air, she saw in herself a look of barefaced audacity which shocked her.

Lisbeth, at Adeline's request, had told her all the circumstances of Wenceslas's infidelity; and the Baroness had learned, to her utter amazement, that in one evening, in one moment, Madame Marneffe had made herself the mistress of the bewitched artist.

'How do these women do it?' the Baroness had asked Lisbeth.

There is no curiosity so great as that of virtuous women on such subjects; they would like to know the arts of vice and remain immaculate.

'Why, they are seductive; it is their business,' said Cousin Bette. 'Valérie that evening, my dear, was, I declare, enough to bring an angel to perdition.'

'But tell me how she set to work.'

'There is no principle, only practice in that walk of life,' said Lisbeth ironically.

The Baroness, recalling this conversation, would have liked to consult Cousin Bette; but there was no time for that. Poor Adeline, incapable of imagining a patch, of pinning a rosebud in the very middle of her bosom, of devising the tricks of the toilet intended to resuscitate the ardours of exhausted nature, was merely well dressed. A woman is not a courtesan for the wishing!

'Woman is soup for man,' as Molière says by the mouth of the judicious Gros-René. This comparison suggests a sort of culinary art in love. Then the virtuous wife would be a Homeric meal, flesh laid on hot cinders. The courtesan, on the contrary, is a dish by Carême, with its condiments, spices, and elegant arrangement. The Baroness could not – did not know how to serve up her fair bosom in a lordly dish of lace, after the manner of Madame Marneffe. She knew nothing of the secrets of certain attitudes, the effect of certain looks. She had no box of mysteries. This high-souled woman might have turned round and round a hundred times, and she would have betrayed nothing to the keen glance of a profligate.

To be a good woman and a prude to all the world, and a courtesan to her husband, is the gift of a woman of genius, and they are few. This is the secret of long fidelity, inexplicable to the women who are not blessed with this double and splendid faculty. Imagine Madame Marneffe virtuous, and you have the Marchesa di Pescara. But such lofty and illustrious women, beautiful as Diane de Poitiers, but virtuous, may be easily counted.

So the scene with which this serious and terrible drama of Paris manners opened was about to be repeated, with this singular difference – that the calamities prophesied then by the captain of the municipal Militia had reversed the parts. Madame Hulot was awaiting Crevel with the same intentions as had brought him to her, smiling down at the Paris crowd from his *milord*, three years ago. And, strangest thing of all, the Baroness was true to herself and to her love, while preparing to yield to the grossest infidelity, such as the storm of passion even does not justify in the eyes of some judges.

'What can I do to become a Madame Marneffe?' she asked herself as she heard the door-bell.

She restrained her tears, fever gave brilliancy to her face, and she meant to be quite the courtesan, poor, noble soul.

'What the devil can that worthy Baronne Hulot want of me?' Crevel wondered as he mounted the stairs. 'She is going to discuss my quarrel with Célestine and Victorin, no doubt; but I will not give way!'

As he went into the drawing-room, shown in by Louise, he said to himself as he noted the bareness of the place (Crevel's word) –

'Poor woman! She lives here like some fine picture stowed in a loft by a man who knows nothing of painting.'

Crevel, seeing Comte Popinot, the Minister of Commerce, buy pictures and statues, wanted also to figure as a Mæcenas of Paris, whose love of Art consists in making good investments.

Adeline smiled graciously at Crevel, pointing to a chair facing her.

'Here am I, fair lady, at your command,' said Crevel.

Monsieur the Mayor, a political personage, now wore black broadcloth. His face, at the top of this solemn suit, shone like a full moon rising above a mass of dark clouds. His shirt, buttoned with three large pearls worth five hundred francs a-piece, gave a great idea of his thoracic capacity, and he was apt to say, 'In me you see the coming athlete of the tribune!' His enormous vulgar hands were encased in yellow gloves even in the morning; his patent leather boots spoke of the chocolate-coloured coupé with one horse in which he drove.

In the course of three years ambition had altered Crevel's pretensions. Like all great artists, he had come to his second manner. In the great world, when he went to the Prince de Wissembourg's, to the Préfecture, to Comte Popinot's, and the like, he held his hat in his hand in an airy manner taught him by Valérie, and he inserted the thumb of the other hand in the armhole of his waistcoat with a knowing air, and a simpering face and expression. This new grace of attitude was due to the satirical inventiveness of Valérie, who, under pretence of rejuvenating her mayor, had given him an added touch of the ridiculous.

'I begged you to come, my dear kind Monsieur Crevel,' said the Baroness in a husky voice, 'on a matter of the greatest importance—'

'I can guess what it is, Madame,' said Crevel, with a knowing air, 'but what you would ask is impossible. – Oh, I am not a brutal father, a man – to use Napoleon's words – set hard and fast on sheer avarice. Listen to me, fair lady. If my children were ruining themselves for their own benefit, I would help them out of the scrape; but as for backing your husband, Madame? It is like trying to fill the vat of the Danaides! Their house is mortgaged for three hundred thousand francs for an incorrigible father! Why, they have nothing left, poor wretches! And they have no fun for their money. All they have to live upon is what Victorin may make in Court. He must wag his tongue more, must Monsieur your son! And he was to have been a Minister, that learned youth! Our hope and pride. A pretty pilot, who runs aground like a land-lubber; for if he had borrowed to enable him to get on, if he had run into debt for feasting Deputies, winning votes, and increasing his influence, I should be the first to say, "Here is my purse – dip your hand in, my friend!" But when it comes to paying for papa's folly – folly I warned you of! – Ah! his father has deprived him of every chance of power. – It is I who shall be Minister!'

'Alas, my dear Crevel, it has nothing to do with the children, poor devoted souls! – If your heart is closed to Victorin and Celéstine, I shall love them so much that perhaps I may soften the bitterness of their souls caused by your anger. You are punishing your children for a good action!'

'Yes, for a good action badly done! That is half a crime,' said Crevel, much pleased with his epigram.

'Doing good, my dear Crevel, does not mean sparing money out of a purse that is bursting with it; it means enduring privations to be generous, suffering for liberality! It is being prepared for ingratitude! Heaven does not see the charity that costs us nothing—'

'Saints, Madame, may if they please go to the workhouse; they know that it is for them the door of heaven. For my part, I am worldly-minded; I fear God, but yet more I fear the hell of poverty. To be destitute is the last depth of misfortune in society as now constituted. I am a man of my time; I respect money.'

'And you are right,' said Adeline, 'from the worldly point of view.'

She was a thousand miles from her point, and she felt herself on a gridiron, like Saint Laurence, as she thought of her uncle, for she could see him blowing his brains out.

She looked down; then she raised her eyes to gaze at Crevel with angelic sweetness – not with the inviting suggestiveness which was part of Valérie's wit. Three years ago she could have bewitched Crevel by that beautiful look.

'I have known the time,' said she, 'when you were more generous – you used to talk of three hundred thousand francs like a grand gentleman—'

Crevel looked at Madame Hulot; he beheld her like a lily in the last of its bloom, vague sensations rose within him, but he felt such respect for this saintly creature that he spurned all suspicions and buried them in the most profligate corner of his heart.

'I, Madame, am still the same; but a retired merchant, if he is a grand gentleman, plays, and must play, the part with method and economy; he carries his ideas of order into everything. He opens an account for his little amusements, and devotes certain profits to that head of expenditure; but as to touching his capital! it would be folly. My children will have their fortune intact, mine and my wife's; but I do not suppose that they wish their father to be dull, a monk and a mummy! My life is a very jolly one; I float gaily down the stream. I fulfil all the duties imposed on me by law, by my affections, and by family ties, just as I always used to be punctual in paying my bills when they fell due. If only my children conduct themselves in their domestic life as I do, I shall be satisfied; and for the present, so long as my follies – for I have committed follies – are no loss to any one but the gulls – excuse me, you do not perhaps understand the slang word – they will have nothing to blame me for, and will find a tidy little sum still left when I die. Your children cannot say as much of their father, who is ruining his son and my daughter by his pranks—'

The Baroness was getting further from her object as he went on.

'You are very unkind about my husband, my dear Crevel – and yet, if you had found his wife obliging, you would have been his best friend—'

She shot a burning glance at Crevel; but, like Dubois, who gave the Regent three kicks, she affected too much, and the rakish perfumer's thoughts jumped at such profligate suggestions, that he said to himself, 'Does she want to turn the tables on Hulot? – Does she think me more attractive as a Mayor than as a National Guardsman? Women are strange creatures!'

And he assumed the position of his second manner, looking at the Baroness with his *Regency* leer.

'I could almost fancy,' she went on, 'that you want to visit on him your resentment against the virtue that resisted you – in a woman whom you loved well enough – to – to buy her,' she added in a low voice.

'In a divine woman,' Crevel replied, with a meaning smile at the Baroness, who looked down while tears rose to her eyes. 'For you have swallowed not a few bitter pills! – in these three years – hey, my beauty?'

'Do not talk of my troubles, dear Crevel; they are too much for the endurance of a mere human being. Ah! if you still love me, you may drag me out of the pit in which I lie. Yes, I am in hell torment! The regicides who were racked and nipped and torn into quarters by four horses were on roses compared with me, for their bodies only were dismembered, and my heart is torn in quarters—'

Crevel's thumb moved from his armhole, he placed his hand on the work-table, he abandoned his attitude, he smiled! The smile was so vacuous that it misled the Baroness; she took it for an expression of kindness.

'You see a woman, not indeed in despair, but with her honour at the point of death, and prepared for everything, my dear friend, to hinder a crime.'

Fearing that Hortense might come in, she bolted the door; then with equal impetuosity she fell at Crevel's feet, took his hand, and kissed it.

'Be my deliverer!' she cried.

She thought there was some generous fibre in this mercantile soul, and full of sudden hope that she might get the two hundred thousand francs without degrading herself –

'Buy a soul – you were once ready to buy virtue!' she went on, with a frenzied gaze. 'Trust to my honesty as a woman, to my honour, of which you know the worth! Be my friend! Save a whole family from ruin, shame, despair; keep it from falling into a bog where the quicksands are mingled with blood! Oh! ask for no explanations,' she exclaimed, at a movement on Crevel's part, who was about to speak. 'Above all, do not say to me, "I told you so!" like a friend who is glad at a misfortune. Come now, yield to her whom you used to love, to the woman whose humiliation at your feet is perhaps the crowning moment of her glory; ask nothing of her, expect what you will from her gratitude! – No, no. Give

me nothing, but lend – lend to me whom you used to call
Adeline—'

At this point her tears flowed so fast, Adeline was sobbing
so passionately, that Crevel's gloves were wet. The words, 'I
need two hundred thousand francs,' were scarcely articulate in
the torrent of weeping, as stones, however large, are invisible
in Alpine cataracts swollen by the melting of the snows.

This is the inexperience of virtue. Vice asks for nothing, as
we have seen in Madame Marneffe; it gets everything offered
to it. Women of that stamp are never exacting till they have
made themselves indispensable, or when a man has to be
worked as a quarry is worked where the lime is rather scarce
– going to ruin, as the quarry-men say.

On hearing these words, 'Two hundred thousand francs,'
Crevel understood all. He cheerfully raised the Baroness, saying insolently –

'Come, come, bear up, mother,' which Adeline, in her
distraction, failed to hear. The scene was changing its character. Crevel was becoming 'master of the situation,' to use his
own words. The vastness of the sum startled Crevel so greatly
that his emotion at seeing this handsome woman in tears at his
feet was forgotten. Besides, however angelical and saintly a
woman may be, when she is crying bitterly her beauty dis-
appears. A Madame Marneffe, as has been seen, whimpers
now and then, a tear trickles down her cheek; but as to melting
into tears and making her eyes and nose red! – never would
she commit such a blunder.

'Come, child, compose yourself. – Deuce take it!' Crevel
went on, taking Madame Hulot's hands in his own and patting
them. 'Why do you apply to me for two hundred thousand
francs? What do you want with them? Whom are they for?'

'Do not,' said she, 'insist on any explanations. Give me the
money! – You will save three lives and the honour of our
children.'

'And do you suppose, my good mother, that in all Paris you
will find a man who at a word from a half-crazy woman will
go off *hic et nunc*, and bring out of some drawer, Heaven knows

where, two hundred thousand francs that have been lying simmering there till she is pleased to scoop them up? Is that all you know of life and of business, my beauty? Your folks are in a bad way; you may send them the last sacraments; for no one in Paris but her Divine Highness Madame la Banque, or the great Nucingen, or some miserable miser who is in love with gold as we other folks are with a woman, could produce such a miracle! The civil list, civil as it may be, would beg you to call again to-morrow. Every one invests his money, and turns it over to the best of his powers.

'You are quite mistaken, my angel, if you suppose that King Louis-Philippe rules us; he himself knows better than that. He knows as well as we do that supreme above the Charter reigns the holy, venerated, substantial, delightful, obliging, beautiful, noble, ever-youthful, and all-powerful five-franc piece! But money, my beauty, insists on interest, and is always engaged in seeking it! "God of the Jews, thou art supreme!" says Racine. The perennial parable of the golden calf, you see! – In the days of Moses there was stock-jobbing in the desert!

'We have reverted to Biblical traditions; the Golden Calf was the first State ledger,' he went on. 'You, my Adeline, have not gone beyond the Rue Plumet. The Egyptians had lent enormous sums to the Hebrews, and what they ran after was not God's people, but their capital.'

He looked at the Baroness with an expression which said, 'How clever I am!'

'You know nothing of the devotion of every city man to his sacred hoard!' he went on, after a pause. 'Excuse me. – Listen to me. Get this well into your head. – You want two hundred thousand francs? No one can produce the sum without selling some security. Now consider! To have two hundred thousand francs in hard cash it would be needful to sell about seven hundred thousand francs' worth of stock at three per cent. Well; and then you could only get the money on the third day. That is the quickest way. To persuade a man to part with a fortune – for two hundred thousand francs is the whole fortune of many a man – he ought at least to know where it is all going to, and for what purpose—'

'It is going, my dear kind Crevel, to save the lives of two men, one of whom will die of grief, and the other will kill himself! And to save me too from going mad! Am I not a little mad already?'

'Not so mad!' said he, taking Madame Hulot round the knees; 'old Crevel has his price, since you thought of applying to him, my angel.'

'They submit to have a man's arms round their knees, it would seem!' thought the saintly woman, covering her face with her hands.

'Once you offered me a fortune!' said she, turning red.

'Ay, mother! but that was three years ago!' replied Crevel. 'Well, you are handsomer now than ever I saw you!' he went on, taking the Baroness's arm and pressing it to his heart. 'You have a good memory, my dear, by Jove! – And now you see how wrong you were to be so prudish, for those three hundred thousand francs that you refused so magnanimously are in another woman's pocket. I loved you then, I love you still; but just look back these three years.

'When I said to you, "You shall be mine," what object had I in view? I meant to be revenged on that rascal Hulot. But your husband, my beauty, found himself a mistress – a jewel of a woman, a pearl, a cunning hussy then aged three-and-twenty, for she is six-and-twenty now. It struck me as more amusing, more complete, more Louis xv., more Maréchal de Richelieu, more first-class altogether, to filch away that charmer, who, in point of fact, never cared for Hulot, and who for these three years has been madly in love with your humble servant.'

As he spoke, Crevel, from whose hands the Baroness had released her own, had resumed his favourite attitude; both thumbs were stuck into his armholes, and he was patting his ribs with his fingers, like two flapping wings, fancying that he was thus making himself very attractive and charming. It was as much as to say, 'And this is the man you would have nothing to say to!'

'There you are, my dear; I had my revenge, and your husband knows it. I proved to him clearly that he was basketed – just where he was before, as we say. Madame Marneffe is my mistress, and when her precious Marneffe kicks the bucket, she will be my wife.'

Madame Hulot stared at Crevel with a fixed and almost dazed look.

'Hector knew it?' she said.

'And went back to her,' replied Crevel. 'And I allowed it, because Valérie wished to be the wife of a head-clerk; but she promised me that she would manage things so that our Baron should be so effectually bowled over that he can never interfere any more. And my little duchess – for that woman is a born duchess, on my soul! – kept her word. She restores you your Hector, Madame, virtuous in perpetuity, as she says – she is so witty! He has had a good lesson, I can tell you! The Baron has had some hard knocks; he will keep no more actresses or fine ladies; he is radically cured; cleaned out like a beer-glass.

'If you had listened to Crevel in the first instance, instead of scorning him and turning him out of the house, you might have had four hundred thousand francs, for my revenge has cost me all of that. – But I shall get my change back, I hope, when Marneffe dies – I have invested in a wife, you see; that is the secret of my extravagance. I have solved the problem of playing the lord on easy terms.'

'Would you give your daughter such a mother-in-law?' cried Madame Hulot.

'You do not know Valérie, Madame,' replied Crevel gravely, striking the attitude of his first manner. 'She is a woman with good blood in her veins, a lady, and a woman who enjoys the highest consideration. Why, only yesterday the vicar of the parish was dining with her. She is pious, and we have presented a splendid monstrance to the church.

'Oh! she is clever, she is witty, she is delightful, well informed – she has everything in her favour. For my part, my dear Adeline, I owe everything to that charming woman; she has opened my mind, polished my speech, as you may

have noticed; she corrects my impetuosity, and gives me
words and ideas. I never say anything now that I ought not.
I have greatly improved; you must have noticed it. And then
she has encouraged my ambition. I shall be a Deputy; and I
shall make no blunders, for I shall consult my Egeria. Every
great politician, from Numa to our present Prime Minister, has
had his Sibyl of the fountain. A score of deputies visit Valérie;
she is acquiring considerable influence; and now that she is
about to be established in a charming house, with a carriage,
she will be one of the occult rulers of Paris.

'A fine locomotive! That is what such a woman is. Oh, I
have blessed you many a time for your stern virtue.'

'It is enough to make one doubt the goodness of God!'
cried Adeline, whose indignation had dried her tears. 'But, no!
Divine justice must be hanging over her head.'

'You know nothing of the world, my beauty,' said the great
politician, deeply offended. 'The world, my Adeline, loves
success! Say, now, has it come to seek out your sublime virtue,
priced at two hundred thousand francs?'

The words made Madame Hulot shudder; the nervous trembling attacked her once more. She saw that the ex-perfumer
was taking a mean revenge on her as he had on Hulot; she felt
sick with disgust, and a spasm rose to her throat, hindering
speech.

'Money!' she said at last. 'Always money!'

'You touched me deeply,' said Crevel, reminded by these
words of the woman's humiliation, 'when I beheld you there,
weeping at my feet! – You perhaps will not believe me, but if I
had my pocket-book about me, it would have been yours. –
Come, do you really want such a sum?'

As she heard this question, big with two hundred thousand
francs, Adeline forgot the odious insults heaped on her by this
cheap-jack fine gentleman, before the tempting picture of
success described by Machiavelli-Crevel, who only wanted to
find out her secrets and laugh over them with Valérie.

'Oh! I will do anything, everything,' cried the unhappy woman.
'Monsieur, I will sell myself – I will be a Valérie, if I must.'

'You would find that difficult,' replied Crevel. 'Valérie is a masterpiece in her way. My good mother, twenty-five years of virtue are always repellent, like a badly treated disease. And your virtue has grown very mouldy, my dear child. But you shall see how much I love you. I will manage to get you your two hundred thousand francs.'

Adeline, incapable of uttering a word, seized his hand and laid it on her heart; a tear of joy trembled in her eyes.

'Oh! don't be in a hurry; there will be some hard pulling. I am a jolly good fellow, a good soul with no prejudices, and I will put things plainly to you. You want to do as Valérie does – very good. But that is not all; you must have a gull, a stockholder, a Hulot. – Well, I know a retired tradesman – in fact, a hosier. He is heavy, dull, has not an idea, I am licking him into shape, but I don't know when he will do me credit. My man is a deputy, stupid and conceited; the tyranny of a turbaned wife, in the depths of the country, has preserved him in a state of utter virginity as to the luxury and pleasures of Paris life. But Beauvisage – his name is Beauvisage – is a millionaire, and, like me, my dear, three years ago, he will give a hundred thousand crowns to be the lover of a real lady. – Yes, you see,' he went on, misunderstanding a gesture on Adeline's part, 'he is jealous of me, you understand; jealous of my happiness with Madame Marneffe, and he is a fellow quite capable of selling an estate to purchase a—'

'Enough, Monsieur Crevel!' said Madame Hulot, no longer controlling her disgust, and showing all her shame in her face. 'I am punished beyond my deserts. My conscience, so sternly repressed by the iron hand of necessity, tells me, at this final insult, that such sacrifices are impossible. – My pride is gone; I do not say now, as I did the first time, "Go!" after receiving this mortal thrust. I have lost the right to do so. I have flung myself before you like a prostitute.

'Yes,' she went on, in reply to a negative on Crevel's part, 'I have fouled my life, till now so pure, by a degrading thought; and I am inexcusable! – I know it! – I deserve every insult you can offer me! God's will be done! If, indeed, He desires the death of two creatures worthy to appear before Him, they must die! I shall mourn them, and pray for them! If it is His will that my family should be humbled to the dust, we must bow to His avenging sword, nay, and kiss it, since we are Christians. – I know how to expiate this disgrace, which will be the torment of all my remaining days.

'I who speak to you, Monsieur, am not Madame Hulot, but a wretched, humble sinner, a Christian whose heart henceforth will know but one feeling, and that is repentance, all my time given up to prayer and charity. With such a sin on my soul, I am the last of women, the first only of penitents. – You have been the means of bringing me to a right mind; I can hear the Voice of God speaking within me, and I can thank you!'

She was shaking with the nervous trembling which from that hour never left her. Her low, sweet tones were quite unlike the fevered accents of the woman who was ready for dishonour to save her family. The blood faded from her cheeks, her face was colourless, and her eyes were dry.

'And I played my part very badly, did I not?' she went on, looking at Crevel with the sweetness that martyrs must have shown in their eyes as they looked up at the Proconsul. 'True love, the sacred love of a devoted woman, gives other pleasures, no doubt, than those that are bought in the open market! – But why so many words?' said she, suddenly bethinking herself, and advancing a step further in the way to perfection. 'They sound like irony, but I am not ironical! Forgive me. Besides, Monsieur, I did not want to hurt any one but myself—'

The dignity of virtue and its holy flame had expelled the transient impurity of the woman who, splendid in her own peculiar beauty, looked taller in Crevel's eyes. Adeline had, at this moment, the majesty of the figures of Religion clinging to the Cross, as painted by the old Venetians; but she expressed, too, the immensity of her love and the grandeur of the Catholic Church, to which she flew like a wounded dove.

Crevel was dazzled, astounded.

'Madame, I am your slave, without conditions,' said he, in an inspiration of generosity. 'We will look into this matter –

and – whatever you want – the impossible even – I will do. I will pledge my securities at the Bank, and in two hours you shall have the money.'

'Good God! a miracle!' said poor Adeline, falling on her knees.

She prayed to Heaven with such fervour as touched Crevel deeply; Madame Hulot saw that he had tears in his eyes when, having ended her prayer, she rose to her feet.

'Be a friend to me, Monsieur,' said she. 'Your heart is better than your words and conduct. God gave you your soul; your passions and the world have given you your ideas. Oh, I will love you truly,' she exclaimed, with an angelic tenderness in strange contrast with her attempts at coquettish trickery.

'But cease to tremble so,' said Crevel.

'Am I trembling?' said the Baroness, unconscious of the infirmity that had so suddenly come upon her.

'Yes; why, look,' said Crevel, taking Adeline by the arm and showing her that she was shaking with nervousness. 'Come, Madame,' he added respectfully, 'compose yourself; I am going to the Bank at once.'

'And come back quickly! Remember,' she added, betraying all her secrets, 'that the first point is to prevent the suicide of our poor Uncle Fischer involved by my husband – for I trust you now, and I am telling you everything. Oh, if we should not be in time, I know my brother-in-law, the Marshal, and he has such a delicate soul, that he would die of it in a few days.'

'I am off, then,' said Crevel, kissing the Baroness's hand. 'But what has that unhappy Hulot done?'

'He has swindled the Government.'

'Good Heavens! I fly, Madame; I understand, I admire you!'

Crevel bent one knee, kissed Madame Hulot's skirt, and vanished, saying, 'You will see me soon.'

Unluckily, on his way from the Rue Plumet to his own house, to fetch the securities, Crevel went along the Rue Vanneau, and he could not resist going in to see his little Duchess. His face still bore an agitated expression.

He went straight into Valérie's room, who was having her
hair dressed. She looked at Crevel in her glass, and, like every
woman of that sort, was annoyed, before she knew anything
about it, to see that he was moved by some strong feeling of
which she was not the cause.

'What is the matter, my dear?' said she. 'Is that a face to
bring in to your little Duchess? I will not be your Duchess any
more, Monsieur, no more than I will be your "little duck," you
old monster.'

Crevel replied by a melancholy smile and a glance at the
maid.

'Reine, child, that will do for to-day; I can finish my hair
myself. Give me my Chinese wrapper; my gentleman seems to
me out of sorts.'

Reine, whose face was pitted like a colander, and who
seemed to have been made on purpose to wait on Valérie,
smiled meaningly in reply, and brought the dressing-gown.
Valérie took off her combing-wrapper; she was in her shift,
and she wriggled into the dressing-gown like a snake into a
clump of grass.

'Madame is not at home?'

'What a question!' said Valérie. – 'Come, tell me, my big
puss, have *Rives Gauches* gone down?'

'No.'

'They have raised the price of the house?'

'No.'

'You fancy that you are not the father of our little Crevel?'

'What nonsense!' replied he, sure of his paternity.

'On my honour, I give it up!' said Madame Marneffe. 'If I am
expected to extract my friends' woes as you pull the cork out of
a bottle of Bordeaux, I let it alone. – Go away, you bore me.'

'It is nothing,' said Crevel. 'I must find two hundred
thousand francs in two hours.'

'Oh, you can easily get them. – I have not spent the fifty
thousand francs we got out of Hulot for that report, and I can
ask Henri for fifty thousand—'

'Henri – it is always Henri!' exclaimed Crevel.

'And do you suppose, you great baby of a Machiavelli, that I will cast off Henri? Would France disarm her fleet? – Henri! why, he is a dagger in a sheath hanging to a nail. That boy serves as a weatherglass to show me if you love me – and you don't love me this morning.'

'I don't love you, Valérie?' cried Crevel. 'I love you as much as a million.'

'That is not nearly enough!' cried she, jumping on to Crevel's knee, and throwing both arms round his neck as if it were a peg to hang on by. 'I want to be loved as much as ten millions, as much as all the gold in the world, and more to that. Henri would never wait a minute before telling me all he had on his mind. What is it, my great pet? Have it out. Make a clean breast of it to your own little duck!'

And she swept her hair over Crevel's face, while she jestingly pulled his nose.

'Can a man with a nose like that,' she went on, 'have any secrets from his *Vava – lélé – ririe*?'

And at *Vava* she tweaked his nose to the right; at *lélé* it went to the left; at *ririe* she nipped it straight again.

'Well, I have just seen—' Crevel stopped and looked at Madame Marneffe.

'Valérie, my treasure, promise me on your honour – ours, you know? – not to repeat a single word of what I tell you.'

'Of course, Mayor, we know all about that. One hand up – so – and one foot – so!' And she put herself in an attitude which, to use Rabelais' phrase, stripped Crevel bare from his brain to his heels, so quaint and delicious was the nudity revealed through the light film of lawn.

'I have just seen virtue in despair.'

'Can despair possess virtue?' said she, nodding gravely and crossing her arms like Napoleon.

'It is poor Madame Hulot. She wants two hundred thousand francs, or else Marshal Hulot and old Johann Fischer will blow their brains out; and as you, my little Duchess, are partly at the bottom of the mischief, I am going to patch matters up.

She is a saintly creature, I know her well; she will repay you every penny.'

At the name of Hulot, at the words two hundred thousand francs, a gleam from Valérie's eyes flashed from between her long eyelids like the flame of a cannon through the smoke.

'What did the old thing do to move you to compassion? Did she show you – what? – her – her religion?'

'Do not make game of her, sweetheart; she is a very saintly, a very noble and pious woman, worthy of all respect.'

'Am I not worthy of respect then, heh?' answered Valérie, with a threatening gaze at Crevel.

'I never said so,' replied he, understanding that the praise of virtue might not be gratifying to Madame Marneffe.

'I am pious too,' Valérie went on, taking her seat in an armchair; 'but I do not make a trade of my religion. I go to church in secret.'

She sat in silence, and paid no further heed to Crevel. He, extremely ill at ease, came to stand in front of the chair into which Valérie had thrown herself, and saw her lost in the reflections he had been so foolish as to suggest.

'Valérie, my little angel!'

Utter silence. A highly problematical tear was furtively dashed away.

'One word, my little duck?'

'Monsieur!'

'What are you thinking of, my darling?'

'Oh, Monsieur Crevel, I was thinking of the day of my first communion! How pretty I was! How pure, how saintly! – immaculate! – Oh! if any one had come to my mother and said, "Your daughter will be a hussy, and unfaithful to her husband; one day a police-officer will find her in a disreputable house; she will sell herself to a Crevel to cheat a Hulot – two horrible old men—" Poof! horrible! – she would have died before the end of the sentence, she was so fond of me, poor dear!—'

'Nay, be calm.'

'You cannot think how well a woman must love a man before she can silence the remorse that gnaws at the heart of an adulterous wife. I am quite sorry that Reine is not here; she would have told you that she found me this morning praying with tears in my eyes. I, Monsieur Crevel, for my part, do not make a mockery of religion. Have you ever heard me say a word I ought not on such a subject?'

Crevel shook his head in negation.

'I will never allow it to be mentioned in my presence. I can make fun of anything under the sun: Kings, politics, finance, everything that is sacred in the eyes of the world – judges, matrimony, and love – old men and maidens. But the Church and God! – There I draw the line. – I know I am wicked; I am sacrificing my future life to you. And you have no conception of the immensity of my love.'

Crevel clasped his hands.

'No, unless you could see into my heart, and fathom the depth of my convictions so as to know the extent of my sacrifice! I feel in me the making of a Magdalen. – And see how respectfully I treat the priests; think of the gifts I make to the Church! My mother brought me up in the Catholic Faith, and I know what is meant by God! It is to sinners like us that His voice is most awful.'

Valérie wiped away two tears that trickled down her cheeks. Crevel was in dismay. Madame Marneffe stood up in her excitement.

'Be calm, my darling – you alarm me!'

Madame Marneffe fell on her knees.

'Dear Heaven! I am not bad all through!' she cried, clasping her hands. 'Vouchsafe to rescue Thy wandering lamb, strike her, crush her, snatch her from foul and adulterous hands, and how gladly she will nestle on Thy shoulder! How willingly she will return to the fold!'

She got up and looked at Crevel; her colourless eyes frightened him.

'Yes, Crevel, and, do you know? I, too, am frightened sometimes. The justice of God is exerted in this nether world as well as in the next. What mercy can I expect at God's hands? His vengeance overtakes the guilty in many ways; it assumes every aspect of disaster. That was what my mother told me on her deathbed, speaking of her own old age. – But if I should lose you,' she added, hugging Crevel with a sort of savage frenzy – 'oh! I should die!'

Madame Marneffe released Crevel, knelt down again at the armchair, folded her hands – and in what a bewitching attitude! – and with incredible fervour poured out the following prayer: –

'And thou, Saint Valérie, my patron saint, why dost thou so rarely visit the pillow of her who was intrusted to thy care? Oh, come this evening, as thou didst this morning, to inspire me with holy thoughts, and I will quit the path of sin; like the Magdalen, I will give up deluding joys and the false glitter of the world, even the man I love so well—'

'My precious duck!'

'No more of the "precious duck," Monsieur!' said she, turning round like a virtuous wife, her eyes full of tears, but dignified, cold, and indifferent.

'Leave me,' she went on, pushing him from her. 'What is my duty? To belong wholly to my husband. – He is a dying man, and what am I doing? Deceiving him on the edge of the grave. He believes your child to be his. I will tell him the truth, and begin by securing his pardon before I ask for God's. – We must part. Good-bye, Monsieur Crevel,' and she stood up to offer him an icy cold hand. 'Good-bye, my friend; we shall meet no more till we meet in a better world. – You have to thank me for some enjoyment, criminal indeed; now I want – oh yes, I shall have your esteem.'

Crevel was weeping bitter tears.

'You great pumpkin!' she exclaimed, with an infernal peal of laughter. 'That is how your pious women go about it to drag from you a plum of two hundred thousand francs. And you, who talk of the Maréchal de Richelieu, the prototype of Lovelace, you can be taken in by such a stale trick as that! I could get hundreds of thousands of francs out of you any day, if I chose, you old ninny! – Keep your money! If you have more than you know what to do with, it is mine. If you give two sous to that "respectable" woman, who is pious forsooth, because she is fifty-six years of age, we shall never meet again, and you may take her for your mistress! You would come back to me next day bruised all over from her bony caresses and sodden with her tears, and sick of her little barmaid's caps and her whimpering, which must turn her favours into showers—'

'In point of fact,' said Crevel, 'two hundred thousand francs is a round sum of money.'

'They have fine appetites, have the goody sort! By the poker! they sell their sermons dearer than we sell the rarest and realest thing on earth – pleasure. – And they can spin a yarn! There, I know them. I have seen plenty in my mother's house. They think everything is allowable for the Church and for— Really, my dear love, you ought to be ashamed of yourself – for you are not so open-handed! You have not given me two hundred thousand francs all told!'

'Oh yes,' said Crevel, 'your little house will cost as much as that.'

'Then you have four hundred thousand francs?' said she thoughtfully.

'No.'

'Then, sir, you meant to lend that old horror the two hundred thousand francs due for my hotel? What a crime, what high treason!'

'Only listen to me.'

'If you were giving the money to some idiotic philanthropic scheme, you would be regarded as a coming man,' she went on, with increasing eagerness, 'and I should be the first to advise it; for you are too simple to write a big political book that might make you famous; as for style, you have not enough to butter a pamphlet; but you might do as other men do who are in your predicament, and who get a halo of glory about their name by putting it at the top of some social, or moral, or general, or national enterprise. Benevolence is out of date, quite vulgar. Providing for old offenders, and making them more comfortable than the poor devils who are honest, is played out. What I should like to see is some invention of your own with an endowment of two hundred thousand francs – something difficult and really useful. Then you would be talked about as a man of mark, a Montyon, and I should be very proud of you!

'But as to throwing two hundred thousand francs into a holy-water shell, or lending them to a bigot – cast off by her husband, and who knows why? there is always some reason: does any one cast me off, I ask you? – is a piece of idiocy which in our days could only come into the head of a retired perfumer. It reeks of the counter. You would not dare look at yourself in the glass two days after.

'Go and pay the money in where it will be safe – run, fly; I will not admit you again without the receipt in your hand. Go, as fast and soon as you can!'

She pushed Crevel out of the room by the shoulders, seeing avarice blossoming in his face once more. When she heard the outer door shut, she exclaimed –

'Then Lisbeth is revenged over and over again! What a pity that she is at her old Marshal's now! We would have had a good laugh! So the old woman wants to take the bread out of my mouth. I will startle her a little!'

Marshal Hulot, being obliged to live in a style suited to the highest military rank, had taken a handsome house in the Rue du Mont-Parnasse, where there are three or four princely residences. Though he rented the whole house, he inhabited only the ground floor. When Lisbeth went to keep house for him, she at once wished to let the first floor, which, as she said, would pay the whole rent, so that the Count would live almost rent-free; but the old soldier would not hear of it.

For some months past the Marshal had had many sad thoughts. He had guessed how miserably poor his sister-in-law was, and suspected her griefs without understanding their cause. The old man, so cheerful in his deafness, became taciturn; he could not help thinking that his house would one day be a refuge for the Baroness and her daughter; and it was for them that he kept the first floor. The smallness of his fortune was so well known at headquarters, that the War

Minister, the Prince de Wissembourg, begged his old comrade to accept a sum of money for his household expenses. This sum the Marshal spent in furnishing the ground floor, which was in every way suitable; for, as he said, he would not accept the Marshal's bâton to walk the streets with it.

The house had belonged to a senator under the Empire, and the ground floor drawing-rooms had been very magnificently fitted with carved wood, white-and-gold, still in very good preservation. The Marshal had found some good old furniture in the same style; in the coach-house he had a carriage with two bâtons in saltire on the panels; and when he was expected to appear in full fig, at the Minister's, at the Tuileries, for some ceremony or high festival, he hired horses for the job.

His servant for more than thirty years was an old soldier of sixty, whose sister was the cook, so he had saved ten thousand francs, adding it by degrees to a little hoard he intended for Hortense. Every day the old man walked along the boulevard, from the Rue du Mont-Parnasse to the Rue Plumet; and every pensioner as he passed stood at attention, without fail, to salute him: then the Marshal rewarded the veteran with a smile.

'Who is the man you always stand at attention to salute?' said a young workman one day to an old captain and pensioner.

'I will tell you, boy,' replied the officer.

The 'boy' stood resigned, as a man does to listen to an old gossip.

'In 1809,' said the captain, 'we were covering the flank of the main army, marching on Vienna under the Emperor's command. We came to a bridge defended by three batteries of cannon, one above another, on a sort of cliff; three redoubts like three shelves, and commanding the bridge. We were under Marshal Masséna. That man whom you see there was Colonel of the Grenadier Guards, and I was one of them. Our columns held one bank of the river, the batteries were on the other. Three times they tried for the bridge, and three times they were driven back. "Go and find Hulot!" said the Marshal; "nobody but he and his men can bolt that

morsel." So we came. The General, who was just retiring from
the bridge, stopped Hulot under fire, to tell him how to do it,
and he was in the way. "I don't want advice, but room to
pass," said our General coolly, marching across at the head of
his men. And then, rattle, thirty guns raking us at once.'

'By Heaven!' cried the workman, 'that accounts for some
of these crutches!'

'And if you, like me, my boy, had heard those words so
quietly spoken, you would bow before that man down to the
ground! It is not so famous as Arcole, but perhaps it was finer.
We followed Hulot at the double, right up to those batteries.
All honour to those we left there!' and the old man lifted his
hat. 'The Austrians were amazed at the dash of it. – The
Emperor made the man you saw a Count; he honoured us all
by honouring our leader; and the King of to-day was very right
to make him a Marshal.'

'Hurrah for the Marshal!' cried the workman.

'Oh, you may shout – shout away! The Marshal is as deaf as
a post from the roar of cannon.'

This anecdote may give some idea of the respect with which
the *Invalides* regarded Marshal Hulot, whose Republican pro-
clivities secured him the popular sympathy of the whole
quarter of the town.

Sorrow taking hold on a spirit so calm and strict and noble,
was a heartbreaking spectacle. The Baroness could only tell
lies, with a woman's ingenuity, to conceal the whole dreadful
truth from her brother-in-law.

In the course of this miserable morning, the Marshal, who,
like all old man, slept but little, had extracted from Lisbeth full
particulars as to his brother's situation, promising to marry her
as the reward of her revelations. Any one can imagine with
what glee the old maid allowed the secrets to be dragged from
her which she had been dying to tell ever since she had come
into the house; for by this means she made her marriage more
certain.

'Your brother is incorrigible!' Lisbeth shouted into the
Marshal's best ear.

Her strong, clear tones enabled her to talk to him, but she wore out her lungs, so anxious was she to prove to her future husband that to her he would never be deaf.

'He has had three mistresses,' said the old man, 'and his wife was an Adeline! Poor Adeline!'

'If you will take my advice,' shrieked Lisbeth, 'you will use your influence with the Prince de Wissembourg to secure her some suitable appointment. She will need it, for the Baron's pay is pledged for three years.'

'I will go to the War Office,' said he, 'and see the Prince, to find out what he thinks of my brother, and ask for his interest to help my sister. Think of some place that is fit for her.'

'The charitable ladies of Paris, in concert with the Archbishop, have formed various beneficent associations; they employ superintendents, very decently paid, whose business it is to seek out cases of real want. Such an occupation would exactly suit dear Adeline; it would be work after her own heart.'

'Send to order the horses,' said the Marshal. 'I will go and dress. I will drive to Neuilly if necessary.'

'How fond he is of her! She will always cross my path wherever I turn!' said Lisbeth to herself.

Lisbeth was already supreme in the house, but not with the Marshal's cognisance. She had struck terror into the three servants – for she had allowed herself a housemaid, and she exerted her old-maidish energy in taking stock of everything, examining everything, and arranging in every respect for the comfort of her dear Marshal. Lisbeth, quite as Republican as he could be, pleased him by her democratic opinions, and she flattered him with amazing dexterity; for the last fortnight the old man, whose house was better kept, and who was cared for as a child is by its mother, had begun to regard Lisbeth as a part of what he had dreamed of.

'My dear Marshal,' she shouted, following him out on to the steps, 'pull up the windows, do not sit in a draught, to oblige me!'

The Marshal, who had never been so cosseted in his life, went off smiling at Lisbeth, though his heart was aching.

At the same hour Baron Hulot was quitting the War Office to call on his chief, Marshal the Prince de Wissembourg, who had sent for him. Though there was nothing extraordinary in one of the Generals on the Board being sent for, Hulot's conscience was so uneasy that he fancied he saw a cold and sinister expression in Mitouflet's face.

'Mitouflet, how is the Prince?' he asked, locking the door of his private room and following the messenger who led the way.

'He must have a crow to pluck with you, Monsieur le Baron,' replied the man, 'for his face is set at stormy.'

Hulot turned pale, and said no more; he crossed the ante-room and reception rooms, and, with a violently beating heart, found himself at the door of the Prince's private study.

The chief, at this time seventy years old, with perfectly white hair, and the tanned complexion of a soldier of that age, commanded attention by a brow so vast that imagination saw in it a field of battle. Under this dome, crowned with snow, sparkled a pair of eyes, of the Napoleon blue, usually sad-looking and full of bitter thoughts and regrets, their fire overshadowed by the penthouse of the strongly projecting brow. This man, Bernadotte's rival, had hoped to find his seat on a throne. But those eyes could flash formidable light-nings when they expressed strong feeling.

Then, his voice, always somewhat hollow, rang with strident tones. When he was angry, the Prince was a soldier once more; he spoke the language of Lieutenant Cottin; he spared nothing – nobody. Hulot d'Ervy found the old lion, his hair shaggy like a mane, standing by the fireplace, his brows knit, his back against the mantel-shelf, and his eyes apparently fixed on vacancy.

'Here! At your orders, Prince!' said Hulot, affecting a grace-ful ease of manner.

The Marshal looked hard at the Baron, without saying a word, during the time it took him to come from the door to within a few steps of where the chief stood. This leaden stare was like the eye of God; Hulot could not meet it; he looked down in confusion.

'He knows everything!' said he to himself.

'Does your conscience tell you nothing?' asked the Marshal, in his deep, hollow tones.

'It tells me, sir, that I have been wrong, no doubt, in ordering *razzias* in Algeria without referring the matter to you. At my age, and with my tastes, after forty-five years of service, I have no fortune. – You know the principles of the four hundred elect representatives of France. Those gentlemen are envious of every distinction; they have pared down even the Ministers' pay – that says everything! Ask them for money for an old servant! – What can you expect of men who pay a whole class so badly as they pay the Government legal officials? – who give thirty sous a day to the labourers on the works at Toulon, when it is a physical impossibility to live there and keep a family on less than forty sous? – who never think of the atrocity of giving salaries of six hundred francs, up to a thousand or twelve hundred perhaps, to clerks living in Paris; and who want to secure our places for themselves as soon as the pay rises to forty thousand? – who, finally, refuse to restore to the Crown a piece of Crown property confiscated from the Crown in 1830 – property acquired, too, by Louis XVI. out of his privy purse! – If you had no private fortune, Prince, you would be left high and dry, like my brother, with your pay and not another sou, and no thought of your having saved the army, and me with it, in the boggy plains of Poland.'

'You have robbed the State! You have made yourself liable to be brought before the bench at Assizes,' said the Marshal, 'like that clerk of the Treasury! And you take this, Monsieur, with such levity.'

'But there is a great difference, Monseigneur!' cried the Baron. 'Have I dipped my hands into a cash-box intrusted to my care?'

'When a man of your rank commits such an infamous crime,' said the Marshal, 'he is doubly guilty if he does it clumsily. You have compromised the honour of our official administration, which hitherto has been the purest in Europe! – And all for two hundred thousand francs and a hussy!' said the Marshal, in a terrible voice. 'You are a Councillor of State – and a private soldier who sells anything belonging to his regiment is punished with death! Here is a story told me one day by Colonel Pourin of the Second Lancers. At Saverne, one of his men fell in love with a little Alsatian girl who had a fancy for a shawl. The jade teased this poor devil of a lancer so effectually, that though he could show twenty years' service, and was about to be promoted to be quartermaster – the pride of the regiment – to buy this shawl he sold some of his company's kit. – Do you know what this lancer did, Baron d'Ervy? He swallowed some window-glass after pounding it down, and died in eleven hours, of an illness, in hospital. – Try, if you please, to die of apoplexy, that we may not see you dishonoured.'

Hulot looked with haggard eyes at the old warrior; and the Prince, reading the look which betrayed the coward, felt a flush rise to his cheeks; his eyes flamed.

'Will you, sir, abandon me?' Hulot stammered.

Marshal Hulot, hearing that only his brother was with the Minister, ventured at this juncture to come in, and, like all deaf people, went straight up to the Prince.

'Oh,' cried the hero of Poland, 'I know what you are here for, my old friend! But we can do nothing.'

'Do nothing?' echoed Marshal Hulot, who had heard only the last word.

'Nothing; you have come to intercede for your brother. But do you know what your brother is?'

'My brother?' asked the deaf man.

'Yes, he is a damned, infernal blackguard, and unworthy of you.'

The Marshal in his rage shot from his eyes those fulminating fires which, like Napoleon's, broke a man's will and judgment.

'You lie, Cottin!' said Marshal Hulot, turning white. 'Throw down your bâton as I throw mine! I am ready.'

The Prince went up to his old comrade, looked him in the face, and shouted in his ear as he grasped his hand –

'Are you a man?'

'You will see that I am.'

'Well, then, pull yourself together! You must face the worst misfortune that can befall you.'

The Prince turned round, took some papers from the table, and placed them in the Marshal's hands, saying, 'Read that.'

The Comte de Forzheim read the following letter, which lay uppermost: –

'To His Excellency the President of the Council.

'*Private and Confidential.*

'ALGIERS.

'MY DEAR PRINCE, – We have a very ugly business on our hands, as you will see by the accompanying documents.

'The story, briefly told, is this: Baron Hulot d'Ervy sent out to the province of Oran an uncle of his as a broker in grain and forage, and gave him an accomplice in the person of a storekeeper. This storekeeper, to curry favour, has made a confession, and finally made his escape. The Public Prosecutor took the matter up very thoroughly, seeing, as he supposed, that only two inferior agents were implicated; but Johann Fischer, uncle to your Chief of the Commissariat Department, finding that he was to be brought up at the Assizes, stabbed himself in prison with a nail.

'That would have been the end of the matter if this worthy and honest man, deceived, it would seem, by his agent and by his nephew, had not thought proper to write to Baron Hulot. This letter, seized as a document, so greatly surprised the Public Prosecutor, that he came to see me. Now, the arrest and public trial of a Councillor of State would be such a terrible thing – of a man high in office too, who has a good record for loyal service – for after the Beresina, it was he who saved us all by reorganising the administration – that I desired to have all the papers sent to me.

'Is the matter to take its course? Now that the principal agent is dead, will it not be better to smother up the affair and sentence the storekeeper in default?

'The Public Prosecutor has consented to my forwarding the documents for your perusal; the Baron Hulot d'Ervy being resident in Paris, the proceedings will lie with your Supreme Court. We have hit on this rather shabby way of ridding ourselves of the difficulty for the moment.

'Only, my dear Marshal, decide quickly. This miserable business is too much talked about already, and it will do as much harm to us as to you all if the name of the principal culprit – known at present only to the Public Prosecutor, the examining judge, and myself – should happen to leak out.'

At this point the letter fell from Marshal Hulot's hands; he looked at his brother; he saw that there was no need to examine the evidence. But he looked for Johann Fischer's letter, and after reading it at a glance, held it out to Hector: –

'FROM THE PRISON AT ORAN.

'DEAR NEPHEW, – When you read this letter, I shall have ceased to live.

'Be quite easy, no proof can be found to incriminate you. When I am dead and your Jesuit of a Chardin fled, the trial must collapse. The face of our Adeline, made so happy by you, makes death easy to me. Now you need not send the two hundred thousand francs. Good-bye.

'This letter will be delivered by a prisoner for a short term whom I can trust, I believe.

'JOHANN FISCHER.'

'I beg your pardon,' said Marshal Hulot to the Prince de Wissembourg with pathetic pride.

'Come, come, say *tu*, not the formal *vous*,' replied the Minister, clasping his old friend's hand. 'The poor lancer killed no one but himself,' he added, with a thunderous look at Hulot d'Ervy.

'How much have you had?' said the Comte de Forzheim to his brother.

'Two hundred thousand francs.'

'My dear friend,' said the Count, addressing the Minister, 'you shall have the two hundred thousand francs within forty- eight hours. It shall never be said that a man bearing the name of Hulot has wronged the public treasury of a single sou.'

'What nonsense!' said the Prince. 'I know where the money is, and I can get it paid back. – Send in your resignation and ask for your pension!' he went on, sending a double sheet of foolscap flying across to where the Councillor of State had sat down by the table, for his legs gave way under him. 'To bring you to trial would disgrace us all. I have already obtained from the superior Board their sanction to this line of action. Since you can accept life with dishonour – in my opinion the last degradation – you will get the pension you have earned. Only take care to be forgotten.'

The Minister rang.

'Is Marneffe, the head-clerk, out there?'

'Yes, Monseigneur.'

'Show him in!'

'You,' said the Minister as Marneffe came in, 'you and your wife have wittingly and intentionally ruined the Baron d'Ervy whom you see.'

'Monsieur le Ministre, I beg your pardon. We are very poor. I have nothing to live on but my pay, and I have two children, and the one that is coming will have been brought into the family by Monsieur le Baron.'

'What a villain he looks!' said the Prince, pointing to Marneffe and addressing Marshal Hulot. – 'No more of Sganarelle speeches,' he went on; 'you will disgorge two hundred thousand francs, or be packed off to Algiers.'

'But, Monsieur le Ministre, you do not know my wife. She has spent it all. Monsieur le Baron asked six persons to dinner every evening. – Fifty thousand francs a year are spent in my house.'

'Leave the room!' said the Minister, in the formidable tones that had given the word to charge in battle. 'You will have notice of your transfer within two hours. Go!'

'I prefer to send in my resignation,' said Marneffe insolently. 'For it is too much to be what I am already, and thrashed into the bargain. That would not satisfy me at all.'

And he left the room.

'What an impudent scoundrel!' said the Prince.

Marshal Hulot, who had stood up throughout this scene, as pale as a corpse, studying his brother out of the corner of his eye, went up to the Prince and took his hand, repeating: –

'In forty-eight hours the pecuniary mischief shall be repaired; but honour? – Good-bye, Marshal. It is the last shot that kills. Yes, I shall die of it!' he said in his ear.

'What the devil brought you here this morning?' said the Prince, much moved.

'I came to see what could be done for his wife,' replied the Count, pointing to his brother. 'She is wanting bread – especially now!'

'He has his pension.'

'It is pledged!'

'The Devil must possess such a man,' said the Prince, with a shrug. 'What philtre do those baggages give you to rob you of your wits?' he went on to Hulot d'Ervy. 'How could you – you, who know the precise details with which in French offices everything is written down at full length, consuming reams of paper to certify to the receipt or outlay of a few centimes – you, who have so often complained that a hundred signatures are needed for a mere trifle, to discharge a soldier, to buy a curry-comb – how could you hope to conceal a theft for any length of time? To say nothing of the newspapers, and the envious, and the people who would like to steal! – those women must rob you of your commonsense! Do they cover your eyes with walnut-shells? or are you yourself made of different stuff from us? – You ought to have left the office as soon as you found that you were no longer a man, but a temperament. If you have complicated your crime with such gross folly, you will end – I will not say where—'

'Promise me, Cottin, that you will do what you can for her,' said the Marshal, who heard nothing, and was still thinking of his sister-in-law.

'Depend on me!' said the Minister.

'Thank you, and good-bye then! – Come, Monsieur,' he said to his brother.

The Prince looked with apparent calmness at the two brothers, so different in their demeanour, conduct, and character – the brave man and the coward, the ascetic and the profligate, the honest man and the peculator – and he said to himself –

'That mean creature will not have courage to die! And my poor Hulot, such an honest fellow! has death in his knapsack I know!'

He sat down again in his big chair and went on reading the despatches from Africa with a look characteristic at once of the coolness of a leader and of the pity roused by the sight of a battle-field! For in reality no one is so humane as a soldier, stern as he may seem in the icy determination acquired by the habit of fighting, and so absolutely essential in the battle-field.

Next morning some of the newspapers contained, under various headings, the following paragraphs: –

'Monsieur le Baron Hulot d'Ervy has applied for his retiring pension. The unsatisfactory state of the Algerian exchequer, which has come out in consequence of the death and disappearance of two employés, has had some share in this distinguished official's decision. On hearing of the delinquencies of the agents whom he had unfortunately trusted, Monsieur le Baron Hulot had a paralytic stroke in the War Minister's private room.

'Monsieur Hulot d'Ervy, brother to the Marshal Comte de Forzheim, has been forty-five years in the service. His determination has been vainly opposed, and is greatly regretted by all who know Monsieur Hulot, whose private virtues are as conspicuous as his administrative capacity. No one can have forgotten the devoted conduct of the Commissary General of the Imperial Guard at Warsaw, or the marvellous promptitude with which he organised supplies for the various sections of the army so suddenly required by Napoleon in 1815.

'One more of the heroes of the Empire is retiring from the stage. Monsieur le Baron Hulot has never ceased, since 1830, to be one of the guiding lights of the State Council and of the War Office.'

———

'ALGIERS. – The case known as the forage supply case, to which some of our contemporaries have given absurd prominence, has been closed by the death of the chief culprit. Johann Wisch has committed suicide in his cell; his accomplice, who had absconded, will be sentenced in default.

'Wisch, formerly an army contractor, was an honest man and highly respected, who could not survive the idea of having been the dupe of Chardin, the storekeeper who has disappeared.'

And in the *Paris News* the following paragraph appeared: –

'Monsieur le Maréchal the Minister of War, to prevent the recurrence of such scandals for the future, has arranged for a regular Commissariat office in Africa. A head-clerk in the War Office, Monsieur Marneffe, is spoken of as likely to be appointed to the post of director.'

———

'The office vacated by Baron Hulot is the object of much ambition. The appointment is promised, it is said, to Monsieur le Comte Martial de la Roche-Hugon, Deputy, brother-in-law to Monsieur le Comte de Rastignac. Monsieur Massol, Master of Appeals, will fill his seat on the Council of State, and Monsieur Claude Vignon becomes Master of Appeals.'

Of all kinds of false gossip, the most dangerous for the Opposition newspapers is the official bogus paragraph. However keen journalists may be, they are sometimes the voluntary or involuntary dupes of the cleverness of those who have risen from the ranks of the Press, like Claude Vignon, to the higher realms of power. The newspaper can only be circumvented by the journalist. It may be said, as a parody on a line by Voltaire –

'The Paris news is never what the foolish folk believe.'

Marshal Hulot drove home with his brother, who took the front seat, respectfully leaving the whole of the back of the carriage to his senior. The two men spoke not a single word. Hector was helpless. The Marshal was lost in thought, like a man who is collecting all his strength, and bracing himself to bear a crushing weight. On arriving at his own house, still without speaking, but by an imperious gesture, he beckoned his brother into his study. The Count had received from the Emperor Napoleon a splendid pair of pistols from the Versailles factory; he took the box, with its inscription, ' *Given by the Emperor Napoleon to General Hulot,*' out of his desk, and placing it on the top, he showed it to his brother, saying, 'There is your remedy.'

Lisbeth, peeping through the chink of the door, flew down to the carriage and ordered the coachman to go as fast as he could gallop to the Rue Plumet. Within about twenty minutes she had brought back Adeline, whom she had told of the Marshal's threat to his brother.

The Marshal, without looking at Hector, rang the bell for his factotum, the old soldier who had served him for thirty years.

'Beau-Pied,' said he, 'fetch my notary, and Count Steinbock, and my niece Hortense, and the stockbroker to the Treasury. It is now half-past ten; they must all be here by twelve. Take hackney cabs – and go faster than *that*!' he added, a republican allusion which in past days had been often on his lips. And he put on the scowl that had brought his soldiers to attention when he was beating the broom on the heaths of Brittany in 1799. (See *Les Chouans*.)

'You shall be obeyed, Maréchal,' said Beau-Pied, with a military salute.

Still paying no heed to his brother, the old man came back into his study, took a key out of his desk, and opened a little malachite box mounted in steel, the gift of the Emperor Alexander.

By Napoleon's orders he had gone to restore to the Russian Emperor the private property seized at the battle of Dresden, in exchange for which Napoleon hoped to get back Vandamme. The Czar rewarded General Hulot very handsomely, giving him this casket, and saying that he hoped one day to show the same courtesy to the Emperor of the French; but he kept Vandamme. The Imperial arms of Russia were displayed in gold on the lid of the box, which was inlaid with gold.

The Marshal counted the bank-notes it contained; he had a hundred and fifty-two thousand francs. He saw this with satisfaction. At the same moment Madame Hulot came into the room in a state to touch the heart of the sternest judge. She flew into Hector's arms, looking alternately with a crazy eye at the Marshal and at the case of pistols.

'What have you to say against your brother? What has my husband done to you?' said she, in such a voice that the Marshal heard her.

'He has disgraced us all!' replied the Republican veteran, who spoke with a vehemence that reopened one of his old wounds. 'He has robbed the Government! He has cast odium on my name, he makes me wish I were dead – he has killed me! – I have only strength enough left to make restitution!

'I have been abased before the Condé of the Republic, the man I esteem above all others, and to whom I unjustifiably gave the lie – the Prince de Wissembourg! – Is that nothing? That is the score his country has against him!'

He wiped away a tear.

'Now, as to his family,' he went on. 'He is robbing you of the bread I had saved for you, the fruit of thirty years' economy, of the privations of an old soldier! Here is what was intended for you,' and he held up the bank-notes. 'He has killed his Uncle Fischer, a noble and worthy son of Alsace who could not – as he can – endure the thought of a stain on his peasant's honour.

'To crown all, God, in His adorable clemency, had allowed him to choose an angel among women; he has had the unspeakable happiness of having an Adeline for his wife! And he has deceived her, he has soaked her in sorrows, he has neglected her for prostitutes, for street-hussies, for ballet-girls, actresses – Cadine, Josépha, Marneffe! – And that is the brother I treated as a son and made my pride!

'Go, wretched man; if you can accept the life of degradation you have made for yourself, leave my house! I have not the heart to curse a brother I have loved so well – I am as foolish about him as you are, Adeline – but never let me see him again. I forbid his attending my funeral or following me to the grave. Let him show the decency of a criminal if he can feel no remorse.'

The Marshal, as pale as death, fell back on the settee, exhausted by his solemn speech. And, for the first time in his life perhaps, tears gathered in his eyes and rolled down his cheeks.

'My poor uncle!' cried Lisbeth, putting a handkerchief to her eyes.

'Brother!' said Adeline, kneeling down by the Marshal, 'live for my sake. Help me in the task of reconciling Hector to the world and making him redeem the past.'

'He!' cried the Marshal. 'If he lives, he is not at the end of his crimes. A man who has misprized an Adeline, who has smothered in his own soul the feelings of a true Republican which I tried to instil into him, the love of his country, of his family, and of the poor – that man is a monster, a swine! – Take him away if you still care for him, for a voice within me cries to me to load my pistols and blow his brains out. By killing him I should save you all, and I should save him too from himself.'

The old man started to his feet with such a terrifying gesture that poor Adeline exclaimed –

'Hector – come!'

She seized her husband's arm, dragged him away, and out of the house; but the Baron was so broken down, that she was obliged to call a coach to take him to the Rue Plumet, where he went to bed. The man remained there for several days in a sort of half-dissolution, refusing all nourishment without a word. By floods of tears, Adeline persuaded him to swallow a little broth; she nursed him, sitting by his bed, and feeling only, of all the emotions that once had filled her heart, the deepest pity for him.

At half-past twelve, Lisbeth showed into her dear Marshal's room – for she would not leave him, so much was she alarmed at the evident change in him – Count Steinbock and the notary.

'Monsieur le Comte,' said the Marshal, 'I would beg you to be so good as to put your signature to a document authorising my niece, your wife, to sell a bond for certain funds of which she at present holds only the reversion. – You, Mademoiselle Fischer, will agree to this sale, thus losing your life interest in the securities.'

'Yes, dear Count,' said Lisbeth without hesitation.

'Good, my dear,' said the old soldier. 'I hope I may live to reward you. But I did not doubt you; you are a true Republican, a daughter of the people.' He took the old maid's hand and kissed it.

'Monsieur Hannequin,' he went on, speaking to the notary, 'draw up the necessary document in the form of a power of attorney, and let me have it within two hours, so that I may sell the stock on the Bourse to-day. My niece, the Countess, holds the security; she will be here to sign the power of attorney when you bring it, and so will Mademoiselle. Monsieur le Comte will be good enough to go with you and sign it at your office.'

The artist, at a nod from Lisbeth, bowed respectfully to the Marshal and went away.

Next morning, at ten o'clock, the Comte de Forzheim sent in to announce himself to the Prince, and was at once admitted.

'Well, my dear Hulot,' said the Prince, holding out the newspapers to his old friend, 'we have saved appearances, you see. – Read.'

Marshal Hulot laid the papers on his comrade's table, and held out to him the two hundred thousand francs.

'Here is the money of which my brother robbed the State,' said he.

'What madness!' cried the Minister. 'It is impossible,' he said into the speaking trumpet handed to him by the Marshal, 'to manage this restitution. We should be obliged to declare your brother's dishonest dealings, and we have done everything to hide them.'

'Do what you like with the money; but the family shall not owe one sou of its fortune to a robbery on the funds of the State,' said the Count.

'I will take the King's commands in the matter. We will discuss it no further,' replied the Prince, perceiving that it would be impossible to conquer the old man's sublime obstinacy on the point.

'Good-bye, Cottin,' said the old soldier, taking the Prince's hand. 'I feel as if my soul were frozen—'

Then, after going a step towards the door, he turned round, looked at the Prince, and seeing that he was deeply moved, he opened his arms to clasp him in them; the two old soldiers embraced each other.

'I feel as if I were taking leave of the whole of the old army in you,' said the Count.

'Good-bye, my good old comrade!' said the Minister.

'Yes, it is good-bye; for I am going where all our brave men are for whom we have mourned—'

Just then Claude Vignon was shown in. The two relics of the Napoleonic phalanx bowed gravely to each other, effacing every trace of emotion.

'You have, I hope, been satisfied by the papers,' said the Master of Appeals elect. 'I contrived to let the Opposition papers believe that they were letting out our secrets.'

'Unfortunately, it is all in vain,' replied the Minister, watching Hulot as he left the room. 'I have just gone through a leave-taking that has been a great grief to me. For, indeed, Marshal Hulot has not three days to live; I saw that plainly enough yesterday. That man, one of those honest souls that are above proof, a soldier respected by the bullets in spite of his valour, received his deathblow – there, in that armchair – and dealt by my hand, in a letter! – Ring and order my carriage. I must go to Neuilly,' said he, putting the two hundred thousand francs into his official portfolio.

Notwithstanding Lisbeth's nursing, Marshal Hulot three days later was a dead man. Such men are the glory of the party they support. To Republicans, the Marshal was the ideal of patriotism; and they all attended his funeral, which was followed by an immense crowd. The army, the State officials, the Court, and the populace all came to do homage to this lofty virtue, this spotless honesty, this immaculate glory. Such a last tribute of the people is not a thing to be had for the asking.

This funeral was distinguished by one of those tributes of delicate feeling, of good taste, and sincere respect which from time to time remind us of the virtues and dignity of the old French nobility. Following the Marshal's bier came the old Marquis de Montauran, the brother of him who, in the great rising of the Chouans in 1799, had been the foe, the luckless foe, of Hulot. That Marquis, killed by the balls of the 'Blues,' had confided the interests of his young brother to the Republican soldier. (See *Les Chouans*.) Hulot had so faithfully acted on the noble Royalist's verbal will, that he succeeded in saving the young man's estates, though he himself was at the time an émigré. And so the homage of the old French nobility was not wanting to the leader who, nine years since, had conquered MADAME.

This death, happening just four days before the banns were cried for the last time, came upon Lisbeth like the thunderbolt that burns the garnered harvest with the barn. The peasant of Lorraine, as often happens, had succeeded too well. The Marshal had died of the blows dealt to the family by herself and Madame Marneffe.

The old maid's vindictiveness, which success seemed to have somewhat mollified, was aggravated by this disappointment of her hopes. Lisbeth went, crying with rage, to Madame Marneffe; for she was homeless, the Marshal having agreed that his lease was at any time to terminate with his life. Crevel, to console Valérie's friend, took charge of her savings, added to them considerably, and invested the capital in five per cents., giving her the life interest, and putting the securities into Célestine's name. Thanks to this stroke of business, Lisbeth had an income of about two thousand francs.

When the Marshal's property was examined and valued, a note was found, addressed to his sister-in-law, to his niece Hortense, and to his nephew Victorin, desiring that they would pay among them an annuity of twelve hundred francs to Mademoiselle Lisbeth Fischer, who was to have been his wife.

Adeline, seeing her husband between life and death, succeeded for some days in hiding from him the fact of his brother's death; but Lisbeth came, in mourning, and the terrible truth was told him eleven days after the funeral.

This crushing blow revived the sick man's energies. He got up, found his family collected in the drawing-room, all in black, and suddenly silent as he came in. In a fortnight, Hulot, as lean as a spectre, looked to his family the mere shadow of himself.

'I must decide on something,' said he in a husky voice, as he seated himself in an easy-chair, and looked round at the party, of whom Crevel and Steinbock were absent.

'We cannot stay here, the rent is too high,' Hortense was saying just as her father came in.

'As to a home,' said Victorin, breaking the painful silence, 'I can offer my mother—'

As he heard these words, which excluded him, the Baron raised his head, which was sunk on his breast as though he were studying the pattern of the carpet, though he did not even see it, and he gave the young lawyer an appealing look. The rights of a father are so indefeasibly sacred, even when he is a villain and devoid of honour, that Victorin paused.

'To your mother,' the Baron repeated. 'You are right, my son.'

'The rooms over ours in our wing,' said Célestine, finishing her husband's sentence.

'I am in your way, my dears?' said the Baron, with the mildness of a man who has judged himself. 'But do not be uneasy as to the future; you will have no further cause for complaint of your father; you will not see him till the time when you need no longer blush for him.'

He went up to Hortense and kissed her brow. He opened his arms to his son, who rushed into his embrace, guessing his father's purpose. The Baron signed to Lisbeth, who came to him, and he kissed her forehead. Then he went to his room, whither Adeline followed him in an agony of dread.

'My brother was quite right, Adeline,' he said, holding her hand. 'I am unworthy of my home life. I dared not bless my children, who have behaved so nobly, but in my heart; tell them that I could only venture to kiss them; for the blessing of a bad man, a father who has been an assassin and the scourge of his family instead of its protector and its glory, might bring evil on them; but assure them that I shall bless them every day. – As to you, God alone, for He is Almighty, can ever reward you according to your merits! – I can only ask your forgiveness!' and he knelt at her feet, taking her hands and wetting them with his tears.

'Hector, Hector! Your sins have been great, but Divine Mercy is infinite, and you may repair all by staying with me. – Rise up in Christian charity, my dear – I am your wife, and not your judge. I am your possession; do what you will with me; take me wherever you go, I feel strong enough to comfort you, to make life endurable to you, by the strength of my love, my care, and respect. – Our children are settled in life; they need me no more. Let me try to be an amusement to you, an occupation. Let me share the pain of your banishment and of your poverty, and help to mitigate it. I could always be of some use, if it were only to save the expense of a servant.'

'Can you forgive, my dearly-beloved Adeline?'

'Yes, only get up, my dear!'

'Well, with that forgiveness I can live,' said he, rising to his feet. 'I came back into this room that my children should not see their father's humiliation. Oh! the sight constantly before their eyes of a father so guilty as I am is a terrible thing; it must undermine parental influence and break every family tie. So I cannot remain among you, and I must go to spare you the odious spectacle of a father bereft of dignity. Do not oppose my departure, Adeline. It would only be to load with your own hand the pistol to blow my brains out. Above all, do not seek me in my hiding-place; you would deprive me of the only strong motive remaining in me, that of remorse.'

Hector's decisiveness silenced his dejected wife. Adeline, lofty in the midst of all this ruin, had derived her courage from her perfect union with her husband; for she had dreamed of having him for her own, of the beautiful task of comforting him, of leading him back to family life, and reconciling him to himself.

'But, Hector, would you leave me to die of despair, anxiety, and alarms!' said she, seeing herself bereft of the mainspring of her strength.

'I will come back to you, dear angel – sent from Heaven expressly for me, I believe. I will come back, if not rich, at least with enough to live in ease. – Listen, my sweet Adeline, I cannot stay here for many reasons. In the first place, my pension of six thousand francs is pledged for four years, so I have nothing. That is not all. I shall be committed to prison within a few days in consequence of the bills held by Vauvinet. So I must keep out of the way until my son, to whom I will give full instructions, shall have bought in the bills. My disappearance will facilitate that. As soon as my pension is my own, and Vauvinet is paid off, I will return to you. – You would be sure to let out the secret of my hiding-place. Be calm; do not cry, Adeline – it is only for a month—'

'Where will you go? What will you do? What will become of you? Who will take care of you now that you are no longer young? Let me go with you – we will go abroad—' said she.

'Well, well, we will see,' he replied.

The Baron rang and ordered Mariette to collect all his things and pack them quickly and secretly. Then, after embracing his wife with a warmth of affection to which she was unaccustomed, he begged her to leave him alone for a few minutes while he wrote his instructions for Victorin, promising that he would not leave the house till dark, or without her.

As soon as the Baroness was in the drawing-room, the cunning old man stole out through the dressing-closet to the anteroom, and went away, giving Mariette a slip of paper, on which was written, 'Address my trunks to go by railway to Corbeil – to Monsieur Hector, cloak-room, Corbeil.'

The Baron jumped into a hackney coach, and was rushing across Paris, by the time Mariette came to give the Baroness this note, and say that her master had gone out. Adeline flew back into her room, trembling more violently than ever; her children followed on hearing her give a piercing cry. They found her in a dead faint; and they put her to bed, for she was seized by a nervous fever which held her for a month between life and death.

'Where is he?' was the only thing she would say.

Victorin sought for him in vain.

And this is why. The Baron had driven to the Place du Palais Royal. There this man, who had recovered all his wits to work out a scheme which he had premeditated during the days he had spent in bed crushed with pain and grief, crossed the Palais Royal on foot, and took a handsome carriage from a livery-stable in the Rue Joquelet. In obedience to his orders, the coachman went to the Rue de la Ville l'Évêque, and into the courtyard of Josépha's mansion, the gates opening at once at the call of the driver of such a splendid vehicle. Josépha came out, prompted by curiosity, for her man-servant had told her that a helpless old gentleman, unable to get out of his carriage, begged her to come to him for a moment.

'Josépha! – it is I—'

The singer recognised her Hulot only by his voice.

'What? you, poor old man? – On my honour, you look like a twenty-franc piece that the Jews have sweated and the money-changers refuse.'

'Alas, yes,' replied Hulot; 'I am snatched from the jaws of death! But you are as lovely as ever. Will you be kind?'

'That depends,' said she; 'everything is relative.'

'Listen,' said Hulot; 'can you put me up for a few days in a servant's room under the roof? I have nothing – not a farthing, not a hope; no food, no pension, no wife, no children, no roof over my head; without honour, without courage, without a friend; and worse than all that, liable to imprisonment for not meeting a bill.'

'Poor old fellow! you are without most things. – Are you also *sans culotte*?'

'You laugh at me! I am done for,' cried the Baron. 'And I counted on you as Gourville did on Ninon.'

'And it was a "real lady," I am told, who brought you to this,' said Josépha. 'Those precious sluts know how to pluck a goose even better than we do! – Why, you are like a corpse that the crows have done with – I can see daylight through!'

'Time is short, Josépha!'

'Come in, old boy. I am alone, as it happens, and my people don't know you. Send away your trap. Is it paid for?'

'Yes,' said the Baron, getting out with the help of Josépha's arm.

'You may call yourself my father if you like,' said the singer, moved to pity.

She made Hulot sit down in the splendid drawing-room where he had last seen her.

'And is it the fact, old man,' she went on, 'that you have killed your brother and your uncle, ruined your family, mort-gaged your children's house over and over again, and robbed the Government till in Africa, all for your princess?'

Hulot sadly bent his head.

'Well, I admire that!' cried Josépha, starting up in her enthusiasm. 'It is a general flare up! It is Sardanapalus! Splen-did, thoroughly complete! I may be a hussy, but I have a soul!

I tell you, I like a spendthrift, like you, crazy over a woman, a thousand times better than those torpid, heartless bankers, who are supposed to be so good, and who ruin no end of families with their rails – gold for them, and iron for their gulls! You have only ruined those who belong to you, you have sold no one but yourself; and then you have excuses, physical and moral.'

She struck a tragic attitude, and spouted –

'"'Tis Venus, whose grasp never parts from her prey."

And there you are!' and she pirouetted on her toe.

Vice, Hulot found, could forgive him; vice smiled on him from the midst of unbridled luxury. Here, as before a jury, the magnitude of a crime was an extenuating circumstance. 'And is your lady pretty at any rate?' asked Josépha, trying, as a preliminary act of charity, to divert Hulot's thoughts, for his depression grieved her.

'On my word, almost as pretty as you are,' said the Baron artfully.

'And monstrously droll? So I have been told. What does she do, I say? Is she better fun than I am?'

'I don't want to talk about her,' said Hulot.

'And I hear she has come round my Crevel, and little Steinbock, and a gorgeous Brazilian?'

'Very likely.'

'And that she has got a house as good as this, that Crevel has given her. The baggage! She is my provost-marshal, and finishes off those I have spoiled. I tell you why I am so curious to know what she is like, old boy; I just caught sight of her in the Bois, in an open carriage – but a long way off. She is a most accomplished harpy, Carabine says. She is trying to eat up Crevel, but he only lets her nibble. Crevel is a knowing hand, good-natured but hard-headed, who will always say Yes, and then go his own way. He is vain and passionate; but his cash is cold. You can never get anything out of such fellows beyond a thousand to three thousand francs a month; they jib at any serious outlay, as a donkey does at a running stream.

'Not like you, old boy. You are a man of passions; you would sell your country for a woman. And, look here, I am ready to do anything for you! You are my father; you started me in life; it is a sacred duty. What do you want? Do you want a hundred thousand francs? I will wear myself to a rag to gain them. As to giving you bed and board – that is nothing. A place will be laid for you here every day; you can have a good room on the second floor, and a hundred crowns a month for pocket-money.'

The Baron, deeply touched by such a welcome, had a last qualm of honour.

'No, my dear child, no; I did not come here for you to keep me,' said he.

'At your age it is something to be proud of,' said she.

'This is what I wish, my child. Your Duc d'Hérouville has immense estates in Normandy, and I want to be his steward, under the name of Thoul. I have the capacity, and I am honest. A man may borrow of the Government, and yet not steal from a cash-box—'

'H'm, h'm,' said Josépha. 'Once drunk, drinks again.'

'In short, I only want to live out of sight for three years—'

'Well, it is soon done,' said Josépha. 'This evening, after dinner, I have only to speak. The Duke would marry me if I wished it, but I have his fortune, and I want something better – his esteem. He is a Duke of the first water. He is high-minded, as noble and great as Louis XIV. and Napoleon rolled into one, though he is a dwarf. Besides, I have done for him what la Schontz did for Rochefide; by taking my advice he has made two millions.

'Now, listen to me, old popgun. I know you; you are always after the women, and you would be dancing attendance on the Normandy girls, who are splendid creatures, and getting your ribs cracked by their lovers and fathers, and the Duke would have to get you out of the scrape. Why, can't I see by the way you look at me that the *young* man is not dead in you – as Fénelon put it. – No, this stewardship is not the thing for you.

A man cannot be off with his Paris and with us, old boy, for the saying! You would die of weariness at Hérouville.'

'What is to become of me?' said the Baron, 'for I will only stay here till I see my way.'

'Well, shall I find a pigeon-hole for you? Listen, you old pirate. Women are what you want. They are consolation in all circumstances. Attend now. – At the end of the Alley, Rue Saint-Maur du Temple, there is a poor family I know of where there is a jewel of a little girl, prettier than I was at sixteen. – Ah! there is a twinkle in your eye already! – The child works sixteen hours a day at embroidering costly pieces for the silk merchants, and earns sixteen sous a day – one sou an hour! – and feeds like the Irish, on potatoes fried in rats' dripping, with bread five times a week – and drinks canal water out of the town pipes, because Seine water costs too much; and she cannot set up on her own account for lack of six or seven thousand francs. Your wife and children bore you to death, don't they? – Besides, one cannot submit to be nobody where one has been a little Almighty. A father who has neither money nor honour can only be stuffed and kept in a glass case.'

The Baron could not help smiling at these abominable jests.

'Well, now, Bijou is to come to-morrow morning to bring me an embroidered wrapper, a gem! It has taken six months to make; no one else will have any stuff like it! Bijou is very fond of me; I give her titbits and my old gowns. And I send orders for bread and meat and wood to the family, who would break the shin-bones of the first comer if I bid them. – I try to do a little good. Ah! I know what I endured from hunger myself! – Bijou has confided to me all her little sorrows. There is the making of a super at the Ambigu-Comique in that child. Her dream is to wear fine dresses like mine; above all, to ride in a carriage. I shall say to her, "Look here, little one, would you like to have a friend of—" How old are you?' she asked, interrupting herself. 'Seventy-two?'

'I have given up counting.'

'"Would you like an old gentleman of seventy-two?" I shall say. "Very clean and neat, and who does not take snuff, who is as sound as a bell, and as good as a young man? He will marry you (in the thirteenth arrondissement) and be very kind to you; he will place seven thousand francs to your account, and furnish you a room all in mahogany; and if you are good, he will sometimes take you to the play. He will give you a hundred francs a month for pocket-money, and fifty francs for housekeeping." – I know Bijou; she is myself at fourteen. I jumped for joy when that horrible Crevel made me his atrocious offers. Well, and you, old man, will be disposed of for three years. She is a good child, well behaved; for three or four years she will have her illusions – not for longer.'

Hulot did not hesitate; he had made up his mind to refuse; but to seem grateful to the kind-hearted singer, who was benevolent after her lights, he affected to hesitate between vice and virtue.

'Why, you are as cold as a paving-stone in winter!' she exclaimed in amazement. 'Come, now. You will make a whole family happy – a grandfather who runs all the errands, a mother who is being worn out with work, and two sisters – one of them very plain – who make thirty-two sous a day while putting their eyes out. It will make up for the misery you have caused at home, and you will expiate your sin while you are having as much fun as a minx at Mabille.'

Hulot, to put an end to this temptation, moved his fingers as if he were counting out money.

'Oh! be quite easy as to ways and means,' replied Josépha. 'My Duke will lend you ten thousand francs; seven thousand to start an embroidery shop in Bijou's name, and three thousand for furnishing; and every three months you will find a cheque here for six hundred and fifty francs. When you get your pension paid you, you can repay the seventeen thousand francs. Meanwhile you will be as happy as a cow in clover, and hidden in a hole where the police will never find you. You must wear a loose serge coat, and you will look like a comfortable householder. Call yourself Thoul, if that is your fancy. I will tell Bijou that you are an uncle of mine come from Germany, having failed in business, and you will be cosseted like a divinity. – There now, Daddy! – And who knows! you may have no regrets. In case you should be bored, keep one Sunday rig-out, and you can come and ask me for a dinner and spend the evening here.'

'I! – and I meant to settle down and behave myself! – Look here, borrow twenty thousand francs for me, and I will set out to make my fortune in America, like my friend d'Aiglemont when Nucingen cleaned him out.'

'You!' cried Josépha. 'Nay, leave morals to work-a-day folks, to raw recruits, to the *worrrthy* citizens who have nothing to boast of but their virtue. You! You were born to be something better than a nincompoop; you are as a man what I am as a woman – a spendthrift of genius.'

'We will sleep on it and discuss it all to-morrow morning.'

'You will dine with the Duke. My d'Hérouville will receive you as civilly as if you were the saviour of the State; and to-morrow you can decide. Come, be jolly, old boy! Life is a garment; when it is dirty, we must brush it; when it is ragged, it must be patched; but we keep it on as long as we can.'

This philosophy of life, and her high spirits, postponed Hulot's keenest pangs.

At noon next day, after a capital breakfast, Hulot saw the arrival of one of those living masterpieces which Paris alone, of all the cities in the world, can produce, by means of the constant concubinage of luxury and poverty, of vice and decent honesty, of suppressed desire and renewed temptation, which makes the French capital the daughter of Nineveh, of Babylon, and of Imperial Rome.

Mademoiselle Olympe Bijou, a child of sixteen, had the exquisite face which Raphael drew for his Virgins; eyes of pathetic innocence, weary with overwork – black eyes, with long lashes, their moisture parched with the heat of laborious nights, and darkened with fatigue; a complexion like porcelain, almost too delicate; a mouth like a partly opened pomegranate; a heaving bosom, a full figure, pretty hands, the whitest teeth, and a mass of black hair; and the whole meagrely set off by a cotton frock at seventy-five centimes the metre, leather shoes

without heels, and the cheapest gloves. The girl, all unconscious of her charms, had put on her best frock to wait on the
fine lady.

The Baron, gripped again by the clutch of profligacy, felt all
his life concentrated in his eyes. He forgot everything on
beholding this delightful creature. He was like a sportsman
in sight of the game; if an emperor were present, he must take
aim!

'And warranted sound,' said Josépha in his ear. 'An
honest child, and wanting bread. This is Paris – I have been
there!'

'It is a bargain,' replied the old man, getting up and rubbing
his hands.

When Olympe Bijou was gone, Josépha looked mischiev-
ously at the Baron.

'If you want things to keep straight, Daddy,' said she, 'be as
firm as the Public Prosecutor on the bench. Keep a tight hand
on her, be a Bartholo! Ware Auguste, Hippolyte, Nestor,
Victor – *or*, that is gold, in every form. When once the child
is fed and dressed, if she gets the upper hand, she will drive
you like a serf. – I will see to settling you comfortably. The
Duke does the handsome; he will lend – that is, give – you ten
thousand francs; and he deposits eight thousand with his
notary, who will pay you six hundred francs every quarter,
for I cannot trust you. – Now, am I nice?'

'Adorable.'

Ten days after deserting his family, when they were gathered round Adeline, who seemed to be dying, as she said again
and again, in a weak voice, 'Where is he?' Hector, under the
name of Thoul, was established in the Rue Saint-Maur, at
the head of a business as embroiderer, under the name of
Thoul and Bijou.

Victorin Hulot, under the overwhelming disasters of his
family, had received the finishing touch which makes or
mars the man. He was perfection. In the great storms of life
we act like the captain of a ship who, under the stress of a

hurricane, lightens the ship of its heaviest cargo. The young lawyer lost his self-conscious pride, his too evident assertiveness, his arrogance as an orator, and his political pretensions. He was as a man what his wife was as a woman. He made up his mind to make the best of his Célestine – who certainly did not realise his dreams – and was wise enough to estimate life at its true value by contenting himself in all things with the second best. He vowed to fulfil his duties, so much had he been shocked by his father's example.

These feelings were confirmed as he stood by his mother's bed on the day when she was out of danger. Nor did this happiness come single. Claude Vignon, who called every day from the Prince de Wissembourg to inquire as to Madame Hulot's progress, desired the re-elected deputy to go with him to see the Minister.

'His Excellency,' said he, 'wants to talk over your family affairs with you.'

The Prince had long known Victorin Hulot, and received him with a friendliness that promised well.

'My dear fellow,' said the old soldier, 'I promised your uncle, in this room, that I would take care of your mother. That saintly woman, I am told, is getting well again; now is the time to pour oil into your wounds. I have for you here two hundred thousand francs; I will give them to you—'

The lawyer's gesture was worthy of his uncle the Marshal.

'Be quite easy,' said the Prince, smiling; 'it is money in trust. My days are numbered; I shall not always be here; so take this sum, and fill my place towards your family. You may use this money to pay off the mortgage on your house. These two hundred thousand francs are the property of your mother and your sister. If I gave the money to Madame Hulot, I fear that, in her devotion to her husband, she would be tempted to waste it. And the intention of those who restore it to you is, that it should procure bread for Madame Hulot and her daughter, the Countess Steinbock. You are a steady man, the worthy son of your noble mother, the true nephew of my friend the Marshal; you are appreciated here, you see – and elsewhere. So be the guardian angel of your family, and take this as a legacy from your uncle and me.'

'Monseigneur,' said Hulot, taking the Minister's hand and pressing it, 'such men as you know that thanks in words mean nothing; gratitude must be proven.'

'Prove yours—' said the old man.

'In what way?'

'By accepting what I have to offer you,' said the Minister. 'We propose to appoint you to be attorney to the War Office, which just now is involved in litigations in consequence of the plan for fortifying Paris; consulting clerk also to the Préfecture of Police; and a member of the Board of the Civil List. These three appointments will secure you salaries amounting to eighteen thousand francs, and will leave you politically free. You can vote in the Chamber in obedience to your opinions and your conscience. Act in perfect freedom on that score. It would be a bad thing for us if there were no national opposition!

'Also, a few lines from your uncle, written a day or two before he breathed his last, suggested what I could do for your mother, whom he loved very truly. – Mesdames Popinot, de Rastignac, de Navarreins, d'Espard, de Grandlieu, de Carigliano, de Lenoncourt, and de la Bâtie have made a place for your mother as a Lady Superintendent of their charities. These ladies, presidents of various branches of benevolent work, cannot do everything themselves; they need a lady of character who can act for them by going to see the objects of their beneficence, ascertaining that charity is not imposed upon, and whether the help given really reaches those who applied for it, finding out the poor who are ashamed to beg, and so forth. Your mother will fulfil an angelic function; she will be thrown in with none but priests and these charitable ladies; she will be paid six thousand francs and the cost of her hackney coaches.

'You see, young man, that a pure and nobly virtuous man can still assist his family, even from the grave. Such a name as your uncle's is, and ought to be, a buckler against misfortune in a well-organised scheme of society. Follow in his path; you have started in it, I know; continue in it.'

'Such delicate kindness cannot surprise me in my uncle's friend,' said Victorin. 'I will try to come up to all your hopes.'

'Go at once, and take comfort to your family. – By the way,' added the Prince, as he shook hands with Victorin, 'your father has disappeared?'

'Alas! yes.'

'So much the better. That unhappy man has shown his wit, in which, indeed, he is not lacking.'

'There are bills of his to be met.'

'Well, you shall have six months' pay of your three appointments in advance. This pre-payment will help you, perhaps, to get the notes out of the hands of the money-lender. And I will see Nucingen, and perhaps may succeed in releasing your father's pension, pledged to him, without its costing you or our office a sou. The peer has not killed the banker in Nucingen; he is insatiable; he wants some concession – I know not what—'

So on his return to the Rue Plumet, Victorin could carry out his plan of lodging his mother and sister under his roof.

The young lawyer, already famous, had, for his sole fortune, one of the handsomest houses in Paris, purchased in 1834 in preparation for his marriage, situated on the boulevard between the Rue de la Paix and the Rue Louis-le-Grand. A speculator had built two houses between the boulevard and the street; and between these, with the gardens and courtyards to the front and back, there remained still standing a splendid wing, the remains of the magnificent mansion of the Verneuils. The younger Hulot had purchased this fine property, on the strength of Mademoiselle Crevel's marriage-portion, for one million francs, when it was put up to auction, paying five hundred thousand down. He lived on the ground floor, expecting to pay the remainder out of letting the rest; but though it is safe to speculate in house-property in Paris, such investments are capricious or hang fire, depending on unforeseen circumstances.

As the Parisian lounger may have observed, the boulevard between the Rue de la Paix and the Rue Louis-le-Grand prospered but slowly; it took so long to furbish and beautify itself, that trade did not set up its display there till 1840 – the gold of the money-changers, the fairy-work of fashion, and the luxurious splendour of shop-fronts.

In spite of two hundred thousand francs given by Crevel to his daughter at the time when his vanity was flattered by this marriage, before the Baron had robbed him of Josépha; in spite of two hundred thousand francs paid off by Victorin in the course of seven years, the property was still burdened with a debt of five hundred thousand francs, in consequence of Victorin's devotion to his father. Happily, a rise in rents and the advantages of the situation had at this time improved the value of the houses. The speculation was justifying itself after eight years' patience, during which the lawyer had strained every nerve to pay the interest and some trifling amounts of the capital borrowed.

The tradespeople were ready to offer good rents for the shops, on condition of being granted leases for eighteen years. The dwelling apartments rose in value by the shifting of the centre of Paris life – henceforth transferred to the region between the Bourse and the Madeleine, now the seat of the political power and financial authority of Paris. The money paid to him by the Minister, added to a year's rent in advance and the premiums paid by his tenants, would finally reduce the outstanding debt to two hundred thousand francs. The two houses, if entirely let, would bring in a hundred thousand francs a year. Within two years more, during which the Hulots could live on his salaries, added to by the Marshal's investments, Victorin would be in a splendid position.

This was manna from heaven. Victorin could give up the first floor of his own house to his mother, and the second to Hortense, excepting two rooms reserved for Lisbeth. With Cousin Bette as the housekeeper, this compound household could bear all these charges, and yet keep up a good appearance, as beseemed a pleader of note. The great stars of the law-courts were rapidly disappearing; and Victorin Hulot, gifted with a shrewd tongue and strict honesty, was listened to by the Bench and Councillors; he studied his cases thoroughly, and advanced nothing that he could not prove. He would not hold every brief that offered; in fact, he was a credit to the bar.

The Baroness's home in the Rue Plumet had become so odious to her, that she allowed herself to be taken to the Rue Louis-le-Grand. Thus, by her son's care, Adeline occupied a fine apartment; she was spared all the daily worries of life; for Lisbeth consented to begin again, working wonders of domestic economy, such as she had achieved for Madame Marneffe, seeing here a way of exerting her silent vengeance on those three noble lives, the object, each, of her hatred, which was kept growing by the overthrow of all her hopes.

Once a month she went to see Valérie, sent, indeed, by Hortense, who wanted news of Wenceslas, and by Célestine, who was seriously uneasy at the acknowledged and well-known connection between her father and a woman to whom her mother-in-law and sister-in-law owed their ruin and their sorrows. As may be supposed, Lisbeth took advantage of this to see Valérie as often as possible.

Thus, about twenty months passed by, during which the Baroness recovered her health, though her palsied trembling never left her. She made herself familiar with her duties, which afforded her a noble distraction from her sorrow and constant food for the divine goodness of her heart. She also regarded it as an opportunity for finding her husband in the course of one of those expeditions which took her into every part of Paris.

During this time, Vauvinet had been paid, and the pension of six thousand francs was almost redeemed. Victorin could maintain his mother as well as Hortense out of the ten thousand francs interest on the money left by Marshal Hulot in trust for them. Adeline's salary amounted to six thousand francs a year; and this, added to the Baron's pension when it was freed, would presently secure an income of twelve thousand francs a year to the mother and daughter.

Thus, the poor woman would have been almost happy but for her perpetual anxieties as to the Baron's fate; for she longed to have him with her to share the improved fortunes that smiled on the family; and but for the constant sight of her forsaken daughter; and but for the terrible thrusts constantly and *unconsciously* dealt her by Lisbeth, whose diabolical character had free course.

A scene which took place at the beginning of the month of March 1843 will show the results of Lisbeth's latent and persistent hatred, still seconded, as she always was, by Madame Marneffe.

Two great events had occurred in the Marneffe household. In the first place, Valérie had given birth to a still-born child, whose little coffin had cost her two thousand francs a year. And then, as to Marneffe himself, eleven months since, this is the report given by Lisbeth to the Hulot family one day on her return from a visit of discovery at the Hôtel Marneffe.

'This morning,' said she, 'that dreadful Valérie sent for Doctor Bianchon to ask whether the medical men who had condemned her husband yesterday had made no mistake. Bianchon pronounced that to-night at latest that horrible creature will depart to the torments that await him. Old Crevel and Madame Marneffe saw the doctor out; and your father, my dear Célestine, gave him five gold pieces for his good news.

'When he came back into the drawing-room, Crevel cut capers like a dancer; he embraced that woman, exclaiming, "Then, at last, you will be Madame Crevel!" – And to me, when she had gone back to her husband's bedside, for he was at his last gasp, your noble father said to me, "With Valérie as my wife, I can become a peer of France! I shall buy an estate I have my eye on – Presles, which Madame de Sérizy wants to sell. I shall be Crevel de Presles, member of the Common Council of Seine-et-Oise, and Deputy. I shall have a son! I shall be everything I have ever wished to be." – "Heh!" said I, "and what about your daughter?" – "Bah!" says he, "she is

only a woman! And she is quite too much of a Hulot. Valérie
has a horror of them all. – My son-in-law has never chosen to
come to this house; why has he given himself such airs as a
Mentor, a Spartan, a Puritan, a philanthropist? Besides, I have
squared accounts with my daughter; she has had all her
mother's fortune, and two hundred thousand francs to that.
So I am free to act as I please. – I shall judge of my son-in-law
and Célestine by their conduct on my marriage; as they
behave, so shall I. If they are nice to their stepmother, I will
receive them. I am a man, after all!" – In short, all his
rhodomontade! And an attitude like Napoleon on the column.'

The ten months' widowhood insisted on by the law had
now elapsed some few days since. The estate of Presles was
purchased. Victorin and Célestine had that very morning sent
Lisbeth to make inquiries as to the marriage of the fascinating
widow to the Mayor of Paris, now a member of the Common
Council of the Department of Seine-et-Oise.

Célestine and Hortense, in whom the ties of affection had
been drawn closer since they had lived under the same roof,
were almost inseparable. The Baroness, carried away by a
sense of honesty which led her to exaggerate the duties of
her place, devoted herself to the work of charity of which she
was the agent; she was out almost every day from eleven till
five. The sisters-in-law, united in their cares for the children
whom they kept together, sat at home and worked. They had
arrived at the intimacy which thinks aloud, and were a touching picture of two sisters, one cheerful and the other sad. The
less happy of the two, handsome, lively, high-spirited, and
clever, seemed by her manner to defy her painful situation;
while the melancholy Célestine, sweet and calm, and as equ-
able as reason itself, might have been supposed to have some
secret grief. It was this contradiction, perhaps, that added to
their warm friendship. Each supplied the other with what she
lacked.

Seated in a little summer-house in the garden, which the
speculator's trowel had spared by some happy fancy of the
builder's, who believed that he was preserving these hundred

feet square of earth for his own pleasure, they were admiring the first green shoots of the lilac-trees, a spring festival which can only be fully appreciated in Paris when the inhabitants have lived for six months oblivious of what vegetation means, among the cliffs of stone where the ocean of humanity tosses to and fro.

'Célestine,' said Hortense to her sister-in-law, who had complained that in such fine weather her husband should be kept at the Chamber, 'I think you do not fully appreciate your happiness. Victorin is a perfect angel, and you sometimes torment him.'

'My dear, men like to be tormented! Certain ways of teasing are a proof of affection. If your poor mother had only been – I will not say exacting, but always prepared to be exacting, you would not have had so much to grieve over.'

'Lisbeth is not come back. I shall have to sing the song of *Malbrouck*,' said Hortense. 'I do long for some news of Wenceslas! – What does he live on? He has not done a thing these two years.'

'Victorin saw him, he told me, with that horrible woman not long ago; and he fancies that she maintains him in idleness. – If you only would, dear soul, you might bring your husband back to you yet.'

Hortense shook her head.

'Believe me,' Célestine went on, 'the position will ere long be intolerable. In the first instance, rage, despair, indignation, gave you strength. The awful disasters that have come upon us since – two deaths, ruin, and the disappearance of Baron Hulot – have occupied your mind and heart; but now you live in peace and silence, you will find it hard to bear the void in your life; and as you cannot, and will never leave the path of virtue, you will have to be reconciled to Wenceslas. Victorin, who loves you so much, is of that opinion. There is something stronger than one's feelings even, and that is Nature!'

'But such a mean creature!' cried the proud Hortense. 'He cares for that woman because she feeds him. – And has she paid his debts, do you suppose? – Good Heaven! I think of that man's position day and night! He is the father of my child, and he is degrading himself.'

'But look at your mother, my dear,' said Célestine.

Célestine was one of those women who, when you have given them reasons enough to convince a Breton peasant, still go back for the hundredth time to their original argument. The character of her face, somewhat flat, dull, and common, her light-brown hair in stiff, neat bands, her very complexion spoke of a sensible woman, devoid of charm, but also devoid of weakness.

'The Baroness would willingly go to join her husband in his disgrace, to comfort him and hide him in her heart from every eye,' Célestine went on. 'Why, she has a room made ready upstairs for Monsieur Hulot, as if she expected to find him and bring him home from one day to the next.'

'Oh yes, my mother is sublime!' replied Hortense. 'She has been so every minute of every day for six-and-twenty years; but I am not like her, it is not my nature. – How can I help it? I am angry with myself sometimes; but you do not know, Célestine, what it would be to make terms with infamy.'

'There is my father!' said Célestine placidly. 'He has certainly started on the road that ruined yours. He is ten years younger than the Baron, to be sure, and was only a tradesman; but how can it end? This Madame Marneffe has made a slave of my father; he is her dog; she is mistress of his fortune and his opinions, and nothing can open his eyes. I tremble when I remember that their banns of marriage are already published! – My husband means to make a last attempt; he thinks it a duty to try to avenge society and the family, and bring that woman to account for all her crimes. Alas! my dear Hortense, such lofty souls as Victorin and hearts like ours come too late to a comprehension of the world and its ways! – This is a secret, dear, and I have told you because you are interested in it, but never by a word or a look betray it to Lisbeth, or your mother, or anybody, for—'

'Here is Lisbeth!' said Hortense. 'Well, cousin, and how is the Inferno of the Rue Barbet going on?'

'Badly for you, my children. – Your husband, my dear Hortense, is more crazy about that woman than ever, and she, I must own, is madly in love with him. – Your father, dear Célestine, is gloriously blind. That, to be sure, is nothing; I have had occasion to see it once a fortnight; really, I am lucky never to have had anything to do with men, they are besotted creatures. – Five days hence you, dear child, and Victorin will have lost your father's fortune.'

'Then the banns are cried?' said Célestine.

'Yes,' said Lisbeth, 'and I have just been arguing your case. I pointed out to that monster, who is going the way of the other, that if he would only get you out of the difficulties you are in by paying off the mortgage on the house, you would show your gratitude and receive your stepmother—'

Hortense started in horror.

'Victorin will see about that,' said Célestine coldly.

'But do you know what Monsieur le Maire's answer was?' said Lisbeth. '"I mean to leave them where they are. Horses can only be broken in by lack of food, sleep, and sugar." – Why, Baron Hulot was not so bad as Monsieur Crevel.

'So, my poor dears, you may say good-bye to the money. And such a fine fortune! Your father paid three million francs for the Presles estate, and he has thirty thousand francs a year in stocks! Oh! – he has no secrets from me. He talks of buying the Hôtel de Navarreins, in the Rue du Bac. Madame Marneffe herself has forty thousand francs a year. – Ah! here is our guardian angel, here comes your mother!' she exclaimed, hearing the rumble of wheels.

And presently the Baroness came down the garden steps and joined the party. At fifty-five, though crushed by so many troubles, and constantly trembling as if shivering with ague, Adeline, whose face was indeed pale and wrinkled, still had a fine figure, a noble outline, and natural dignity. Those who saw her said, 'She must have been beautiful!' Worn with the grief of not knowing her husband's fate, of being unable to share with him this oasis in the heart of Paris, this peace and seclusion and the better fortune that was dawning on the family, her beauty was the beauty of a ruin. As each gleam of hope died out, each day of search proved vain, Adeline sank into fits of deep melancholy that drove her children to despair.

The Baroness had gone out that morning with fresh hopes, and was anxiously expected. An official, who was under obligations to Hulot, to whom he owed his position and advancement, declared that he had seen the Baron in a box at the Ambigu-Comique theatre with a woman of extraordinary beauty. So Adeline had gone to call on the Baron Verneuil. This important personage, while asserting that he had positively seen his old patron, and that his behaviour to the woman indicated an illicit establishment, told Madame Hulot that to avoid meeting him the Baron had left long before the end of the play.

'He looked like a man at home with the damsel, but his dress betrayed some lack of means,' said he in conclusion.

'Well?' said the three women as the Baroness came towards them.

'Well, Monsieur Hulot is in Paris; and to me,' said Adeline, 'it is a gleam of happiness only to know that he is within reach of us.'

'But he does not seem to have mended his ways,' Lisbeth remarked when Adeline had finished her report of her visit to Baron Verneuil. 'He has taken up some little work-girl. But where can he get the money from? I could bet that he begs of his former mistresses – Mademoiselle Jenny Cadine or Josépha.'

The Baroness trembled more severely than ever; every nerve quivered; she wiped away the tears that rose to her eyes and looked mournfully up to heaven.

'I cannot think that a Grand Commander of the Legion of Honour will have fallen so low,' said she.

'For his pleasure what would he not do?' said Lisbeth. 'He robbed the State, he will rob private persons, commit murder – who knows?'

'Oh, Lisbeth!' cried the Baroness, 'keep such thoughts to yourself.'

At this moment Louise came up to the family group, now increased by the arrival of the two Hulot children and little Wenceslas to see if their grandmother's pockets did not contain some sweetmeats.

'What is it, Louise?' asked one and another.

'A man who wants to see Mademoiselle Fischer.'

'Who is the man?' asked Lisbeth.

'He is in rags, Mademoiselle, and covered with flue like a mattress-picker; his nose is red, and he smells of brandy.—He is one of those men who work half the week at most.'

This uninviting picture had the effect of making Lisbeth hurry into the courtyard of the house in the Rue Louis-le-Grand, where she found a man smoking a pipe coloured in a style that showed him an artist in tobacco.

'Why have you come here, Père Chardin?' she asked. 'It is understood that you go, on the first Saturday in every month, to the gate of the Hôtel Marneffe, Rue Barbet-de-Jouy. I have just come back after waiting there for five hours, and you did not come.'

'I did go there, good and charitable lady!' replied the mattress-picker. 'But there was a game at pool going on at the Café des Savants, Rue du Cerf-Volant, and every man has his fancy. Now, mine is billiards. If it wasn't for billiards, I might be eating off silver plate. For, I tell you this,' and he fumbled for a scrap of paper in his ragged trousers pocket, 'it is billiards that leads on to a dram and plum-brandy. – It is ruinous, like all fine things, in the things it leads to. I know your orders, but the old 'un is in such a quandary that I came on to forbidden ground. – If the hair was all hair, we might sleep sound on it; but it is mixed. God is not for all, as the saying goes. He has His favourites – well, He has the right. Now, here is the writing of your estimable relative and my very good friend – his political opinion.'

Chardin attempted to trace some zigzag lines in the air with the forefinger of his right hand.

Lisbeth, not listening to him, read these few words: –

'DEAR COUSIN, – Be my Providence; give me three hundred francs this day.

'HECTOR.'

'What does he want so much money for?'

'The lan'lord!' said Chardin, still trying to sketch arabesques. 'And then my son, you see, has come back from Algiers through Spain and Bayonne, and, and – he has *found* nothing – against his rule, for a sharp cove is my son, saving your presence. How can he help it, he is in want of food; but he will repay all we lend him, for he is going to get up a company. He has ideas, he has, that will carry him—'

'To the police court,' Lisbeth put in. 'He murdered my uncle; I shall not forget that.'

'He – why, he could not bleed a chicken, honourable lady.'

'Here are the three hundred francs,' said Lisbeth, taking fifteen gold pieces out of her purse. 'Now, go, and never come here again.'

She saw the father of the Oran storekeeper off the premises, and pointed out the drunken old creature to the porter.

'At any time when that man comes here, if by chance he should come again, do not let him in. If he should ask whether Monsieur Hulot junior or Madame la Baronne Hulot lives here, tell him you know of no such persons.'

'Very good, Mademoiselle.'

'Your place depends on it if you make any mistake, even without intending it,' said Lisbeth in the woman's ear. – 'Cousin,' she went on to Victorin, who just now came in, 'a great misfortune is hanging over your head.'

'What is that?' said Victorin.

'Within a few days Madame Marneffe will be your wife's stepmother.'

'That remains to be seen,' replied Victorin.

For six months past Lisbeth had very regularly paid a little allowance to Baron Hulot, her former protector, whom she now protected; she knew the secret of his dwelling-place, and relished Adeline's tears, saying to her, as we have seen, when she saw her cheerful and hopeful, 'You may expect to find my poor cousin's name in the papers some day under the heading "Police Report."'

But in this, as on a former occasion, she let her vengeance carry her too far. She had aroused the prudent suspicions of Victorin. He had resolved to be rid of this Damocles' sword so constantly flourished over them by Lisbeth, and of the female demon to whom his mother and the family owed so many woes. The Prince de Wissembourg, knowing all about Madame Marneffe's conduct, approved of the young lawyer's secret project; he had promised him, as a President of the Council can promise, the secret assistance of the police, to enlighten Crevel and rescue a fine fortune from the clutches of the diabolical courtesan, whom he could not forgive either for causing the death of Marshal Hulot or for the Baron's utter ruin.

The words spoken by Lisbeth, 'He begs of his former mistresses,' haunted the Baroness all night. Like sick men given over by the physicians, who have recourse to quacks, like men who have fallen into the lowest Dantesque circle of despair, or drowning creatures who mistake a floating stick for a hawser, she ended by believing in the baseness of which the mere idea had horrified her; and it occurred to her that she might apply for help to one of those terrible women.

Next morning, without consulting her children or saying a word to anybody, she went to see Mademoiselle Josépha Mirah, prima donna of the Royal Academy of Music, to find or to lose the hope that had gleamed before her like a will o' the wisp. At midday, the great singer's waiting-maid brought her in the card of the Baronne Hulot, saying that this person was waiting at the door, having asked whether Mademoiselle could receive her.

'Are the rooms done?'

'Yes, Mademoiselle.'

'And the flowers fresh?'

'Yes, Mademoiselle.'

'Just tell Jean to look round and see that everything is as it should be before showing the lady in, and treat her with the greatest respect. Go, and come back to dress me – I must look my very best.'

She went to study herself in the long glass.

'Now, to put our best foot foremost!' said she to herself. 'Vice under arms to meet virtue! – Poor woman, what can she want of me? I cannot bear to see

'" The noble victim of outrageous fortune!"'

And she sang through the famous aria as the maid came in again.

'Madame,' said the girl, 'the lady has a nervous trembling—'

'Offer her some orange-flower water, some rum, some broth—'

'I did, Mademoiselle; but she declines everything, and says it is an infirmity, a nervous complaint—'

'Where is she?'

'In the big drawing-room.'

'Well, make haste, child. Give me my smartest slippers, the dressing-gown embroidered by Bijou, and no end of lace frills. Do my hair in a way to astonish a woman. – This woman plays a part against mine; and tell the lady – for she is a real, great lady, my girl; nay, more, she is what you will never be, a woman whose prayers can rescue souls from your purgatory – tell her I was in bed, as I was playing last night, and that I am just getting up.'

The Baroness, shown into Josépha's handsome drawing-room, did not note how long she was kept waiting there, though it was a long half hour. This room, entirely redecorated even since Josépha had had the house, was hung with silk in purple and gold colour. The luxury which fine gentlemen were wont to lavish on their *petites maisons*, the scenes of their profligacy, of which the remains still bear witness to the follies from which they were so aptly named, was displayed to perfection, thanks to modern inventiveness, in the four rooms opening into each other, where the warm temperature was maintained by a system of hot-air pipes with invisible openings.

The Baroness, quite bewildered, examined each work of art with the greatest amazement. Here she found the fortunes accounted for that melt in the crucible under which pleasure and vanity feed the devouring flames. This woman, who for twenty-six years had lived among the dead relics of imperial magnificence, whose eyes were accustomed to carpets patterned with faded flowers, rubbed gilding, silks as forlorn as her heart, half understood the powerful fascinations of vice as she studied its results. It was impossible not to wish to possess these beautiful things, these admirable works of art, the creation of the unknown talent which abounds in Paris in our day and produces treasures for all Europe. Each thing had the novel charm of unique perfection. The models being destroyed, every vase, every figure, every piece of sculpture was the original. This is the crowning grace of modern luxury. To own the thing which is not vulgarised by the two thousand wealthy citizens whose notion of luxury is the lavish display of the splendours that shops can supply, is the stamp of true luxury – the luxury of the fine gentlemen of the day, the shooting stars of the Paris firmament.

As she examined the flower-stands, filled with the choicest exotic plants, mounted in chased brass and inlaid in the style of Boulle, the Baroness was scared by the idea of the wealth in this apartment. And this impression naturally shed a glamour over the person round whom all this profusion was heaped. Adeline imagined that Josépha Mirah – whose portrait by Joseph Bridau was the glory of the adjoining boudoir – must be a singer of genius, a Malibran, and she expected to see a real star. She was sorry she had come. But she had been prompted by so strong and so natural a feeling, by such purely disinterested devotion, that she collected all her courage for the interview. Besides, she was about to satisfy her urgent curiosity, to see for herself what was the charm of this kind of women, that they could extract so much gold from the miserly ore of Paris mud.

The Baroness looked at herself to see if she were not a blot on all this splendour; but she was well dressed in her velvet gown, with a little cape trimmed with beautiful lace, and her velvet bonnet of the same shade was becoming. Seeing herself still as imposing as any queen, always a queen even in her fall, she reflected that the dignity of sorrow was a match for the dignity of talent.

At last, after much opening and shutting of doors, she saw Josépha. The singer bore a strong resemblance to Allori's *Judith*, which dwells in the memory of all who have ever seen it in the Pitti palace, near the door of one of the great rooms. She had the same haughty mien, the same fine features, black hair simply knotted, and a yellow wrapper with little embroidered flowers, exactly like the brocade worn by the immortal homicide conceived of by Bronzino's nephew.

'Madame la Baronne, I am quite overwhelmed by the honour you do me in coming here,' said the singer, resolved to play her part as a great lady with a grace.

She pushed forward an easy-chair for the Baroness and seated herself on a stool. She discerned the faded beauty of the woman before her, and was filled with pity as she saw her shaken by the nervous palsy that, on the least excitement, became convulsive. She could read at a glance the saintly life described to her of old by Hulot and Crevel; and she not only ceased to think of a contest with her, she humiliated herself before a superiority she appreciated. The great artist could admire what the courtesan laughed to scorn.

'Mademoiselle, despair brought me here. It reduces us to any means—'

A look in Josépha's face made the Baroness feel that she had wounded the woman from whom she hoped for so much, and she looked at her. Her beseeching eyes extinguished the flash in Josépha's; the singer smiled. It was a wordless dialogue of pathetic eloquence.

'It is now two years and a half since Monsieur Hulot left his family, and I do not know where to find him, though I know that he lives in Paris,' said the Baroness with emotion. 'A dream suggested to me the idea – an absurd one perhaps – that you may have interested yourself in Monsieur Hulot. If you could enable me to see him – oh! Mademoiselle, I would pray Heaven for you every day as long as I live in this world—'

Two large tears in the singer's eyes told what her reply would be.

'Madame,' said she, 'I have done you an injury without knowing you; but, now that I have the happiness of seeing in you the most perfect image of virtue on earth, believe me I am sensible of the extent of my fault; I repent sincerely, and believe me, I will do all in my power to remedy it!'

She took Madame Hulot's hand, and before the lady could do anything to hinder her, she kissed it respectfully, even humbling herself to bend one knee. Then she rose, as proud as when she stood on the stage in the part of *Mathilde*, and rang the bell.

'Go on horseback,' said she to the man-servant, 'and kill the horse if you must, to find little Bijou, Rue Saint-Maur-du-Temple, and bring her here. Put her into a coach and pay the coachman to come at a gallop. Do not lose a moment – or you lose your place.

'Madame,' she went on, coming back to the Baroness, and speaking to her in respectful tones, 'you must forgive me. As soon as the Duc d'Hérouville became my protector, I dismissed the Baron, having heard that he was ruining his family for me. What more could I do? In an actress's career a protector is indispensable from the first day of her appearance on the boards. Our salaries do not pay half our expenses; we must have a temporary husband. I did not value Monsieur Hulot, who took me away from a rich man, a conceited idiot. Old Crevel would undoubtedly have married me—'

'So he told me,' said the Baroness, interrupting her.

'Well, then, you see, Madame, I might at this day have been an honest woman, with only one legitimate husband!'

'You have many excuses, Mademoiselle,' said Adeline, 'and God will take them into account. But, for my part, far from reproaching you, I came, on the contrary, to make myself your debtor in gratitude—'

'Madame, for nearly three years I have provided for Monsieur le Baron's necessities—'

'You?' interrupted the Baroness, with tears in her eyes. 'Oh, what can I do for you? I can only pray—'

'I and Monsieur le Duc d'Hérouville,' the singer said, 'a noble soul, a true gentleman—' and Josépha related the settling and *marriage* of Monsieur Thoul.

'And so, thanks to you, Mademoiselle, the Baron has wanted nothing?'

'We have done our best to that end, Madame.'

'And where is he now?'

'About six months ago, Monsieur le Duc told me that the Baron, known to the notary by the name of Thoul, had drawn all the eight thousand francs that were to have been paid to him in fixed sums once a quarter,' replied Josépha. 'We have heard no more of the Baron, neither I nor Monsieur d'Hérouville. Our lives are so full, we artists are so busy, that I really have not time to run after old Thoul. As it happens, for the last six months, Bijou, who works for me – his – what shall I say—?'

'His mistress,' said Madame Hulot.

'His mistress,' repeated Josépha, 'has not been here. Mademoiselle Olympe Bijou is perhaps divorced. Divorce is common in the thirteenth arrondissement.'

Josépha rose, and foraging among the rare plants in her stands, made a charming bouquet for Madame Hulot, whose expectations, it may be said, were by no means fulfilled. Like those worthy folks who take men of genius to be a sort of monsters, eating, drinking, walking, and speaking unlike other people, the Baroness had hoped to see Josépha the opera singer, the witch, the amorous and amusing courtesan; she saw a calm and well-mannered woman, with the dignity of talent, the simplicity of an actress who knows herself to be at night a queen, and also, better than all, a woman of the town whose eyes, attitude, and demeanour paid full and ungrudging homage to the virtuous wife, the *Mater dolorosa* of the sacred hymn, and who was crowning her sorrows with flowers, as the Madonna is crowned in Italy.

'Madame,' said the man-servant, reappearing at the end of half an hour, 'Madame Bijou is on her way, but you are not to expect little Olympe. Your needlewoman, Madame, is settled in life; she is married—'

'More or less?' said Josépha.

'No, Madame, really married. She is at the head of a very fine business; she has married the owner of a large and fashionable shop, on which they have spent millions of francs, on the Boulevard des Italiens; and she has left the embroidery business to her sister and mother. She is Madame Grenouville. The fat tradesman—'

'A Crevel?'

'Yes, Madame,' said the man. 'Well, he has settled thirty thousand francs a year on Mademoiselle Bijou by the marriage articles. And her elder sister, they say, is going to be married to a rich butcher.'

'Your business looks rather hopeless, I am afraid,' said Josépha to the Baroness. 'Monsieur le Baron is no longer where I lodged him.'

Ten minutes later Madame Bijou was announced. Josépha very prudently placed the Baroness in the boudoir, and drew the curtain over the door.

'You would scare her,' said she to Madame Hulot. 'She would let nothing out if she suspected that you were interested in the information. Leave me to catechise her. Hide there, and you will hear everything. It is a scene that is played quite as often in real life as on the stage—

'Well, Mother Bijou,' she said to an old woman dressed in tartan stuff, and who looked like a porter's wife in her Sunday best, 'so you are all very happy? Your daughter is in luck.'

'Oh, happy? As for that! – My daughter gives us a hundred francs a month, while she rides in a carriage and eats off silver plate – she is a millionary, is my daughter! Olympe might have lifted me above labour. To have to work at my age? Is that being good to me?'

'She ought not to be ungrateful, for she owes her beauty to you,' replied Josépha; 'but why did she not come to see me? It was I who placed her in ease by settling her with my uncle.'

'Yes, Madame, with old Monsieur Thoul, but he is very old and broken—'

'But what have you done with him? Is he with you? She was very foolish to leave him; he is worth millions now.'

'Heaven above us!' cried the mother. 'What did I tell her when she behaved so badly to him, and he as mild as milk, poor old fellow? Oh! didn't she just give it him hot? – Olympe was perverted, Madame!'

'But how?'

'She got to know a *claqueur*, Madame, saving your presence, a man paid to clap, you know, the grandnephew of an old mattress-picker of the Faubourg Saint-Marceau. This good-for-nought, as all your good-looking fellows are, paid to make a piece go, is the cock of the walk out on the Boulevard du Temple, where he works up the new plays, and takes care that the actresses get a reception, as he calls it. First, he has a good breakfast in the morning; then, before the play, he dines, to be "up to the mark," as he says; in short, he is a born lover of billiards and drams. "But that is not following a trade," as I said to Olympe.'

'It is a trade men follow, unfortunately,' said Josépha.

'Well, the rascal turned Olympe's head, and he, Madame, did not keep good company – when I tell you he was very near being nabbed by the police in a tavern where thieves meet. 'Wever, Monsieur Braulard, the leader of the claque, got him out of that. He wears gold earrings, and he lives by doing nothing, hanging on to women, who are fools about these good-looking scamps. He spent all the money Monsieur Thoul used to give the child.

'Then the business was going to grief; what embroidery brought in went out across the billiard table. 'Wever, the young fellow had a pretty sister, Madame, who, like her brother, lived by hook and by crook, and no better than she should be neither, over in the students' quarter.'

'One of the sluts at the Chaumière,' said Josépha.

'So, Madame,' said the old woman. 'So Idamore – his name is Idamore, leastways that is what he calls himself, for his real name is Chardin – Idamore fancied that your uncle had a deal more money than he owned to, and he managed to send his sister Élodie – and that was a stage name he gave her – to send her to be a workwoman at our place, without my daughter's knowing who she was; and, gracious goodness! but that girl turned the whole place topsy-turvy; she got all those poor girls into mischief – impossible to whitewash them, saving your presence—

'And she was so sharp, she won over poor old Thoul, and took him away, and we don't know where, and left us in a pretty fix, with a lot of bills coming in. To this day as ever is we have not been able to settle up; but my daughter, who knows all about such things, keeps an eye on them as they fall due. – Then, when Idamore saw he had got hold of the old man, through his sister, you understand, he threw over my daughter, and now he has got hold of a little actress at the *Funambules*. – And that was how my daughter came to get married, as you will see—'

'But you know where the mattress-picker lives?' said Josépha.

'What! old Chardin? As if he lived anywhere at all! – He is drunk by six in the morning; he makes a mattress once a month; he hangs about the wineshops all day; he plays at pools—'

'He plays at pools?' said Josépha.

'You do not understand, Madame; pools of billiards, I mean, and he wins three or four a day, and then he drinks.'

'Water out of the pools, I suppose?' said Josépha. 'But if Idamore haunts the Boulevard, by inquiring through my friend Braulard, we could find him.'

'I don't know, Madame; all this was six months ago. Idamore was one of the sort who are bound to find their way into the police court, and from that to Melun – and then – who knows—?'

'To the prison yard!' said Josépha.

'Well, Madame, you know everything,' said the old woman, smiling. 'Well, if my girl had never known that scamp, she would now be— Still, she was in luck, all the same, you will say, for Monsieur Grenouville fell so much in love with her that he married her—'

'And what brought that about?'

'Olympe was desperate, Madame. When she found herself left in the lurch for that little actress – and she took a rod out of pickle for her, I can tell you; my word, but she gave her a dressing! – and when she had lost poor old Thoul, who worshipped her, she would have nothing more to say to the men. 'Wever, Monsieur Grenouville, who had been dealing largely with us – to the tune of two hundred embroidered China-crape shawls every quarter – he wanted to console her; but whether or no, she would not listen to anything without the mayor and the priest. "I mean to be respectable," says she, "or perish!" and she stuck to it. Monsieur Grenouville consented to marry her, on condition of her giving us all up, and we agreed—'

'For a handsome consideration?' said Josépha, with her usual perspicacity.

'Yes, Madame, ten thousand francs, and an allowance to my father, who is past work.'

'I begged your daughter to make old Thoul happy, and she has thrown me over. That is not fair. I will take no interest in any one for the future! That is what comes of trying to do good! Benevolence certainly does not answer as a speculation! – Olympe ought, at least, to have given me notice of this jobbing. Now, if you find the old man Thoul within a fortnight, I will give you a thousand francs.'

'It will be a hard task, my good lady; still, there are a good many five-franc pieces in a thousand francs, and I will try to earn your money.'

'Good morning, then, Madame Bijou.'

On going into the boudoir, the singer found that Madame Hulot had fainted; but in spite of having lost consciousness, her nervous trembling kept her still perpetually shaking, as the pieces of a snake that has been cut up still wriggle and move. Strong salts, cold water, and all the ordinary remedies were applied to recall the Baroness to her senses, or rather, to the apprehension of her sorrows.

'Ah! Mademoiselle, how far has he fallen!' cried she, recognising Josépha, and finding that she was alone with her.

'Take heart, Madame,' replied the actress, who had seated herself on a cushion at Adeline's feet, and was kissing her hands. 'We shall find him; and if he is in the mire, well, he must wash himself. Believe me, with people of good breeding it is all a matter of clothes. – Allow me to make up for the harm I have done you, for I see how much you are attached to your husband, in spite of his misconduct – or you would not have come here. – Well, you see, the poor man is so fond of the women. If you had had a little of our dash, you would have kept him from running about the world; for you would have been what we can never be – all the women man wants.

'The State ought to subsidise a school of manners for honest women! But governments are so prudish! Still, they are guided by the men, whom we privately guide. My word, I pity nations!

'But the matter in question is how you can be helped, and not to laugh at the world. – Well, Madame, be easy, go home again, and do not worry. I will bring your Hector back to you as he was as a man of thirty.'

'Ah, Mademoiselle, let us go to see that Madame Grenouville,' said the Baroness. 'She surely knows something! Perhaps I may see the Baron this very day, and be able to snatch him at once from poverty and disgrace.'

'Madame, I will show you the deep gratitude I feel towards you by not displaying the stage-singer Josépha, the Duc d'Hérouville's mistress, in the company of the noblest, saintliest image of virtue. I respect you too much to be seen by your side. This is not acted humility; it is sincere homage. You make me sorry, Madame, that I cannot tread in your footsteps, in spite of the thorns that tear your feet and hands. – But it cannot be helped! I am one with art, as you are one with virtue.'

'Poor child!' said the Baroness, moved amid her own sorrows by a strange sense of compassionate sympathy; 'I will pray to God for you; for you are the victim of society, which must have theatres. When you are old, repent – you will be heard if God vouchsafes to hear the prayers of a—'

'Of a martyr, Madame,' Josépha put in, and she respectfully kissed the Baroness's skirt.

But Adeline took the actress's hand, and drawing her towards her, kissed her on the forehead. Colouring with pleasure, Josépha saw the Baroness into the hackney coach with the humblest politeness.

'It must be some visiting Lady of Charity,' said the manservant to the maid, 'for she does not do so much for any one, not even for her dear friend Madame Jenny Cadine.'

'Wait a few days,' said she, 'and you will see him, Madame, or I renounce the God of my fathers – and that from a Jewess, you know, is a promise of success.'

At the very time when Madame Hulot was calling on Josépha, Victorin, in his study, was receiving an old woman of about seventy-five, who, to gain admission to the lawyer, had used the terrible name of the head of the detective force. The man in waiting announced –

'Madame de Saint-Estève.'

'I have assumed one of my business names,' said she, taking a seat.

Victorin felt a sort of internal chill at the sight of this dreadful old woman. Though handsomely dressed, she was terrible to look upon, for her flat, colourless, strongly-marked face, furrowed with wrinkles, expressed a sort of cold malignity. Marat, as a woman of that age, might have been like this creature, a living embodiment of the Reign of Terror.

This sinister old woman's small, pale eyes twinkled with a tiger's bloodthirsty greed. Her broad, flat nose, with nostrils expanded into oval cavities, breathed the fires of hell, and resembled the beak of some evil bird of prey. The spirit of intrigue lurked behind her low, cruel brow. Long hairs had grown from her wrinkled chin, betraying the masculine character of her schemes. Any one seeing that woman's face would have said that artists had failed in their conceptions of Mephistopheles.

'My dear sir,' she began, with a patronising air, 'I have long since given up active business of any kind. What I have come to you to do, I have undertaken, for the sake of my dear nephew, whom I love more than I could love a son of my own. – Now, the Head of the Police – to whom the President of the Council said two words in his ear as regards yourself, in talking to Monsieur Chapuzot – thinks as the police ought not to appear in a matter of this description, you understand. They gave my nephew a free hand, but my nephew will have nothing to say to it, except as before the Council; he will not be seen in it.'

'Then your nephew is—'

'You have hit it, and I am rather proud of him,' said she, interrupting the lawyer, 'for he is my pupil, and he soon could teach his teacher. – We have considered this case, and have come to our own conclusions. Will you hand over thirty thousand francs to have the whole thing taken off your hands? I will make a clean sweep of it all, and you need not pay till the job is done.'

'Do you know the persons concerned?'

'No, my dear sir; I look for information from you. What we are told is, that a certain old idiot has fallen into the clutches of a widow. This widow, of nine-and-twenty, has played her cards so well, that she has forty thousand francs a year, of which she has robbed two fathers of families. She is now about to swallow down eighty thousand francs a year by marrying an old boy of sixty-one. She will thus ruin a respectable family, and hand over this vast fortune to the child of some lover by getting rid at once of the old husband. – That is the case as stated.'

'Quite correct,' said Victorin. 'My father-in-law, Monsieur Crevel—'

'Formerly a perfumer; a mayor – yes, I live in his district under the name of Ma'ame Nourrisson,' said the woman.

'The other person is Madame Marneffe.'

'I do not know her,' said Madame de Saint-Estève. 'But within three days I will be in a position to count her shifts.'

'Can you hinder the marriage?' asked Victorin.

'How far have they got?'

'To the second time of asking.'

'We must carry off the woman. – To-day is Sunday – there are but three days, for they will be married on Wednesday, no doubt; it is impossible. – But she may be killed—'

Victorin Hulot started with an honest man's horror at hearing these five words uttered in cold blood.

'Murder?' said he. 'And how could you do it?'

'For forty years, now, Monsieur, we have played the part of fate,' replied she, with terrible pride, 'and do just what we will in Paris. More than one family – even in the Faubourg Saint-Germain – has told me all its secrets, I can tell you! I have made and spoiled many a match, I have destroyed many a will, and saved many a man's honour. I have in there,' and she tapped her forehead, 'a store of secrets which are worth thirty-six thousand francs a year to me; and you – you will be one of my lambs, hoh! Could such a woman as I am be what I am if she revealed her ways and means? I act.

'Whatever I may do, sir, will be the result of an accident; you need feel no remorse. You will be like a man cured by a clairvoyant; by the end of a month, it seems all the work of Nature.'

Victorin broke out in a cold sweat. The sight of an executioner would have shocked him less than this prolix and pretentious Sister of the Hulks. As he looked at her purple-red gown, she seemed to him dyed in blood.

'Madame, I do not accept the help of your experience and skill if success is to cost anybody's life, or the least criminal act is to come of it.'

'You are a great baby, Monsieur,' replied the woman; 'you wish to remain blameless in your own eyes, while you want your enemy to be overthrown.'

Victorin shook his head in denial.

'Yes,' she went on, 'you want this Madame Marneffe to drop the prey she has between her teeth. But how do you expect to make a tiger drop his piece of beef? Can you do it by patting his back and saying, "Poor Puss"? You are illogical. You want a battle fought, but you object to blows. – Well, I grant you the innocence you are so careful over. I have always found that there was material for hypocrisy in honesty! One day, three months hence, a poor priest will come to beg of you forty thousand francs for a pious work – a convent to be rebuilt in the Levant – in the desert. – If you are satisfied with your lot, give the good man the money. You will pay more than that into the treasury. It will be a mere trifle in comparison with what you will get, I can tell you.'

She rose, standing on the broad feet that seemed to overflow her satin shoes; she smiled, bowed, and vanished.

'The Devil has a sister,' said Victorin, rising.

He saw the hideous stranger to the door, a creature called up from the dens of the police, as on the stage a monster comes up from the third cellar at the touch of a fairy's wand in a ballet-extravaganza.

After finishing what he had to do at the Courts, Victorin went to call on Monsieur Chapuzot, the head of one of the most important branches of the Central Police, to make some inquiries about the stranger. Finding Monsieur Chapuzot alone in his office, Victorin thanked him for his help.

'You sent me an old woman who might stand for the incarnation of the criminal side of Paris.'

Monsieur Chapuzot laid his spectacles on his papers and looked at the lawyer with astonishment.

'I should not have taken the liberty of sending any body to see you without giving you notice beforehand, or a line of introduction,' said he.

'Then it was Monsieur le Préfet——?'

'I think not,' said Chapuzot. 'The last time that the Prince de Wissembourg dined with the Minister of the Interior, he spoke to the Préfet of the position in which you find yourself – a deplorable position – and asked him if you could be helped in any friendly way. The Préfet, who was interested by the regrets his Excellency expressed as to this family affair, did me the honour to consult me about it.

'Ever since the present Préfet has held the reins of this department – so useful and so vilified – he has made it a rule that family matters are never to be interfered in. He is right in principle and in morality; but in practice he is wrong. In the forty-five years that I have served in the police, it did, from 1799 till 1815, great service in family concerns. Since 1820 a constitutional government and the press have completely altered the conditions of existence. So my advice, indeed, was not to intervene in such a case, and the Préfet did me the honour to agree with my remarks. The Head of the detective branch had orders, in my presence, to take no steps; so if you have had any one sent to you by him, he will be reprimanded. It might cost him his place. "The Police will do this or that," is easily said; the Police, the Police! But, my dear sir, the Marshal and the Ministerial Council do not know what the Police is. The Police alone knows the Police. The Kings, Napoleon and Louis XVIII., knew their Police; but as for ours, only Fouché, Monsieur Lenoir, and Monsieur de Sartines have had any notion of it. – Everything is changed now; we are reduced and disarmed! I have seen many private disasters develop, which I could have checked with five grains of despotic power. – We shall be regretted by the very men who have crippled us when they, like you, stand face to face with some moral monstrosities, which ought to be swept away as we sweep away mud! In public affairs the Police is expected to foresee everything, or when the safety of the public is involved – but the family? – It is sacred! I would do my utmost to discover and hinder a plot against the King's life, I would see through the walls of a house; but as to laying a finger on a household, or peeping into private interests – never, so long as I sit in this office. I should be afraid.'

'Of what?'

'Of the Press, Monsieur le Député, of the left centre.'

'What, then, can I do?' said Hulot, after a pause.

'Well, you are the Family,' said the official. 'That settles it; you can do what you please. But as to helping you, as to using the Police as an instrument of private feelings and interests, how is it possible? There lies, you see, the secret of the persecution, necessary, but pronounced illegal by the Bench, which was brought to bear against the predecessor of our present chief detective. Bibi-Lupin undertook investigations for the benefit of private persons. This might have led to great social dangers. With the means at his command, the man would have been formidable, an underlying fate—'

'But in my place?' said Hulot.

'What, you ask my advice? You who sell it!' replied Monsieur Chapuzot. 'Come, come, my dear sir, you are making fun of me.'

Hulot bowed to the functionary, and went away without seeing that gentleman's almost imperceptible shrug as he rose to open the door.

'And he wants to be a statesman!' said Chapuzot to himself as he returned to his reports.

Victorin went home, still full of perplexities which he could confide to no one.

At dinner the Baroness joyfully announced to her children that within a month their father might be sharing their comforts, and end his days in peace among his family.

'Oh, I would gladly give my three thousand six hundred francs a year to see the Baron here!' cried Lisbeth. 'But, my dear Adeline, do not dream beforehand of such happiness, I entreat you!'

'Lisbeth is right,' said Célestine. 'My dear mother, wait till the end.'

The Baroness, all feeling and all hope, related her visit to Josépha, expressed her sense of the misery of such women in the midst of good fortune, and mentioned Chardin the mattress-picker, the father of the Oran storekeeper, thus showing that her hopes were not groundless.

By seven next morning Lisbeth had driven in a hackney coach to the Quai de la Tournelle, and stopped the vehicle at the corner of the Rue de Poissy.

'Go to the Rue des Bernardins,' said she to the driver, 'No. 7, a house with an entry and no porter. Go up to the fourth floor, ring at the door to the left, on which you will see "Mademoiselle Chardin – Lace and shawls mended." She will answer the door. Ask for the Chevalier. She will say he is out. Say in reply, "Yes, I know, but find him, for his *bonne* is out on the quay in a coach, and wants to see him."'

Twenty minutes later, an old man, who looked about eighty, with perfectly white hair, and a nose reddened by the cold, and a pale, wrinkled face like an old woman's, came shuffling slowly along in list slippers, a shiny alpaca overcoat hanging on his stooping shoulders, no ribbon at his buttonhole, the sleeves of an under-vest showing below his coat-cuffs, and his shirt-front unpleasantly dingy. He approached timidly, looked at the coach, recognised Lisbeth, and came to the window.

'Why, my dear cousin, what a state you are in!'

'Élodie keeps everything for herself,' said Baron Hulot. 'Those Chardins are a blackguard crew.'

'Will you come home to us?'

'Oh, no, no!' cried the old man. 'I would rather go to America.'

'Adeline is on the scent.'

'Oh, if only some one would pay my debts!' said the Baron, with a suspicious look, 'for Samanon is after me.'

'We have not paid up the arrears yet; your son still owes a hundred thousand francs.'

'Poor boy!'

'And your pension will not be free before seven or eight months. – If you will wait a minute, I have two thousand francs here.'

The Baron held out his hand with fearful avidity.

'Give it me, Lisbeth, and may God reward you! Give it me; I know where to go.'

'But you will tell me, old wretch?'

'Yes, yes. Then I can wait eight months, for I have discovered a little angel, a good child, an innocent thing not old enough to be depraved.'

'Do not forget the police court,' said Lisbeth, who flattered herself that she would some day see Hulot there.

'No. – It is in the Rue de Charonne,' said the Baron, 'a part of the town where no fuss is made about anything. No one will ever find me there. I am called Père Thorec, Lisbeth, and I shall be taken for a retired cabinetmaker; the girl is fond of me, and I will not allow my back to be shorn any more.'

'No, that has been done,' said Lisbeth, looking at his coat. 'Supposing I take you there.'

Baron Hulot got into the coach, deserting Mademoiselle Élodie without taking leave of her, as he might have tossed aside a novel he had finished.

In half an hour, during which Baron Hulot talked to Lisbeth of nothing but little Atala Judici – for he had fallen by degrees to those base passions that ruin old men – she set him down with two thousand francs in his pocket, in the Rue de Charonne, Faubourg Saint-Antoine, at the door of a doubtful and sinister-looking house.

'Good day, Cousin; so now you are to be called Thorec, I suppose? Send none but commissionaires if you need me, and always take them from different parts.'

'Trust me! Oh, I am really very lucky!' said the Baron, his face beaming with the prospect of new and future happiness.

'No one can find him there,' said Lisbeth; and she paid the coach at the Boulevard Beaumarchais, and returned to the Rue Louis-le-Grand in the omnibus.

On the following day Crevel was announced at the hour when all the family were together in the drawing-room, just after breakfast. Célestine flew to throw her arms round her father's neck, and behaved as if she had seen him only the day before, though in fact he had not called there for more than two years.

'Good morning, father,' said Victorin, offering his hand.

'Good morning, children,' said the pompous Crevel. 'Madame la Baronne, I throw myself at your feet! Good Heavens, how the children grow! they are pushing us off the perch – "Grand-pa'," they say, "we want our turn in the sunshine." – Madame la Comtesse, you are as lovely as ever,' he went on, addressing Hortense. – 'Ah, ha! and here is the best of good money: Cousin Bette, the Wise Virgin.'

'Why, you are really very comfortable here,' said he, after scattering these greetings with a cackle of loud laughter that hardly moved the rubicund muscles of his broad face.

He looked at his daughter with some contempt.

'My dear Célestine, I will make you a present of all my furniture out of the Rue des Saussayes; it will just do here. Your drawing-room wants furbishing up. – Ha! there is that little rogue Wenceslas. Well, and are we very good children, I wonder? You must have pretty manners, you know.'

'To make up for those who have none,' said Lisbeth.

'That sarcasm, my dear Lisbeth, has lost its sting. I am going, my dear children, to put an end to the false position in which I have so long been placed; I have come, like a good father, to announce my approaching marriage without any circumlocution.'

'You have a perfect right to marry,' said Victorin. 'And for my part, I give you back the promise you made me when you gave me the hand of my dear Célestine—'

'What promise?' said Crevel.

'Not to marry,' replied the lawyer. 'You will do me the justice to allow that I did not ask you to pledge yourself, that you gave your word quite voluntarily and in spite of my desire, for I pointed out to you at the time that you were unwise to bind yourself.'

'Yes, I do remember, my dear fellow,' said Crevel, ashamed of himself. 'But, on my honour, if you will but live with Madame Crevel, my children, you will find no reason to repent. – Your good feeling touches me, Victorin, and you will find that generosity to me is not unrewarded. – Come, by the Poker! welcome your stepmother and come to the wedding.'

'But you have not told us the lady's name, papa,' said Célestine.

'Why, it is an open secret,' replied Crevel. 'Do not let us play at guess who can! Lisbeth must have told you.'

'My dear Monsieur Crevel,' replied Lisbeth, 'there are certain names we never utter here—'

'Well, then, it is Madame Marneffe.'

'Monsieur Crevel,' said the lawyer very sternly, 'neither my wife nor I can be present at that marriage; not out of interest, for I spoke in all sincerity just now. Yes, I am most happy to think that you may find happiness in this union; but I act on considerations of honour and good feeling which you must understand, and which I cannot speak of here, as they reopen wounds still ready to bleed—'

The Baroness telegraphed a signal to Hortense, who tucked her little one under her arm, saying, 'Come, Wenceslas, and have your bath! – Good-bye, Monsieur Crevel.'

The Baroness also bowed to Crevel without a word; and Crevel could not help smiling at the child's astonishment when threatened with this impromptu tubbing.

'You, Monsieur,' said Victorin, when he found himself alone with Lisbeth, his wife, and his father-in-law, 'are about to marry a woman loaded with the spoils of my father; it was she who, in cold blood, brought him down to such depths; a woman who is the son-in-law's mistress after ruining the father-in-law; who is the cause of constant grief to my sister! – And you fancy that I shall be seen to sanction your madness by my presence? I deeply pity you, dear Monsieur Crevel; you have no family feeling; you do not understand the unity of the honour which binds the members of it together. There is no arguing with passion – as I have too much reason to know. The slaves of their passions are as deaf as they are blind. Your daughter Célestine has too strong a sense of her duty to proffer a word of reproach.'

'That would, indeed, be a pretty thing!' cried Crevel, trying to cut short this harangue.

'Célestine would not be my wife if she made the slightest remonstrance,' the lawyer went on. 'But I, at least, may try to stop you before you step over the precipice, especially after giving you ample proof of my disinterestedness. It is not your fortune, it is you that I care about. Nay, to make it quite plain to you, I may add, if it were only to set your mind at ease with regard to your marriage-contract, that I am now in a position which leaves me with nothing to wish for—'

'Thanks to me!' exclaimed Crevel, whose face was purple.

'Thanks to Célestine's fortune,' replied Victorin. 'And if you regret having given to your daughter, as a present from yourself, a sum which is not half what her mother left her, I can only say that we are prepared to give it back.'

'And do you not know, my respected son-in-law,' said Crevel, striking an attitude, 'that under the shelter of my name Madame Marneffe is not called upon to answer for her conduct excepting as my wife – as Madame Crevel?'

'That is, no doubt, quite the correct thing,' said the lawyer; 'very generous so far as the affections are concerned and the vagaries of passion; but I know of no name, nor law, nor title that can shelter the theft of three hundred thousand francs so meanly wrung from my father! – I tell you plainly, my dear father-in-law, your future wife is unworthy of you; she is false to you, and is madly in love with my brother-in-law, Stein-bock, whose debts she has paid.'

'It was I who paid them!'

'Very good,' said Hulot; 'I am glad for Count Steinbock's sake; he may some day repay the money. But he is loved, much loved, and often—'

'Loved!' cried Crevel, whose face showed his utter bewilderment. 'It is cowardly, and dirty, and mean, and cheap, to calumniate a woman! – When a man says such things, Monsieur, he must bring proof.'

'I will bring proof.'

'I shall expect it.'

'By the day after to-morrow, my dear Monsieur Crevel, I shall be able to tell you the day, the hour, the very minute when I can expose the horrible depravity of your future wife.'

'Very well; I shall be delighted,' said Crevel, who had recovered himself.

'Good-bye, my children, for the present; good-bye, Lisbeth.'

'See him out, Lisbeth,' said Célestine in an undertone.

'And is this the way you take yourself off?' cried Lisbeth to Crevel.

'Ah, ha!' said Crevel, 'my son-in-law is too clever by half; he is getting on. The Courts and the Chamber, judicial trickery and political dodges, are making a man of him with a vengeance! – So he knows I am to be married on Wednesday, and on a Sunday my gentleman proposes to fix the hour, within three days, when he can prove that my wife is unworthy of me. That is a good story! – Well, I am going back to sign the contract. Come with me, Lisbeth – yes, come. They will never know. I meant to have left Célestine forty thousand francs a year; but Hulot has just behaved in a way to alienate my affection for ever.'

'Give me ten minutes, Père Crevel; wait for me in your carriage at the gate. I will make some excuse for going out.'

'Very well – all right.'

'My dears,' said Lisbeth, who found all the family reassembled in the drawing-room, 'I am going with Crevel: the marriage-contract is to be signed this afternoon, and I shall hear what he has settled. It will probably be my last visit to that woman. Your father is furious; he will disinherit you—'

'His vanity will prevent that,' said the son-in-law. 'He was bent on owning the estate of Presles, and he will keep it; I know him. Even if he were to have children, Célestine would still have half of what he might leave; the law forbids his giving away all his fortune. – Still, these questions are nothing to me; I am thinking only of our honour. – Go then, Cousin,' and he pressed Lisbeth's hand, 'and listen carefully to the contract.'

Twenty minutes after, Lisbeth and Crevel reached the house in the Rue Barbet, where Madame Marneffe was awaiting, in mild impatience, the result of a step taken by her commands. Valérie had in the end fallen a prey to the absorbing love which, once in her life, masters a woman's heart. Wenceslas was its object, and, a failure as an artist, he became in Madame Marneffe's hands a lover so perfect that he was to her what she had been to Baron Hulot.

Valérie was holding a slipper in one hand, and Steinbock clasped the other, while her head rested on his shoulder. The rambling conversation in which they had been engaged ever since Crevel went out may be ticketed, like certain lengthy literary efforts of our day, '*All rights reserved*,' for it cannot be reproduced. This masterpiece of personal poetry naturally brought a regret to the artist's lips, and he said, not without some bitterness –

'What a pity it is that I married; for if I had but waited, as Lisbeth told me, I might now have married you.'

'Who but a Pole would wish to make a wife of a devoted mistress?' cried Valérie. 'To change love into duty, and pleasure into a bore.'

'I know you to be so fickle,' replied Steinbock. 'Did I not hear you talking to Lisbeth of that Brazilian, Baron Montès?'

'Do you want to rid me of him?'

'It would be the only way to hinder his seeing you,' said the ex-sculptor.

'Let me tell you, my darling – for I tell you everything,' said Valérie – 'I was saving him up for a husband. – The promises I have made to that man! – Oh, long before I knew you,' said she, in reply to a movement from Wenceslas. 'And those promises, of which he avails himself to plague me, oblige me to get married almost secretly; for if he should hear that I am marrying Crevel, he is the sort of man that – that would kill me.'

'Oh, as to that!' said Steinbock, with a scornful expression, which conveyed that such a danger was small indeed for a woman beloved by a Pole.

And in the matter of valour there is no brag or bravado in a Pole, so thoroughly and seriously brave are they all.

'And that idiot Crevel,' she went on, 'who wants to make a great display and indulge his taste for inexpensive magnificence in honour of the wedding, places me in difficulties from which I see no escape.'

Could Valérie confess to this man, whom she adored, that, since the discomfiture of Baron Hulot, this Baron Henri Montès had inherited the privilege of calling on her at all hours of the day or night; and that, notwithstanding her cleverness, she was still puzzled to find a cause of quarrel in which the Brazilian might seem to be solely in the wrong? She knew the Baron's almost savage temper – not unlike Lisbeth's – too well not to quake as she thought of this Othello of Rio de Janeiro.

As the carriage drove up, Steinbock released Valérie, for his arm was round her waist, and took up a newspaper, in which he was found absorbed. Valérie was stitching with elaborate care at the slippers she was working for Crevel.

'How they slander her!' whispered Lisbeth to Crevel, pointing to this picture as they opened the door. 'Look at her hair – not in the least tumbled. To hear Victorin, you might have expected to find two turtledoves in a nest.'

'My dear Lisbeth,' replied Crevel, in his favourite position, 'you see that to turn Lucretia into Aspasia, you have only to inspire a passion!'

'And have I not always told you,' said Lisbeth, 'that women like a burly profligate like you?'

'And she would be most ungrateful too,' said Crevel; 'for as to the money I have spent here, Grindot and I alone can tell!'

And he waved a hand at the staircase.

In decorating this house, which Crevel regarded as his own, Grindot had tried to compete with Cleretti, in whose hands the Duc d'Hérouville had placed Josépha's villa. But Crevel, incapable of understanding art, had, like all sordid souls, wanted to spend a certain sum fixed beforehand. Grindot, fettered by a contract, had found it impossible to embody his architectural dream.

The difference between Josépha's house and that in the Rue Barbet was just that between the individual stamp on things and commonness. The objects you admired at Josépha's were to be seen nowhere else; those that glittered at Crevel's were to be bought in any shop. These two types of luxury are divided by the river Million. A mirror, if unique, is worth six thousand francs; a mirror designed by a manufacturer who turns them out by the dozen costs five hundred. A genuine lustre by Boulle will sell at a public auction for three thousand francs; the same thing reproduced by casting may be made for a thousand or twelve hundred; one is archæologically what a picture by Raphael is in painting, the other is a copy. At what would you value a copy of a Raphael? Thus Crevel's mansion was a splendid example of the luxury of idiots, while Josépha's was a perfect model of an artist's home.

'War is declared,' said Crevel, going up to Madame Marneffe. She rang the bell.

'Go and find Monsieur Berthier,' said she to the man-servant, 'and do not return without him. – If you had succeeded,' said she, embracing Crevel, 'we would have postponed our happiness, my dear Daddy, and have given a really splendid entertainment; but when a whole family is set against a match, my dear, decency requires that the wedding shall be a quiet one, especially when the lady is a widow.'

'On the contrary, I intend to make a display of magnificence *à la* Louis xiv.,' said Crevel, who of late had held the eighteenth century rather cheap. 'I have ordered new carriages; there is one for Monsieur and one for Madame, two neat coupés; and a chaise, a handsome travelling carriage with a splendid hammer-cloth, on springs that tremble like Madame Hulot.'

'Oh, ho! *You intend?* – Then you have ceased to be my lamb? – No, no, my friend, you will do what *I* intend. We will sign the contract quietly – just ourselves – this afternoon. Then, on Wednesday, we will be regularly married, really married, in mufti, as my poor mother would have said. We will walk to church, plainly dressed, and have only a low mass. Our witnesses are Stidmann, Steinbock, Vignon, and Massol, all wide-awake men, who will be at the mairie by chance, and who will so far sacrifice themselves as to attend mass.

'Your colleague will perform the civil marriage, for once in a way, as early as half-past nine. Mass is at ten; we shall be at home to breakfast by half-past eleven.

'I have promised our guests that we will sit at table till the evening. There will be Bixou, your old official chum du Tillet, Lousteau, Vernisset, Léon de Lora, Vernou, all the wittiest men in Paris, who will not know that we are married. We will play them a little trick, we will get just a little tipsy, and Lisbeth must join us. I want her to study matrimony; Bixiou shall make love to her, and – and enlighten her darkness.'

For two hours Madame Marneffe went on talking nonsense, and Crevel made this judicious reflection –

'How can so light-hearted a creature be utterly depraved? Feather-brained, yes! but wicked? Nonsense!'

'Well, and what did the young people say about me?' said Valérie to Crevel at a moment when he sat down by her on the sofa. 'All sorts of horrors?'

'They will have it that you have a criminal passion for Wenceslas – you, who are virtue itself.'

'I love him! – I should think so, my little Wenceslas!' cried Valérie, calling the artist to her, taking his face in her hands, and kissing his forehead. 'A poor boy with no fortune, and no one to depend on! Cast off by a carrotty giraffe! What do you expect, Crevel? Wenceslas is my poet, and I love him as if he were my own child, and make no secret of it. Bah! your virtuous women see evil everywhere and in everything. Bless me, could they not sit by a man without doing wrong? I am a spoilt child who has had all it ever wanted, and bonbons no longer excite me. – Poor things! I am sorry for them!

'And who slandered me so?'

'Victorin,' said Crevel.

'Then why did you not stop his mouth, the odious legal macaw! with the story of the two hundred thousand francs and his mamma?'

'Oh, the Baroness had fled,' said Lisbeth.

'They had better take care, Lisbeth,' said Madame Marneffe, with a frown. 'Either they will receive me and do it hand-somely, and come to their stepmother's house – all the party! – or I will see them in lower depths than the Baron has reached, and you may tell them I said so! – At last I shall turn nasty. On my honour, I believe that evil is the scythe with which to cut down the good.'

At three o'clock Monsieur Berthier, Cardot's successor, read the marriage-contract, after a short conference with Crevel, for some of the articles were made conditional on the action taken by Monsieur and Madame Victorin Hulot.

Crevel settled on his wife a fortune consisting, in the first place, of forty thousand francs in dividends on specified securities; secondly, of the house and all its contents; and thirdly, of three million francs not invested. He also assigned to his wife every benefit allowed by law; he left all the property free of duty; and in the event of their dying without issue, each devised to the survivor the whole of their property and real estate.

By this arrangement the fortune left to Célestine and her husband was reduced to two millions of francs in capital. If Crevel and his second wife should have children, Célestine's share was limited to five hundred thousand francs, as the life-interest in the rest was to accrue to Valérie. This would be about the ninth part of his whole real and personal estate.

Lisbeth returned to dine in the Rue Louis-le-Grand, despair written on her face. She explained and bewailed the terms of the marriage-contract, but found Célestine and her husband insensible to the disastrous news.

'You have provoked your father, my children. Madame Marneffe swears that you shall receive Monsieur Crevel's wife and go to her house,' said she.

'Never!' said Victorin.

'Never!' said Célestine.

'Never!' said Hortense.

Lisbeth was possessed by the wish to crush the haughty attitude assumed by all the Hulots.

'She seems to have arms that she can turn against you,' she replied. 'I do not know all about it, but I shall find out. – She spoke vaguely of some history of two hundred thousand francs in which Adeline is implicated.'

The Baroness fell gently backward on the sofa she was sitting on in a fit of hysterical sobbing.

'Go there, go, my children!' she cried. 'Receive the woman! Monsieur Crevel is an infamous wretch. He deserves the worst punishment imaginable. – Do as the woman desires you! She is a monster – she knows all!'

After gasping out these words with tears and sobs, Madame Hulot collected her strength to go to her room, leaning on her daughter and Célestine.

'What is the meaning of all this?' cried Lisbeth, left alone with Victorin.

The lawyer stood rigid, in very natural dismay, and did not hear her.

'What is the matter, my dear Victorin?'

'I am horrified!' said he, and his face scowled darkly. 'Woe to anybody who hurts my mother! I have no scruples then. I would crush that woman like a viper if I could! – What, does she attack my mother's life, my mother's honour?'

'She said, but do not repeat it, my dear Victorin – she said you should all fall lower even than your father. And she scolded Crevel roundly for not having shut your mouths with this secret that seems to be such a terror to Adeline.'

A doctor was sent for, for the Baroness was evidently worse. He gave her a draught containing a large dose of opium, and Adeline, having swallowed it, fell into a deep sleep; but the whole family were greatly alarmed.

Early next morning Victorin went out, and on his way to the Courts called at the Préfecture of the Police, where he begged Vautrin, the head of the detective department, to send him Madame de Saint-Estève.

'We are forbidden, Monsieur, to meddle in your affairs; but Madame de Saint-Estève is in business, and will attend to your orders,' replied this famous police-officer.

On his return home, the unhappy lawyer was told that his mother's reason was in danger. Doctor Bianchon, Doctor Larabit, and Professor Angard had met in consultation, and were prepared to apply heroic remedies to hinder the rush of blood to the head. At the moment when Victorin was listening to Doctor Bianchon, who was giving him, at some length, his reasons for hoping that the crisis might be got over, the man-servant announced that a client, Madame de Saint-Estève, was waiting to see him. Victorin left Bianchon in the middle of a sentence and flew downstairs like a madman.

'Is there any hereditary lunacy in the family?' said Bianchon, addressing Larabit.

The doctors departed, leaving a hospital attendant, instructed by them, to watch Madame Hulot.

'A whole life of virtue!—' was the only sentence the sufferer had spoken since the attack.

Lisbeth never left Adeline's bedside; she sat up all night, and was much admired by the two younger women.

'Well, my dear Madame de Saint-Estève,' said Victorin, showing the dreadful old woman into his study and carefully shutting the doors, 'how are we getting on?'

'Ah, ha! my dear friend,' said she, looking at Victorin with cold irony. 'So you have thought things over?'

'Have you done anything?'

'Will you pay fifty thousand francs?'

'Yes,' replied Victorin, 'for we must get on. Do you know that by one single phrase that woman has endangered my mother's life and reason? So, I say, get on.'

'We have got on!' replied the old woman.

'Well?' cried Victorin, with a gulp.

'Well, you do not cry off the expenses?'

'On the contrary.'

'They run up to twenty-three thousand francs already.'

Victorin looked helplessly at the woman.

'Well, could we hoodwink you, you, one of the shining lights of the law?' said she. 'For that sum we have secured a maid's conscience and a picture by Raphael. – It is not dear.'

Hulot, still bewildered, sat with wide open eyes.

'Well, then,' his visitor went on, 'we have purchased the honesty of Mademoiselle Reine Tousard, a damsel from whom Madame Marneffe has no secrets—'

'I understand!'

'But if you shy, say so.'

'I will pay blindfold,' he replied. 'My mother has told me that that couple deserve the worst torments—'

'The rack is out of date,' said the old woman.

'You answer for the result?'

'Leave it all to me,' said the woman; 'your vengeance is simmering.'

She looked at the clock; it was six.

'Your avenger is dressing; the fires are lighted at the *Rocher de Cancale*; the horses are pawing the ground; my irons are getting hot. – Oh, I know your Madame Marneffe by heart! – Everything is ready. And there are some boluses in the rat-trap; I will tell you to-morrow morning if the mouse is poisoned. I believe she will be; good evening, my son.'

'Good-bye, Madame.'

'Do you know English?'

'Yes.'

'Have you ever seen *Macbeth* in English?'

'Yes.'

'Well, my son, Thou shalt be King. That is to say, you shall come into your inheritance,' said the dreadful old witch, foreseen by Shakespeare, and who seemed to know her Shakespeare.

She left Hulot amazed at the door of his study.

'The consultation is for to-morrow!' said she, with the gracious air of a regular client.

She saw two persons coming, and wished to pass in their eyes as a pinchbeck countess.

'What impudence!' thought Hulot, bowing to his pretended client.

Baron Montès de Montejanos was a *lion*, but a lion not accounted for. Fashionable Paris, Paris of the turf and of the town, admired the ineffable waistcoats of this foreign gentle-man, his spotless patent-leather boots, his incomparable sticks, his much-coveted horses, and the negro servants who rode the horses and who were entirely slaves and most consumedly thrashed.

His fortune was well known; he had a credit account up to seven hundred thousand francs in the great banking house of du Tillet; but he was always seen alone. When he went to 'first nights,' he was in a stall. He frequented no drawing-rooms. He had never given his arm to a girl on the streets. His name could not be coupled with that of any pretty woman of the world. To pass his time he played whist at the Jockey-Club. The world was reduced to calumny, or, which it thought funnier, to laughing at his peculiarities; he went by the name of Combabus.

Bixiou, Léon de Lora, Lousteau, Florine, Mademoiselle Héloïse Brisetout and Nathan, supping one evening with the notorious Carabine, with a large party of *lions* and *lionesses*, had invented this name with an excessively burlesque explanation. Massol, as being on the Council of State, and Claude Vignon, erewhile Professor of Greek, had related to the ignorant damsels the famous anecdote, preserved in Rollin's *Ancient History*, concerning Combabus, that voluntary Abelard who was placed in charge of the wife of a King of Assyria, Persia, Bactria, Mesopotamia, and other geographical divisions peculiar to old Professor du Bocage, who continued the work of d'Anville, the creator of the East of antiquity. This nickname, which gave Carabine's guests laughter for a quarter of an hour, gave rise to a series of over-free jests, to which the Academy could not award the Montyon prize; but among which the name was taken up, to rest thenceforth on the curly mane of the handsome Baron, called by Josépha the splendid Brazilian – as one might say a splendid *Catoxantha*.

Carabine, the loveliest of her tribe, whose delicate beauty and amusing wit had snatched the sceptre of the thirteenth arrondissement from the hands of Mademoiselle Turquet, better known by the name of Malaga – Mademoiselle Séraphine Sinet (this was her real name) was to du Tillet the banker what Josépha Mirah was to the Duc d'Hérouville.

Now, on the morning of the very day when Madame de Saint-Estève had prophesied success to Victorin, Carabine had said to du Tillet at about seven o'clock –

'If you want to be very nice, you will give me a dinner at the *Rocher de Cancale* and bring Combabus. We want to know, once for all, whether he has a mistress. – I bet that he has, and I should like to win.'

'He is still at the Hôtel des Princes; I will call,' replied du Tillet. 'We will have some fun. Ask all the youngsters – the youngster Bixiou, the youngster Lora, in short, all the clan.'

At half-past seven that evening, in the handsomest room of the restaurant where all Europe has dined, a splendid silver service was spread, made on purpose for entertainments where vanity pays the bill in bank-notes. A flood of light fell in ripples on the chased rims; waiters, whom a provincial might have taken for diplomatists but for their age, stood solemnly, as knowing themselves to be overpaid.

Five guests had arrived, and were waiting for nine more. These were first and foremost Bixiou, still flourishing in 1843, the salt of every intellectual dish, always supplied with fresh wit – a phenomenon as rare in Paris as virtue is; Léon de Lora, the greatest living painter of landscape and the sea, who has this great advantage over all his rivals, that he has never fallen below his first successes. The courtesans could never dispense with these two kings of ready wit. No supper, no dinner, was possible without them.

Séraphine Sinet, *dite* Carabine, as the mistress *en titre* of the Amphitryon, was one of the first to arrive; and the brilliant lighting showed off her shoulders, unrivalled in Paris, her throat, as round as if turned in a lathe, without a crease, her saucy face, and dress of satin brocade in two shades of blue, trimmed with Honiton lace enough to have fed a whole village for a month.

Pretty Jenny Cadine, not acting that evening, came in a dress of incredible splendour; her portrait is too well known to need any description. A party is always a Longchamps of evening dress for these ladies, each anxious to win the prize for her millionaire by thus announcing to her rivals –

'This is the price I am worth!'

A third woman, evidently at the initial stage of her career, gazed, almost shamefaced, at the luxury of her two established and wealthy companions. Simply dressed in white cashmere trimmed with blue, her head had been dressed with real flowers by a coiffeur of the old-fashioned school, whose awkward hands had unconsciously given the charm of ineptitude to her fair hair. Still unaccustomed to any finery, she showed the timidity – to use a hackneyed phrase – inseparable from a first appearance. She had come from Valognes to find in Paris some use for her distracting youthfulness, her innocence that might have stirred the senses of a dying man, and her beauty, worthy to hold its own with any that Normandy has ever supplied to the theatres of the capital. The lines of that unblemished face were the ideal of angelic purity. Her milk-white skin reflected the light like a mirror. The delicate pink in her cheeks might have been laid on with a brush. She was called Cydalise, and, as will be seen, she was an important pawn in the game played by Ma'ame Nourrisson to defeat Madame Marneffe.

'Your arm is not a match for your name, my child,' said Jenny Cadine, to whom Carabine had introduced this masterpiece of sixteen, having brought her with her.

And, in fact, Cydalise displayed to public admiration a fine pair of arms, smooth and satiny, but red with healthy young blood.

'What do you want for her?' said Jenny Cadine, in an undertone to Carabine.

'A fortune.'

'What are you going to do with her?'

'Well – Madame Combabus!'

'And what are you to get for such a job?'

'Guess.'

'A service of plate?'

'I have three.'

'Diamonds?'

'I am selling them.'

'A green monkey?'

'No. A picture by Raphael.'

'What maggot is that in your brain?'

'Josépha makes me sick with her pictures,' said Carabine. 'I want some better than hers.'

Du Tillet came with the Brazilian, the hero of the feast; the Duc de Hérouville followed with Josépha. The singer wore a plain velvet gown, but she had on a necklace worth a hundred and twenty thousand francs, pearls hardly distinguishable from her skin like white camellia petals. She had stuck one scarlet camellia in her black hair – a patch – the effect was dazzling, and she had amused herself by putting eleven rows of pearls on each arm. As she shook hands with Jenny Cadine, the actress said, 'Lend me your mittens!'

Josépha unclasped them one by one and handed them to her friend on a plate.

'There's style!' said Carabine. 'Quite the Duchess! You have robbed the ocean to dress the nymph, Monsieur le Duc,' she added, turning to the little Duc d'Hérouville.

The actress took two of the bracelets; she clasped the other twenty on the singer's beautiful arms, which she kissed.

Lousteau, the literary cadger, la Palférine and Malaga, Massol, Vauvinet, and Théodore Gaillard, a proprietor of one of the most important political newspapers, completed the party. The Duc d'Hérouville, polite to everybody, as a fine gentleman knows how to be, greeted the Comte de la Palférine with the particular nod which, while it does not imply either esteem or intimacy, conveys to all the world, 'We are of the same race, the same blood – equals!' – And this greeting, the shibboleth of the aristocracy, was invented to be the despair of the upper citizen class.

Carabine placed Combabus on her left, and the Duc d'Hérouville on her right. Cydalise was next to the Brazilian, and beyond her was Bixiou. Malaga sat by the Duke.

Oysters appeared at seven o'clock; at eight they were drinking iced punch. Every one is familiar with the bill of fare of such a banquet. By nine o'clock they were talking as people talk after forty-two bottles of various wines, drunk by fourteen persons. Dessert was on the table, the odious dessert of the month of April. Of all the party, the only one affected by the heady atmosphere was Cydalise, who was humming a tune. None of the party, with the exception of the poor country girl, had lost their reason; the drinkers and the women were the experienced *élite* of the society that sups. Their wits were bright, their eyes glistened, but with no loss of intelligence, though the talk drifted into satire, anecdote, and gossip. Conversation, hitherto confined to the inevitable circle of racing, horses, hammerings on the Bourse, the different occupations of the *lions* themselves, and the scandals of the town, showed a tendency to break up into intimate *tête-a-tête*, the dialogues of two hearts.

And at this stage, at a signal from Carabine to Léon de Lora, Bixiou, la Palférine, and du Tillet, love came under discussion.

'A doctor in good society never talks of medicine, true nobles never speak of their ancestors, men of genius do not discuss their works,' said Josépha; 'why should we talk business? If I got the opera put off in order to dine here, it was assuredly not to work. – So let us change the subject, dear children.'

'But we are speaking of real love, my beauty,' said Malaga, 'of the love that makes a man fling all to the dogs – father, mother, wife, children – and retire to Clichy.'

'Talk away, then, "don't know yer,"' said the singer.

The slang words, borrowed from the street Arab, and spoken by these women, may be a poem on their lips, helped by the expression of the eyes and face.

'What, do not I love you, Josépha?' said the Duke in a low voice.

'You, perhaps, may love me truly,' said she in his ear, and she smiled. 'But I do not love you in the way they describe, with such love as makes the world dark in the absence of the man beloved. You are delightful to me, useful – but not indispensable; and if you were to throw me over to-morrow, I could have three dukes for one.'

'Is true love to be found in Paris?' asked Léon de Lora. 'Men have not even time to make a fortune; how can they give themselves over to true love, which swamps a man as water melts sugar? A man must be enormously rich to indulge in it, for love annihilates him – for instance, like our Brazilian friend over there. As I said long ago, "Extremes defeat – themselves." A true lover is like an eunuch; women have ceased to exist for him. He is mystical; he is like the true Christian, an anchorite of the desert! – See our noble Brazilian.'

Every one at table looked at Henri Montès de Montejanos, who was shy at finding every eye centred on him.

'He has been feeding there for an hour without discovering, any more than an ox at pasture, that he is sitting next to – I will not say, in such company, the loveliest – but the freshest woman in all Paris.'

'Everything is fresh here, even the fish; it is what the house is famous for,' said Carabine.

Baron Montès looked good-naturedly at the painter, and said –

'Very good! I drink to your very good health,' and bowing to Léon de Lora, he lifted his glass of port wine and drank it with much dignity.

'Are you then truly in love?' asked Malaga of her neighbour, thus interpreting his toast.

The Brazilian refilled his glass, bowed to Carabine, and drank again.

'To the lady's health then!' said the courtesan, in such a droll tone that Lora, du Tillet, and Bixiou burst out laughing.

The Brazilian sat like a bronze statue. This impassibility provoked Carabine. She knew perfectly well that Montès was devoted to Madame Marneffe, but she had not expected this dogged fidelity, this obstinate silence of conviction.

A woman is as often gauged by the attitude of her lover as a man is judged from the tone of his mistress. The Baron was proud of his attachment to Valérie, and of hers to him; his smile had, to these experienced connoisseurs, a touch of irony; he was really grand to look upon; wine had not flushed him;

and his eyes, with their peculiar lustre as of tarnished gold, kept the secrets of his soul. Even Carabine said to herself –

'What a woman she must be! How she has sealed up that heart!'

'He is a rock!' said Bixiou in an undertone, imagining that the whole thing was a practical joke, and never suspecting the importance to Carabine of reducing this fortress.

While this conversation, apparently so frivolous, was going on at Carabine's right, the discussion of love was continued on her left between the Duc d'Hérouville, Lousteau, Josépha, Jenny Cadine, and Massol. They were wondering whether such rare phenomena were the result of passion, obstinacy, or affection. Josépha, bored to death by it all, tried to change the subject.

'You are talking of what you know nothing about. Is there a man among you who ever loved a woman – a woman beneath him – enough to squander his fortune and his children's, to sacrifice his future and blight his past, to risk going to the hulks for robbing the Government, to kill an uncle and a brother, to let his eyes be so effectually blinded that he did not even perceive that it was done to hinder his seeing the abyss into which, as a crowning jest, he was being driven? Du Tillet has a cash-box under the left breast; Léon de Lora has his wit; Bixiou would laugh at himself for a fool if he loved any one but himself; Massol has a minister's portfolio in the place of a heart; Lousteau can have nothing but viscera, since he could endure to be thrown over by Madame de Baudraye; Monsieur le Duc is too rich to prove his love by his ruin; Vauvinet is not in it – I do not regard a bill-broker as one of the human race; and you have never loved, nor I, nor Jenny Cadine, nor Malaga. For my part, I never but once even saw the phenomenon I have described. It was,' and she turned to Jenny Cadine, 'that poor Baron Hulot, whom I am going to advertise for like a lost dog, for I want to find him.'

'Oh, ho!' said Carabine to herself, and looking keenly at Josépha, 'then Madame Nourrisson has two pictures by Raphael, since Josépha is playing my hand!'

'Poor fellow,' said Vauvinet, 'he was a great man! Magnificent! And what a figure, what a style, the air of Francis I.! What a volcano! and how full of ingenious ways of getting money! He must be looking for it now, wherever he is, and I make no doubt he extracts it even from the walls built of bones that you may see in the suburbs of Paris near the city gates—'

'And all that,' said Bixiou, 'for that little Madame Marneffe! There is a precious hussy for you!'

'She is just going to marry my friend Crevel,' said du Tillet.

'And she is madly in love with my friend Steinbock,' Léon de Lora put in.

These three phrases were like so many pistol-shots fired point blank at Montès. He turned white, and the shock was so painful that he rose with difficulty.

'You are a set of blackguards!' cried he. 'You have no right to speak the name of an honest woman in the same breath with those of fallen creatures – above all, not to make it a mark for your slander!'

He was interrupted by unanimous bravos and applause. Bixiou, Léon de Lora, Vauvinet, du Tillet, and Massol set the example, and there was a chorus.

'Hurrah for the Emperor!' said Bixiou.

'Crown him! crown him!' cried Vauvinet.

'Three groans for such a good dog! Hurrah for Brazil!' cried Lousteau.

'So, my copper-coloured Baron, it is our Valérie that you love; and you are not disgusted?' said Léon de Lora.

'His remark is not parliamentary, but it is grand!' observed Massol.

'But, my most delightful customer,' said du Tillet, 'you were recommended to me; I am your banker; your innocence reflects on my credit.'

'Yes, tell me, you who are a reasonable creature—' said the Brazilian to the banker.

'Thanks on behalf of the company,' said Bixiou with a bow.

'Tell me the real facts,' Montès went on, heedless of Bixiou's interjection.

'Well, then,' replied du Tillet, 'I have the honour to tell you that I am asked to the Crevel wedding.'

'Ah, ha! Combabus holds a brief for Madame Marneffe!' said Josépha, rising solemnly.

She went round to Montès with a tragic look, patted him kindly on the head, looked at him for a moment with comical admiration, and nodded sagely.

'Hulot was the first instance of love through fire and water,' said she; 'this is the second. But it ought not to count, as it comes from the Tropics.'

Montès had dropped into his chair again, when Josépha gently touched his forehead and looked at du Tillet as he said –

'If I am the victim of a Paris jest, if you only wanted to get at my secret – ' and he sent a flashing look round the table, embracing all the guests in a flaming glance that blazed with the sun of Brazil, – 'I beg of you as a favour to tell me so,' he went on, in a tone of almost childlike entreaty; 'but do not vilify the woman I love.'

'Nay, indeed,' said Carabine in a low voice; 'but if, on the contrary, you are shamefully betrayed, cheated, tricked by Valérie, if I should give you the proof in an hour, in my own house, what then?'

'I cannot tell you before all these Iagos,' said the Brazilian.

Carabine understood him to say *magots* (baboons).

'Well, well, say no more!' she replied, smiling. 'Do not make yourself a laughing-stock for all the wittiest men in Paris; come to my house, we will talk it over.'

Montès was crushed. 'Proofs,' he stammered; 'consider—'

'Only too many,' replied Carabine; 'and if the mere suspicion hits you so hard, I fear for your reason.'

'Is this creature obstinate, I ask you? He is worse than the late lamented King of Holland! – I say, Lousteau, Bixiou, Massol, all the crew of you, are you not invited to breakfast

with Madame Marneffe the day after to-morrow?' said Léon de
Lora.

'*Ya*,' said du Tillet; 'I have the honour of assuring you,
Baron, that if you had by any chance thought of marrying
Madame Marneffe, you are thrown out like a bill in Parliament,
beaten by a blackball called Crevel. My friend, my old comrade
Crevel, has eighty thousand francs a year; and you, I suppose,
did not show such a good hand, for if you had, you, I imagine,
would have been preferred.'

Montès listened with a half-absent, half-smiling expression,
which struck them all with terror.

At this moment the head-waiter came to whisper to Carabine that a lady, a relation of hers, was in the drawing-room
and wished to speak to her.

Carabine rose and went out to find Madame Nourrisson,
decently veiled with black lace.

'Well, child, am I to go to your house? Has he taken the
hook?'

'Yes, mother; and the pistol is so fully loaded, that my only
fear is that it will burst,' said Carabine.

About an hour later, Montès, Cydalise, and Carabine,
returning from the *Rocher de Cancale*, entered Carabine's little
sitting-room in the Rue Saint-Georges. Madame Nourrisson
was sitting in an armchair by the fire.

'Here is my worthy old aunt,' said Carabine.

'Yes, child, I came in person to fetch my little allowance.
You would have forgotten me, though you are kind-hearted,
and I have some bills to pay to-morrow. Buying and selling
clothes, I am always short of cash. Who is that at your heels?
The gentleman looks very much put out about something.'

The dreadful Madame Nourrisson, at this moment so completely disguised as to look like a respectable old body, rose to
embrace Carabine, one of the hundred and odd courtesans she
had launched on their horrible career of vice.

'He is an Othello who is not to be taken in, whom I have
the honour of introducing to you – Monsieur le Baron Montès
de Montejanos.'

'Oh! I have heard him talked about, and know his name. – You are nicknamed Combabus, because you love but one woman; and in Paris, that is the same as loving no one at all. And is it by chance the object of your affections who is fretting you? Madame Marneffe, Crevel's woman? I tell you what, my dear sir, you may bless your stars instead of cursing them. She is a good-for-nothing baggage, is that little woman. I know her tricks!'

'Get along,' said Carabine, into whose hand Madame Nourrisson had slipped a note while embracing her, 'you do not know your Brazilians. They are wrong-headed creatures that insist on being impaled through the heart. The more jealous they are, the more jealous they want to be. Monsieur talks of dealing death all round, but he will kill nobody because he is in love. – However, I have brought him here to give him the proofs of his discomfiture, which I have got from that little Steinbock.'

Montès was drunk; he listened as if the women were talking about somebody else.

Carabine went to take off her velvet wrap, and read a facsimile of a note, as follows: –

'DEAR PUSS, – He dines with Popinot this evening, and will come to fetch me from the Opera at eleven. I shall go out at about half-past five and count on finding you at our paradise. Order dinner to be sent in from the *Maison d'or*. Dress, so as to be able to take me to the Opera. We shall have four hours to ourselves. Return this note to me; not that your Valérie doubts you – I would give you my life, my fortune, and my honour, but I am afraid of the tricks of chance.'

'Here, Baron, this is the note sent to Count Steinbock this morning; read the address. The original document is burnt.'

Montès turned the note over and over, recognised the writing, and was struck by a rational idea, which is sufficient evidence of the disorder of his brain.

'And, pray,' said he, looking at Carabine, 'what object have you in torturing my heart, for you must have paid very dear for the privilege of having the note in your possession long enough to get it lithographed?'

'Foolish man!' said Carabine, at a nod from Madame Nourrisson, 'don't you see that poor child Cydalise – a girl of sixteen, who has been pining for you these three months, till she has lost her appetite for food or drink, and who is heartbroken because you have never even glanced at her?'

Cydalise put her handkerchief to her eyes with an appearance of emotion – 'She is furious,' Carabine went on, 'though she looks as if butter would not melt in her mouth, furious to see the man she adores duped by a villainous hussy; she would kill Valérie—'

'Oh, as for that,' said the Brazilian, 'that is my business!'

'What, killing?' said old Nourrisson. 'No, my son, we don't do that here nowadays.'

'Oh!' said Montès, 'I am not a native of this country. I live in a parish where I can laugh at your laws; and if you give me proof—'

'Well, that note. Is that nothing?'

'No,' said the Brazilian. 'I do not believe in the writing. I must see for myself.'

'See!' cried Carabine, taking the hint at once from a gesture of her supposed aunt. 'You shall see, my dear Tiger, all you can wish to see – on one condition.'

'And that is?'

'Look at Cydalise.'

At a wink from Madame Nourrisson, Cydalise cast a tender look at the Baron.

'Will you be good to her? Will you make her a home?' asked Carabine. 'A girl of such beauty is well worth a house and a carriage! It would be a monstrous shame to leave her to walk the streets. And besides – she is in debt. – How much do you owe?' asked Carabine, nipping Cydalise's arm.

'She is worth all she can get,' said the old woman. 'The point is that she can find a buyer.'

'Listen!' cried Montès, fully aware at last of this masterpiece of womankind, 'you will show me Valérie—'

'And Count Steinbock. – Certainly!' said Madame Nourrisson.

For the past ten minutes the old woman had been watching the Brazilian; she saw that he was an instrument tuned up to the murderous pitch she needed; and, above all, so effectually blinded, that he would never heed who had led him on to it, and she spoke –

'Cydalise, my Brazilian jewel, is my niece, so her concerns are partly mine. All this catastrophe will be the work of a few minutes, for a friend of mine lets the furnished room to Count Steinbock where Valérie is at this moment taking coffee – a queer sort of coffee, but she calls it her coffee. So let us understand each other, Brazil! – I like Brazil, it is a hot country. – What is to become of my niece?'

'You old ostrich,' said Montès, the plumes in the woman's bonnet catching his eye, 'you interrupted me. – If you show me – if I see Valérie and that artist together—'

'As you would wish to be—' said Carabine; 'that is understood.'

'Then I will take this girl and carry her away—'

'Where?' asked Carabine.

'To Brazil,' replied the Baron. 'I will make her my wife. My uncle left me ten leagues square of entailed estate; that is how I still have that house and home. I have a hundred negroes – nothing but negroes and negresses and negro brats, all bought by my uncle—'

'Nephew to a nigger-driver,' said Carabine, with a grimace. 'That needs some consideration. – Cydalise, child, are you fond of the blacks?'

'Pooh! Carabine, no nonsense,' said the old woman. 'The deuce is in it! Monsieur and I are doing business.'

'If I take up another Frenchwoman, I mean to have her to myself,' the Brazilian went on. 'I warn you, Mademoiselle, I am king there, and not a constitutional king. I am Czar; my subjects are mine by purchase, and no one can escape from my kingdom, which is a hundred leagues from any human settlement, hemmed in by savages on the interior, and divided from the sea by a wilderness as wide as France.'

'I should prefer a garret here.'

'So thought I,' said Montès, 'since I sold all my land and possessions at Rio to come back to Madame Marneffe.'

'A man does not make such a voyage for nothing,' remarked Madame Nourrisson. 'You have a right to look for love for your own sake, particularly being so good-looking. – Oh, he is very handsome!' said she to Carabine.

'Very handsome, handsomer than the *Postillon de Longjumeau*,' replied the courtesan.

Cydalise took the Brazilian's hand, but he released it as politely as he could.

'I came back for Madame Marneffe,' the man went on where he had left off, 'but you do not know why I was three years thinking about it.'

'No, Savage!' said Carabine.

'Well, she had so repeatedly told me that she longed to live with me alone in a desert—'

'Oh, ho! he is not a savage after all,' cried Carabine, with a shout of laughter. 'He is of the highly-civilised tribe of Flats!'

'She had told me this so often,' Montès went on, regardless of the courtesan's mockery, 'that I had a lovely house fitted up in the heart of that vast estate. I came back to France to fetch Valérie, and the first evening I saw her—'

'Saw her is very proper!' said Carabine. 'I will remember it.'

'She told me to wait till that wretched Marneffe was dead; and I agreed, and forgave her for having admitted the attentions of Hulot. Whether the devil had her in hand I don't know, but from that instant that woman has humoured my every whim, complied with all my demands – never for one moment has she given me cause to suspect her!—'

'That is supremely clever!' said Carabine to Madame Nourrisson, who nodded in sign of assent.

'My faith in that woman,' said Montès, and he shed a tear, 'was a match for my love. Just now, I was ready to fight everybody at table—'

'So I saw,' said Carabine.

'And if I am cheated, if she is going to be married, if she is at this moment in Steinbock's arms, she deserves a thousand deaths! I will kill her as I would smash a fly—'

'And how about the gendarmes, my son?' said Madame Nourrisson, with a smile that made your flesh creep.

'And the police agents, and the judges, and the assizes, and all the set out?' added Carabine.

'You are bragging, my dear fellow,' said the old woman, who wanted to know all the Brazilian's schemes of vengeance.

'I will kill her,' he calmly repeated. 'You called me a savage. – Do you imagine that I am fool enough to go, like a Frenchman, and buy poison at the chemist's shop? – During the time while we were driving here, I thought out my means of revenge, if you should prove to be right as concerns Valérie. One of my negroes has the most deadly of animal poisons, that gives a disease more fatal than any vegetable poison, and incurable anywhere but in Brazil. I will administer it to Cydalise, who will give it to me; then by the time when death is a certainty to Crevel and his wife, I shall be beyond the Azores with your cousin, who will be cured, and I will marry her. We have our own little tricks, we savages! – Cydalise,' said he, looking at the country girl, 'is the animal I need. – How much does she owe?'

'A hundred thousand francs,' said Cydalise.

'She says little – but to the purpose,' said Carabine, in a low tone to Madame Nourrisson.

'I am going mad!' cried the Brazilian, in a husky voice, dropping on to a sofa. 'I shall die of this! But I must see, for it is impossible! – A lithographed note! What is to assure me that it is not a forgery? – Baron Hulot was in love with Valérie?' said he, recalling Josépha's harangue. 'Nay; the proof that he did not love is that she is still alive – I will not leave her living for anybody else, if she is not wholly mine.'

Montès was terrible to behold. He bellowed, he stormed; he broke everything he touched; rosewood was as brittle as glass.

'How he destroys things!' said Carabine, looking at the old woman. 'My good boy,' said she, giving the Brazilian a little slap, 'Roland the Furious is very fine in a poem; but in a drawing-room he is prosaic and expensive.'

'My son,' said old Nourrisson, rising to stand in front of the crestfallen Baron, 'I am of your way of thinking. When you love in that way, and are joined "till death does you part," life must answer for love. The one who first goes, carries everything away; it is a general wreck. You command my esteem, my admiration, my consent, especially for your inoculation, which will make me a Friend of the Negro. – But you love her! You will hark back?'

'I? – If she is so infamous, I—'

'Well, come now, you are talking too much, it strikes me. A man who means to be avenged, and who says he has the ways and means of a savage, doesn't do that. – If you want to see your "object" in her paradise, you must take Cydalise and walk straight in with her on your arm, as if the servant had made a mistake. But no scandal! If you mean to be revenged, you must eat the leek, seem to be in despair, and allow her to bully you. – Do you see?' said Madame Nourrisson, finding the Brazilian quite amazed by so subtle a scheme.

'All right, old ostrich,' he replied. 'Come along: I understand.'

'Good-bye, little one!' said the old woman to Carabine.

She signed to Cydalise to go on with Montès, and remained a minute with Carabine.

'Now, child, I have but one fear, and that is that he will strangle her! I should be in a very tight place; we must do everything gently. I believe you have won your picture by Raphael; but they tell me it is only a Mignard. Never mind, it is much prettier; all the Raphaels are gone black, I am told, whereas this one is as bright as a Girodet.'

'All I want is to crow over Josépha; and it is all the same to me whether I have a Mignard or a Raphael! – That thief had on such pearls this evening! – you would sell your soul for them.'

Cydalise, Montès, and Madame Nourrisson got into a hackney coach that was waiting at the door. Madame Nourrisson whispered to the driver the address of a house in the same block as the Italian Opera House, which they could have reached in five or six minutes from the Rue Saint-Georges; but Madame Nourrisson desired the man to drive along the Rue le Peletier, and to go very slowly, so as to be able to examine the carriages in waiting.

'Brazilian,' said the old woman, 'look out for your angel's carriage and servants.'

The Baron pointed out Valérie's carriage as they passed it.

'She has told them to come for her at ten o'clock, and she is gone in a cab to the house where she visits Count Stein-bock. She has dined there, and will come to the Opera in half an hour. – It is well contrived!' said Madame Nourrisson. 'Thus you see how she has kept you so long in the dark.'

The Brazilian made no reply. He had become the tiger, and had recovered the imperturbable cool ferocity that had been so striking at dinner. He was as calm as a bankrupt the day after he has stopped payment.

At the door of the house stood a hackney coach with two horses, of the kind known as a *Compagnie Générale*, from the Company that runs them.

'Stay here in the box,' said the old woman to Montès. 'This is not an open house like a tavern. I will send for you.'

The paradise of Madame Marneffe and Wenceslas was not at all like that of Crevel – who, finding it useless now, had just sold his to the Comte Maxime de Trailles. This paradise, the paradise of all comers, consisted of a room on the fourth floor opening to the landing, in a house close to the Italian Opera. On each floor of this house there was a room which had originally served as the kitchen to the apartments on that floor. But the house having become a sort of inn, let out for clandestine love affairs at an exorbitant price, the owner, the real Madame Nourrisson, an old-clothes buyer in the Rue Neuve Saint-Marc, had wisely appreciated the great value of these kitchens, and had turned them into a sort of dining-rooms. Each of these rooms, built between thick party-walls and with windows to the street, was entirely shut in by very thick double doors on the landing. Thus the most important secrets could be discussed over a dinner, with no risk of being overheard. For greater security, the windows had shutters inside and out. These rooms, in consequence of this peculiarity, were let for twelve hundred francs a month. The whole house, full of such paradises and mysteries, was rented by Madame Nourrisson the First for twenty-eight thousand francs a year, and one year with another she made twenty thousand francs of clear profit, after paying her housekeeper, Madame Nourrisson the Second, for she did not manage it herself.

The paradise let to Count Steinbock had been hung with chintz; the cold, hard floor, of common tiles reddened with encaustic, was not felt through a soft, thick carpet. The furniture consisted of two pretty chairs and a bed in an alcove, just now half hidden by a table loaded with the remains of an elegant dinner, while two bottles with long necks and an empty champagne-bottle in ice strewed the field of Bacchus cultivated by Venus.

There were also – the property, no doubt, of Valérie – a low easy-chair and a man's smoking-chair, and a pretty toilet chest of drawers in rosewood, the mirror handsomely framed *à la* Pompadour. A lamp hanging from the ceiling gave a subdued light, increased by wax candles on the table and on the chimney-shelf.

This sketch will suffice to give an idea, *urbi et orbi*, of clandestine passion in the squalid style stamped on it in Paris in 1840. How far, alas! from the adulterous love, symbolised by Vulcan's nets, three thousand years ago.

When Montès and Cydalise came upstairs, Valérie, standing before the fire, where a log was blazing, was allowing Wenceslas to lace her stays.

This is a moment when a woman who is neither too fat nor too thin, but, like Valérie, elegant and slender, displays divine beauty. The rosy skin, moistly soft, invites the sleepiest eye. The lines of her figure, so little hidden, are so charmingly outlined by the white pleats of the shift and the support of the stays, that she is irresistible – like everything that must be parted from.

With a happy face smiling at the glass, a foot impatiently marking time, a hand put up to restore order among the tumbled curls, and eyes expressive of gratitude; with the glow of satisfaction which, like a sunset, warms the least details of the countenance – everything makes such a moment a mine of memories.

Any man who dares look back on the early errors of his life may, perhaps, recall some such reminiscences, and understand, though not excuse, the follies of Hulot and Crevel. Women are so well aware of their power at such a moment, that they find in it what may be called the aftermath of the meeting.

'Come, come; after two years' practice, you do not yet know how to lace a woman's stays! You are too much a Pole! – There, it is ten o'clock, my Wenceslas!' said Valérie, laughing at him.

At this very moment, a mischievous waiting-woman, by inserting a knife, pushed up the hook of the double doors that formed the whole security of Adam and Eve. She hastily pulled the door open – for the servants of these dens have little time to waste – and discovered one of the bewitching *tableaux de genre* which Gavarni has so often shown at the Salon.

'In here, Madame,' said the girl; and Cydalise went in, followed by Montès.

'But there is some one here. – Excuse me, Madame,' said the country girl, in alarm.

'What? – Why! it is Valérie!' cried Montès, violently slamming the door.

Madame Marneffe, too genuinely agitated to dissemble her feelings, dropped on to the chair by the fireplace. Two tears rose to her eyes, and at once dried away. She looked at Montès, saw the girl, and burst into a cackle of forced laughter. The dignity of the insulted woman redeemed the scantiness of her attire; she walked close up to the Brazilian, and looked at him so defiantly that her eyes glittered like knives.

'So that,' said she, standing face to face with the Baron, and pointing to Cydalise – 'that is the other side of your fidelity? You, who have made me promises that might convert a disbeliever in love! You, for whom I have done so much – have even committed crimes! – You are right, Monsieur, I am not to compare with a child of her age and of such beauty!

'I know what you are going to say,' she went on, looking at Wenceslas, whose undress was proof too clear to be denied. 'This is my concern. If I could love you after such gross treachery – for you have spied upon me, you have paid for every step up these stairs, paid the mistress of the house, and the servant, perhaps even Reine – a noble deed! – If I had any remnant of affection for such a mean wretch, I could give him reasons that would renew his passion! – But I leave you, Monsieur, to your doubts, which will become remorse. – Wenceslas, my gown!'

She took her dress and put it on, looked at herself in the glass, and finished dressing without heeding the Baron, as calmly as if she had been alone in the room.

'Wenceslas, are you ready? – Go first.'

She had been watching Montès in the glass and out of the corner of her eye, and fancied she could see in his pallor an indication of the weakness which delivers a strong man over to a woman's fascinations; she now took his hand, going so close to him that he could not help inhaling the terrible perfumes which men love, and by which they intoxicate themselves; then, feeling his pulses beat high, she looked at him reproachfully.

'You have my full permission to go and tell your history to Monsieur Crevel; he will never believe you. I have a perfect right to marry him, and he becomes my husband the day after to-morrow. – I shall make him very happy. – Good-bye; try to forget me.'

'Oh! Valérie,' cried Henri Montès, clasping her in his arms, 'that is impossible! – Come to Brazil!'

Valérie looked in his face, and saw him her slave.

'Well, if you still love me, Henri, two years hence I will be your wife; but your expression at this moment strikes me as very suspicious.'

'I swear to you that they made me drink, that false friends threw this girl on my hands, and that the whole thing is the outcome of chance!' said Montès.

'Then I am to forgive you?' she asked, with a smile.

'But you will marry, all the same?' asked the Baron, in an agony of jealousy.

'Eighty thousand francs a year!' said she, with almost comical enthusiasm. 'And Crevel loves me so much that he will die of it!'

'Ah! I understand,' said Montès.

'Well, then, in a few days we will come to an understanding,' said she.

And she departed triumphant.

'I have no scruples,' thought the Baron, standing transfixed for a few minutes. 'What! That woman believes she can make use of his passion to be quit of that dolt, as she counted on Marneffe's decease! – I shall be the instrument of divine wrath.'

Two days later those of du Tillet's guests who had demolished Madame Marneffe tooth and nail, were seated round her table an hour after she had shed her skin and changed her name for the illustrious name of a Paris mayor. This verbal treason is one of the commonest forms of Parisian levity.

Valérie had had the satisfaction of seeing the Brazilian in the church; for Crevel, now so entirely the husband, had invited him out of bravado. And the Baron's presence at the breakfast astonished no one. All these men of wit and of the world were familiar with the meanness of passion, the compromises of pleasure.

Steinbock's deep melancholy – for he was beginning to despise the woman whom he had adored as an angel – was considered to be in excellent taste. The Pole thus seemed to convey that all was at an end between Valérie and himself. Lisbeth came to embrace her dear Madame Crevel, and to excuse herself for not staying to the breakfast on the score of Adeline's sad state of health.

'Be quite easy,' said she to Valérie, 'they will call on you, and you will call on them. Simply hearing the words *two hundred thousand francs* has brought the Baroness to death's door. Oh, you have them all hard and fast by that tale! — But you must tell it to me.'

Within a month of her marriage, Valérie was at her tenth quarrel with Steinbock; he insisted on explanations as to Henri Montès, reminding her of the words spoken in their paradise; and, not content with speaking to her in terms of scorn, he watched her so closely that she never had a moment of liberty, so much was she fettered by his jealousy on one side and Crevel's devotion on the other.

Bereft now of Lisbeth, whose advice had always been so valuable, she flew into such a rage as to reproach Wenceslas for the money she had lent him. This so effectually roused Steinbock's pride, that he came no more to the Crevels' house. So Valérie had gained her point, which was to be rid of him for a time, and enjoy some freedom. She waited till Crevel should make a little journey into the country to see Comte Popinot, with a view to arranging for her introduction to the Countess, and was then able to make an appointment to meet the Baron, whom she wanted to have at her command for a whole day to give him those 'reasons' which were to make him love her more than ever.

On the morning of that day, Reine, who estimated the magnitude of her crime by that of the bribe she received, tried to warn her mistress, in whom she naturally took more interest than in strangers. Still, as she had been threatened with madness, and ending her days in the Salpétrière in case of indiscretion, she was cautious.

'Madame, you are so well off now,' said she. 'Why take on again with that Brazilian? — I do not trust him at all.'

'You are very right, Reine, and I mean to be rid of him.'

'Oh, Madame, I am glad to hear it; he frightens me, does that big Moor! I believe him to be capable of anything.'

'Silly child! you have more reason to be afraid for him when he is with me.'

At this moment Lisbeth came in.

'My dear little pet Nanny, what an age since we met!' cried Valérie. 'I am so unhappy! Crevel bores me to death; and Wenceslas is gone – we quarrelled.'

'I know,' said Lisbeth, 'and that is what brings me here. Victorin met him at about five in the afternoon going into an eating-house at five-and-twenty sous, and he brought him home, hungry, by working on his feelings, to the Rue Louis-le-Grand. – Hortense, seeing Wenceslas lean and ill and badly dressed, held out her hand. This is how you throw me over—'

'Monsieur Henri, Madame,' the man-servant announced in a low voice to Valérie.

'Leave me now, Lisbeth; I will explain it all to-morrow.' But, as will be seen, Valérie was ere long not in a state to explain anything to anybody.

Towards the end of May, Baron Hulot's pension was released by Victorin's regular payments to Baron Nucingen. As everybody knows, pensions are paid half-yearly, and only on the presentation of a certificate that the recipient is alive; and as Hulot's residence was unknown, the arrears unpaid on Vauvinet's demand remained to his credit in the Treasury. Vauvinet now signed his renunciation of any further claims, and it was still indispensable to find the pensioner before the arrears could be drawn.

Thanks to Bianchon's care, the Baroness had recovered her health; and to this Josépha's good heart had contributed by a letter, of which the orthography betrayed the collaboration of the Duc d'Hérouville. This was what the singer wrote to the Baroness, after twenty days of anxious search: –

'MADAME LA BARONNE, – Monsieur Hulot was living, two months since, in the Rue des Bernardins, with Élodie Chardin, a lace-mender, for whom he had left Mademoiselle Bijou; but he went away without a word, leaving everything behind him, and no one knows where he went. I am not without hope, however, and I have put a man on his track who believes he has already seen him in the Boulevard Bourdon.

'The poor Jewess means to keep the promise she made to the Christian. Will the angel pray for the devil? That must sometimes happen in heaven. – I remain, with the deepest respect, always your humble servant,

JOSÉPHA MIRAH.'

The lawyer, Maître Hulot d'Ervy, hearing no more of the dreadful Madame Nourrisson, seeing his father-in-law married, having brought back his brother-in-law to the family fold, suffering from no importunity on the part of his new stepmother, and seeing his mother's health improve daily, gave himself up to his political and judicial duties, swept along by the tide of Paris life, in which the hours count for days.

One night, towards the end of the session, having occasion to write up a report to the Chamber of Deputies, he was obliged to sit at work till late at night. He had gone into his study at nine o'clock, and, while waiting till the man-servant should bring in the candles with green shades, his thoughts turned to his father. He was blaming himself for leaving the inquiry so much to the singer, and had resolved to see Monsieur Chapuzot himself on the morrow, when he saw in the twilight, outside the window, a handsome old head, bald and yellow, with a fringe of white hair.

'Would you please to give orders, sir, that a poor hermit is to be admitted, just come from the Desert, and who is instructed to beg for contributions towards rebuilding a holy house.'

This apparition, which suddenly reminded the lawyer of a prophecy uttered by the terrible Nourrisson, gave him a shock.

'Let in that old man,' said he to the servant.

'He will poison the place, sir,' replied the man. 'He has on a brown gown which he has never changed since he left Syria, and he has no shirt—'

'Show him in,' repeated the master.

The old man came in. Victorin's keen eye examined this so-called pilgrim hermit, and he saw a fine specimen of the

Neapolitan friars, whose frocks are akin to the rags of the *lazzaroni*, whose sandals are tatters of leather, as the friars are tatters of humanity. The get-up was so perfect that the lawyer, though still on his guard, was vexed with himself for having believed it to be one of Madame Nourrisson's tricks.

'How much do you want of me?'

'Whatever you feel that you ought to give me.'

Victorin took a five-franc piece from a little pile on his table, and handed it to the stranger.

'That is not much on account of fifty thousand francs,' said the pilgrim of the desert.

This speech removed all Victorin's doubts.

'And has Heaven kept its word?' he said, with a frown.

'The question is an offence, my son,' said the hermit. 'If you do not choose to pay till after the funeral, you are in your rights. I will return in a week's time.'

'The funeral!' cried the lawyer, starting up.

'The world moves on,' said the old man, as he withdrew, 'and the dead move quickly in Paris!'

When Hulot, who stood looking down, was about to reply, the stalwart old man had vanished.

'I don't understand one word of all this,' said Victorin to himself. 'But at the end of the week I will ask him again about my father, if we have not yet found him. Where does Madame Nourrisson – yes, that was her name – pick up such actors?'

On the following day, Doctor Bianchon allowed the Baroness to go down into the garden, after examining Lisbeth, who had been obliged to keep to her room for a month by a slight bronchial attack. The learned doctor, who dared not pronounce a definite opinion on Lisbeth's case till he had seen some decisive symptoms, went into the garden with Adeline to observe the effect of the fresh air on her nervous trembling after two months of seclusion. He was interested and allured by the hope of curing this nervous complaint. On seeing the great physician sitting with them and sparing them a few minutes, the Baroness and her family conversed with him on general subjects.

'Your life is a very full and a very sad one,' said Madame Hulot. 'I know what it is to spend one's days in seeing poverty and physical suffering.'

'I know, Madame,' replied the doctor, 'all the scenes of which charity compels you to be a spectator; but you will get used to it in time, as we all do. It is the law of existence. The confessor, the magistrate, the lawyer would find life unendurable if the spirit of the State did not assert itself above the feelings of the individual. Could we live at all but for that? Is not the soldier in time of war brought face to face with spectacles even more dreadful than those we see? And every soldier that has been under fire is kind-hearted. We medical men have the pleasure now and again of a successful cure, as you have that of saving a family from the horrors of hunger, depravity, or misery, and of restoring it to social respectability. But what comfort can the magistrate find, the police agent, or the attorney, who spend their lives in investigating the basest schemes of self-interest, the social monster whose only regret is when it fails, but on whom repentance never dawns?

'One-half of society spends its life in watching the other half. A very old friend of mine is an attorney, now retired, who told me that for fifteen years past notaries and lawyers have distrusted their clients quite as much as their adversaries. Your son is a pleader; has he never found himself compromised by the client for whom he held a brief?'

'Very often,' said Victorin, with a smile.

'And what is the cause of this deep-seated evil?' asked the Baroness.

'The decay of religion,' said Bianchon, 'and the preeminence of finance, which is simply solidified selfishness. Money used not to be everything; there were some kinds of superiority that ranked above it – nobility, genius, service done to the State. But nowadays the law takes wealth as the universal standard, and regards it as the measure of public capacity. Certain magistrates are ineligible to the Chamber; Jean-Jacques Rousseau would be ineligible! The perpetual subdivision of estates compels every man to take care of himself from the age of twenty.

'Well, then, between the necessity for making a fortune and the depravity of speculation there is no check or hindrance; for the religious sense is wholly lacking in France, in spite of the laudable endeavours of those who are working for a Catholic revival. And this is the opinion of every man who, like me, studies society at the core.'

'And you have few pleasures?' said Hortense.

'The true physician, Madame, is in love with his science,' replied the doctor. 'He is sustained by that passion as much as by the sense of his usefulness to society.

'At this very time you see me in a sort of scientific rapture, and many superficial judges would regard me as a man devoid of feeling. I have to announce a discovery to-morrow to the College of Medicine, for I am studying a disease that had disappeared – a mortal disease for which no cure is known in temperate climates, though it is curable in the West Indies – a malady known here in the Middle Ages. A noble fight is that of the physician against such a disease. For the last ten days I have thought of nothing but these cases – for there are two, a husband and wife. – Are they not connections of yours? For you, Madame, are surely Monsieur Crevel's daughter?' said he, addressing Célestine.

'What, is my father your patient?' asked Célestine. 'Living in the Rue Barbet-de-Jouy?'

'Precisely so,' said Bianchon.

'And the disease is inevitably fatal?' said Victorin in dismay.

'I will go to see him,' said Célestine, rising.

'I positively forbid it, Madame,' Bianchon quietly said. 'The disease is contagious.'

'But you go there, Monsieur,' replied the young woman. 'Do you think that a daughter's duty is less binding than a doctor's?'

'Madame, a physician knows how to protect himself against infection, and the rashness of your devotion proves to me that you would probably be less prudent than I.'

Célestine, however, got up and went to her room, where she dressed to go out.

'Monsieur,' said Victorin to Bianchon, 'have you any hope of saving Monsieur and Madame Crevel?'

'I hope, but I do not believe that I may,' said Bianchon. 'The case is to me quite inexplicable. The disease is peculiar to negroes and the American tribes, whose skin is differently constituted to that of the white races. Now I can trace no connection with the copper-coloured tribes, with negroes or half-castes, in Monsieur or Madame Crevel.

'And though it is a very interesting disease to us, it is a terrible thing for the sufferers. The poor woman, who is said to have been very pretty, is punished for her sins, for she is now squalidly hideous if she is still anything at all. She is losing her hair and teeth, her skin is like a leper's, she is a horror to herself; her hands are horrible, covered with greenish pustules, her nails are loose, and the flesh is eaten away by the poisoned humours.'

'And the cause of such a disease?' asked the lawyer.

'Oh!' said the doctor, 'the cause lies in a form of rapid blood-poisoning; it degenerates with terrific rapidity. I hope to act on the blood; I am having it analysed; and I am now going home to ascertain the result of the labours of my friend Professor Duval, the famous chemist, with a view to trying one of those desperate measures by which we sometimes attempt to defeat death.'

'The hand of God is there!' said Adeline, in a voice husky with emotion. 'Though that woman has brought sorrows on me which have led me in moments of madness to invoke the vengeance of Heaven, I hope – God knows I hope – you may succeed, doctor.'

Victorin felt dizzy. He looked at his mother, his sister, and the physician by turns, quaking lest they should read his thoughts. He felt himself a murderer.

Hortense, for her part, thought God was just.

Célestine came back to beg her husband to accompany her.

'If you insist on going, Madame, and you too, Monsieur, keep at least a foot between you and the bed of the sufferer, that is the chief precaution. Neither you nor your wife must dream of kissing the dying man. And, indeed, you ought to go with your wife, Monsieur Hulot, to hinder her from disobeying my injunctions.'

Adeline and Hortense, when they were left alone, went to sit with Lisbeth. Hortense had such a virulent hatred of Valérie that she could not contain the expression of it.

'Cousin Lisbeth,' she exclaimed, 'my mother and I are avenged! That venomous snake is herself bitten – she is rotting in her bed!'

'Hortense, at this moment you are not a Christian. You ought to pray to God to vouchsafe repentance to this wretched woman.'

'What are you talking about?' said Bette, rising from her couch. 'Are you speaking of Valérie?'

'Yes,' replied Adeline; 'she is past hope – dying of some horrible disease of which the mere description makes one shudder—'

Lisbeth's teeth chattered, a cold sweat broke out all over her; the violence of the shock showed how passionate her attachment to Valérie had been.

'I must go there,' said she.

'But the doctor forbids your going out.'

'I do not care – I must go! – Poor Crevel! what a state he must be in; for he loves that woman.'

'He is dying too,' replied Countess Steinbock. 'Ah! all our enemies are in the devil's clutches—'

'In God's hands, my child—'

Lisbeth dressed in the famous yellow Indian shawl and her black velvet bonnet, and put on her boots; in spite of her relations' remonstrances, she set out as if driven by some irresistible power.

She arrived in the Rue Barbet a few minutes after Monsieur and Madame Hulot, and found seven physicians there, brought by Bianchon to study this unique case; he had just joined them. The physicians, assembled in the drawing-room, were discussing the disease; now one and now another went into Valérie's room or Crevel's to take a note, and returned with an opinion based on this rapid study.

These princes of science were divided in their opinions. One, who stood alone in his views, considered it a case of poisoning, of private revenge, and denied its identity with the disease known in the Middle Ages. Three others regarded it as a specific deterioration of the blood and the humours. The rest, agreeing with Bianchon, maintained that the blood was poisoned by some hitherto unknown morbid infection. Bianchon produced Professor Duval's analysis of the blood. The remedies to be applied, though absolutely empirical and without hope, depended on the verdict in this medical dilemma.

Lisbeth stood as if petrified three yards away from the bed where Valérie lay dying, as she saw a priest from Saint-Thomas d'Aquin standing by her friend's pillow, and a sister of charity in attendance. Religion could find a soul to save in a mass of rottenness which, of the five senses of man, had now only that of sight. The sister of charity who alone had been found to nurse Valérie stood apart. Thus the Catholic religion, that divine institution, always actuated by the spirit of self-sacrifice, under its twofold aspect of the Spirit and the Flesh, was tending this horrible and atrocious creature, soothing her death-bed by its infinite benevolence and inexhaustible stores of mercy.

The servants, in horror, refused to go into the room of either their master or mistress; they thought only of themselves, and judged their betters as righteously stricken. The smell was so foul that in spite of open windows and strong perfumes, no one could remain long in Valérie's room. Religion alone kept guard there.

How could a woman so clever as Valérie fail to ask herself to what end these two representatives of the Church remained with her? The dying woman had listened to the words of the priest. Repentance had risen on her darkened soul as the devouring malady had consumed her beauty. The fragile Valérie had been less able to resist the inroads of the disease than Crevel; she would be the first to succumb, and, indeed, had been the first attacked.

'If I had not been ill myself, I would have come to nurse you,' said Lisbeth at last, after a glance at her friend's sunken eyes. 'I have kept my room this fortnight or three weeks; but when I heard of your state from the doctor, I came at once.'

'Poor Lisbeth, you at least love me still, I see!' said Valérie. 'Listen. I have only a day or two left to think, for I cannot say to live. You see, there is nothing left of me – I am a heap of mud! They will not let me see myself in a glass. – Well, it is no more than I deserve. Oh, if I might only win mercy, I would gladly undo all the mischief I have done.'

'Oh!' said Lisbeth, 'if you can talk like that, you are indeed a dead woman.'

'Do not hinder this woman's repentance, leave her in her Christian mind,' said the priest.

'There is nothing left!' said Lisbeth in consternation. 'I cannot recognise her eyes or her mouth! Not a feature of her is there! And her wit has deserted her! Oh, it is awful!'

'You don't know,' said Valérie, 'what death is; what it is to be obliged to think of the morrow of your last day on earth, and of what is to be found in the grave. – Worms for the body – and for the soul, what? – Lisbeth, I know there is another life! And I am given over to terrors which prevent my feeling the pangs of my decomposing body. – I, who could laugh at a saint, and say to Crevel that the vengeance of God took every form of disaster. – Well, I was a true prophet. – Do not trifle with sacred things, Lisbeth; if you love me, repent as I do.'

'I!' said Lisbeth. 'I see vengeance wherever I turn in nature; insects even die to satisfy the craving for revenge when they are attacked. And do not these gentlemen tell us' – and she looked at the priest – 'that God is revenged, and that His vengeance lasts through all eternity?'

The priest looked mildly at Lisbeth and said –

'You, Madame, are an atheist!'

'But look what I have come to,' said Valérie.

'And where did you get this gangrene?' asked the old maid, unmoved from her peasant incredulity.

'I had a letter from Henri which leaves me in no doubt as to my fate. He has murdered me. And – just when I meant to live honestly – to die an object of disgust!

'Lisbeth, give up all notions of revenge. Be kind to that family to whom I have left by my will everything I can dispose of. Go, child, though you are the only creature who, at this hour, does not avoid me with horror – go, I beseech you, and leave me. – I have only time to make my peace with God!'

'She is wandering in her wits,' said Lisbeth to herself, as she left the room.

The strongest affection known, that of a woman for a woman, had not such heroic constancy as the Church. Lisbeth, stifled by the miasma, went away. She found the physicians still in consultation. But Bianchon's opinion carried the day, and the only question now was how to try the remedies.

'At any rate, we shall have a splendid *post-mortem*,' said one of his opponents, 'and there will be two cases to enable us to make comparisons.'

Lisbeth came in again with Bianchon, who went up to the sick woman without seeming aware of the malodorous atmosphere.

'Madame,' said he, 'we intend to try a powerful remedy which may save you—'

'And if you save my life,' said she, 'shall I be as good-looking as ever?'

'Possibly,' said the judicious physician.

'I know your *possibly*,' said Valérie. 'I shall look like a woman who has fallen into the fire! No, leave me to the Church. I can please no one now but God. I will try to be reconciled to Him, and that will be my last flirtation; yes, I must try to come round God!'

'That is my poor Valérie's last jest; that is all herself!' said Lisbeth in tears.

Lisbeth thought it her duty to go into Crevel's room, where she found Victorin and his wife sitting about a yard away from the stricken man's bed.

'Lisbeth,' said he, 'they will not tell me what state my wife is in; you have just seen her – how is she?'

'She is better; she says she is saved,' replied Lisbeth, allowing herself this play on the word to soothe Crevel's mind.

'That is well,' said the Mayor. 'I feared lest I had been the cause of her illness. A man is not a traveller in perfumery for nothing; I had blamed myself. – If I should lose her, what would become of me? On my honour, my children, I worship that woman.'

He sat up in bed and tried to assume his favourite position.

'Oh, papa!' cried Célestine, 'if only you could be well again, I would make friends with my stepmother – I make a vow!'

'Poor little Célestine!' said Crevel, 'come and kiss me.'

Victorin held back his wife, who was rushing forward.

'You do not know, perhaps,' said the lawyer gently, 'that your disease is contagious, Monsieur.'

'To be sure,' replied Crevel. 'And the doctors are quite proud of having rediscovered in me some long lost plague of the Middle Ages, which the Faculty has had cried like lost property – it is very funny!'

'Papa,' said Célestine, 'be brave, and you will get the better of this disease.'

'Be quite easy, my children; Death thinks twice of it before carrying off a Mayor of Paris,' said he, with monstrous composure. 'And if, after all, my district is so unfortunate as to lose a man it has twice honoured with its suffrages – you see, what a flow of words I have! – Well, I shall know how to pack up and go. I have been a commercial traveller; I am experienced in such matters. Ah! my children, I am a man of strong mind.'

'Papa, promise me to admit the Church—'

'Never,' replied Crevel. 'What is to be said? I drank the milk of Revolution; I have not Baron Holbach's wit, but I have his strength of mind. I am more *Régence* than ever, more Musketeer, Abbé Dubois, and Maréchal de Richelieu! By the Holy Poker! – My wife, who is wandering in her head, has just sent me a man in a gown – to me! the admirer of Béranger, the friend of Lisette, the son of Voltaire and Rousseau. – The doctor, to feel my pulse, as it were, and see if sickness had subdued me – "You saw Monsieur l'Abbé?" said he. – Well, I imitated the great Montesquieu. Yes, I looked at the doctor – see, like this,' and he turned to show three-quarters face, like his portrait, and extended his hand authoritatively – 'and I said –

> "The slave was here,
> He showed his order, but he nothing gained."

'*His order* is a pretty jest, showing that even in death Monsieur le Président de Montesquieu preserved his elegant wit, for they had sent him a Jesuit. I admire that passage – I cannot say of his life, but of his death – the passage – another joke! The passage from life to death – the Passage Montesquieu!'

Victorin gazed sadly at his father-in-law, wondering whether folly and vanity were not forces on a par with true greatness of soul. The causes that act on the springs of the soul seem to be quite independent of the results. Can it be that the fortitude which upholds a great criminal is the same as that with which a Champcenetz so proudly walks to the scaffold?

By the end of the week Madame Crevel was buried, after dreadful sufferings; and Crevel followed her within two days. Thus the marriage-contract was annulled. Crevel was heir to Valérie.

On the very day after the funeral, the friar called again on the lawyer, who received him in perfect silence. The monk held out his hand without a word, and without a word Victorin Hulot gave him eighty thousand-franc notes, taken from a sum of money found in Crevel's desk.

Young Madame Hulot inherited the estate of Presles and thirty thousand francs a year.

Madame Crevel had bequeathed a sum of three hundred thousand francs to Baron Hulot. Her scrofulous boy Stanislas was to inherit, at his majority, the Hôtel Crevel and eighty thousand francs a year.

Among the many noble associations founded in Paris by Catholic charity, there is one, originated by Madame de la Chanterie, for promoting civil and religious marriages between persons who have formed a voluntary but illicit union. Legislators, who draw large revenues from the registration fees, and the Bourgeois dynasty, which benefits by the notary's profits, affect to overlook the fact that three-fourths of the poorer class cannot afford fifteen francs for the marriage-contract. In this the corporation of notaries is inferior to that of the pleaders in Paris. The pleaders, a sufficiently vilified body, gratuitously defend the cases of the indigent, while the notaries have not as yet agreed to charge nothing for the marriage-contract of the poor. As to the revenue collectors, the whole machinery of Government would have to be dislocated to induce the authorities to relax their demands. The registrar's office is deaf and dumb.

Then the Church, too, receives a duty on marriages. In France the Church depends largely on such revenues; even in the House of God it traffics in chairs and kneeling stools in a way that offends foreigners; though it cannot have forgotten the anger of the Saviour who drove the money-changers out of the Temple. If the Church is so loth to relinquish its dues, it must be supposed that these dues, known as Vestry dues, are one of its sources of maintenance, and then the fault of the Church is the fault of the State.

The co-operation of these conditions, at a time when charity is too greatly concerned with the negroes and the petty offenders discharged from prison to trouble itself about honest folks in difficulties, results in the existence of a number of decent couples who have never been legally married for lack of thirty francs, the lowest figure for which the Notary, the Registrar, the Mayor, and the Church will unite two citizens of Paris. Madame de la Chanterie's fund, founded to restore poor households to their religious and legal status, hunts up such couples, and with all the more success because it helps them in their poverty before attacking their unlawful union.

As soon as Madame Hulot had recovered, she returned to her occupations. And then it was that the admirable Madame de la Chanterie came to beg that Adeline would add the legalisation of these voluntary unions to the other good works of which she was the instrument.

One of the Baroness's first efforts in this cause was made in the ominous-looking district, formerly known as la Petite Pologne – Little Poland – bounded by the Rue du Rocher, Rue de la Pépinière, and Rue de Miroménil. There exists there a sort of offshoot of the Faubourg Saint-Marceau. To give an idea of this part of the town, it is enough to say that the landlords of some of the houses tenanted by working men without work, by dangerous characters, and by the very poor employed in unhealthy toil, dare not demand their rents, and can find no bailiffs bold enough to evict insolvent lodgers. At the present time speculating builders, who are fast changing the aspect of this corner of Paris, and covering the waste ground lying between the Rue d'Amsterdam and the Rue Faubourg-du-Roule, will no doubt alter the character of the inhabitants; for the trowel is a more civilising agent than is generally supposed. By erecting substantial and handsome houses, with porters at the doors, by bordering the streets with footwalks and shops, speculation, while raising the rents, disperses the squalid class, families bereft of furniture, and lodgers that cannot pay. And so these districts are cleared of such objectionable residents, and the dens vanish into which the police never venture but under the sanction of the law.

In June 1844, the purlieus of the Place de Laborde were still far from inviting. The genteel pedestrian, who, by chance, should turn out of the Rue de la Pépinière into one of these dreadful side-streets, would have been dismayed to see how vile a bohemia dwelt cheek by jowl with the aristocracy. In such places as these, haunted by ignorant poverty and misery driven to bay, flourish the last public letter-writers who are to be found in Paris. Wherever you see the two words 'Écrivain Public' written in a fine copy hand on a sheet of letter-paper stuck to the window pane of some low entresol or mud-

splashed ground-floor room, you may safely conclude that the
neighbourhood is the lurking place of many unlettered folks,
and of much vice and crime, the outcome of misery; for
ignorance is the mother of all sorts of crime. A crime is, in
the first instance, a defect of reasoning powers.

While the Baroness had been ill, this quarter, to which she
was a minor Providence, had seen the advent of a public
writer who settled in the Passage du Soleil – Sun Alley – a
spot of which the name is one of the antitheses dear to the
Parisian, for the passage is especially dark. This writer, supposed to be a German, was named Vyder, and he lived on
matrimonial terms with a young creature of whom he was so
jealous that he never allowed her to go anywhere excepting to
some honest stove and flue-fitters, in the Rue Saint-Lazare,
Italians, as such fitters always are, but long since established in
Paris. These people had been saved from a bankruptcy, which
would have reduced them to misery, by the Baroness, acting in
behalf of Madame de la Chanterie. In a few months comfort
had taken the place of poverty, and Religion had found a
home in hearts which once had cursed Heaven with the energy
peculiar to Italian stove-fitters. So one of Madame Hulot's first
visits was to this family.

She was pleased at the scene that presented itself to her eyes
at the back of the house where these worthy folks lived in the
Rue Saint-Lazare, not far from the Rue du Rocher. High
above the stores and workshops, now well filled, where toiled
a swarm of apprentices and workmen – all Italians from the
valley of Domo d'Ossola – the master's family occupied a set
of rooms, which hard work had blessed with abundance. The
Baroness was hailed like the Virgin Mary in person.

After a quarter of an hour's questioning, Adeline, having to
wait for the father to inquire how his business was prospering,
pursued her saintly calling as a spy by asking whether they
knew of any families needing help.

'Ah! dear lady, you who could save the damned from hell!'
said the Italian wife, 'there is a girl quite near here to be saved
from perdition.'

'A girl well known to you?' asked the Baroness.

'She is the granddaughter of a master my husband formerly worked for, who came to France in 1798, after the Revolution, by name Judici. Old Judici, in Napoleon's time, was one of the principal stove-fitters in Paris; he died in 1819, leaving his son a fine fortune. But the younger Judici wasted all his money on bad women; till, at last, he married one who was sharper than the rest, and she had this poor little girl, who is just turned fifteen.'

'And what is wrong with her?' asked Adeline, struck by the resemblance between this Judici and her husband.

'Well, Madame, this child, named Atala, ran away from her father, and came to live close by here with an old German of eighty at least, named Vyder, who does odd jobs for people who cannot read and write. Now, if this old sinner, who bought the child of her mother, they say, for fifteen hundred francs, would but marry her, as he certainly has not long to live, and as he is said to have some few thousands of francs a year – well, the poor thing, who is a sweet little angel, would be out of mischief, and above want, which must be the ruin of her.'

'Thank you very much for the information. I may do some good, but I must act with caution. – Who is the old man?'

'Oh! Madame, he is a good old fellow; he makes the child very happy, and he has some sense too, for he left the part of town where the Judicis live, as I believe, to snatch the child from her mother's clutches. The mother was jealous of her, and I dare say she thought she could make money out of her beauty and make a *Mademoiselle* of the girl.

'Atala remembered us, and advised her gentleman to settle near us; and as the good man sees how decent we are, he allows her to come here. But get them married, Madame, and you will do an action worthy of you. Once married, the child will be independent and free from her mother, who keeps an eye on her, and who, if she could make money by her, would like to see her on the stage, or successful in the wicked life she meant her to lead.'

'Why doesn't the old man marry her?'

'There was no necessity for it, you see,' said the Italian. 'And though old Vyder is not a bad old fellow, I fancy he is sharp enough to wish to remain the master, while if he once got married – why, the poor man is afraid of the stone that hangs round every old man's neck.'

'Could you send for the girl to come here?' said Madame Hulot. 'I should see her quietly, and find out what could be done—'

The stove-fitter's wife signed to her eldest girl, who ran off. Ten minutes later she returned, leading by the hand a child of fifteen and a half, a beauty of the Italian type. Mademoiselle Judici inherited from her father that ivory skin which, rather yellow by day, is by artificial light of lily-whiteness; eyes of Oriental beauty, form, and brilliancy, close curling lashes like black feathers, hair of ebony hue, and that native dignity of the Lombard race which makes the foreigner, as he walks through Milan on a Sunday, fancy that every porter's daughter is a princess.

Atala, told by the stove-fitter's daughter that she was to meet the great lady of whom she had heard so much, had hastily dressed in a black silk gown, a smart little cape, and neat boots. A cap with a cherry-coloured bow added to the brilliant effect of her colouring. The child stood in an attitude of artless curiosity, studying the Baroness out of the corner of her eye, for her palsied trembling puzzled her greatly.

Adeline sighed deeply as she saw this jewel of womanhood in the mire of prostitution, and determined to rescue her to virtue.

'What is your name, my dear?'

'Atala, Madame.'

'And can you read and write?'

'No, Madame; but that does not matter, as Monsieur can.'

'Did your parents ever take you to church? Have you been to your first Communion? Do you know your Catechism?'

'Madame, papa wanted to make me do something of the kind you speak of, but mamma would not have it—'

'Your mother?' exclaimed the Baroness. 'Is she bad to you, then?'

'She was always beating me. I don't know why, but I was always being quarrelled over by my father and mother—'

'Did you never hear of God?' cried the Baroness.

The girl looked up wide-eyed.

'Oh yes, papa and mamma often said "Good God," and "In God's name," and "God's thunder,"' said she, with perfect simplicity.

'Then you never saw a church? Did you never think of going into one?'

'A church? – Notre-Dame, the Panthéon? – I have seen them from a distance, when papa took me into town; but that was not very often. There are no churches like those in the Faubourg.'

'Which Faubourg did you live in?'

'In the Faubourg.'

'Yes, but which?'

'In the Rue de Charonne, Madame.'

The inhabitants of the Faubourg Saint-Antoine never call that notorious district other than *the* Faubourg. To them it is the one and only Faubourg; and manufacturers generally understand the words as meaning the Faubourg Saint-Antoine.

'Did no one ever tell you what was right or wrong?'

'Mamma used to beat me when I did not do what pleased her.'

'But did you not know that it was very wicked to run away from your father and mother to go to live with an old man?'

Atala Judici gazed at the Baroness with a haughty stare, but made no reply.

'She is a perfect little savage,' murmured Adeline.

'There are a great many like her in the Faubourg, Madame,' said the stove-fitter's wife.

'But she knows nothing – not even what is wrong. Good Heavens! – Why do you not answer me?' said Madame Hulot, putting out her hand to take Atala's.

Atala indignantly withdrew a step.

'You are an old fool!' said she. 'Why, my father and mother had had nothing to eat for a week. My mother wanted me to do much worse than that, I think, for my father thrashed her and called her a thief! However, Monsieur Vyder paid all their debts, and gave them some money – oh, a bagful! And he brought me away, and poor papa was crying. But we had to part! – Was it wicked?' she asked.

'And are you very fond of Monsieur Vyder?'

'Fond of him?' said she. 'I should think so! He tells me beautiful stories, Madame, every evening; and he has given me nice gowns, and linen, and a shawl. Why, I am figged out like a princess, and I never wear sabots now. And then, I have not known what it is to be hungry these two months past. And I don't live on potatoes now. He brings me bonbons and burnt almonds, and chocolate almonds. – Aren't they good? – I do anything he pleases for a bag of chocolate. – Then my old Daddy is very kind; he takes such care of me, and is so nice; I know now what my mother ought to have been. – He is going to get an old woman to help me, for he doesn't like me to dirty my hands with cooking. For the last month, too, he has been making a little money, and he gives me three francs every evening that I put into a money-box. Only he will never let me go out except to come here – and he calls me his little kitten! Mamma never called me anything but bad names – and thief, and vermin!'

'Well, then, my child, why should not Daddy Vyder be your husband?'

'But he is, Madame,' said the girl, looking at Adeline with calm pride, without a blush, her brow smooth, her eyes steady. 'He told me I was his little wife; but it is a horrid bore to be a man's wife – if it were not for the burnt almonds!'

'Good Heavens!' said the Baroness to herself, 'what monster can have had the heart to betray such perfect, such holy innocence? To restore this child to the ways of virtue would surely atone for many sins. – I knew what I was doing,' thought she, remembering the scene with Crevel. 'But she – she knows nothing.'

'Do you know Monsieur Samanon?' asked Atala, with an insinuating look.

'No, my child; but why do you ask?'

'Really and truly?' said the artless girl.

'You have nothing to fear from this lady,' said the Italian woman. 'She is an angel.'

'It is because my good old boy is afraid of being caught by Samanon. He is hiding, and I wish he could be free—'

'Why?'

'Oh! then he would take me to Bobino, perhaps to the Ambigu.'

'What a delightful creature!' said the Baroness, kissing the girl.

'Are you rich?' asked Atala, who was fingering the Baroness's lace ruffles.

'Yes, and No,' replied Madame Hulot. 'I am rich for dear little girls like you when they are willing to be taught their duties as Christians by a priest, and to walk in the right way.'

'What way is that?' said Atala; 'I walk on my two feet.'

'The way of virtue.'

Atala looked at the Baroness with a crafty smile.

'Look at Madame,' said the Baroness, pointing to the stove-fitter's wife, 'she has been quite happy because she was received into the bosom of the Church. You married like the beasts that perish.'

'I?' said Atala. 'Why, if you will give me as much as Daddy Vyder gives me, I shall be quite happy unmarried again. It is a grind. – Do you know what it is to—?'

'But when once you are united to a man as you are,' the Baroness put in, 'virtue requires you to remain faithful to him.'

'Till he dies,' said Atala, with a knowing flash. 'I shall not have to wait long. If you only knew how Daddy Vyder coughs and blows. – Poof, poof,' and she imitated the old man.

'Virtue and morality require that the Church, representing God, and the Mayor, representing the law, should consecrate your marriage,' Madame Hulot went on. 'Look at Madame; she is legally married—'

'Will it make it more amusing?' asked the girl.

'You will be happier,' said the Baroness, 'for no one then could blame you. You would satisfy God! Ask her if she was married without the sacrament of marriage!'

Atala looked at the Italian.

'How is she any better than I am?' she asked. 'I am prettier than she is.'

'Yes, but I am an honest woman,' said the wife, 'and you may be called by a bad name.'

'How can you expect God to protect you if you trample every law, human and divine, under foot?' said the Baroness. 'Don't you know that God has Paradise in store for those who obey the injunctions of His Church?'

'What is there in Paradise? Are there playhouses?'

'Paradise!' said Adeline, 'is every joy you can conceive of. It is full of angels with white wings. You see God in all His glory, you share His power, you are happy for every minute of eternity!'

Atala listened to the lady as she might have listened to music; but Adeline, seeing that she was incapable of understanding her, thought she had better take another line of action and speak to the old man.

'Go home, then, my child, and I will go to see Monsieur Vyder. Is he a Frenchman?'

'He is an Alsatian, Madame. But he will be quite rich soon. If you would pay what he owes to that vile Samanon, he would give you back your money, for in a few months he will be getting six thousand francs a year, he says, and we are to go to live in the country a long way off, in the Vosges.'

At the word *Vosges* the Baroness sat lost in reverie. It called up the vision of her native village. She was roused from her melancholy meditation by the entrance of the stove-fitter, who came to assure her of his prosperity.

'In a year's time, Madame, I can repay the money you lent us, for it is God's money, the money of the poor and wretched. If ever I make a fortune, come to me for what you want, and I will render through you the help to others which you first brought us.'

'Just now,' said Madame Hulot, 'I do not need your money, but I ask your assistance in a good work. I have just seen that little Judici, who is living with an old man, and I mean to see them regularly and legally married.'

'Ah! old Vyder; he is a very worthy old fellow, with plenty of good sense. The poor old man has already made friends in the neighbourhood, though he has been here but two months. He keeps my accounts for me. He is, I believe, a brave Colonel who served the Emperor well. And how he adores Napoleon! – He has some orders, but he never wears them. He is waiting till he is straight again, for he is in debt, poor old boy! In fact, I believe he is hiding, threatened by the law—'

'Tell him that I will pay his debts if he will marry the child.'

'Oh, that will soon be settled. – Suppose you were to see him, Madame; it is not two steps away, in the Passage du Soleil.'

So the lady and the stove-fitter went out.

'This way, Madame,' said the man, turning down the Rue de la Pépinière.

The alley runs, in fact, from the bottom of this street through to the Rue du Rocher. Halfway down this passage, recently opened through, where the shops let at a very low rent, the Baroness saw on a window, screened up to a height with a green gauze curtain, which excluded the prying eyes of the passer-by, the words –

'ÉCRIVAIN PUBLIC'; and on the door the announcement –

BUSINESS TRANSACTED.

Petitions Drawn Up, Accounts Audited, Etc.

With Secrecy and Dispatch.

The shop was like one of the little offices where travellers by omnibus await the vehicles to take them on to their destination. A private staircase led up, no doubt, to the living rooms on the entresol which were let with the shop. Madame Hulot saw a dirty writing-table of some light wood, some letter-boxes, and a wretched second-hand chair. A cap with a peak and a greasy green shade for the eyes suggested either precautions for disguise, or weak eyes, which was not unlikely in an old man.

'He is upstairs,' said the stove-fitter. 'I will go up and tell him to come down.'

Adeline lowered her veil and took a seat. A heavy step made the narrow stairs creak, and Adeline could not restrain a piercing cry when she saw her husband, Baron Hulot, in a grey knitted jersey, old grey flannel trousers, and slippers.

'What is your business, Madame?' said Hulot, with a flourish.

She rose, seized Hulot by the arm, and said in a voice hoarse with emotion –

'At last – I have found you!'

'Adeline!' exclaimed the Baron in bewilderment, and he locked the shop door. 'Joseph, go out the back way,' he added to the stove-fitter.

'My dear!' she said, forgetting everything in her excessive joy, 'you can come home to us all; we are rich. Your son draws a hundred and sixty thousand francs a year! Your pension is released; there are fifteen thousand francs of arrears you can get on showing that you are alive. Valérie is dead, and left you three hundred thousand francs.

'Your name is quite forgotten by this time; you may re-appear in the world, and you will find a fortune awaiting you at your son's house. Come; our happiness will be complete. For nearly three years have I been seeking you, and I felt so sure of finding you that a room is ready waiting for you. Oh! come away from this, come away from the dreadful state I see you in!'

'I am very willing,' said the bewildered Baron, 'but can I take the girl?'

'Hector, give her up! Do that much for your Adeline, who has never before asked you to make the smallest sacrifice. I promise you I will give the child a marriage portion; I will see that she marries well, and has some education. Let it be said of one of the women who have given you happiness that she too is happy; and do not relapse into vice, into the mire.'

'So it was you,' said the Baron, with a smile, 'who wanted to see me married? – Wait a few minutes,' he added; 'I will go upstairs and dress; I have some decent clothes in a trunk.'

Adeline, left alone, and looking round the squalid shop, melted into tears.

'He has been living here, and we rolling in wealth!' said she to herself. 'Poor man, he has indeed been punished – he who was elegance itself.'

The stove-fitter returned to make his bow to his benefactress, and she desired him to fetch a coach. When he came back, she begged him to give little Atala Judici a home, and to take her away at once.

'And tell her that if she will place herself under the guidance of Monsieur the Curé of the Madeleine, on the day when she attends her first Communion I will give her thirty thousand francs and find her a good husband, some worthy young man.'

'My eldest son, then, Madame! He is two-and-twenty, and he worships the child.'

The Baron now came down; there were tears in his eyes.

'You are forcing me to desert the only creature who has ever begun to love me at all as you do!' said he in a whisper to his wife. 'She is crying bitterly, and I cannot abandon her so—'

'Be quite easy, Hector. She will find a home with honest people, and I will answer for her conduct.'

'Well, then, I can go with you,' said the Baron, escorting his wife to the cab.

Hector, the Baron d'Ervy once more, had put on a blue coat and trousers, a white waistcoat, a black stock, and gloves. When the Baroness had taken her seat in the vehicle, Atala slipped in like an eel.

'Oh, Madame,' she said, 'let me go with you. I will be so good, so obedient; I will do whatever you wish; but do not part me from my Daddy Vyder, my kind Daddy who gives me such nice things. I shall be beaten—'

'Come, come, Atala,' said the Baron, 'this lady is my wife – we must part—'

'She! As old as that! and shaking like a leaf!' said the child. 'Look at her head!' and she laughingly mimicked the Baroness's palsy.

The stove-fitter, who had run after the girl, came to the carriage door.

'Take her away!' said Adeline. The man put his arms round Atala and fairly carried her off.

'Thanks for such a sacrifice, my dearest,' said Adeline, taking the Baron's hand and clutching it with delirious joy. 'How much you are altered! you must have suffered so much! What a surprise for Hortense and for your son!'

Adeline talked as lovers talk who meet after a long absence, of a hundred things at once.

In ten minutes the Baron and his wife reached the Rue Louis-le-Grand, and there Adeline found this note awaiting her: –

'MADAME LA BARONNE, –

'Monsieur le Baron Hulot d'Ervy lived for one month in the Rue de Charonne under the name of Thorec, an anagram of Hector. He now is in the Passage du Soleil by the name of Vyder. He says he is an Alsatian, and does writing, and he lives with a girl named Atala Judici. Be very cautious, Madame, for search is on foot; the Baron is wanted, on what score I know not.

'The actress has kept her word, and remains, as ever,
'Madame la Baronne, your humble servant,'

'J. M.'

The Baron's return was hailed with such joy as reconciled him to domestic life. He forgot little Atala Judici, for excesses of profligacy had reduced him to the volatility of feeling that is characteristic of childhood. But the happiness of the family was dashed by the change that had come over him. He had been still hale when he had gone away from his home; he had come back almost a hundred, broken, bent, and his expression even debased.

A splendid dinner, improvised by Célestine, reminded the old man of the singer's banquets; he was dazzled by the splendour of his home.

'A feast in honour of the return of the prodigal father?' said he in a murmur to Adeline.

'Hush!' said she, 'all is forgotten.'

'And Lisbeth?' he asked, not seeing the old maid.

'I am sorry to say she is in bed,' replied Hortense. 'She can never get up, and we shall have the grief of losing her ere long. She hopes to see you after dinner.'

At daybreak next morning Victorin Hulot was informed by the porter's wife that soldiers of the municipal guard were posted all round the premises; the police demanded Baron Hulot. The bailiff, who had followed the woman, laid a summons in due form before the lawyer, and asked him whether he meant to pay his father's debts. The claim was for ten thousand francs at the suit of an usurer named Samanon, who had probably lent the Baron two or three thousand at most. Victorin desired the bailiff to dismiss his men, and paid.

'But is it the last?' he anxiously wondered.

Lisbeth, miserable already at seeing the family so prosperous, could not survive this happy event. She grew so rapidly worse that Bianchon gave her but a week to live, conquered at last in the long struggle in which she had scored so many victories.

She kept the secret of her hatred even through a painful death from pulmonary consumption. And, indeed, she had the supreme satisfaction of seeing Adeline, Hortense, Hulot, Victorin, Steinbock, Célestine, and their children standing in tears round her bed and mourning for her as the angel of the family.

Baron Hulot, enjoying a course of solid food such as he had not known for nearly three years, recovered flesh and strength, and was almost himself again. This improvement was such a

joy to Adeline that her nervous trembling perceptibly diminished.

'She will be happy after all,' said Lisbeth to herself on the
day before she died, as she saw the veneration with which
the Baron regarded his wife, of whose sufferings he had heard
from Hortense and Victorin.

And vindictiveness hastened Cousin Bette's end. The family
followed her, weeping, to the grave.

The Baron and Baroness, having reached the age which
looks for perfect rest, gave up the handsome rooms on the
first floor to the Count and Countess Steinbock, and took
those above. The Baron by his son's exertions found an
official position in the management of a railroad, in 1845,
with a salary of six thousand francs, which, added to the six
thousand of his pension and the money left to him by
Madame Crevel, secured him an income of twenty-four thousand francs. Hortense having enjoyed her independent income
during the three years of separation from Wenceslas, Victorin
now invested the two hundred thousand francs he had in
trust, in his sister's name, and he allowed her twelve thousand
francs.

Wenceslas, as the husband of a rich woman, was not
unfaithful, but he was an idler; he could not make up his
mind to begin any work, however trifling. Once more he
became the artist *in partibus*; he was popular in society, and
consulted by amateurs; in short, he became a critic, like all the
feeble folk who fall below their promise.

Thus each household, though living as one family, had its
own fortune. The Baroness, taught by bitter experience, left
the management of matters to her son, and the Baron was
thus reduced to his salary, in the hope that the smallness of his
income would prevent his relapsing into mischief. And by
some singular good fortune, on which neither the mother
nor the son had reckoned, Hulot seemed to have forsworn
the fair sex. His subdued behaviour, ascribed to the course of
nature, so completely reassured the family, that they enjoyed
to the full his recovered amiability and delightful qualities. He

was unfailingly attentive to his wife and children, escorted them to the play, reappeared in society, and did the honours of his son's house with exquisite grace. In short, this reclaimed prodigal was the joy of his family.

He was a most agreeable old man, a ruin, but full of wit, having retained no more of his vice than made it an added social grace.

Of course, everybody was quite satisfied and easy. The young people and the Baroness lauded the model father to the skies, forgetting the death of the two uncles. Life cannot go on without much forgetting!

Madame Victorin, who managed this enormous household with great skill, due, no doubt, to Lisbeth's training, had found it necessary to have a man-cook. This again necessitated a kitchen-maid. Kitchen-maids are in these days ambitious creatures, eager to detect the *chef's* secrets, and to become cooks as soon as they have learnt to stir a sauce. Consequently, the kitchen-maid is liable to frequent change.

At the beginning of 1845 Célestine engaged as kitchen-maid a sturdy Normandy peasant come from Isigny – short-waisted, with strong red arms, a common face, as dull as an 'occasional piece' at the play, and hardly to be persuaded out of wearing the classical linen cap peculiar to the women of Lower Normandy. This girl, as buxom as a wet-nurse, looked as if she would burst the blue cotton check in which she clothed her person. Her florid face might have been hewn out of stone, so hard were its tawny outlines.

Of course no attention was paid to the advent in the house of this girl, whose name was Agathe – an ordinary, wide-awake specimen, such as is daily imported from the provinces. Agathe had no attractions for the cook, her tongue was too rough, for she had served in a suburban inn, waiting on carters; and instead of making a conquest of her chief and winning from him the secrets of the high art of the kitchen, she was the object of his great contempt. The *chef's* attentions were, in fact, devoted to Louise, the Countess Steinbock's maid. The country girl, thinking herself ill-used, complained bitterly that she was always sent out of the way on some pretext when the *chef* was finishing a dish or putting the crowning touch to a sauce.

'I am out of luck,' said she, 'and I shall go to another place.'

And yet she stayed, though she had twice given notice to quit.

One night, Adeline, roused by some unusual noise, did not see Hector in the bed he occupied near hers; for they slept side by side in two beds, as beseemed an old couple. She lay awake an hour, but he did not return. Seized with a panic, fancying some tragic end had overtaken him – an apoplectic attack, perhaps – she went upstairs to the floor occupied by the servants, and there was attracted to the room where Agathe slept, partly by seeing a light below the door, and partly by the murmur of voices. She stood still in dismay on recognising the voice of her husband, who, a victim to Agathe's charms, to vanquish this strapping wench's not disinterested resistance, went to the length of saying –

'My wife has not long to live, and if you like you may be a Baroness.'

Adeline gave a cry, dropped her candlestick, and fled.

Three days later the Baroness, who had received the last sacraments, was dying, surrounded by her weeping family.

Just before she died, she took her husband's hand and pressed it, murmuring in his ear –

'My dear, I had nothing left to give up to you but my life. In a minute or two you will be free, and can make another Baronne Hulot.'

And, rare sight, tears oozed from her dead eyes.

This desperateness of vice had vanquished the patience of the angel, who, on the brink of eternity, gave utterance to the only reproach she had ever spoken in her life.

The Baron left Paris three days after his wife's funeral. Eleven months later Victorin heard indirectly of his father's marriage to Mademoiselle Agathe Piquetard, solemnised at Isigny, on the 1st February 1846.

'Parents may hinder their children's marriage, but children cannot interfere with the insane acts of their parents in their second childhood,' said Maître Hulot to Maître Popinot, the second son of the Minister of Commerce, who was discussing this marriage.

THE END

ABOUT THE INTRODUCER

MICHAEL TILBY is Fellow and Lecturer in French, Selwyn College, Cambridge. He is the author of *Gide: 'Les Faux-Monnayeurs'* and the editor of *Balzac* (an anthology of Balzac criticism), and *Beyond the Nouveau Roman. Essays on the Contemporary French Novel.* He has also edited works by Mérimée and Pascal Lainé, and written numerous articles on nineteenth- and twentieth-century French literature.

CHINUA ACHEBE
Things Fall Apart

THE ARABIAN NIGHTS
(2 vols, tr. Husain Haddawy)

AUGUSTINE
The Confessions

JANE AUSTEN
Emma
Mansfield Park
Northanger Abbey
Persuasion
Pride and Prejudice
Sanditon and Other Stories
Sense and Sensibility

HONORÉ DE BALZAC
Cousin Bette
Eugénie Grandet
Old Goriot

SIMONE DE BEAUVOIR
The Second Sex

SAUL BELLOW
The Adventures of Augie March

WILLIAM BLAKE
Poems and Prophecies

JORGE LUIS BORGES
Ficciones

JAMES BOSWELL
The Life of Samuel Johnson

CHARLOTTE BRONTË
Jane Eyre
Villette

EMILY BRONTË
Wuthering Heights

MIKHAIL BULGAKOV
The Master and Margarita

SAMUEL BUTLER
The Way of all Flesh

ITALO CALVINO
If on a winter's night a traveler

ALBERT CAMUS
The Outsider

MIGUEL DE CERVANTES
Don Quixote

GEOFFREY CHAUCER
Canterbury Tales

ANTON CHEKHOV
My Life and Other Stories
The Steppe and Other Stories

KATE CHOPIN
The Awakening

CARL VON CLAUSEWITZ
On War

S. T. COLERIDGE
Poems

WILKIE COLLINS
The Moonstone
The Woman in White

CONFUCIUS
The Analects

JOSEPH CONRAD
Heart of Darkness
Lord Jim
Nostromo
The Secret Agent
Typhoon and Other Stories
Under Western Eyes
Victory

THOMAS CRANMER
The Book of Common Prayer

DANTE ALIGHIERI
The Divine Comedy

DANIEL DEFOE
Moll Flanders
Robinson Crusoe

CHARLES DICKENS
Bleak House
David Copperfield
Dombey and Son
Great Expectations
Hard Times
Little Dorrit
Martin Chuzzlewit
Nicholas Nickleby
The Old Curiosity Shop
Oliver Twist
Our Mutual Friend
The Pickwick Papers
A Tale of Two Cities

DENIS DIDEROT
Memoirs of a Nun

JOHN DONNE
The Complete English Poems